WARS OF THE
COLD WAR

WARS OF THE COLD WAR

CAMPAIGNS AND CONFLICTS
1945–1990

DAVID STONE

BRASSEY'S

First published in 2004 by
Brassey's
The Chrysalis Building
Bramley Road
London W10 6SP

An imprint of **Chrysalis** Books Group plc

Distributed in North America by
Casemate Publishing
2114 Darby Road
Havertown
PA 19083
USA

David J. A. Stone has asserted his moral right
to be identified as the author of this work.

British Library Cataloguing in Publication Data:
A catalogue record for this book is available
from the British Library

ISBN 1 85753 342 9

Edited and designed by DAG Publications Ltd
Designed by David Gibbons
Edited by Michael Boxall
Printed in Great Britain

CONTENTS

CONTENTS

AUTHOR'S NOTE
AND ACKNOWLEDGEMENTS

Very many books have already been written about the Cold War. Some were produced while it was still in progress; not surprisingly, some authors seized the opportunity to publish in the immediate aftermath of the fall of the Berlin Wall in 1989, albeit possibly a little prematurely, given the various turns of events that followed that historic event. These many accounts and analyses of the Cold War have included the full range of eyewitness accounts, biographies, autobiographies, and academic and strategic works at all levels of detail and from various perspectives. Several of these have been learned, informed and highly thought-provoking. Inevitably, the authors of a majority of these accounts are the international statesmen, politicians, academics and senior military commanders for whom the Cold War was 'their war', and whose knowledge of the ebb and flow of its actions and conflicts was based upon first-hand knowledge, personal involvement and vivid recollection. For the student or reader who seeks to know about the detail of the international relationships, strategy and politics of the Cold War era there are thus many such sources upon which he or she may draw. However, the use of these works does provoke a note of caution, as those involved in the development and implementation of such strategic and political decisions will inevitably – even if entirely unintentionally – colour their perspective of events in their own favour. To do so is human nature and the 'top down' recording of history has ever been such. Also, the majority of these works have not surprisingly approached the subject from the author's particular area of interest or involvement; or (as is so with many of the Cold War analyses by academics) by a broad history of the Cold War in all its aspects. Inevitably, the latter approach, whilst usually informative and full of facts, does on occasion lose sight of the human element of a war that although 'undeclared' was nevertheless a conflict in which very many human beings, civilians and soldiers, sailors and airmen alike, died in combat across the world.

Wars of the Cold War does not seek to be a full military history of all aspects of the Cold War – the reader who seeks such a text will find it hard to better David Miller's excellent functional approach to the subject in *The Cold War: A Military History*.[1] Similarly, the detail of the strategic nuclear arms race and potentially cataclysmic ballistic missile conflict between the United States and the Soviet Union is meticulously documented and analysed in works such as that by Miller and a host of other studies[2] of this complex subject. Indeed, many people identify this aspect of post-Second

World War history as the true Cold War, to the exclusion of the peripheral conflicts and limited wars that occurred between 1945 and 1990. However, these lesser conflicts cannot realistically be decoupled from the strategic conflict of the superpowers. Given the existence of such works, *Wars of the Cold War* seeks neither to duplicate nor to compete directly with them.

The intention in *Wars of the Cold War* is, therefore, to document, to bring to life and to analyse the proposition that, far from being a period of relative peace, the Cold War deserves a status in the military and political history of the world every bit as important as that accorded to the two World Wars that immediately preceded it, together with the great armed conflicts of previous centuries. This proposition is based primarily upon the perception that the several actual wars, together with the 'war in waiting' in Central Europe, which occurred between 1945 and 1990, were but military campaigns within a wider conflict that was a war in its own right: a war that lasted for almost half a century and was in many respects a modern version of the ideological struggle that raged across Europe from 1618 to 1648, to which history has accorded the title the 'Thirty Years' War'. In parallel with this, the author (himself a former 'Cold War Warrior')[3] seeks to highlight the often extraordinary dedication, professionalism and self-sacrifice of the hundreds of thousands of Cold War warriors of the armed forces on both sides of the political divide. Whether of the communist or non-communist bloc, their contribution to the needs of their countries and their unquestioning response to the direction, and sometimes the whims, of their political leaders has been consigned all too speedily to the past by many of today's political leaders. Arguably this is especially so in Western Europe – within those countries that number themselves among the victors of the Cold War – where may be found those politicians who today appear all too eager to bask in the reflected glory of the actions of their nations' armed forces, and so exploit the high profile, 'quick fix' conflicts of the 'New World Order' for their own political ends. While by no means universal, such actions have diminished the stature of many of today's professional politicians and have tended to confirm that the era of the true statesmen of former times is truly at an end.

From all this it follows that *Wars of the Cold War* is necessarily selective, and that selectivity inevitably involves an element of personal judgement by an author who lived through the whole Cold War period and was a member of the British Army for the final twenty-five years of that conflict, and for a decade beyond. The work therefore treats the Cold War as a single conflict, whilst focusing upon the related campaigns and crises of the period. Inevitably, the clashes in Korea, Indochina and Vietnam, the Cuban missile crisis, and those members of the armed forces at the front line of the Cold

War in Europe attract particular attention. Of the communist insurgencies, that which was defeated by the British in Malaya merits close attention. The failed national uprisings against Soviet rule in East Berlin, Hungary and Czechoslovakia were also key events in the Cold War. Similarly, although they were not direct clashes of arms between West and East, capitalism and communism, the Arab–Israeli conflicts, together with other Middle East wars and the importance of that region's oil supplies, are linked inextricably to the Cold War, and are therefore dealt with as such. This treatment allows a global view to be taken of the subject. Inevitably, however, this approach precludes detailed coverage of much of the high-level political manoeuvring that formed a backdrop to these campaigns. Similarly, where it is assessed that a conflict's linkage to the Cold War is non-existent or tenuous, its non-inclusion or only passing treatment reflects this. It follows that certain lesser conflicts – while unquestionably of historical significance in their own right – are generally not considered in the detail accorded to the more major Cold War conflicts, except where their progress or outcome bore directly on the global confrontation between East and West. Similarly, the major war that India and Pakistan fought in 1971, which resulted in the creation of Bangladesh, was only of Cold War significance inasmuch as it contributed to assessments of the effectiveness of each side's Western or Soviet-supplied equipment in combat – albeit that both India and Pakistan were then in the process of developing their own nuclear capability (although this was at a very early stage in 1971).

Whilst this degree of selectivity may result in the omission of a conflict that another might deem important, the historical context and significance or otherwise of a given conflict or event can be no more than the personal view of the author. Accordingly, it is freely acknowledged that the responsibility for this work, and therefore for any consequent omissions, inaccuracies or misperceptions therein, rests finally and entirely with him. He therefore apologises in advance to any reader who might vainly seek an account of a favourite Cold War era campaign, crisis or conflict within its pages, but which has been omitted or afforded less than full treatment.

However, whilst obviating the need to document the course of each campaign or conflict in detail, and to omit some altogether, this selectivity also allows for an informed track back into those momentous years and a wider analysis on a case-by-case basis of the consequences and lessons of the Cold War campaigns and conflicts, and of the process of cause and effect. Then, on the premise that the most important function of history is to learn from it, *Wars of the Cold War* finally provides an assessment of some of the crises and conflicts that the post-Cold War world may be destined to experience in the twenty-first century.

Inevitably, an authoritative study of such a broad subject as the Cold War era involved extensive research, and the bibliography reflects this. In consequence of that, I am most grateful to all of the many authors, publishers, agents and other organisations and copyright holders who so readily agreed that I might reproduce extracts from their own works where appropriate. A number of specific acknowledgements are indicated at the bibliography. Although every reasonable effort was made to contact each one of the copyright holders involved, a very few proved to be entirely untraceable. Therefore, where such material has necessarily been included in *Wars of the Cold War* nonetheless, it has been fully referenced and credited on the basis of the information about the author and publisher as shown in the original source document or book, albeit that these publishing details must now be assumed realistically to be no longer current.

Finally, my particular thanks are due to Rod Dymott of Brassey's for his continued support, advice and faith in my literary abilities. But, most importantly, I must conclude by thanking my former military colleague Ian Wilkinson for allowing me to inflict yet another draft manuscript upon him, just when the prospect of a somewhat more immediate military conflict was no doubt occupying much of his thoughts and time. The resultant text of *Wars of the Cold Wars* has benefited immeasurably from his informed, pragmatic and invariably constructive comments.

David Stone

INTRODUCTION

The true starting point of the Cold War might have been marked by any one of a number of historic events. Foremost among these was the famous 'Iron Curtain' speech by Winston Churchill at Fulton, Missouri on 5 March 1946, which illustrated so dramatically the rift that had occurred between East and West. Then again, perhaps it really all began with the dropping of the first atomic bomb on Hiroshima on 6 August 1945, when the Soviet Union had finally to come to terms with the fact that the non-communist West had won the race to harness atomic power for military purposes. However, some would argue that the seeds of the Cold War had actually been planted some three decades earlier, with the assassination of an Austrian Archduke in the obscure Balkan town of Sarajevo, which triggered the First World War, precipitated the Russian Revolution, and subsequently spawned a communist superpower in the form of the Soviet Union.

Yet whatever the start point of the Cold War may truly be, it is undeniable that its principal focus throughout was always the struggle between the Soviets and their erstwhile Western Allies in the war against Nazi Germany: the United States, Great Britain and the British Empire, and France. And, although it later diverged from the Soviet form of communism, the People's Republic of China also became an important player in the global struggle between communism and capitalism. Thus, when these great powers, together with the forces they controlled and the ideology they espoused, finally came physically and militarily into close proximity with one another, all that followed was more or less inevitable.

Accordingly, the start point of the Cold War may actually have been during the final days of a bright but still chilly spring of 1945, in the final days of the Second World War in Europe. The very first East and West 'confrontation' almost certainly took place on 25 April, when a patrol from the 69th US Infantry Division, led by a Lieutenant Albert Kotzebue, encountered a lone Soviet cavalryman near Stehla, a nondescript German village situated on the west bank of the Elbe, some twenty miles to the south-east of the town of Torgau. Significantly, Kotzebue's subsequent radio report of the incident to his command post indicated that there had been 'no casualties'! Next, on 27 April, the first officially recorded meeting of the Americans and the Russians took place. This happened when other soldiers of 69th US Infantry Division linked up with their Soviet allies of the 1st Ukrainian Army on the River Elbe at Torgau. The first such meeting of British and Russian troops did not occur until four days later. On that day, a group of weary soldiers of the

British 6th Airborne Division, then under the command of General Ridgway's 18th US Airborne Corps, were advancing rapidly along the north coast of Germany and had just seized the Baltic port of Wismar. They were continuing to push forward out of the town when they encountered 'two motorcycle combinations, followed by two lease-lend American scout cars containing seven ragged soldiers and one buxom female soldier armed with a tommy-gun'.[4] These turned out to be the leading troops of Marshal Rokossovsky's 2nd Byelorussian Front of the Red Army. The time was about 9 p.m. on 1 May 1945.

After almost six years of war, the ground forces of the East had finally met those of the West, communism had met capitalism, and two mighty war machines had no option but to acknowledge and come to terms with each other's existence. That acknowledgement was speedily followed by a growing awareness at all levels of the sheer military power and fundamental differences of ideology between the two great power blocs that had emerged from the Second World War.

Following that first meeting on the Baltic coast, the natural bonhomie and genuine comradeship of the ordinary soldiers of both sides – one serving the red star, the other the white star – was modified and transformed all too rapidly by their respective armies' political masters. The change was first manifested by an uneasy reserve, then by a mutual suspicion, and finally by an open hostility that was destined to perpetuate for almost fifty years.

Ironically, however, throughout that time the only reliably recorded and direct combat between soldiers of the Red Army and the Western Allies occurred just two days later, on the evening of 3 May 1945. This was an entirely avoidable and rather sordid little Anglo-Soviet affair, which was precipitated by the arrival of a score of very drunk Russian soldiers at Wismar's main hospital, by then occupied by soldiers of the British 7th Parachute Battalion. The Russians' principal interest in the hospital that night was the large number of German Red Cross sisters and female auxiliaries who had earlier taken refuge inside. The immovable determination of the paratroopers to protect the women met the irresistible force of the Russian insistence on access to the hospital, and this soon degenerated into a short firefight that left six Russian soldiers lying dead on the cobbled street of the little German seaport.[5]

For the next forty-five years the Soviet Union and the West were locked into an undeclared state of war; but it was a war in which the main protagonists never again engaged in open combat, face-to-face, on land.[6] It was in reality a war of many wars, fought out through a host of proxy conflicts that together comprised the wider Cold War – a period of conflict that for almost half a century affected the lives and fortunes of the majority of the world's population. And wherever the subsequent conflict moved beyond the political and diplomatic arenas, there were to be found the soldiers, sailors and airmen of both sides: ready as always to answer their country's call to arms, and to reinforce time and again the truth of the oft-quoted statement by Major General Karl Philip Gottlieb von Clausewitz that war is indeed 'a true political instrument, a continuation of political intercourse, carried on by other means'.[7] To that axiom might be added the observation that in the modern age wars are also so often the evidence of moral weakness and professional failures on the part of politicians and diplomats inexperienced in the real implications and art of war; whose errors of judgement and responsibilities are then passed on to the military men for what may be – in some if not all cases – their less than ideal resolution by force of arms.

Now that the Cold War has finally drawn to an end, the events of those momentous years are rapidly being consigned to the past, to the texts of academics and to the political and military memoirs of those involved. Indeed, with the so-called hot wars in the Gulf in 1990–1, in the Balkans from 1995 and the plethora of low intensity military operations conducted under the auspices of the UN or NATO since 1990, the focus has increasingly relegated the Cold War to virtual irrelevance in light of the 'new world order' so beloved of many of today's politicians. Even in military circles, the imperative to prepare for 'today's conflicts' and the 'sort of conflicts that we can expect in the future' (those that primarily involve peacekeeping, peace support and peace enforcement operations, or the achievement of a satisfactory outcome primarily by the use of air power) are increasingly degrading the ability of many nations to wage war on a significant scale. And, for those politicians who postulate that this need will never arise again, it would perhaps be appropriate to remind them that if they learn no more than one lesson from history it should be that the only absolute certainty is that the future is entirely uncertain.

Typical of that uncertainty was the terrorist attack on the World Trade Centre on 11 September 2001. Although its immediate categorisation by the United States and NATO as an 'act of war' would probably not now bear close and objective scrutiny, it effectively brought about an albeit fairly one-sided war between the in-place Taliban government of Afghanistan and the United States, the latter nation being supported in relatively small measure by Great Britain, and by a few of its other allies. But the future course of the so-called 'war against terrorism' is still very uncertain, as is the precise form of the forces needed to conduct it. There is a danger, however, that the long-term committal of forces to an open-ended campaign to suit these current needs will eventually further dissipate, degrade and diminish the skills of war-fighting that were developed and honed during the Cold War years.

Then, when some as yet entirely unexpected and previously unimaginable threat manifests itself, the necessary military response may not be forthcoming.

There is, therefore, a very real risk of forgetting too quickly the experience of strategic and operational deterrence and warfare gained between 1945 and 1990. The risk also exists of losing sight of the fact that the Cold War was, in many theatres of operations, far from 'cold' in nature. Even at the epicentre of the conflict – in Central Europe – although no combat took place (notwithstanding that the populations of East Germany, Hungary and Czechoslovakia might, with some justification, disagree with that statement!) the forces of East and West faced each other on a permanent war footing throughout the conflict: a fact that, ironically, provided the deterrent balance to ensure that a full scale 'hot war' never broke out. However, nobody should be under any illusion that these forces, on both sides of the Inner German Border (IGB), were other than entirely ready for immediate committal to combat. They lived with that individual and corporate commitment, and with the necessary levels of operational readiness and training to sustain it, through every day of their service. No official commemorative medal was struck by NATO or by its individual member states to mark the end of the Cold War, or to recognise military service during it. This unfortunate omission tends to diminish the contribution of hundreds of thousands of regular and conscripted servicemen and servicewomen for whom the Cold War was 'their war', just as the First and Second World Wars were, respectively, the wars of their grandparents and parents. The lack of any such tangible symbol of Cold War involvement inevitably gives credence to the view that this was a war that never was.

But of course such a perception would be entirely misplaced and factually very far from the truth. Those soldiers, sailors and airmen of all sides and many nations who fought in the steaming jungles of South-east Asia, in the sub-zero temperatures of Korea, in the rocky *djebel* of the Arabian Peninsula, at Suez and in the Sinai, in the mountains of Afghanistan, and in a score of other war zones across the world are testimony to the very real nature of this diverse war. And, while these easily recognisable and limited conflicts were being fought out to their often bloody end, the strategic bombers of the US, British and Soviet air forces played cat and mouse with each other in the skies above, while the submarines of the nuclear powers conducted their own game of hide and seek in the cold darkness deep in the world's oceans. Then there were the missiles: thousands of nuclear-tipped rockets, poised ready to be launched from their underground silos, or from their mobile launchers. And throughout, there were the mighty armies and air forces of NATO and the Warsaw Pact which faced each other across the IGB – the Iron Curtain that Churchill had so vividly identified in March 1946.

Thus the Cold War was played out simultaneously at the strategic, operational and tactical levels. The ultimate aim of what became by default the new 'Great Game'[8] was clear to all, but the rules of the conflict were regularly modified as the war progressed and as the international situation and political agendas of the major players changed, and then changed again and again.

CHAPTER ONE

1945: THE FOUNDATIONS OF CONFLICT

The world that found itself finally at peace following the defeat of Japan in August 1945 was very different from the one that had taken the road to war in the late summer of 1939. Although the defeat of the German Axis powers and subsequently of Japan meant that the Western Allies and the Soviet Union had won the war, the new task of winning the peace would prove in different ways to be just as difficult and infinitely more complex than had been that of confronting the territorial aspirations and excesses of fascism and Japanese imperialism. Consequently, the goal of peace in the post-1945 era proved every bit as elusive as it had been throughout all of history, as the long and difficult process that began while the radioactive dust was still settling on to the debris of Hiroshima and Nagasaki was punctuated all too frequently by the many conflicts, campaigns and wars of the Cold War period.

In 1945, with the notable exception of the United States, many of the world's countries were metaphorically, economically and physically in bits, and the task of picking up the pieces, rebuilding and rehabilitating, was indeed formidable. In much of the world – but particularly in many of the overseas territories of the European powers – new political movements and a surge of nationalism provided an early indication that this process would produce end-state situations that were very far removed from those that had existed prior to 1939. But, amid the post-war euphoria and general sense of relief of late 1945, relatively few leaders of the once-great European powers had the vision or inclination to comprehend this; or to understand the embryo new world order and the serious implications of resisting the developing international trends and political movements within it. Many in Europe also failed to understand or accept the pre-eminent position that the United States now occupied in the world. Meanwhile, on the other side of the Atlantic, a number of influential politicians and decision-makers in Washington, supported by a significant groundswell of post-war public opinion, were determined that American lives should never again be sacrificed in the defence of Europe, or to preserve what they perceived to be an outdated, undemocratic and un-American system of colonialism and imperialism.

In May 1945 the 'Victory in Europe' (VE) celebrations were conducted against a backdrop of destruction, economic collapse, mass migration, political unrest and a future that was anything but certain. Upon this chaotic situation were laid the foundations of the Cold War. Almost all of mainland

Europe had suffered the horrors of ground warfare and foreign occupation. Of the principal nations, only Britain had escaped the ultimate trauma of invasion and occupation, although the German bombing campaign had torn the heart out of many British towns and cities. Some areas of London that escaped the massed air raids of the blitz finally succumbed to German V-1 and V-2 rocket attacks in the closing months of the war. Overseas, a British empire still existed, although a wind of change was wafting across Britain's overseas territories and gaining strength – spurred on by a growing tide of nationalism. Meanwhile, Britain was still a nation in arms, with its economy and industry entirely geared to the war effort. Consequently, Britain emerged from the war as militarily the most powerful West European nation. But after six years at war the country was virtually bankrupt, and the post-war Labour government faced a Herculean task for which it was in many ways ill-prepared; a situation exacerbated by the sweeping programme of social and welfare reforms that the new government was determined to introduce. In order to meet its funding commitments, Britain borrowed 4.3 billion US dollars in autumn 1945, and this loan placed Britain in debt to the United States for at least the next sixty years.[9]

France also suffered very extensive war damage, although Paris had escaped relatively unscathed. The destruction was especially apparent in northern France, consequent upon the Allied landings in Normandy and the breakout campaign after D-Day. But whereas the physical destruction was repairable, the human damage was less easily rectified, and with the coming of peace the population of France began to come to terms with its recent past. Collaborators, informers, anti-Semitism, Vichy, and the fact of the French military defeat in 1940 all made for a divided and unhappy nation – one in which the communists (who had played an important role in the resistance movement) prospered better than anywhere else in Western Europe. France also had a pre-war overseas empire, and in 1945 the Paris government fervently desired both to retain it and to regain its former position as the major continental European power. In both these aspirations it was destined to fail, as its military defeat, followed by Vichy's policies and performance in the war, created external perceptions of France's post-war impotence that at first ignited and then fanned the flames of nationalism in its overseas territories. Nowhere was this more evident than in its territories in French Indochina and North Africa.

Throughout continental Western Europe the story was much the same: ruined countries, shattered lives, wrecked industries, and destroyed roads, railways and infrastructure. And everywhere new governments with new political agendas set about the monumental task of reconstruction, with varying degrees of success.

Germany had been the final focus of the war in Europe, and very many of its towns and cities had been reduced to rubble. Berlin, Dresden, Hamburg, Cologne, the Ruhr and a hundred other once-proud centres of German culture, learning and industry were almost unrecognisable under the towering piles of smashed bricks and broken concrete that had virtually obliterated their former glory and buried the bodies of thousands of their soldiers and citizens. Much of Germany's population was traumatised, homeless and starving. The country's industrial base had been comprehensively destroyed, and a great deal of the machinery which had survived in the zones now occupied by US, British and French forces was in any case destined to be removed to the Soviet Union as war reparations, in accordance with the agreements made by the Allies at Potsdam – although a reciprocal undertaking given by Stalin to send food from the mainly agricultural Soviet zone of occupation in eastern Germany to help feed the Germans living in the western zones was not honoured.

Everywhere in Europe people were on the move – possibly in excess of thirty million of them in 1945. The Jews who had survived the concentration camps and now sought new homes and new lives in Palestine, America and other countries were an identifiable group that attracted much attention (and would provide the focus of much more during the next five decades). But there were also thousands of demobilised German soldiers, liberated prisoners of war and slave labourers, former impressed foreign workers, homeless refugees and a multiplicity of other categories of displaced persons (DP) of every nationality on the roads and few surviving railways of Europe. Although their plight was often desperate, these were people who had retained a measure of control over their own destiny. However, there were also many thousands more in enforced transit, due to the Soviet policy of relocating to Siberia and elsewhere many people from the Baltic, East Prussia, the Crimea and the Caucasus, and from Karelia. The Potsdam agreements and other accommodations between the 'Big Three' allies – many of which were undoubtedly naïve on the part of the Western Allies and patently pandered to Stalin's agenda – produced numerous inequities which further exacerbated the problem. Forces that had fought for the Germans, together with some of those who had fought for the Western Allies, now found their homelands under Soviet domination, and their forcible repatriation by the West to face death or imprisonment at the hands of the communists was one of the less honourable stories of the time. The Soviets' mass eviction of the ethnic German populations of Hungary, Czechoslovakia and Poland added to the turmoil and led to the death of more than three million ethnic Germans in the immediate post-war period.

Much of the blame for the continued turbulence in Europe was due to Stalin's fear of attack by the West, and to his need to preserve the power of the Communist Party of the Soviet Union (CPSU) internally, while simultaneously expanding communism (and Soviet control and influence) internationally. In Soviet-occupied eastern Germany communist control was both obsessive and absolute, and during the few years following the German defeat communists seized control in Yugoslavia, Poland, Romania, Czechoslovakia, Hungary, Bulgaria and Albania, which enabled the Soviet Union to create an almost unbroken defensive shield on its western borders, a shield that was later transformed into a formal defensive alliance. But elsewhere in Europe – in Greece, in France and in Italy – the communists were less successful. Despite its initial occupation by the Soviets in 1945 and its willing participation in the German cause in 1939, Austria finally emerged from the post-war turmoil as a neutral state.

Meanwhile, far from the devastated countryside of central Europe, much of Asia and the Far East had also suffered enormously from the war with Japan. Many of the towns and cities of the Philippines, Thailand, Burma, Indochina, Korea, the Pacific islands and the southern region of China had sustained significant damage, as had the great cities of Singapore and Hong Kong. Japan itself had ultimately paid a particularly high price for its wartime policies, becoming the first country in the world to suffer an atomic attack, with the bombing of Hiroshima and Nagasaki in August 1945. In Asia and the Far East, just as in Europe, people set about the task of rebuilding their lives following the Japanese surrender in August 1945. And in many of the countries of South-east Asia, much of which had endured a Japanese occupation unparalleled in modern times for its inhumanity and savagery, the inability of the European powers to counter the Japanese aggression had been well noted by those who now sought a new future for their nations. Foremost among these were communist leaders such as Ho Chi Minh and Mao Tse-tung; the latter already engaged in an epic struggle with Chiang Kai-shek's nationalists for control of China. Indeed, much of the conflict to come would centre upon South-east Asia, where the Cold War contest between East and West, communism and capitalism, was be fought out in a succession of proxy wars.

In 1945 the different circumstances of the two superpowers – one already established, the other rapidly emerging – could not have been more distinct. By and large, the United States had had a relatively 'good war' following its late entry to the conflict after the Japanese bombing of Pearl Harbor in December 1941. By then Europe had already endured two years of warfare, during which US industry had benefited enormously from supporting the war against Germany through the lend-lease arrangement with Britain. It had also begun the process of reinvigorating a military machine that successive budget cuts in the 1930s had left with a capability that was in many respects no greater than that of Germany under the terms of the 1920 Treaty of Versailles. After some uncertain starts (in the Philippines and in North Africa), the US armed forces had generally acquitted themselves well, and their casualties during the war had not been excessive. But, most importantly, at no time had the continental United States been subjected to direct enemy action. Therefore, no part of that huge country (apart from Pearl Harbor) had been bombed, shelled or occupied by enemy forces throughout the entire war. Small wonder perhaps that a serious terrorist attack on a sunny 11 September 2001 in New York, fifty-six years after the end of the Second World War, should have so traumatised the government and people of the most powerful nation in the world.

America's Second World War experience contrasted starkly with that of the Soviet Union. Some twenty-seven million Soviet servicemen and civilians had died since 1941. The western Soviet Union had suffered an oppressive enemy occupation founded upon German ideological and racial philosophies that espoused the evils of Bolshevism and the ethnic inferiority of the Russian and Slav peoples. The levels of destruction and the almost total disregard of the invaders for human life on the Eastern Front reflected the very different nature of the German army's campaign in Russia from that it had fought in the West. In the Soviet Union, the Second World War was and still is termed 'The Great Patriotic War', with the additional words 'against fascism' often added. The significant differences between the situation and perceptions of the United States and the Soviet Union in 1945 played a defining role in establishing their future priorities, policies, roles and destinies during the Cold War. A post-war American commentator noted:

> There were only two first-class powers in the world at the end of the war. Both the United States and the Soviet Union had harnessed their vast resources in people and industrial capacity to win the war for the [Allied cause]. While the United States became the 'arsenal of democracy' to equip and sustain much of the Allied war effort, the Soviet Union made a Herculean effort to focus its industry on war production and gained the wherewithal for its mass armies to grind down and overwhelm the enemy. In some respects, World War II represents a culmination of some of the main trends in American history in that it was pre-eminently a war of mass and concentration militarily, industrial capacity (the first of the so-called 'gross national product wars'), and organizational and managerial necessity, all the things at which Americans had historically come to excel. So great were the resources and managerial capacity of the United States that it could fight two

major but separate wars [in Northwest Europe and in the Pacific region] and still raise its standard of living appreciably. Built with the sweat and blood of its people, the Soviet war effort was cruder but still resulted in the emergence of a true nation-state possessing military power second only to that of the United States, coupled with the confidence born of having beaten in open battle the world's most modern and impressive [German] war machine.[10]

In 1945 the world was still populated by the great military forces that had waged the war. Whilst the United States, the Western Allies and the Soviet Union all had millions of personnel under arms, America was the only nation that possessed the atomic bomb. Now, with Germany and Japan defeated, the Western Allies at last set about the complex process of demobilising and repatriating their forces scattered across the world. However, the bulk of the Soviet ground forces were deployed as occupation troops in the eastern part of Europe and the western Soviet Union, and Stalin decided to maintain in existence and (in many instances) in place the Soviet war machine that had been developed so assiduously since 1941. The Soviet leader had looked pragmatically at the nature of the new world order, and had concluded that there would be further work for the armed forces of the Soviet Union in the years ahead. As 1945 drew to a close the opening moves of the Cold War were already under way.

CHAPTER TWO

BACKGROUND TO CONFLICT:
THE AGE OF THE SUPERPOWER

Never the Twain: The United States and the Soviet Union

The many conflicts and campaigns of the Cold War period were all conducted against the background of the global power struggle between the United States and the Soviet Union. This strategic contest was affected by virtually every one of the more visible armed conflicts that occurred between 1945 and 1990. Indeed, the 1991 Gulf War – although it took place after what was generally acknowledged to be the end of the Cold War – was directly influenced by it; for had the Cold War not concluded by 1990 it is unlikely that the coalition's campaign in Kuwait and Iraq could ever have taken place. The fact that it did is perhaps one of the best pieces of evidence that the Cold War had indeed ended by 1990, although it is also a moot point whether or not Saddam Hussein's invasion of Kuwait would have been possible had the Cold War still been in progress; with the Soviet Union as strong in 1990 as it had been in former times.

As well as the international politics, power-plays, brinkmanship and diplomacy that characterised Soviet–US relations throughout the Cold War, their parallel and complementary technological contest was at its most visible in the struggle for nuclear dominance. Although the nuclear balance was maintained and nuclear deterrence worked (inasmuch as the oft-predicted nuclear war between the United States and the Soviet Union never took place) the considerable holdings of nuclear weapons and the means to deliver them, both strategically and (later) as tactical or battlefield weapons, was an ever-present backdrop for everything else that happened between 1945 and 1990. It follows that the specific campaigns and conflicts that occurred during the Cold War can only be understood in the context of the superpower contest and later that between the two great Cold War alliances: NATO and the Warsaw Pact. Without the titanic struggle between the United States and the Soviet Union many of the localised or limited wars that flared up between 1945 and 1990 would simply not have happened, and the world of the early twenty-first century would undoubtedly have been a very different place from that which it is today.

Blame for the East–West confrontation that emerged at the end of the Second World War cannot be attributed to either side exclusively. The Soviet Union under Stalin was to a great extent a prisoner both of recent events of 1941–5 and of its old pre-1917 imperial history. These on the one hand underlined the threat posed by the West and need to maintain an effective buffer against a future invasion, while on the other they indicated the need to acquire territory and worldwide influence. Meanwhile, the United States was not reticent in trumpeting its military, technological and economic pre-eminence. It had provided the military forces that ensured the final victory against the Germans in the West. It had won its own war against the Japanese in the Pacific. To a significant extent it had underwritten and resourced the Allied campaigns in both the East and the West. Its scientists had won the race to produce the first viable atomic weapon; and American industry had benefited enormously from the government contracts to manufacture vast quantities of war matériel for the US forces and their allies. The post-war Marshall Aid Plan, whilst vital to the regeneration of Europe, also served to emphasise the economic strength of the United States and the almost total dependence of Western Europe on America for decades to come. And unlike the Soviet Union, Europe and the Far East, the conti-nental United States had been physically untouched by hostile action. Only Hawaii had experienced the horrors of war at first-hand.

In victorious post-war America a fierce belief in the power of capitalism was matched by a growing ideological hostility to communism and all that it represented. For the American people, communism threatened their way of life, their future prosperity, and the continued global supremacy of the nation. Small wonder then that President Harry S. Truman, more a politi-cian and less a statesmen than his predecessor, set the United States firmly on a course to contain the communist threat wherever it manifested itself: a course that was maintained by his successors into the 1980s. Small wonder also that Stalin and all of his successors until Gorbachev in the late 1980s identified the United States as the principal post-war threat to a Soviet state that had, since 1917, been firmly founded on the principles and practices of Marxist-Leninism. The collapse of the Nationalist Chinese in 1949 only served to increase American fears of a red tide of communism expanding from the Soviet Union and the newly established People's Republic of China to engulf a United States that had been largely untouched by foreign powers and influences ever since it gained its independence from Great Britain in 1783.[11] That fear fuelled the obsessive anti-communist purges by Senator Joseph Raymond McCarthy from 1950, which in turn reinforced the Kremlin's perception of the antipathy of the United States to the ideology on which the Soviet system was based.

The creation of NATO in 1949 provided the West with an effective defensive barrier against communist expansion westward and, seen through Western eyes, it was a benign and logical extension of the military co-operation that the Allies had exercised through the Second World War. In Moscow, however, it was viewed as an offensive alliance – one underwritten by the American nuclear capability – designed to restart and complete the crusade against

Bolshevism begun by Nazi Germany in 1941. This Soviet assessment gained additional substance with the accession of the Federal Republic of Germany (FRG) to full NATO membership in 1955. The creation of the Warsaw Pact in May 1955 was, therefore, a not unreasonable Soviet response to a NATO Alliance that had by then existed for almost six years, and which had just extended membership to the state that had invaded Russia and the Soviet Union twice within the previous four decades.[12] It also followed the January 1954 announcement by American Secretary of State John Foster Dulles of the US doctrine of massive nuclear retaliation, which took full account of the Soviet Union's first successful thermonuclear explosion on 12 August 1953.[13] Meanwhile, albeit under UN auspices, the United States and others had just fought a major war against communist North Korea and its Chinese allies, while in Malaya the British were engaged in a successful campaign against communist insurgents. Both conflicts could reasonably be regarded by Moscow as evidence of the West's readiness to use armed force to confront communism far from the United States and Europe. And, even though the Korean War had cost the Democrats the 1952 presidential election, the new Republican administration, headed by Dwight D. Eisenhower and his unequivocally anti-communist Secretary of State, gave the Soviets no reason to believe that American attitudes and policies were about to change.

During the late 1950s NATO and the Warsaw Pact sought to strengthen their forces both quantitatively and qualitatively, with the Soviet Union striving ever more vigorously to close the considerable East–West nuclear capability gap. The Warsaw Pact also provided a means by which Moscow could exert closer ideological and military control over the Soviet satellite states. In East Berlin in 1953 and Hungary in 1956 it demonstrated that it would maintain that control by force of arms if necessary. In both cases, but especially so in Hungary, the failure of the Western powers to intervene indicated that a de facto acceptance of East–West spheres of influence and interest was beginning to emerge from the game of international relations between the Soviet Union and the United States.

The development of the Warsaw Pact also provided some reassurance within the Kremlin at a time when Moscow was still experiencing the unsatisfactory and potentially destabilising period of so-called 'collective leadership' that followed the death of Stalin in 1953. From then until February 1955 the Soviet Union was ruled jointly by Georgii Malenkov, Nikita Khrushchev and Vyacheslav Molotov. Malenkov resigned as Chairman of the Council of Ministers in 1955 and by 1957 Khrushchev's position as overall leader of the Soviet Union was assured.

While the Soviets consolidated the strength of the Warsaw Pact, the United States continued to pursue its anti-communism policies, and to expand its own power and influence beyond Europe through treaties and organisations – such as the 1954 treaty signed with the beleaguered Nationalist Chinese government in Formosa, the South-east Asia Treaty Organisation (SEATO) also in 1954, and the Baghdad Pact in 1955. Following the French defeat at Dien Bien Phu in 1954, the late-1950s also saw growing US involvement in the former French Indochina, which led it into one of the greatest of the Cold War conflicts: the Vietnam War.

However, US support for its NATO allies Britain and France, and for Israel, did not extend to the Anglo-French attack on Egypt in 1956 to recapture and safeguard the strategically vital Suez Canal. On that occasion Washington's objections to an invasion by two former European imperial and colonial powers even overrode the fact of Soviet military support for Egypt and Moscow's hostility to the invasion – the failure of which was finally attributable to the pressure exerted upon the British and French governments by Secretary of State Dulles. Nevertheless, only two years later, in July 1958, America and Britain acted in concert to deal with another crisis in the Middle East centred on the Baghdad Pact region. On this occasion, the Iraqi royal family was overthrown by a coup, and the leftist takeover of Iraq was countered by US marines landing on the beaches of the Lebanon to deal with communist forces in Beirut and at Tripoli. Concurrently, elements of the same British 16th Independent Parachute Brigade that had landed in the Suez Canal Zone in 1956 parachuted into the Jordanian capital Amman to support the authority of King Hussein. During 1959, Iraq formally left the Baghdad Pact organisation, which subsequently adopted the better-known name of the Central Treaty Organisation (CENTO).

But throughout the Cold War the main focus of East–West tension was always the Central Region of Europe, and within that region the epicentre of the undeclared war was invariably Berlin. The tensions and power struggle between East and West, and the imminent crisis within East Germany in mid-1961, culminated in the construction of the Berlin Wall in August that year. Thus was created a physical Iron Curtain across a divided Europe that more than matched the metaphorical image provided so eloquently by Winston Churchill during his historic speech at Fulton, Missouri in March 1946.

The existence of the Berlin Wall emphasised the clear line that had been drawn between the communist world and the West – the 'Free World'. Shortly thereafter the undeclared but de facto existence of Soviet and US spheres of influence was graphically illustrated by the only direct Soviet–US armed confrontation of the Cold War: the Cuban missile crisis of 1962. The world was possibly closer to a full-scale nuclear war on that occasion than at any other time during the Cold War. However, the lessons of that crisis undoubtedly assisted the development of better arrangements for the management of these ultimate weapons of destruction – even though it did not check the accelerating nuclear arms race of the 1960s. But above all else Cuba did demonstrate a grudging acceptance by Khrushchev that Cuba was placed both geographically and strategically well within the US sphere of vital interest. Thus was the nuclear balance – the balance of power or of terror – refined, as the two superpowers continued to learn the art of co-existing in the nuclear age.

Two years later, on 16 October 1964, the sleeping dragon of China awoke to the flash of light, blast and heat produced by the first successful test deto-nation of its own atomic device, which was followed on 17 June 1967 by its first thermonuclear explosion. Although it had a great deal of catching up to do, communist China – with its huge population and commensurately large conventional armed forces – had effectively laid its claim to being the third world superpower in waiting. The emergence of China as a superpower made the international scene infinitely more complex, not least due to the ideological differences and worsening relations between the People's Republic of China and the Soviet Union – and their various proxy and client states – during the 1960s. The involvement of both countries in the so-called wars of liberation, insurgencies and limited wars in the Middle East, South-east Asia and Africa also created numerous situations in which the United States, the Soviet Union and communist China became engaged in proxy wars during the 1960s and 1970s.

In a number of those conflicts described as 'insurgencies' the descriptive line between 'nationalist' and 'communist' was often so blurred that it became virtually indistinguishable. Whilst all of these lesser conflicts influ-enced to varying extents the global and ideological struggle between the superpowers, their true significance for the Cold War often lay in the entirely practical strategic advantages (such as deep-sea ports, airbases, access to oil and minerals and so on) that either the United States or the Soviet Union derived from the successful campaign of its client state or insurgent organisation. These wars also provided useful opportunities for the superpowers to test in combat – but by proxy – much of the new mili-tary technology and equipment that both of them developed as the Cold War progressed.

The Soviet policy of supporting wars of liberation wherever they were waged was a direct contributor to its second priority of reducing the power and influence of the United States and NATO. The achievement of this second priority in turn enabled achievement of the Soviets' first priority – the security of the Soviet Union and communist bloc against any and all forms of ideological and military attack; and central to this overriding need was Soviet awareness of the constantly growing nuclear capability of the United States.

At the conclusion of the US military involvement in Vietnam in 1973, the way was open for new relationships to be formed between the communist and capitalist worlds. Significant political changes had taken place in Washington through the 1960s, with the assassination of John F. Kennedy in 1963 and the escalating media (and consequently domestic) opposition to the Vietnam War – especially after Tet 1968 – which finally destroyed Lyndon B. Johnson politically and personally, and facilitated Richard M. Nixon's presidential victory in 1968. Then, in August 1974, the very institution of US president was severely damaged by Nixon's resignation following the Watergate affair, when Gerald Ford succeeded him. Rightly or wrongly, the office of president had been seriously diminished in world eyes. Throughout the Ford administration, and that of Jimmy Carter which followed it, America was perceived by the Soviet Union to be a weaker state – politically, militarily, economically and morally – than the superpower that had confronted it prior to 1968. Although but one incident, the seizing of the US Embassy staff in Tehran as hostages by Iranian Islamic revolutionaries on 4 November 1979, followed by the ill-fated rescue attempt by Delta Force in late-April the following year, exemplified the decline in America's power since the 1960s, that of its military in particular.[14] As if to emphasise this fact, just after Christmas 1979, the Soviet Union invaded Afghanistan.

Only when President Ronald Reagan was elected in 1980 did the Soviet Union recognise in America a resurgence of the superpower qualities with which it had been familiar in previous decades. The election of Margaret Thatcher and the Conservative Party in the United Kingdom in 1979 also restored that country's economic and military fortunes. Together, the United States and Great Britain at the start of the 1980s presented a new, united and forward-looking challenge to communism that had lain dormant for almost a decade. Although not by definition a 'Cold War conflict', the British victory against the Argentines in the Falklands War of 1982 provided a major boost for Britain's armed forces and for the country as a whole. However, the Falklands campaign also highlighted numerous war-fighting deficiencies in all three services and provided justification for remedying these matters. This in turn led to a real terms increase in UK defence expenditure and so raised the overall operational capability of the British armed forces to meet their wider Cold War challenges and NATO obligations effectively.

The renewed strength of the Anglo-American alliance during this period was a vital contributor to the eventual end of the Cold War. But although the Western Alliance's final Cold War victory came at the end of the 1980s, the less confrontational approach of the United States during the previous decade had also enabled it to engage in substantive negotiations with the Soviet leadership with a view to containing and managing the vast numbers of nuclear weapons that both sides had by then accumulated.

A Superpower in Embryo: The People's Republic of China

Early in the 1970s, in a major transformation of US foreign policy that had only been made possible by the steadily reducing American military involvement in South Vietnam, a bilateral rapprochement between the United States and the People's Republic of China (PRC) took place. In 1972, in an historic move, the then President Richard Nixon visited Beijing and conducted face-to-face talks with Chairman Mao Tse-tung. This momentous change of American foreign policy subsequently reduced US direct military involvement in Taiwan and also signalled Washington's acceptance of the PRC as representative of the whole of the Chinese people. And this in turn facilitated communist China's recognition and acceptance as a full member of the UN.

Understandably, these improved relations between Washington and Beijing did not sit well with Moscow; where the growing threat posed by the emerging superpower on its southern border was viewed with increasing concern. Nixon's visit to Beijing came just three years after a major Sino–Soviet border clash concerning Damansky Island in the late summer of 1969, in which more than 200 had died; and other sporadic incidents had continued to occur in the border region. China's readiness to resort to force and attack another communist state was again evident five years later, when it invaded Soviet-supported Vietnam in February 1979. On this occasion some 20,000 communist Chinese and 27,000 Vietnamese died. Previously, the People's Liberation Army (PLA) had engaged UN forces in Korea from 1950 to 1953, had suppressed the Tibetan uprising in 1954 to 1959, and had clashed with India in a border dispute from April to September 1965. The Soviets, therefore, had some cause for concern over the developing Sino-American relationship from 1972.

Moscow's concern was magnified considerably by the fact that China had carried out its first atomic explosion in October 1964. Beijing had followed this success with its first thermonuclear explosion in the summer of 1967 and China's first hydrogen bomb came into service about a year later. But even more significantly, the PRC had its first ICBM operational in 1971. If the new Sino–US rapprochement were ever translated into any form of military alliance it would mean that the Soviet Union was effectively surrounded. To the west were NATO's European states – notably the nuclear-capable United Kingdom and France, and the US and West German forces in the FRG. To the south lay China, by 1972 also a nuclear power. Meanwhile, over the North Pole and to the east was the United States with its huge nuclear arsenal. During the 1970s, the Soviet Union's perceptions of nuclear encirclement were further exacerbated by the development of nuclear capabilities by India, Pakistan and – it was generally assessed – Israel; although it was unlikely that the Soviet Union would be a primary target for an ICBM from any of these three countries.

The nuclear balance and the gradual rise of communist China to super-power status were two major and ever-present issues throughout the Cold War. Another was the growing level of terrorism that impinged increasingly upon everyday life worldwide from the 1960s, which has continued right up to the present day. A full account and analysis of the horrors that have scarred the Middle East and Western Europe in particular – but which since the end of the Cold War have also impacted directly upon the former Soviet Union and the United States – is beyond the scope of this text, although its escalation and general significance deserve a word of explanation.

The Rise of International Terrorism

As ever, the line between the terrorist and the freedom fighter is finely drawn, and depends entirely upon one's political standpoint and percep-tions. Therefore, however much their actions may be abhorrent to a rational observer or to a member of legitimate security forces seeking to impose and maintain the rule of law, the actions of those described as terrorists will usually provoke debate. The role of the Irgun and the Stern Gang against the British in Palestine, that of ZAPU and ZANU against the Salisbury regime in Rhodesia, and that of the FLN against the French in Algeria are but three such examples. Perceptions of terrorism are invariably complex and usually comprise a mixture of history (itself often a very subjective matter), precedent, politics and emotion. Religion, culture, language and ethnicity may also impinge upon the nature of terrorist campaigns to various extents. But if such campaigns are not themselves 'Cold War conflicts' what then has been their significance for the Cold War?

First, much as the wars of the period provided opportunities for the superpowers of East and West to further their national interests by proxy, so also did various terrorist campaigns. Given that a declared policy aim of the Soviet Union was 'to support wars of liberation', and that a number of terrorist organisations were 'revolutionary' and followed to varying degrees the teachings of Marx and Lenin, the extensive support provided to terrorist organisations by Moscow (or indirectly via another Eastern bloc country or Soviet client state) was predictable. As an adjunct to the Cold War strategic struggle, the actions of terrorist groups in the West also had the potential to destabilise these states and to divert and weaken the military effort directed against the Soviet Union and Warsaw Pact. The impact of the FLN and ALN campaign in Algeria upon a France already shaken politically and militarily by the outcome of the war in Indochina was enormous, and the French army revolts in 1960 and 1961 sent shock waves through what was – after the United States, Britain and the Federal Republic of Germany – one of the principal military powers within NATO. But the particular significance of any weakening or destabilising of France at that time was that it had just entered the nuclear weapons club, with the detonation of its first atomic bomb on 2 March 1960.

Terrorism was greatly assisted by the often naïve and over-liberal policies of the irresolute and politically weak governments of some Western states in the 1960s and 1970s. This provided favourable operating conditions and battlegrounds for organisations and groups such as Black September, the Palestine Liberation Organisation (PLO), the Red Army Faction, the Basque nationalists, the Baader-Meinhof Gang, the Red Brigades, the Japanese Red Army, the Irish Republican Army (IRA), and a host of others. In many cases the weapons and explosives of choice used by terrorist groups were of Eastern European origin, such as the ubiquitous AK-47 or Kalashnikov assault rifle employed extensively by the PLO, or the Czech-manufactured Semtex high explosive used by the Provisional IRA.[15] These items were either provided by the Soviet Union or (more often) via those states that tradition-ally sponsored terror and provided safe havens for terrorists. Libya and Syria are examples of such states. Soviet support for non-communist regimes and for Arab terrorist movements within or operating from the Muslim world exemplified Moscow's sometimes ambiguous but invariably pragmatic approach to the furtherance of its Cold War aims; and while US support for Israel remained inviolable, the Soviet Union's support for the PLO was entirely predictable. The United States and (later) Britain both supported the mujahedin in their fight against the Soviet forces in Afghanistan from 1980; actions that Moscow certainly regarded as aid to terrorists and insurgents. However, with a certain grim irony, it was the mujahedin victory in Afghanistan that subsequently enabled Islamic extremist terrorism to be visited so devastatingly upon New York on 11 September, 2001.

Dealing with insurgency and international terrorism became yet another violent strand of the forty-five-year-long Cold War. It also led to the formation, expansion and capability enhancement of various military special purpose forces – such as the British SAS, the West German Bundesgrenzschutz GSG-9, and the US Delta Force – all of which acquired operational skills that were readily transferable on to the conventional or nuclear battlefield.

Yet although terrorism became a part of all too many people's lives and consciousness during the Cold War, it remained very much a subsidiary form of conflict. However murderous and callous the actions of the terrorists were, their groups usually had a declared political aim or agenda, whether or not it was remotely achievable in practice. Therefore, no matter how inhuman or despicable a terrorist act might have been (especially where it was carried out against a non-military, non-political target), the reason for it was usually made abundantly clear. Only in recent times, with the indiscriminate action of the Al-Qaeda suicide bombers in the United States and those of Hamas and Islamic *jihad* against Israel in the Middle East, have today's Islamic terrorists effectively dehumanised both themselves and their cause. In the case of the Israeli–Palestinian conflict that is at the heart of this, the indiscriminate suicide bombings have moved the Palestinian movement so far beyond the accepted rules of armed conflict that Israel may soon have no room for further negotiation. If this is indeed so, then the time may be approaching when Israel will be forced into a final, decisive, full-scale war against the Palestinians – an Armageddon that would undoubtedly inflame the whole Middle East, with consequences extending far beyond that region. In the course of such a conflict, the supply of oil to the industrialised world would certainly be disrupted and invite outside intervention to safeguard it.

But irrespective of the levels of violence achieved and atrocities perpetrated by the terrorists, they could never match the awesome destructive power of the nuclear weapons developed and deployed by the principal protagonists of the Cold War. And, although they were never used in battle, these weapons of mass destruction came to be identified with the Cold War era more than any other category of weapon system.

THE NUCLEAR DIMENSION

Enabling Apocalypse

The respective development of the Soviet and US nuclear strategies during the Cold War followed separate courses, and very much reflected the different national characters of the two superpowers, which in turn flowed from their individual experiences during the Second World War. From the mid-1950s, the Soviet Union, then led by Khrushchev, assumed that a future war would inevitably be nuclear and prepared its offensive and defensive options accordingly. Initially, the Soviet strategic nuclear delivery capability focused on manned bombers such as the Myasischev Mya-4 Bison, the Tupolev Tu-20 Bear and the Tu-16 Badger. However, Khrushchev subsequently determined that the key nuclear weapon was the missile, and on 7 May 1960, the strategic rocket forces (*Raketnye Voiska Strategicheskogo Naznacheniya*) were created as a separate arm of the Soviet armed forces, and all missiles with ranges in excess of 620 miles came under their command. In addition to the long-range intercontinental missiles, the Soviets also developed a series of short-range tactical free-flight rockets with ranges up to about twenty miles. Just as the United States capitalised upon Second World War missile technology to advance its own missile programme, so the Soviet Union made extensive use of the V-2 missiles, scientists and technicians that the Red Army had captured in 1945; thus the terror weapons of Nazi Germany provided the foundation of knowledge from which were developed what many commentators categorised as the terror weapons of the Cold War.

Throughout the late 1940s and most of the 1950s the United States also favoured the manned bomber as its nuclear delivery means of choice. The Strategic Air Command (SAC) B-29 Superfortress of the Second World War was succeeded by the B-50, B-45, B-47 and then the B-52 Stratofortress. Generally, the American strategic bombers were technologically superior to their Soviet equivalents, and they were promoted at the expense of missile research and development, despite the potentially decisive lead in this field conferred on the United States by its direct access to the former German rocket scientist Werner von Braun, and the former head of the German V-2 rocket project at Peenemünde, Major General Walter Dornberger. However, developments in the Soviet Union prompted a revival of the missile programme in the mid-1950s, which was then considerably accelerated following the success of the Sputnik satellite launched by the Soviets on 4 October 1957. With massive funding available, the United States developed solid fuel technology, which enhanced significantly its missile readiness and deployment options. It also initiated a development programme for submarine-launched missiles. At the other end of the nuclear scale it developed a series of short-range tactical (or 'battlefield') nuclear missiles and artillery-fired atomic munitions.

So began the nuclear arms race – the contest between the United States and the Soviet Union to achieve nuclear superiority, both in qualitative and quantitative terms. In parallel with this both countries formulated policies for the management and potential use of these weapons, a process that culminated in the mutually assured destruction (MAD) concept, which was founded on the premise that a first-strike by either side could not eliminate the other's ability to launch a counter-strike, and that therefore a nuclear war was unwinnable and non-viable. In practice the MAD concept worked very well, inasmuch as no nuclear exchange took place between the Soviet Union and the United States throughout the Cold War period. However, it also fuelled the nuclear arms race, as neither side could afford to let the other believe that a nuclear war could be won: a situation that would have invalidated the MAD concept. Consequently, from the mid-1950s, the development, production and deployment by both superpowers of ever more sophisticated and varied types of missiles and nuclear warheads proceeded apace.[16]

Caribbean Crisis: Cuba, 1962

In 1962, just a year after the physical delineation of the East–West divide by the construction of the Berlin Wall, another major crisis arose. Although it was centred upon the Caribbean island of Cuba and so was several thousand miles away from the main focus of the Cold War conflict in Europe, it nevertheless impacted directly upon the struggle between the Soviet Union and the United States for strategic supremacy. It also brought these two superpowers to the brink of nuclear war.

Ever since 1 January 1959, when General Fulgencio Batista, the dictatorial ruler of Cuba, fled to safety in the United States, and so cleared the way for the victorious entry of Dr Fidel Castro's communist insurgents into Havana eight days later, the island that lay off the south coast of Florida and close to Central America had been a continuing source of irritation for Washington. Not only had Castro prevailed against all the odds and the accepted principles of counter-revolutionary warfare of the time, but his success had shown the revolutionary movements in several other Central and South American countries that despite US support for the government forces an insurgency could still succeed. The possibilities opened up by such perceptions threatened to destabilise the region, and by extension to diminish

American power and influence therein. But perhaps the greatest source of worry for Washington was the fact that Castro had openly courted the Soviet Union, and so when President Castro established his new communist government in Havana serious concerns were raised in Washington. Future years proved that the Cuban revolution was in reality unique, and none of the several other Central and South American revolutions that followed it were able to emulate its success. But in 1959 (the same year in which the first Soviet ICBM became operational) the existence of a Soviet-armed and supported communist state – potentially but the first of many – at the very heart of the US sphere of interest, posed an all too real threat to American security. However, although the events of 1961 and 1962 which flowed from Castro's success brought the United States and the Soviet Union into direct conflict and created possibly the most dangerous crisis of the Cold War, the resolution of what became known as the 'Cuban missile crisis' was also a watershed in East–West relations that enabled many of the unwritten protocols by which the two superpowers subsequently managed their strategic affairs.

When President John F. Kennedy was elected to office in 1961 he inherited a Central Intelligence Agency (CIA) plan to invade Cuba using a force of Cuban exiles and escapees who had been trained and equipped for the mission by the Americans. The invasion was intended to overthrow Castro's communist regime, which accorded directly with America's anti-communist policies of the 1950s. The ill-conceived operation was mounted in April 1961 at the Bay of Pigs, where forewarned and superior numbers of Cuban troops awaited the invaders, all of whom were killed or captured on the landing beaches. The failure was mainly attributable to the United States rather than to the Cuban exiles and while Castro's prestige was enhanced, the Soviet leader, Khrushchev, assessed that the new US president lacked sound judgement and that, in light of the Bay of Pigs débâcle, he would seek to avoid further military confrontations.

Accordingly, Khrushchev decided to test US resolve and at the same time redress recent American advances in missile technology and intercontinental strike capability by placing Soviet missiles on Cuba, with the clear capability to hit American cities and so restore what was (in Khrushchev's view) an equitable strategic balance. However, when a U-2 aircraft's aerial surveillance cameras revealed the presence of part-constructed medium-range ballistic missile (MRBM) sites in western Cuba near San Cristobal and on the northern coast at Sagua La Grande, Washington refused to share Khrushchev's view of an equitable strategic balance.

Indeed, as at 14 October, there were already some 20,000 Soviet personnel in Cuba, so any US military action against Cuba would almost certainly have brought them into direct conflict with these Soviet forces. The Soviet military assets and equipment in Cuba included 140 SAMs, forty-two MiG-21 fighters and forty Ilyushin Il-28 bombers. But most significantly, there were also forty MRBMs and twelve intermediate-range ballistic missiles (IRBM) on the island.

Once activated, missiles from these sites would be able to strike targets throughout the United States. Washington could be hit just twelve minutes after launch and New York or Chicago a few minutes later; longer-range missiles would be able to strike cities as far away as Los Angeles less than twenty minutes after launch. The strategic implications were clear, and their potential enormity indicated Khrushchev's failure to understand both the nature of the United States and the wider global realities of the time. Clearly, the United States could not allow the missile sites to become operational, and Kennedy advised the Soviets that they should be removed within fourteen days. This requirement was reinforced by the deployment of a naval task force to prevent the balance of missiles – then in transit in Soviet ships on the high seas – from reaching Cuba. Wherever they were intercepted, these cargo vessels were to be given the choice either of returning whence they came, sailing to a non-Cuban port, or being sunk by the US Navy (USN). The crisis became acute when, on 22 October, US intelligence staffs briefed that sixteen of the MRBM sites 'appeared to be operational' (in fact, this intelligence assessment actually underestimated the true extent of operational readiness of the Soviet missiles on Cuba).[17] That day, Kennedy dispelled any lingering doubts that Khrushchev might have had concerning his resolve, when he indicated in a broadcast to the nation that in the event of a missile attack from Cuba against any state in the Western Hemisphere, the United States would regard it as an attack against its own territory – one that would be met with 'a full retaliatory response upon the Soviet Union'. In a further television statement he added: 'We will not prematurely or unnecessarily risk the costs of worldwide nuclear war in which even the fruits of victory would be ashes in our mouth – but neither will we shrink from that risk at any time it must be faced.'[18] Within the language of international diplomacy, the message for Khrushchev could not have been expressed more plainly: the United States was if necessary prepared to embark upon a nuclear war over Cuba.

Both sides must have known that the United States could have destroyed much of the Soviet Union in a strategic nuclear exchange (including a counterforce strike that would have severely reduced Moscow's ability to carry out its own retaliation) and that the price of solving the Cuban situation was certainly not worth a nuclear war. Nevertheless, the Soviet freighters sailed on. Meanwhile, the US forces moved to Alert Condition Two, NATO forces in

Europe prepared for the war they had anticipated and trained for since 1949, and diplomatic activity reached fever-pitch. In London, on 27 October (the same day on which an American U-2 strayed into Siberian airspace – an act that could well have been misinterpreted by the Kremlin as a final reconnaissance prior to a nuclear first strike),[19] Prime Minister Harold MacMillan authorised Britain's nuclear delivery V-bomber force to move to Alert Condition Three, which meant that they were at fifteen minutes' notice to take off from their Lincolnshire bases to attack their targets in the Soviet Union. In the United States a task force of 280,000 men stood ready to invade Cuba and eliminate the missile threat by force.

The crisis peaked on Wednesday 24 October. A convoy of Soviet vessels was observed moving towards the so-called 'quarantine line' of some sixty American warships that had been deployed about 500 miles east of Cuba in a huge arc to block the Atlantic approaches to the island. Maritime patrol aircraft had already provided photo-imagery that showed the missiles aboard these craft. As the world held its breath, two Soviet freighters – the *Gagarin* and the *Komiles*, with a Soviet submarine close at hand to support them if necessary – approached a group of nineteen American warships in the quarantine line. Washington assessed that the freighters would reach these warships shortly after 10.00 hours. Meanwhile, from their bases in the United States, the B-52 bombers were already airborne, fully prepared, if so required, to fly to the Soviet Union with their loads of nuclear bombs.

By 10.25 hours the freighters were in direct sight of the American warships. Then, just as an armed confrontation seemed inevitable, they hove to. They paused in place for a while; then they laboriously turned and steamed away from Cuba, heading back to their home ports. Although Khrushchev had pushed the crisis to the very brink – and had argued (and from Moscow's perspective had probably believed) the 'defensive' nature of the missiles bound for Cuba – common-sense had prevailed at the last minute and the two-week crisis drew to an end.

Although clearly the victor in the affair, President Kennedy responded positively to a request made by Khrushchev the next day, the 25th, for an assurance that the United States would not subsequently invade Cuba. Khrushchev also linked an acceptable resolution of the crisis to a reduction (albeit much later) of the US intermediate-range Jupiter missiles then stationed in Turkey, close to the southern border of the Soviet Union. This assurance and the withdrawal of the now-superfluous naval blockade were the only concessions made by Washington. Then, following Kennedy's positive reaction to the Soviet bid to save face and salvage something from the crisis, on 28 October Khrushchev indicated that the missiles on Cuba would all be removed. He was also forced by the Americans to remove the Soviet bombers that were based there. Khrushchev's climb-down concluded the Cuban missile crisis: the only occasion on which United States and Soviet Union opposed each other so directly, with both sides just a step away from global nuclear war.

In retrospect, the Cuban affair had several positive outcomes for the future conduct of the Cold War. It forced Moscow and Washington – the former in particular – to understand the true nature and implications of nuclear weapons. Although the Soviets continued to regard their early use (together with that of chemical weapons) much more routinely than the Western Powers ever did, Soviet attitudes to these weapons were undoubtedly modified by the events of October 1962. At the same time, Kennedy's position was strengthened immeasurably, whereas Khrushchev's was weakened. The latter's flawed judgement over the Cuba crisis undoubtedly contributed to his final removal from office in 1964.

One of the most positive consequences of the crisis was the establishment of the 'hot line' between Washington and Moscow some months later, which allowed the US and Soviet heads of state to communicate directly during future East–West crises. Such communication during the Cuban crisis had involved the tortuous transmission of all messages via numerous levels of staffing, encoding and decoding before they eventually reached the decision makers. The final stage of these potentially world-changing transmissions from Moscow was surreal, in that they were carried by an ordinary bicycle courier from the Soviet Embassy in Washington to the White House administration. Perhaps the crisis might have been avoided altogether if a direct line between Khrushchev and Kennedy had existed prior to October 1962? Certainly such a real-time means of international dialogue could have reduced the extent of the Soviet leader's underestimation of Kennedy's resolve.

After the crisis, both the United States and Great Britain assigned certain of their nuclear forces to NATO. Finally, the Americans withdrew the sixty Jupiter IRBM systems from Italy and Turkey by the end of 1965 (by which time the real effectiveness of these older missiles had been substantially diminished by other technological advances) in accordance with the undertaking given by Kennedy in his reply to Khrushchev's request of 25 October.

Meanwhile, the Soviet leaders had noted and learned from the inability of their naval forces to confront the USN on the high seas. This capability gap directly influenced the Kremlin's decision to expand the Soviet global maritime capability significantly during the next two decades – a move promoted energetically and successfully by Admiral of the Fleet Sergei Georgiyevich Gorshkov, albeit at enormous financial cost to the Soviet Union and at the expense of some other parts of the Soviet armed forces.

Perhaps one of the most telling anecdotes of the 1962 Cuban crisis was that recounted by Peter Hennessy in his book *The Secret State*. It provided a very British perspective on the business of nuclear war and of the myriad of related sub-plots and issues that attended its Cold War development. Hennessy described the arrest of a highly placed Western-controlled agent or spy, one Colonel Oleg Penkovsky, by the Soviet authorities on 22 October (the very same day that President Kennedy was addressing the American people concerning the developing Cuban crisis), although at the time Penkovsky's arrest was not disclosed by the KGB. Despite this fact, 'various things convinced his MI6 controller that something was amiss', then, in Hennessy's own words:

> On 2 November 1962, nearly a week after the Cuban missile crisis had eased (but when British V-bombers still stood on Alert Condition 3), a pre-arranged set of noises came down the MI6 officer's telephone which Penkovsky was to use if and when a Soviet nuclear attack on the West was imminent (three blows of breath, repeated in another call one minute later). Shortly before he died, I asked Gervase Cowell, the SIS [Secret Intelligence Service] man who took the call, what he did on hearing those sounds. Certain that Penkovsky was captive and had had information extracted from him about call-signs, rendezvous and so on, Cowell decided to do nothing. He neither alerted his ambassador, Sir Frank Roberts, nor his chief in London, Sir Dick White. Mr Cowell, a small, humorous, unassuming man, delivered himself of this recollection without personal grandeur or historical drama. He is, however, the only man I have ever met who has found himself in such a precarious and classically Cold War position. *For the bomb made error so terrible and potentially terminal, from virtually the beginning to the end of the East–West confrontation* [author's italics].[20]

Thus the Cuban missile crisis was a defining moment of the Cold War. It was the point at which both the United States and the Soviet Union began fully to understand the potentially apocalyptic power that each had at its disposal, and the consequent responsibility that devolved upon the leaders of both states to manage and control that capability with great care. In fact, many years later it was revealed that nuclear war had been even closer than those involved had judged in 1962. Not only had a Soviet submarine under sustained depth charge attack by US warships off Cuba been on the verge of responding with a nuclear torpedo – a situation averted by the clear thinking of Vassily Arkhipov, one of the three officers required to authorise its use[21] – but it became clear that the Soviet forces on Cuba were in fact already fully prepared to use tactical nuclear missiles to counter any US invasion of the island: which would undoubtedly have provoked a strategic nuclear response by the United States. In a radio interview in 2002, on the fortieth anniversary of the Cuban crisis, Robert MacNamara readily acknowledged in hindsight that a peaceful outcome of the crisis had been a matter of 'sheer luck'.[22]

In any event, the momentous lessons learned in Washington and Moscow during that October of 1962 were also lost neither upon the governments of Great Britain and France, nor those of the non-nuclear Western Powers. Therefore, in several ways the Cuban crisis actually contributed to reducing the possibility of a nuclear conflict in the future; although this in turn indirectly fuelled the fires of many lesser proxy wars and conflicts that occurred during the succeeding years.

The Nuclear Balance and Arms Control

By the end of 1969 – the same year in which America finally beat the Soviets in the race to achieve a manned moon landing – the United States possessed some 1,054 land-based ICBMs, 656 maritime ballistic missiles, 450 long-range heavy bombers and sixty medium bombers. Multiple warhead technology meant that each nuclear missile could attack several targets. The Soviet Union's nuclear weapons holdings were 1,050 land-based ICBMs, 160 maritime ballistic missiles, 200 long-range heavy bombers and 1,050 medium bombers. Significantly, the Soviets also had 700 of the shorter-range IRBMs and MRBMs, which reflected Soviet doctrine for nuclear war-fighting at a tactical and operational level.[23] It should be said, however, that various US battlefield missile systems of the time also had the capability to be fitted with nuclear or conventional warheads. Thus, both East and West possessed sufficient nuclear weapons to destroy each other – and much of the rest of the world – several times over.

Yet despite the construction of the Berlin Wall in 1961, the Cuban crisis in 1962 and the continuing conflict in Vietnam, détente between the United States and the Soviet Union haltingly emerged in the 1960s from what Khrushchev had, in the late 1950s, euphemistically termed a policy of peaceful co-existence; and by 1970 both Washington and Moscow understood the need to put in place some sort of agreed constraints and controls over the escalating strategic arms race.

Accordingly, in 1972 the first Strategic Arms Limitation Treaty (SALT 1) was signed by both countries. The same year, an anti-ballistic missile (ABM) treaty was also signed, which limited the allowable defences against long-range strategic missile attack.[24] Work on a SALT 2 agreement then began, but this was frustrated and delayed by both sides seeking to maintain an advantage whilst limiting the capability of the other. The degree of mutual trust and impetus that had obtained in 1972 was largely absent from the SALT 2 negotiations, and made for a difficult process. Meanwhile, the accelerating pace of rocket, warhead and related technology meant that multiple warheads, increased missile accuracy, the use of mobile launchers and so on all provided ways in which the total number of weapons allowed could be circumvented in terms of actual capability. Nevertheless, the SALT 2 agreement was finally ready for ratification by the US Congress at the end of 1979. But when the Soviet forces invaded Afghanistan at the end of December, President Carter recommended a postponement of ratification, and SALT 2 was rendered non-effective. In parallel with this, in December 1979 NATO announced the intended future deployment of 108 Pershing II MRBMs and 464 ground-launched cruise missiles (GLCM) in Western Europe to offset the significantly greater size of the Warsaw Pact conventional forces in the Central Region, as well as the threat posed by Soviet MRBMs. By late 1980, the nuclear balance totalled 1,054 ICBMs (with 2,154 warheads) and 656 submarine-launched ballistic missiles (SLBMs) (with 5,120 warheads) for the United States, while there were 1,398 ICBMs (4,306 warheads), 600 MRBMs and 1,003 SLBMs (1,309 warheads) in the Soviet nuclear inventory. Also in 1980, the United States had 338 long-range bombers and sixty-five medium-range bombers, compared with the Soviet Union's 156 and 518 of each category. Finally, there were forty-one US ballistic missile submarines, as against eighty-seven in the Soviet fleet; although the Soviets had also some sixty-eight submarines carrying cruise missiles.[25] Although the specifics of throw-weight, accuracy and delivery means are without the scope of this text, the significance of the advances in multiple warhead technology and the sheer scale of the US and Soviet nuclear arsenals were indicative of the central (if dormant in practice) role that the nuclear confrontation played in the Cold War, and the extent to which the nuclear threat understandably overshadowed all other superpower considerations and decisions.

Another issue linked to the main nuclear debate followed US development of the enhanced radiation (ER) W70-3 warhead for its Lance SSM tactical nuclear delivery system, and the one-kiloton W70-9 warhead for the nuclear-capable 8in (or 203 mm) howitzer. In simple terms, the ER warhead was designed to release up to eighty per cent of its yield in very high-energy, deadly (but quite short-term) neutrons, with a longer range than the neutrons generated by standard fission weapons. It therefore had a much larger effective radius against personnel than normal fission weapons of the same nominal yield. This meant that the destruction due to the heat and blast of a nuclear explosion was minimised, while the fatal effect on human beings was increased significantly. Consequently, the ER was an ideal defensive and deterrent weapon for NATO in Europe – what better way could there be to stop the Warsaw Pact armoured formations literally in their tracks as they raced west across the North German Plain? Hopefully the German civilian population could have been evacuated or protected beforehand, and the forewarned NATO troops would have been able to take appropriate protective measures before the ER weapon was used. Meanwhile, although the exposed Warsaw Pact aggressors in their tanks, armoured personnel carriers and trucks would be killed in their hundreds and possibly thousands, the industrial infrastructure, bridges, roadways, buildings and forestation of West Germany would (when compared to the effects of a standard non-ER nuclear explosion) be left relatively unscathed.

The ER weapon should therefore have been both a war-winner and a real deterrent to war. However, the Soviet propaganda machine presented an emotive image of the ER weapon – or 'neutron bomb' – as the ultimate capitalist weapon: one that killed people while preserving property. Remarkably, this proposition gained so much credibility in the West – ably assisted by some sensationalised media reporting – that public opinion forced its withdrawal from service (although the United States retained the W-79-0 ten kiloton and W-79-1 one- to two-kiloton artillery ER warheads, and the one-kiloton Lance SSM ER warhead, but these were never deployed to units). Thus it was that Soviet propaganda and public opinion so pressured Western political leaders in the late 1970s that NATO forces were denied access to an important technological advance which, by its very existence, could have significantly reduced the likelihood of a conventional Warsaw Pact attack in central Europe. At the same time, this ill-judged political decision denied those same NATO forces the ability to deal effectively – and at least physical cost to Western Europe – with the invaders, if the Soviet and Warsaw Pact forces had ever chosen to launch such an attack. The neutron bomb issue showed the power of the media to influence defence policy, and also illustrated its susceptibility to well-orchestrated manipulation by the communists. The demise of the neutron bomb as a NATO weapon also showed the degree to which the American political leadership was, by the late 1970s, reluctant to support the needs of its military commanders in the wake of its recent Vietnam War experience.[26]

After the Cold War the process of nuclear arms limitation was transformed into one of nuclear arms reduction by the US–Soviet START agreements. On 5 December 2001, both countries announced that they had complied with the START 1 agreement of 1991, which reduced their nuclear weapons ceilings to 1,600 delivery vehicles and 6,000 warheads. For various reasons START 2 and START 3 agreements – although negotiated – were never implemented. However, a so-called 'Treaty of Moscow' signed by US President Bush and Russian President Putin reduced their nuclear arsenals to 2,200 warheads each, although additional warheads might be stored independently of the missiles.

The metaphorical nuclear fall-out of 1945 has already existed for more than half a century, with the rapidly developing Cold War that made the East–West nuclear arms race inevitable. Although the Cold War has now ended, the vital process of managing and controlling nuclear weapons and their proliferation will undoubtedly continue far into the future – in a world where access to nuclear material today is probably easier than at any time since the invention of the atom bomb.

By the way. the kiss on page 37 was a dude. How did it feel? if it made you feel good you are gay. if it didn't do nothing for you, you are still straight.

CHAPTER FOUR

THE COLD WAR COMBATANTS

Terrorism was one of the lowest levels of violent activity during the Cold War, and nuclear war potentially the highest; but central to all aspects of the conflict were the two great alliances that, from the mid-1950s, represented the military power, principles and ideology of East and West: the Warsaw Pact and NATO. They also embodied the military and political doctrine of the two superpowers that led them: the Soviet Union and the United States. Remarkably, despite the scale and capability of the huge forces commanded by these alliances, their role throughout the Cold War proved to be deterrence, not combat. Indeed, each side's awareness of the other's power provided a balance of forces – some would say a balance of fear – that made their committal to war if not unthinkable, then at least ill-advised.

Thus the respective perceptions by East and West of the strengths and capabilities of NATO and the Warsaw Pact meant in practice that the much predicted and extensively planned war between the communist East and the democratic (or capitalist) West in Central Europe never took place, although on numerous occasions the abyss was but a short step or single error of judgement away, and had such a war begun it would almost certainly have led to a global nuclear conflict. Accordingly, the part played by NATO and the Warsaw Pact during the Cold War was another vitally important aspect of the overall conflict. Indeed, the very existence and actions short of war carried out by these forces were a form of conflict in their own right; one in which NATO was finally triumphant. And throughout the strategic struggle, the threat of nuclear war was ever-present.

The North Atlantic Treaty Organisation

The NATO Treaty, signed on 4 April 1949, was the birth of what was undoubtedly one of the most important and successful military alliances of all time. The original twelve member states were the United States, Great Britain, France,[27] Canada, Norway, Iceland, Denmark, Italy, Portugal, and the three Benelux countries. Later, West Germany, Spain, Greece and Turkey also became NATO members.[28] Despite its relatively large and disparate membership, and the numerous practical difficulties that flowed from this, from 1949 to 1990 it undeniably fulfilled its mission of deterring a Soviet and (from 1955) Warsaw Pact attack on Western Europe. Subsequently, it has provided a mechanism for the expansion of its membership within Eastern Europe, where it has also produced an important stabilising influence and point of contact and dialogue with Russia on defence and security matters.

Finally, the post-1990 NATO alliance has adapted itself to match the so-called 'new world order' and today provides an effective military framework for global peacekeeping that has already been tested operationally in the former Yugoslavia and Kosovo.

The NATO organisation developed and grew through the 1950s, and in September 1950 it adopted the strategic concept of 'forward defence', which meant that it would engage any Soviet aggression in Europe as far to the east as possible. This in turn meant implicitly that NATO forces would need to be stationed in West Germany, which would be the European focus of any future war. It also highlighted the significant advantages of West German armed forces being included in NATO. This led, on 23 October 1954, to the creation of the FRG as a sovereign state within NATO, with foreign NATO troops stationed in West Germany by invitation of the government.

The ministerial-level diplomatic and policy lead for NATO was provided by the North Atlantic Council and by its Defence Council, while its military focus was embodied in the Military Committee – all of which bodies were based at NATO headquarters in Fontainebleau, France until 1966, and thereafter at Brussels, Belgium. During the 1950s the three major NATO commands (MNC) were formed as Allied Command Atlantic (based in the United States), Allied Command Europe and Allied Command Channel. Below the MNCs were the NATO regional major subordinate commands and these in turn commanded a number of principal subordinate commands.[29]

NATO's evolving strategy reflected the changing political, technological and military world, and the 'tripwire' concept endorsed by NATO in 1956 was succeeded by 'flexible response' in 1967. The former supported the militarily questionable (but politically necessary) concept of forward defence and called for an immediate and massive retaliation to counter any Soviet aggression. However, flexible response recognised the much increased range of nuclear and conventional options that were by then available, and also that the implications and management of modern warfare had by 1967 become significantly more complex. In practice, NATO's conventional capability suffered from two important weaknesses. The first was the maldeployment of its forces – a legacy of geography and of the positions in which the Allies had found themselves at the end of the Second World War. The heavily armoured American forces were based mainly in the picturesque mountainous and heavily forested countryside of southern Germany and Bavaria, while the much more lightly equipped British and Benelux forces were stationed adjacent to the gently undulating Hanover Plain. Although a redeployment of the Americans northward to counter what was assessed to be the area of the greatest Warsaw Pact tank threat against NATO was impracticable, the relative inappropriateness of the NATO deployment to deal with the specific forces that would oppose them was a problem that endured throughout the Cold War. The issue was further exacerbated by the numbers of national forces that remained stationed in their home countries, which therefore had to move considerable distances eastward to their battle positions in time of war. NATO's second important capability gap was in logistic stocks and resupply. In simple terms, it is unlikely that the planned stocks held in the forward areas could have sustained the probable expenditure rates – of ammunition in particular – or that Warsaw Pact interdiction of NATO lines of communication would have permitted the necessary resupply of NATO forward units.

Although several post-1945 conflicts (notably the Arab–Israeli wars, the Falklands War, the Vietnam War and the Korean conflict) all indicated the new intensity and increasing tempo of modern warfare – both of which would have been maximised in a war between NATO and the Warsaw Pact – it was not until the final decade of the Cold War that significant steps were taken to rectify this deficiency in the NATO Central Region. However, even then these measures would probably have been inadequate to meet NATO's needs in an unreinforced ground war in West Germany. But despite this, any substantive moves to rectify either the maldeployment or the logistic issues invariably foundered on financial grounds, as the Western democracies were simply unwilling to bear the huge cost of putting right these operational deficiencies. Nevertheless, despite the risk imposed by these important operational constraints, NATO still managed to maintain a sufficiently robust deterrent military posture throughout the Cold War. This meant that the Soviet leadership never felt sufficiently confident of its ultimate success to launch its armoured formations across the IGB in a bid to destroy NATO and dominate the whole of Western Europe.

NATO strategy was also affected and modified by a plethora of world events. Especially significant were the Berlin crisis in 1953; the war in Indochina, with the defeat of the French in 1954; the Hungarian uprising and the Anglo-French attack at Suez in 1956; the Sputnik I satellite launch in 1957; the Soviet shooting down in 1960 of an American U-2 surveillance aircraft over Russia and the capture of its pilot, Francis Gary Powers; the Cuban missile crisis in 1962; the successful detonation by communist China of its first atomic bomb in 1964; and, finally, the withdrawal of France from NATO's integrated command structure in 1966. By 1968, albeit at the apparent price of accepting that a Soviet sphere of influence existed to the east of the 'Iron Curtain', NATO had achieved a more or less workable relationship with its potential foes and the two great alliances provided a balance of power and influence across Europe. The existence of this undeclared status quo was confirmed by NATO's pragmatic and generally passive reaction to the Warsaw Pact invasion of Czechoslovakia in 1968. Subsequently, through the 1970s, there were bilateral talks between East and West Germany, and others between the Soviets and the three Western Powers in Berlin[30] concerning the city's future status. There were initiatives by the United States and the Soviet Union to achieve nuclear arms limitation and better control of these weapons. A 1968 NATO proposal for talks on mutual and balanced force reductions received a positive Soviet response in 1971. There were also wider talks about military security and co-operation in Europe. All this indicated an improving security situation between West and East in Europe; despite the growth of Soviet and Warsaw Pact military capability throughout the decade.

Indeed, the Soviet Union astutely used the improvement in East–West relations to weaken Western resolve in a number of NATO member states. Inevitably, as the apparent threat of war retreated, so certain Western governments and electorates questioned the need to maintain their high levels of forces and NATO military readiness, with the level of national defence expenditure this necessitated. Even the effects of the 1973 Yom Kippur War were largely limited to a short-term increase in nuclear alert states, an increased understanding of the nature of modern warfare, and a new awareness of the war's impact upon the Middle East oil industry on which the West so depended. However, in late December 1979, NATO received its first real wake-up call since the much more turbulent and difficult days of the 1960s. On 27 December, Soviet armoured forces rolled across the Soviet-Afghan border at the start of Moscow's ten-year war to subjugate and dominate its Muslim neighbour.

The West's diplomatic response to the Soviet invasion was led by the United States, and President Carter demonstrated an uncharacteristically robust response to the Soviet action. Perhaps this very fact was indicative of Moscow's misjudgement of the extent to which the West had been lulled into complacency by the improved East–West relations during the 1970s. In any event, the Soviet Union's military action demonstrated both its possible wider expansionist intentions and its military capability to carry out those intentions should it so choose; and the threat of Soviet action to deal with civil unrest in Poland two years later served further to underline the still-present threat posed by the Soviet Union and Warsaw Pact.

In Afghanistan, the Soviet campaign became an important factor in the declining morale and combat effectiveness of the Soviet armed forces, and was thus an indirect contributor to NATO's Cold War victory. It also provided an opportunity for the United States and Great Britain (plus Pakistan and several other Muslim countries) to provide financial and limited military support for the mujahedin insurgents – a policy that the future governments of both countries undoubtedly regretted in later years, but which did match their containment and counter-communism policies of the early 1980s. The Afghanistan conflict also coincided with the return to power of the Republicans in the United States and the Conservatives in the United Kingdom – political events that reinvigorated the transatlantic link and meeting of minds on security and defence issues. This common under-standing and awareness of the ever-present and increasing Soviet and Warsaw Pact threat precipitated an unprecedented flurry of NATO activity: first, to publicise the realities and sheer scale of the Soviet threat, and then to justify its measures to counter it.

An unclassified NATO worst-case (with both sides fully reinforced) assess-ment in 1986 indicated that its forces were outnumbered by those of the Warsaw Pact by 121 to 230 divisions, 24,250 to 52,000 tanks, 22,580 to 28,000 anti-armour guided weapon launchers, 18,350 to 42,000 artillery pieces, heavy mortars and multi-barrelled rocket launchers, and 41,500 to 54,000 armoured personnel carriers and other armoured fighting vehicles. Only in the area of dedicated attack helicopters did NATO enjoy a numerical supe-riority, with 1,250 against the Warsaw Pact holding of 970. In an unrein-forced scenario, such as a surprise attack launched against NATO without time for its US-based forces to move to Europe, the Warsaw Pact forces enjoyed an overall quantitative superiority in all manpower and matériel categories. The Soviet Union and Warsaw Pact also had more reconnais-sance and combat aircraft of all types at their disposal than NATO, although once it had completed its full reinforcement NATO would probably have had available a greater number of fighter-bomber ground attack aircraft than the Warsaw Pact forces. However, in all other categories of aircraft the Warsaw Pact would have maintained its superiority.[31]

NATO actions to redress the significant threat posed to its forces in Europe included the deployment of Pershing II and GLCMs in West Germany and the United Kingdom respectively to counter the Soviet SS-20 intermediate range missile threat, the announcement of the US strategic defence initiative (SDI) to counter the ICBM threat, and finally a new NATO operational concept of follow-on forces attack (FOFA). The FOFA concept provided for the early destruction of the Soviet and Warsaw Pact forces in depth that were essential to maintain the momentum of any ground attack launched against NATO in Europe. By the mid-1980s NATO's target acquisi-tion capability was able to support this concept, and could therefore invali-date the strategy upon which Soviet offensive plans for a war against NATO had depended for the previous four decades. As the Soviet Union became more deeply embroiled in its vicious and domestically unpopular war in

Afghanistan, it was gradually losing the Cold War against NATO. Only by its propaganda success against the intended deployment by the United States in the early 1980s of ER weapons could Moscow claim to have redressed the otherwise irresistible military, economic and political tide that was flowing against its Cold War aspirations. By the second half of the decade an East–West dialogue on a range of security issues was again in progress, and the appointment of the reforming Mikhail Gorbachev as the CPSU General Secretary in 1985 provided the catalyst that subsequently changed the Soviet Union for ever.

The fundamental nature and future extent of these changes was illustrated by Prime Minister Margaret Thatcher's relationship with Gorbachev, when she, together with President Ronald Reagan, declared that here at last was 'a man with whom we could do business'. She provided an informal conduit between Gorbachev and Reagan, as well as being a sounding-board for Gorbachev on American attitudes and on Washington's possible responses to his own ideas and intentions.

'No sparer of persons, she told him [Gorbachev] that she thought communism was a rotten system and the sooner he got rid of it the better. Also that Chernenko, then [December 1984] General Secretary, made no sense at all, and that the Soviet Union was the cause of most of the world's problems and it should take a lead in disarming. Many would have got huffy or retreated into a shell, or terminated the conversation, but the good thing about Gorbachev was that he didn't – he hit back in similar terms.' ... [Later on] for her visit to the Soviet Union in March 1987 [Gorbachev] agreed to arrange whatever she wanted. Her presence was to have an electrifying effect, especially in a famous television interview when she routed three Russian journalists put up to attack her. The Soviet audience heard from her that they had more weapons than any other country, and that the information they were fed was worthless. 'With Gorbachev the discussions were tough. She spoke of the damage that communism had done to the Soviet Union and the rest of the world ... An awful lot, I think, he was hearing for the first time, being exposed to the outside world in a crude and powerful form. Increasingly from 1987 onwards he found it useful to test out his views [during his discussions with Mrs Thatcher].'[32]

The great policy changes in the Soviet Union in turn precipitated the irrelevance and subsequent collapse of the Warsaw Pact, and thus enabled NATO to claim the final victory over its Soviet and Warsaw Pact enemies of some forty years' standing. Somewhat bizarrely, during the decade following the end of the Cold War, a number of the former Warsaw Pact nations (actively encouraged by the NATO 'Partnership for Peace' initiative and other initiatives, programmes and inducements) abrogated their Cold War ties with almost indecent haste, and sought to transfer their military and political allegiance to NATO and the European Union. In 2002, although still denied membership of NATO, Russia itself was offered representative access to important aspects of NATO policy-making and high-level deliberations on global defence and security issues. Truly the end of the Cold War had created a new world order, together with an uncertain future both for the victorious West and NATO and for the vanquished – the former Soviet Union and its old allies of the now defunct Warsaw Pact.

The Warsaw Pact

The Warsaw Pact Treaty supplemented and strengthened a number of existing military aid agreements between the Eastern bloc countries. Although the states involved (the Soviet Union, Poland, East Germany, Czechoslovakia, Hungary, Romania, Bulgaria and Albania[33]) were moving towards such a military organisation by 1954 in any case, the admission of West Germany to NATO on 5 May 1955 was cited as the formal justification for the creation of the Warsaw Pact. It was signed on 14 May 1955 and came fully into effect during 1957, when bilateral agreements between the Soviet Union and East Germany, Poland, Hungary and Romania concerning the stationing of Soviet forces on their territory were concluded. Also, in time of war, all of the national forces of the member states would come under the command of the Soviet-dominated Combined Supreme Command of the Warsaw Pact.[34] The Soviet forces that were permanently stationed in member states comprised respectively the Group of Soviet Forces Germany (GSFG) (twenty divisions, plus an artillery division), the Northern Group of Forces (NGF) in Poland (two divisions), and the Southern Group of Forces (SGF) in Hungary (four divisions). Following the Soviet intervention in 1968, a further bilateral agreement was also concluded with Czechoslovakia on 16 October that year, concerning the stationing of a Soviet Central Group of Forces (CGF) (five divisions) in that country.

In 1978 the combat potential of the Warsaw Pact was formidable. The Soviet Union alone could field an army of two million soldiers, with 60,000 tanks and 36,000 guns and rocket launchers; organised in fifty armoured divisions, 110 motor-rifle (mechanised) divisions and seven airborne divisions. The Soviet ground forces were supported by an air force equipped with about 10,000 operational aircraft, plus the ability to call on a trained reserve of twenty million men. A force of about 200,000 strategic rocket troops manned some 1,600 ICBM silos and 800 MRBMs. Meanwhile, on the high seas a Soviet fleet of two aircraft carriers, two helicopter carriers, thirty-three cruisers, eighty-four destroyers, 136 frigates and 400 submarines (including sixty-six equipped with ballistic missiles) enabled the Soviet Union to project its maritime power across the globe. A further 270,000 border troops and eleven million militia troops were available for the defence of the Soviet homeland.

Although the military quality of the Warsaw Pact member states varied considerably, if all had been committed to an offensive against NATO, they could have added to the land campaign up to a further fifty-seven armoured and mechanised divisions, with a total of almost 12,000 tanks and about 6,000 artillery guns and rocket launchers; plus the support of more than 2,000 additional combat aircraft.[35]

Despite the development and deployment of some nationally produced weapons, vehicles and equipment the Warsaw Pact nations generally used equipment of Soviet origin, thereby achieving a significantly greater degree of standardisation and interoperability than could ever have been achieved within NATO.

Conceptually, the Warsaw Pact differed fundamentally from NATO in that it was not an alliance of international equals, as all its member states were ultimately subordinate to the Soviet Union.[36] This was demonstrated all too clearly by Moscow's intervention or threatened intervention in East Germany, Hungary, Czechoslovakia and Poland in 1953, 1956, 1968 and 1981 respectively. Thus, while the Warsaw Pact was certainly a counterbalance to NATO, with a well-defined external military mission, it was also the principal means by which the Soviet Union – applying the 'Brezhnev doctrine' which limited the sovereignty of the non-Soviet socialist states – maintained its day-to-day domination of the Eastern bloc; a domination invariably charac-terised by the Soviet Union's national interests.

For all its apparent military strength, the Warsaw Pact's real capability to conduct a successful offensive against NATO was probably illusory, although that view only really emerged in the West during the 1980s. Nevertheless, the Pact's very frequent large-scale training exercises during the Cold War demonstrated an always impressive war-fighting capability, and thus served to ensure continued caution by NATO, whilst also discouraging any poten-tial political dissent from Warsaw Pact members. Certainly, had NATO not presented an effective guard against the communist forces ranged against it in the East, the Soviet Union might well have been tempted to pre-empt a war against NATO that for more than three decades Moscow had judged to be inevitable. In these circumstances, if a successful assault against NATO had taken place, it would certainly not have been unreasonable for the Warsaw Pact nations to throw in their lot entirely with the Soviets. Indeed, in such a situation, it would probably have been remiss of them not to do so. But, despite the numerous East–West crises, no such apocalyptic campaign ever took place, and the Warsaw Pact's primary function was to provide the mechanism by which the Soviet Union maintained its control of Eastern Europe, protected itself from a NATO attack, and furthered its ideological, commercial and wider strategic policies. As the Cold War continued, these truths became increasingly evident to the member states, together with an awareness of the improbability of NATO carrying out an attack against the Eastern bloc. While NATO would of course have responded decisively to a Warsaw Pact attack, its failure to intervene in any of the crises that occurred in Berlin, Hungary, Czechoslovakia or Poland was clear evidence of the West's cautiousness, and of its inability to match the stereotype of military aggressor that was portrayed by Moscow.

The end of the Warsaw Pact on 31 March 1991 was a clear indication of the end of the Cold War; but the fact that the NATO alliance still exists today provides a clear indication that the West and NATO did indeed triumph over the Soviet Union and the Warsaw Pact in the forty-five-year conflict. However, this conclusion, whilst valid, is also somewhat simplistic, as the Warsaw Pact was not defeated on any battlefield; rather it collapsed internally as its original reasons for existence lost credibility and diminished in parallel with the decline of Soviet military power during the 1980s. Although it could undoubtedly have been an effective military defensive alliance, as an offensive military organisation it was weakened from the outset by the antipathy of many Eastern bloc citizens towards the Soviet Union after the Second World War. Large numbers of the populations of some Warsaw Pact countries – notably Poland, Czechoslovakia and Hungary – were certainly not communists, and in most cases they had for centuries owed their ideological faith and allegiance to Roman Catholicism rather than to the relatively new teachings of Marx and Lenin. The cohesion of the Warsaw Pact was, therefore, maintained principally by the will and martial might of the Soviet Union, and when Mikhail Gorbachev gained power as the new General Secretary of the CPSU, following the unexpected death of Konstantin Chernenko in March 1985, the scene was set for dramatic changes within the Soviet Union.

Over the next six years the Cold War drew to an end, while East–West and US–Soviet Union relations were the best since 1945. The Soviet Union was finally consigned to the history books, as it broke up into independent states, with the re-emergence of an independent Russia. Meanwhile, Gorbachev's personal fortunes rose and finally fell in parallel with the momentous events that he had set in train. The enduring symbol of East–West division and confrontation, the Berlin Wall, was opened for free movement in November

1989. Just one year later East and West Germany were reunified; and the armed forces of the German Democratic Republic (GDR) were disbanded. While these historic events were taking place in Germany, the Soviet forces based in East Germany and in the other Warsaw Pact countries quietly withdrew in 1990. Across the Eastern bloc the communist regimes collapsed or were progressively replaced by democratically elected administrations. Meanwhile, with no credible reason for its continued existence, and no more pressure for that existence from Moscow, the military organisation that had represented the single greatest threat to NATO for more than forty years simply dissolved away. By the spring of 1991 the Warsaw Pact had ceased to exist.

EUROPE: FOCUS OF CONFLICT

Greece, 1945–9

The Greek Civil War was the first of the post-1945 communist insurgencies in Europe, and in many ways it established the broad principles by which future communist expansionism would be countered by financial and military aid from the United States. This aid, plus the increasing effectiveness of the Greek national army (GNA), eventually resulted in the defeat of the communist forces. Another important contributory factor was the reducing support provided to the communists from neighbouring Albania, Bulgaria and Yugoslavia. A fundamental requirement for the success of a guerrilla insurgency is access to a supportive state adjacent to the country that is home to the conflict and, as American aid poured into Greece to bolster the government forces, this external assistance for the insurgents diminished rapidly. Finally, a misjudgement by the communists of the efficacy of terrorism to further their campaign also negated much of the support that they might otherwise have enjoyed from within a civilised European population. Indeed, much of the history of the late twentieth century shows that terror tactics used in a civilised country rarely achieve the political goals that most terrorist organisations seek, but merely harden the resolve of the security forces against them.

In October 1944 it had been agreed by Stalin and Churchill that after the Second World War the future of Greece would initially be a British responsibility. However, throughout the war the principal Greek resistance movement had been centred on the Greek Communist Party (KKE), headed by George Siantos, who had raised a sizeable Liberation Army (ELAS) some 40,000 strong. The KKE had the long-term aim of filling the vacuum left by the Greek monarch, who had fled Greece in 1941 when the Germans invaded the country. Clearly Churchill had no intention of allowing Greece to be turned into a communist state, and when ELAS marched upon Athens in early 1945 it was swiftly defeated by British forces. Although the Greek communist organisation ceased to exist as a viable army, many of its members evaded the general round-up by the British and established a presence in the hills and mountains of the notoriously rugged Greek–Albanian–Yugoslav border region. For many it was but a short step to revert to the existence that they had experienced during the previous four years. The communists chose initially to forgo the armed struggle and sought to promote their cause within the Greek political system. However, they effectively ruled themselves out of that process less than a year later when they refused to participate in the national elections, and so by default allowed King George II to return to the Greek throne. With the legitimate political route to power now closed to them, the communists looked to their comrades in the mountains to carry forward their aspirations through guerrilla warfare. From the outset they also counted upon the neighbouring communist states within which the Greek communists had established their bases to provide support and sanctuary for the campaign against the government in Athens.

The newly formed Democratic Army of Greece (DSE) was headed by General Markos Vaphiadis, a competent commander well versed in the skills of guerrilla warfare. In accordance with the communist doctrine for revolutionary conflict, Vaphiadis spent the next twelve months organising and training an active guerrilla army of 23,000 for the coming struggle. In addition, he had available a further 8,000 reserves, plus more volunteers in DSE training camps outside Greece. Almost twenty per cent of the DSE fighters were female. The DSE claimed to be supported within Greece by an underground organisation about 50,000 strong, and to enjoy the support of a further 500,000 sympathisers. Prior to 1947, the DSE operations were deliberately limited to the classic insurgent activities of reconnaissance, sabotage, consolidation and recruiting; while simultaneously dominating the border region and maintaining a regular but transient military presence throughout all of Greece to the north of Athens.

Meanwhile, the GNA, some 180,000 strong and headed by its equally competent commander General Alexandros Papagos, suffered from an excess of political direction and interference. This resulted in its wholesale commitment to thinly spread static defensive locations at the main population centres, which made the GNA reactive rather than pro-active and handed the operational initiative to the communist forces from the outset. Papagos was all too aware of the flawed nature of this strategy and that 'the national forces were in danger of losing the war without fighting it'.[37] Indeed, at no stage of the war was the GNA able to seal the porous northern border of Greece and, although the DSE and ELAS were until the latter part of the conflict able to move across it at will and even to call upon cross-border artillery fire support, the Greek government chose not to conduct operations into Albania, Yugoslavia or Bulgaria for fear of precipitating their formal military support for the communist forces.

Although the government in Great Britain had both the responsibility and the will to ensure that the communists did not triumph in Greece, the country's resources and its armed forces were literally exhausted by six years of war, and so the Greek government turned elsewhere for help. Inevitably, it looked to the United States. The appeal was made in March 1946, and it led directly to the formulation of the so-called 'Truman

Doctrine' which subsequently had important implications for the future conduct of the Cold War.

On 12 March 1947 President Truman asked the US Congress to grant 400 million dollars of aid for both Turkey and Greece, in order to back 'the policy of the United States to support free peoples who are resisting attempted subjugation by armed minorities or by outside pressures'. Congress approved the grant, and the impact of this major policy initiative was almost immediate. By August, military and other equipment was pouring into Greece, and a military advisory group had been installed in Athens to co-ordinate the American support and assist the GNA campaign as necessary. Prior to the American involvement the GNA had been equipped mainly with British weapons, but as US supplies flooded into Greece they supplanted the older British equipment. In 1949, the US aid contribution included fifty Curtiss Helldiver fighter dive-bombers, consituting a decisive form of fire support in the mountains that were virtually no-go areas for tanks and most other forms of tracked and wheeled vehicles.

The communists saw the initiative slipping from their grasp, and on 24 December 1947 they announced the establishment of a 'Free Democratic Government'. They followed this declaration with an abortive assault by about 2,000 fighters on Konitsa in north-west Greece, where it was intended to create an alternative Greek capital. This and other attacks produced a surge of some 700,000 refugees southward to the coastal regions, where the Greek government was forced to bear the burden of their day-to-day support. But whereas this additional pressure on the government achieved one of the communist aims, their failures on the battlefield were significant, and the defeat at Konitsa highlighted the DSE's inability to succeed in conventional military operations. This lesson was not lost on General Vaphiadis. Accordingly, the DSE reverted to guerrilla warfare and terrorism to further its political aims. This policy change in early 1948 coincided with a GNA offensive against the guerrilla mountain strongholds in the Albanian border region. Despite the extensive American support, the GNA achieved only limited success, although the very fact that the GNA had moved on from its former policy of static defence was a significant development in its own right. Meanwhile, the DSE campaign of murder, abduction and mayhem within the more heavily populated areas to the south had precisely the opposite effect to that which they desired. International support for the communists waned, the mass abduction of 'recruits' and children to fight for the DSE attracted the condemnation of the UN; even the Soviet Union failed to recognise the 'Free Democratic Greek Government' in waiting. Indeed, in 1948 Stalin was increasingly focused on events then developing in Germany, where a war of infinitely greater proportions than the guerrilla conflict in Greece was becoming ever more possible.

The defining year of the Greek conflict, both politically and militarily, was 1949. Just as the GNA was gaining in confidence and effectiveness, command of the DSE passed from General Vaphiadis to General Nikos Zachariades. The latter assessed that the time had come to move the guerrilla campaign on to the next doctrinal level of conflict, in order to confront the GNA in conventional warfare before it could bring the full benefit of US support to bear. However, he misjudged the strategic situation, as the GNA was in reality already well prepared to conclude the war, and the restructuring of the DSE from its guerrilla organisation into conventional military units and formations simply provided better targets for the GNA's new firepower, especially the Curtiss Helldivers. Accordingly, General Papagos continued to make progress against the DSE. First he secured the Peloponnese, which was essential to the security of Athens. Then he gradually pushed the GNA area of control northward to the provincial towns and the mountains that lay beyond. The GNA successes were matched by the DSE casualty figures, which rose dramatically throughout 1948. Meanwhile, GNA units newly based in the north of the country denied the DSE much of its earlier freedom to move and operate beyond its mountain bases. Simultaneously, while the GNA's conventional operations moved on apace, special security force units identified and destroyed the 50,000-strong ELAS underground organisation. The mass arrest and internment of communist sympathisers across the country comprehensively destroyed the DSE's baseline of support.

Having secured central Greece, in August General Papagos launched a two-pronged attack towards the communist bases at Vitsi and Grammos. The latter thrust was a feint and so the full weight of the GNA fell upon the 7,500 DSE fighters at Vitsi. Despite Vitsi's comprehensively prepared and well fortified positions, within two weeks the GNA had annihilated its defenders. The few survivors of the battle who escaped to join their comrades in the remaining guerrilla bastion at Grammos subsequently endured a similar defeat on 24 August.

In parallel with the DSE's declining fortunes on the battlefield, external political influences in 1949 had further undermined the communists' prospects of success. First, in July, Marshal Tito's deteriorating relations with the Soviet bloc resulted in the closure of the Yugoslav border to the DSE, denying the communists their bases and sanctuary in Yugoslavia. Thus, just as the GNA was closing in on Grammos and Vitsi, the guerrillas' traditional escape route to the north was sealed. At the same time, a move by nine national communist parties to promote the Greek region of Macedonia as an independent state sounded alarm bells throughout Greece, which persuaded many previously uncommitted Greeks that the time had come to give their unqualified support to the national government. The alternative was to risk the break-up of the country.

So it was that military failure and political isolation converged, and by the autumn of 1949 the Greek Civil War was at an end. Since the start of the war in 1945, about 38,000 communists of ELAS and the DSE had been killed, with a further 40,000 captured. The GNA had lost 12,777 dead, 37,732 wounded and 4,527 missing. Allegedly, some 4,289 civilians had been murdered by the communists, including 165 priests. An additional 931 civilian deaths had resulted from landmines.[38]

Although the war was over, this bitter conflict had created a festering sore of mistrust, political instability and friction for decades to come. However, in the wider scheme of things, the KKE had forfeited any realistic prospect of a return to prominence or gaining power in Greece. Therefore, by the end of 1949, the westward advance of communism had been halted, and the American and British governments could be well pleased with this successful first application of the Truman Doctrine. The Americans and the British could also congratulate themselves on the fact that the West's Cold War success 'by proxy' in Greece had been accomplished in parallel with a Soviet climb-down over a potentially much more serious conflict at the very heart of the divided Germany – at its occupied and rubble-strewn former capital, the city of Berlin.

Germany and Berlin, 1945–8

A constant throughout the whole process that finally resulted in the Cold War was Germany. At the end of the Second World War the dissolution of a comprehensively defeated Third Reich resulted in a power vacuum at the heart of Europe, which did not bode well for the stability of the war-ravaged continent. At the same time, the demise of German fascism unfettered the bonds that had, of necessity, ensured since 1941 that the Western Allies and the Soviet Union would work together. The signs of the discord to come were already very evident at the Yalta Conference before the end of the war, but it was at the follow-on conference at Potsdam in July 1945 that the seeds of future crises were truly sown.

Two issues had dominated the Potsdam meeting: the future control of Germany and the arrangements for the recovery of German reparations. From the unsatisfactory agreements made at that gathering of Churchill (and later Attlee), Stalin and Truman flowed a chain of events that eventually culminated in the 1961 construction of the Berlin Wall and what the GDR government termed the 'modern frontier' along the length of the IGB. At Potsdam the interests of the 'Big Three' had been generally different and mutually exclusive. The United States took the view that Germany should be rehabilitated rather than punished. This was a sensible approach, given the significant part that the Treaty of Versailles had played in enabling the rise of National Socialism in Germany through the 1920s and 1930s, which culminated in the Second World War. However, American awareness of the course and lessons of world and European history has often been ill-informed, and the line taken by Truman at Potsdam was prompted as much by a parochial desire to disengage the United States from Europe and to form a bulwark against Soviet territorial ambitions as it was to assist the defeated Germany. Even the discovery of the succession of concentration camps during the spring of 1945 did not sway American policy appreciably at that time.

Meanwhile, Stalin was quite clear about the future of Germany. He sought nothing less than its punishment and the negation of its military and indus-trial base, with any salvageable assets being removed post-haste to support his own plans for the development of the Soviet empire. Of course, his historical perspective was fundamentally different from that of Truman. The Soviet Union had been invaded, occupied, and had lost up to twenty-seven million of its population since the start of Operation Barbarossa in mid-1941. Many of its major cities had played host to protracted periods of combat and were reduced almost entirely to rubble, whilst much of the civilian popula-tion had been savagely and deliberately exterminated by the German forces. Although the Soviet line undoubtedly stemmed from concern over the recent past, and an understandable determination that Germany should not be able to invade Russia again in the future, it also indicated Stalin's desire to keep Germany weak so that his longer-term aspirations for Soviet expan-sion (both ideological and military) into Western Europe could be realised. For less complex reasons, and with the German invasions of 1870, 1914 and 1940 in mind, France generally supported the Soviet line.

With the United States and the Soviet Union diametrically opposed on this fundamental matter of principle, Churchill (although he already had grave misgivings about Soviet future intentions, which were later stated openly at Fulton, Missouri in March 1946) attempted to steer a middle course by advo-cating a solution that guaranteed the stability of post-1945 Europe. Inevitably perhaps, these divergent views resulted in a thoroughly unsatisfactory compromise on the reparations issue and the division of Germany, which less than twelve months later brought about the first major Cold War conflict within that country. Finally, the atmosphere at these crucial negoti-ations was not improved by Truman disclosing in an aside to Stalin that the Manhattan Project had been successfully concluded, and that the United States now possessed the first viable atomic bomb.

In May 1946 the reparations arrangements for Germany broke down entirely, and the autonomous US, British and French Zones of Occupation were amalgamated; this effectively split Germany between the Western powers on the one hand and the Soviets on the other. East–West tension rose, and on 12 March 1947 President Truman announced the Truman Doctrine to a joint session of the US Congress. This formalisation of US policy to counter communism was prompted by the Greek Civil War then in progress, and reflected Washington's fears of communist expansion in the Balkans and the need to bolster Greece and Turkey to counter that threat.

The Truman Doctrine identified the United States as the primary source of support for any country threatened by communist insurgency in the future – a principle that would cost its armed forces dearly in Korea and Vietnam in later years. At the same time it confirmed the fact that two mutually exclusive ideologies were already engaged in a new conflict.

So, with constitutional authority to pursue this policy on the record, the time had come for the United States to set about resolving the German issue, together with other measures to strengthen Europe against what was now openly acknowledged to be a communist threat. This goal could only be achieved by the revival of European industry and commerce through economic aid, and so was born the Marshall Aid Plan, named for General George C. Marshall, the US Secretary of State, who declared that the United States would provide economic aid for all countries, including those that were communist. The resultant package totalled some thirteen billion US dollars, with twelve West European countries, plus Yugoslavia, receiving various amounts; of which Great Britain, France, Italy, West Germany and Holland were the main beneficiaries.

But the Truman Doctrine and the Marshall Aid Plan were unacceptable to Stalin, and the Soviets refused to involve themselves further with the latter: the capitalist nature of which was in any case totally at odds with Marxist ideology. The Soviet reaction was understandable, as the Truman Doctrine indicated the US intention to counter communism directly, whereas Marshall Aid could be readily interpreted as a commitment to do so on the familiar battleground of Central Europe. Relations between the Soviet Union and the West deteriorated rapidly as the year drew on, and in the spring of 1948 the Cold War almost became a 'hot war'. Predictably, the confrontation was focused on the enduring epicentre of the Cold War: the city of Berlin.

The Berlin Blockade and Airlift, 1948–9

In April 1948 the Western Powers announced that they intended to reform the West German economy, in order to place it on a viable footing and so enable its recovery; which would involve fundamental changes to the West German currency arrangements. This was closely followed by the announcement of an intention to establish a new West German state. The Russians perceived this to be a thinly veiled attempt to reconstitute Germany as a military power that would yet again spearhead a future invasion of the Soviet Union.

Berlin lay one hundred miles to the east of the main boundary between the Soviet Zone of Occupation and the three zones or sectors occupied by the Western Powers. However, the city was itself divided and occupied by Soviet, US, British and French forces. This meant that the Western Allies needed regular and unrestricted access to their sectors of the city via the Soviet Zone. But in response to the West's plans for West Germany Stalin ordered that land access to Berlin was to be denied, and by June 1948 the divided city had been blockaded. Stalin's ultimate objective was to make the presence of the Western Allies in Berlin untenable, so that they would be forced to leave and give control of the whole city to the Russians. The stage was thus set for an event that many believed presaged the next World War, as the Western Allies once again prepared for armed conflict, while at the same time examining their options for resolving the crisis by other means.

New indicators of the growing severity of the crisis were identified almost daily. Since the beginning of 1948 the Soviets had imposed ever-increasing pressures and delays upon the movement of traffic between Berlin and the West, but now the level of tension rose still further. During March the US Commandant in Berlin, General Lucius D. Clay, proposed that each of the Western Allies should deploy a division to the border crossing in the British Zone of Germany at Helmstedt, and that this force should then advance to Berlin, engaging in combat if necessary, in order to demonstrate unequivo-cally the Western Powers' continued right of access to the city. Plans for this robust military action, however, were subsequently modified extensively, and the proposed force was reduced to a single convoy of 200 trucks. This patently non-aggressive convoy would be escorted by a US military force comprising a military police regiment, an engineer battalion and a detach-ment of infantry, plus a British infantry battalion and a detachment of French anti-tank troops. Yet the several plans produced for the military relief of Berlin by land remained plans only, as the crisis finally came to a head.[39]

On 24 June the Soviets finally severed all road and rail connections on the pretext of 'technical difficulties'. They also cut the electrical supply gener-ated in the East, which caused particular hardship to hospitals and forced many commercial enterprises to close. At that time there was only enough food for thirty-six days and coal for forty-five days stocked in the Western sectors of the city.

Initially, the US, British and French garrisons made independent arrangements for their provisioning by air, but it was not long before these separate operations were combined in a co-ordinated multinational airlift, using the three air corridors that ran from Frankfurt-am-Main, Hanover and Hamburg into the Berlin [Air] Control Zone: a twenty-mile radius circle centred on the Allied Control Council building. Each air lane was twenty miles wide.

In fact, in light of the deteriorating situation in Berlin and in addition to General Clay's more extreme military options, the Americans had already carried out various exercises to test the feasibility of supplying Berlin by air alone. These exercises had been conducted from 2 April by the USAF 61st Troop Carrier Group (which was equipped with twenty-five of the ubiquitous Douglas C-47 (Dakota) transports) at the vast Rhein-Main airbase at Frankfurt. They developed a concept proposed to General Clay by General Albert Wedemeyer, who had benefited from the successful use of air transports to supply the US and Chinese forces in China over 'the Hump' from Assam during the recently ended war.

The risks inherent in this East–West brinkmanship had already been demonstrated dramatically on 5 April, when a Soviet Yak-3 fighter pilot miscalculated his turn while harassing a BEA Vickers Viking aircraft on a scheduled flight into Berlin. The fighter crashed into the airliner, killing the pilot plus the ten civilian passengers and crew on the Viking. This incident was but one of many that led the British government to deploy a squadron of eight Hawker Tempest fighter bombers to RAF Gatow on 22 June, although these aircraft were withdrawn on 14 July, when it became clear that the Soviets did not intend to take direct action against either civil air traffic or the aircraft engaged in the airlift.

The effects of the blockade were quickly felt. At the political level President Truman was determined to pursue a firm line against the Soviets, although a number of his advisers sounded a note of caution. However, the British had already put in place their own airlift, albeit on the assumption that the need for it would not be overly long, and this persuaded the Americans of the viability of a much expanded operation to sustain Berlin by air. At the end of July, Major General William H. Tunner USAF was appointed to command the operation (he had previously overseen 'the Hump' airlift in China). Tunner immediately set to work to develop a co-ordinated operation from the somewhat ad hoc national arrangements that had been instituted at the start of the blockade on 24 June. At the outset his staff and advisers calculated that a minimum 4,500 tons of supplies would be required by the Western sectors each day if they were to survive the blockade. This was the bare minimum, and contrasted with the 13,000 tons that had previously been brought into West Berlin daily by rail, canal and road.

Initially, the airlift available to the Western Allies fell well short of the required carrying capacity. In practical terms, it was centred exclusively on US and British aircraft, as in 1948 the French air force was embroiled in the escalating conflict in Indochina, with few aircraft still in Europe. Thus, as the airlift took shape, there were only about 170 C-47s (110 USAF and 60 RAF) and some 50 RAF Avro Yorks available, with a total airlift capacity of about 700 tons per day. Clearly this capability needed rapid augmentation, and over the succeeding months this was achieved through the introduction of a mix of civil and military transport aircraft. These included American DC-4 Skymasters, a C-97 Stratofreighter, more RAF Avro Yorks, plus ten RAF Short Sunderland flying-boats (which operated between Finkenwerder on the River Elbe, near Hamburg, and the Havel Lake in Berlin near to Gatow). As more and

EUROPE AND
BERLIN, 1945–90

more aircraft were brought into the airlift, the overall command and control, air traffic control, maintenance and associated ground supply, loading and unloading arrangements were all expanded and refined to match the increasing scale and sophistication of the operation. The progress made was remarkable, and by late August 1948 more than 5,000 tons of stores were being flown daily into Tempelhof and Gatow airfields in the US and British Sectors – some 500 tons more than the minimum amount required to sustain life in the west of the city. In mid-December Tegel Airport in the French sector was activated to provide a third airhead. Meanwhile, additional airfields were opened in West Germany, from which increasing numbers and types of US and British aircraft flew into the beleaguered city. Night and day reverberated incessantly with the throb of aero engines; for the citizens of West Berlin and the military garrisons that protected them this noise became the very heartbeat of the city.

But the airlift was not without human cost, and some seventy-three Allied military personnel and five German civilians lost their lives through air crashes and accidents. Remarkably, despite in-air harassment, offset anti-aircraft fire and the use of searchlights by the Soviets to dazzle the Western pilots, none of these fatalities were attributed directly to Soviet action.

These tragedies were balanced not only by the overall success of the oper-ation but also by tales such as that of USAF Lieutenant Gail S. Halverson – the 'Schokolade Flieger' – who would drop candy and chewing gum on impro-vised parachutes to the ever-growing crowds of children that gathered each day on the north side of the Tempelhof runway. 'Day by day, the crowds of kids waiting for the drop got bigger,' recalled Halverson, 'and day by day my supply of old shirts, GI sheets and old shorts, all of which I used for parachutes, got smaller.'[40]

Meanwhile, a counter-blockade had been put in place by the Western Allies as soon as the Soviet blockade began. This halted coal and steel deliv-eries to the Soviet Zone as well as restricting other trading arrangements. Internationally, any support for the Soviets rapidly dissipated, as all attempts by relief agencies – including the Swedish Red Cross – to move vital supplies through the Soviet Zone by land were balked. To add to Moscow's discom-fort, an American intelligence source revealed that there had been no prior consultation between the Soviet military authorities and the East German economic experts before the blockade was imposed. All in all it was there-fore not surprising when negotiations conducted under UN auspices early in 1949 produced a Soviet offer to end the blockade, subject to the Western Allies' agreement to a Four-Power meeting to resolve the issue of currency reform. The Allies readily acquiesced to this and the Berlin blockade was lifted at 00.01 hours on 12 May 1949; although the airlift continued until 30

September, in order to create a large stockpile of supplies against the possibility of another Soviet blockade in the future.

The crisis had lasted for eleven months. During the airlift the USAF contribution had been 76.7 per cent, the RAF 17 per cent and that by British civil aviation 6.3 per cent. A total 2,325,809 tons of supplies were flown to West Berlin between June 1948 and September 1949, of which 1,586,500 tons were coal, 538,016 tons were food and 92,282 tons were fuel oils. During the 318 days of the actual blockade, from 24 June 1948 to 12 May 1949, more than 200,000 flights had lifted in excess of 1,500,000 tons of supplies into the city. At the same time, the USAF had evacuated 1,500 tuberculosis patients from the city, and the RAF had flown out 15,426 children to foster-homes in West Germany during the airlift. Although the blockade had continued throughout a bitterly cold Berlin winter, not one death from cold or starvation was recorded during the period.[41]

In terms of its impact on the wider Cold War, however, the Berlin blockade and the consequent airlift had considerable significance. Over eleven critical months the role of the Western Allies in Berlin, and thus by implication in West Germany as well, was transformed from that of 'occupying powers' to that of 'protectors'. At the same time, the events of June 1948 to September 1949 reinforced the need for West Germany to become a state in its own right, in order that it might contribute actively to what had by default become a counter-communist military alliance. Thus, hard on the heels of the Berlin blockade and with the follow-on airlift still in progress, on 23 May 1949 the Federal Republic of Germany came into being.

Berlin, Post-1949
Berlin continued to be the most high-profile symbol and focus of the Cold War in the years that followed the blockade. Meanwhile, the burgeoning economic success of West Germany – supported by Marshall Aid and the sheer determination, energy and industry of its population – added another factor into the East–West equation, as any hint of the resurgence, militarisation or possible reunification of Germany was anathema to the Soviet leadership. Berlin was easily accessible to the communists and was an obvious point upon which Moscow's concerns could be focused. Inevitably, therefore, a succession of incidents occurred during the years after the Berlin blockade and establishment of the FRG. These created a permanent environment of tension within and about the city, and produced various actions and reactions at every political and military level.

A second blockade seemed in prospect in May 1950, when overland travel to the city was once again halted and all telephone links between Berlin and the West were severed. This Soviet action followed hard on the reinforcement of the Western Powers' garrisons the previous November, when some thirty Comet tanks were deployed to the British garrison and an additional infantry regiment had been moved into the US sector. Predictably, most of these incidents involved access to and from the city by air, road and waterway, and from 1950 to 1952 the Soviets targeted the autobahn routes into Berlin and the waterways along which the giant barges moved goods and supplies from West Germany into the isolated city. Many incidents were recorded, but whereas they were by and large merely irritations for the Western Allies – all of whom were very aware of the rules of what was rapidly becoming an almost surreal political game – for the German residents of communist-dominated East Germany the implications were more significant.

In May 1952 the Soviets and their East German allies declared a five-kilometre security zone along the length of the inter-zone land border and along the Baltic coast. This militarisation of the internal border of the divided Germany caused the enforced relocation of the many hundreds of East Germans unfortunate enough to live within the newly designated security zone, and provided an early indication of the way in which events would subsequently develop along the entire inter-zone border almost a decade later. But within East Berlin growing disquiet over the situation in East Germany resulted in violence much earlier than that.

On 16 June 1953 an industrial dispute by building workers over production quotas and pay was transformed within just twenty-four hours into a major political protest. The Red Flag was torn down from the Brandenburg Gate and strikes and demonstrations occurred in 270 separate places across East Germany. The East German civilian police, the *Volkspolizei* or '*Vopos*', were unable to contain the demonstrations, and shortly after midday on 17 June the Soviet Commandant ordered Soviet Army units – including tanks – into Berlin to suppress the rioting. Less than ten years after they had spearheaded the Red Army's final attacks on the Reichstag and Brandenburg Gate, T-34 tanks again clattered through the heart of the city and along once-fashionable streets and boulevards such as Leipziger Strasse, Wilhelmstrasse, Pariser Platz and Potsdamer Platz.

The Soviet armour was opposed by no more than a hail of sticks and stones. Despite this, at least thirty-five East Germans were killed and 378 injured in the fighting (some accounts put the number of those killed as high as 260 civilians and 100 policemen), while many more were arrested and subsequently suffered death or imprisonment for their part in what was treated by the East German authorities and the Soviets as an uprising. Significantly, some Soviet troops refused to fire on the demonstrators and, although such dissent was on a small scale and those involved were severely disciplined, the mere possibility of unreliability within the Red Army in East Germany no doubt caused substantial concern in Moscow.

Not surprisingly, the events of 17 June attracted significant protest from the Western Allied commandants, although there was little that they could do to affect events within the Soviet sector. However, Charlottenburger Chaussee, which runs westward from the Brandenburg Gate within the British sector, was subsequently named 'Strasse des 17 Juni' to commemorate the uprising.

But the real significance of the events of 16 and 17 June 1953 was threefold. First, it provided an indication of Soviet readiness to use overwhelming military force to maintain order within what they clearly regarded as their area of interest. This lesson was not fully appreciated by the people of Hungary, as subsequent events showed some three years later. Second, the relative impotence of the West to respond effectively to events within the Soviet Zone of Occupation was very evident; another lesson understood neither by the Hungarians in 1956, nor by the Czechs more than a decade later. Finally, the Soviet response demonstrated Moscow's implacable determination not to countenance any action that might eventually lead to a united Germany. The memories of a country whose armies had invaded the Soviet Union twice during the previous three decades, and which had caused some twenty-seven million Soviet deaths (the majority of them civilians) between 1941 and the end of the Second World War, were still much too recent.

The confrontations over Berlin continued. Most were concerned with access to the city, its diplomatic status and the plethora of associated agreements, rules and regulations. The career civil servants and diplomats who administered the city's four-power status coped with an infinite spectrum of incidents: these included numerous Soviet ploys to achieve recognition of the GDR, the detention in 1956 of two US Congressmen and the wife of one of them, and the frequent harassment of aircraft flying into Berlin and of the military personnel and convoys using the authorised autobahn routes. But all in all the rules of the game were well known by the Western and Soviet authorities, and so a balance of action, reaction and diplomatic protest maintained the uneasy peace in Berlin. Meanwhile, the quality of life for the civilian population of the Soviet-dominated GDR declined markedly with each passing year compared with that of their West German countrymen.

Yet it was not only in East Germany that seeds of discontent were germinating within Soviet-controlled Eastern Europe. In Poland in June 1956 an uprising was speedily and decisively put down by Soviet troops. In Yugoslavia Marshal Tito pursued national rather than Soviet policies and was isolated by Stalin for this, whilst nevertheless demonstrating to other communist bloc nations that a disagreement with the Soviet Union did not necessarily attract an armed response. However, it was in Hungary (which had had the double misfortune to have supported Germany during the Second World War and then to have been occupied by the Red Army rather than by the Western Allies in 1945) that talk of freedom and independence gained more momentum with each day that passed. And it was in the picturesque Hungarian capital on the Danube that the true meaning of Soviet military domination was graphically demonstrated by an event which also proved to be the high-water mark of the Stalinist concept of total control of Eastern Europe.

The Hungarian Uprising, 1956

After the Red Army's occupation of Hungary in 1945 a coalition government was formed, within which the communists were a minority group. However, this situation changed in 1949. During that year's national elections (in which no opposition candidates were permitted and which followed five years of the progressive elimination of all non-communists) the communists won overall control of Hungary. The Hungarian communist leader Mátyás Rákosi became de facto the head of state.

While the people of Hungary looked enviously towards an isolated but still relatively free Yugoslavia, Stalin determined that no more Soviet satellite states should be allowed to adopt the Yugoslavian model, and in 1949 the order was issued that henceforth all such dissent was to be suppressed. In Hungary this decree resulted in the arrest, trial and execution or imprisonment of some 1,000 people. But then in March 1953 Stalin died and the Soviet Politburo, sensing the increasing unrest in the occupied countries, directed a relaxation of this policy of total control. Rákosi remained in place, but the more enlightened, moderate and popular Imre Nagy was appointed prime minister. Despite constant opposition from the old-style Stalinists, he promptly set about a programme of reform. This included the slowing down or reversal of ideological policies for the collectivisation of agriculture and the industrialisation of Hungary. Unfortunately, Nagy suffered a heart attack in April 1955, which provided those who opposed him with a convenient excuse to remove him from office. But by then precedents had been set and the potential for further progress exposed. Meanwhile, other events had also fuelled the growing unrest in Hungary.

First, the tacit acceptance by the Soviet leadership in mid-1955 of Tito's form of communism had signalled that there were alternatives to the Soviet way, and that opposition to the Soviet Union did not necessarily invite national disaster. Next, the signing of the Warsaw Pact in May 1955 had provided a sense of national military identity for the various East European states involved. Lastly, in February 1956 the historic denunciation of Stalin's policies by the new Soviet leader, Nikita Khrushchev, at the Twentieth Congress of the Communist Party appeared to provide those nations seeking release from Soviet domination with real hope for the future. By spring of 1956 Mátyás Rákosi and his supporters were becoming increasingly vulnerable, while support for Imre Nagy was growing apace.

The Soviet suppression of the East German unrest in 1953 should have provided a reason for the Hungarians to tread carefully, as also might the much more recent use of Soviet troops to deal with the riots in Poznan, Poland in June 1956. However, the tide of Hungarian nationalism was in full flow and the replacement in July of Rákosi by Ernö Gerö at Soviet instigation signalled what many interpreted as a weakening of Moscow's power and resolve. This perception was further reinforced by Khrushchev's intervention to halt the Red Army's operation to deal with yet more unrest in Poland during October. This was followed on 21 October by the appointment of Wladyslaw Gomulka, an enlightened communist in the mould of Tito, as First Secretary of the Polish Communist Party. Apparently a wind of change really was blowing through Eastern Europe, and the time had come for Hungary to assert its independence from the Soviet monolith. Events moved fast thereafter; but too fast and too precipitately.

On 22 October the students of Budapest's Technological University in Buda produced a manifesto for the future of Hungary that sought to emulate the progress made in Poland. Among its fourteen points was a demand for the removal of all Soviet troops from Hungary, and for a new government led by Imre Nagy to be elected. A range of other political rights, freedoms and civil liberties were also addressed. Publication of the manifesto was followed the next day by a mass demonstration to indicate Hungary's support for the people of Poland. The Soviet authorities and Hungarian security troops watched these events with increasing concern; but no direct military intervention was ordered, and the euphoria of a population that increasingly believed their liberation was at hand grew by the hour. By the evening of 23 October the formal demonstration had ended with the destruction of a large statue of Stalin near Heroes' Square during the night. However, some 200,000 people were still on the streets in front of the parliament building, where they called for their supposed saviour Imre Nagy to address them. He did so, but – no longer the man that he had been prior to his heart attack the previous year – his response to the call of the people was uninspiring. Rákosi now saw an opportunity to regain his position of power and at eight o'clock that evening he broadcast on national radio a hard-line rebuttal of the demonstrators' aspirations. From this point the security situation deteriorated by the hour.

An angry crowd went to the headquarters of the radio station in Pest, with the intention of broadcasting the manifesto. It was countered by the paramilitary state security troops: at first using tear gas, but eventually resorting to live ammunition. The Hungarian authorities and Soviets were losing control, and although they appointed Imre Nagy prime minister, they also ordered Soviet army units to move to the capital. Meanwhile, the still-euphoric but now increasingly angry crowds ebbed and flowed through the streets of Budapest during the rest of the night, engaging in further clashes with the security troops. At the same time, revolutionary councils of the people appeared in many parts of Hungary, promoting the concepts of Hungarian nationalism, neutrality and the withdrawal of all Soviet forces from the country. Outside Hungary, Radio Free Europe fuelled the unrest by urging the demonstrators on, and irresponsibly implying that their struggle for freedom would be fully supported by the West. This was plainly never an option in the autumn of 1956, due to the Anglo-French (and US) preoccupation with the rapidly escalating crisis over Egypt and the Suez Canal.

By midnight two motor rifle divisions of the Red Army were approaching Budapest from their bases in Hungary, and at two o'clock on the morning of 24 October the streets echoed to the sound of steel tank tracks on cobbles, as columns of olive-green T-54 tanks and armoured personnel carriers rumbled along the city streets. Had they been deployed much earlier, their deterrent effect might have been decisive; but now it was too late, as a battle began between the Red Army's tanks and a civilian population armed mainly with a variety of small-arms, some light anti-armour weapons, hand grenades and petrol bombs. Ironically, many of the younger members of the civilian population had previously benefited from the guerrilla warfare training that they had received in school as part of the Soviet-mandated national curriculum. Also, in addition to the military expertise that some members of the Hungarian national army brought to the barricades, many of the insurgents had combat experience from the Second World War. By and large, however, the Hungarian army (which, as with all non-Soviet Warsaw Pact forces, had Soviet officers at all key levels of command) was not involved in the uprising.

Despite the unequal nature of the struggle, as Anastas Mikoyan and Mikhail Suslov, representing the Moscow Politburo, flew into Budapest airport on 24 October, the flames and plumes of greasy black smoke from a number of T-54 tanks destroyed by petrol bombs were all too visible. Meanwhile, the violence was spreading beyond Budapest. In one such confrontation in Magyarovar the security troops shot eighty-seven demonstrators. Everywhere the pace of the insurgency was accelerating and after just a couple of days the Soviet delegation decided it had seen enough. Before they went, Ernö Gerö was replaced as First Secretary of the Hungarian Communist Party by János Kádár. Ostensibly, he was a progressive, but subsequently he proved to be very much Moscow's man. As the two Russians left Budapest on 26 October it must have appeared to the people that the Soviets had accepted the inevitability of Hungarian national self-determination – a perception significantly reinforced by the fact that before it left Budapest the delegation gave Imre Nagy (who had not supported the use of the Soviet tanks on 24 October) the task of forming a new government. On 27 October a new Hungarian administration was established and the last Soviet tanks drove – or were dragged – from the streets of the capital. It appeared that the cause of freedom had indeed triumphed over military might in Hungary. But then events took a more sinister turn, as the impact of the Cold War's global conflicts directly affected the situation in Hungary.

On 26 July 1956 President Gamal Abdel Nasser of Egypt had nationalised the strategically vital Suez Canal. Subsequently, despite strong objections from the United States, Britain and France determined upon military intervention to regain international control of the canal. These Anglo-French intentions were made clear in the autumn, just as the freedom movement in Hungary was gaining momentum. Meanwhile, Israel took advantage of the impending Anglo-French invasion at Suez to attack Egypt from the east in the Sinai, with a view to neutralising what was then the principal military threat to the nine-year-old state of Israel. At last light on 29 October a parachute brigade dropped on to the Mitla Pass, while three more brigades of Israeli armour and infantry rolled across the Sinai, destroying the Egyptian forces wherever they were encountered. Then, on 31 October, waves of British and French aircraft began to bomb the Egyptian airbases. This action was followed by Anglo-French airborne and seaborne landings on 5 and 6 November.

Undoubtedly, the Soviets were well aware of the Anglo-French intentions regarding Suez. Ever since 29 October the potential neutralisation of one of the Soviet Union's principal candidate states and supporters in the region, together with the imminent prospect of Anglo-French control of the Suez Canal, had been watched with growing concern by a Politburo still smarting from the Red Army's humiliation during the October riots in Budapest. Moscow was also very aware of the need to restore its authority both within its own immediate area of interest and on the world stage. Strategically, the removal of the Hungarian buffer between the Soviet Union and the West was unacceptable to Moscow; while Hungary's common borders with a potentially unstable Czechoslovakia, a semi-neutral Yugoslavia, a neutral but plainly pro-West Austria, and with the communist stalwart Romania, heightened dramatically the level of Soviet concern. Even without the benefit of hindsight, the sheer ingenuousness of the Hungarian nationalists in not appreciating the vital strategic importance of Hungary to the Soviet Union in 1956 was both irresponsible and remarkable.

By 1 November it was clear to all but the most naïve Hungarians that the Soviet withdrawal from Budapest on 29 October had not been repeated throughout Hungary. The withdrawal of the tanks and grant of political concessions had simply been to gain the Politburo a temporary respite – and time to prepare their real response to the crisis. Meanwhile, the Kremlin had noted the dangers of using locally based units for internal security operations; when some of the troops of the two motor rifle divisions deployed to Budapest on 23 October had shown considerably less enthusiasm for their task than their political masters had expected of them. The Soviet commanders had also relearned the lessons of 1945 concerning the command, control and target acquisition problems incurred by tank-heavy units operating against a non-armoured and elusive enemy in urban areas. All this they took into account as they formulated their plans for Hungary.

During the first three days of November 1956, a force of some 250,000 Soviet troops was assembled from bases in Russia, Czechoslovakia and Romania and moved across the borders into Hungary. In parallel with these deployments the Soviets continued to negotiate with Imre Nagy and the new Hungarian government. However, this was no more than a deception designed to allay Hungarian fears and to buy time for the invasion plans to be completed. At midnight on 3 November, Soviet armour again rumbled into Budapest, and at five o'clock the next morning Imre Nagy broadcast to the nation and the world that Budapest was under direct attack by Soviet forces.

This time the Soviet intentions were unequivocal. The Kremlin launched about twelve divisions with 2,500 armoured vehicles into the city of Budapest, and parts of the Hungarian capital soon assumed a state of destruction reminiscent of Budapest's wartime liberation from the Germans by the Red Army just a decade before.

Many of the attackers had undoubtedly been involved in the battle for Berlin and, although on a much smaller scale, the battle for Budapest must have evoked still-recent memories of that urban battle for some of the more senior Soviet troops. First the city was surrounded. Next, massed artillery and echelons of the multi-barrelled rocket launchers that had proved so devastatingly effective on the Eastern Front just over eleven years earlier were deployed on the high ground to the west of the city. Finally, the bombardment began, with all the insurgent strongholds and centres of resistance speedily reduced to rubble. Bridges, barracks and other key points were seized by tank units that moved in during the closing stages of the bombardment. These troops were followed shortly afterwards by infantry-heavy all-arms units, with tanks and artillery supporting the motor rifle troops as they set about clearing each building in detail. The Soviet operation within the city was completed on 7 November, although resistance continued – and was dealt with in similar fashion – in some other urban areas for a further week, while in the wider countryside isolated instances of resistance continued until the end of the year. Some 25,000 Hungarian citizens and about 7,000 Soviet soldiers died between 4 and 14 November.[42] In addition, a further 20,000 people were arrested, of whom some 2,000 were subsequently executed. Finally, more than 25,000 Hungarians fled to Austria during November 1956, considerably exacerbating an already serious refugee crisis for that officially neutral (but undeniably pro-West) state.

On 22 November Imre Nagy was persuaded by a false promise of safe conduct to leave the Yugoslav Embassy where he had taken refuge. He, together with those resistance leaders and members of his short-lived government who had sought sanctuary there with him, were promptly arrested by the Soviets and transported to Romania, where they were imprisoned. Their ultimate fate was inevitable. One day in June 1958, once the Soviet Politburo was certain that the new government of their preferred candidate János Kádár was secure, Nagy and those still imprisoned with him in Romania were taken from their cells and summarily shot. But by then world events and the Cold War had moved on, and beyond Hungary the memories of the heroic but hopeless battles fought on the streets of Budapest during that fateful autumn of 1956 had faded as new crises loomed in Europe and elsewhere. Yet, even some forty years later, bullet holes and shrapnel marks still scar a number of buildings in Budapest (mainly in Pest) – a poignant reminder of the street battles of October and November 1956.

The hard lessons of Hungary were duly noted by the other Warsaw Pact member states. But with the passage of time people's perceptions and beliefs change, and ten years later – in the 'Prague Spring' of 1968 – yet another state was destined to experience the consequences of challenging the authority of Moscow.

In December 1956, the West's predisposition not to provide assistance to the insurgents during any such uprisings in the future was the subject of a British Joint Intelligence Committee report. This document stated that recent events in Hungary had demonstrated 'the view that we have always held that the Soviet leaders would go to almost any lengths to retain their hold on the Satellites ... Any action by the West to assist a Satellite to free itself from Soviet domination would be likely to result in violent Soviet reaction, and, through a confused series of events, including threats made under mounting nervous pressure, could lead up to a global war.'[43] The key phrase here was 'the view that we have always held', for it indicated quite clearly that the Hungarian uprising was doomed from the outset, as no outside support would have been countenanced. Throughout the 1950s, containment and restraint rather than intervention were the fundamental principles that determined Western policy, and the recent experience of US and British Commonwealth intervention (albeit under UN auspices) in Korea from 1950 to 1953 was no doubt a significant factor in the formulation of that policy. In addition, Western strategic planners were also very aware that in 1949 the Soviet Union had joined the ranks of the nuclear powers; which made the stakes in any risk-taking infinitely higher than had been the case previously. Meanwhile, new crises threatened to bring the nuclear powers of East and West into direct conflict; and the first major Cold War crisis of the 1960s occurred in Germany, when Berlin became yet again the focus of the conflict during the balmy late summer days of 1961.

The Berlin Wall, 1961

Although a posting to the GDR was generally regarded as highly desirable by the troops of the Red Army (and by officers in particular, who enjoyed a standard of accommodation and living which far exceeded that of their colleagues based in the Soviet Union), life in East Germany for the country's civilian population was less than idyllic and was becoming worse with each passing year. At the same time, there was a growing awareness in the East of the increasing prosperity and standard of living of the citizens of West Germany. Despite the existence of the border security zone, escape to West Germany and West Berlin from East Germany in the late 1950s was still not overly difficult. As the decade drew to a close the annual stream of refugees that had numbered some 129,245 in 1945 and peaked at 331,390 in 1953, had settled down to an annual average of about 200,000. Then, following the disastrous collectivisation of the GDR farming industry from 1959, which was completed in mid-1960, about 15,000 farmers fled to the West and left behind them yet another food crisis in East Germany. As the human crisis escalated, 30,000 people fled in July 1961, with 20,000 more between 1 and 12 August. Four thousand people registered as refugees at the Marienborn processing centre on the single day of 12 August. Clearly something had to be done if the GDR was to survive, and the solution produced what quickly became the most enduring symbol of the Cold War.

Last light on Saturday 12 August 1961, and the Soviet and GDR governments prepared to implement a radical plan to deal with the crisis. Although the impending operation was underwritten by some two divisions of Soviet troops of Marshal Koniev's GSFG, it was portrayed as a GDR operation directed by Walter Ulbricht, the East German leader. Final briefings were conducted, and at midnight a force of more than 40,000 policemen (*Vopos*), border security troops, East German army – the *Nationale Volksarmee* (NVA) – units and workmen began deploying to the East–West inter-sector boundaries within and about Berlin. At 2.30 a.m. they proceeded to seal them off. Surprise was absolute. Europe awoke on 13 August to find that East and West Berlin had been physically divided, and that the precedent set in Berlin would shortly be repeated along the border between East and West Germany. As the work proceeded in Berlin, West Europeans must have wondered if this was the precursor of the long-anticipated war with the Soviet Union. However, the Kremlin leaders had already assessed quite correctly that the crisis would be dealt with in Washington, Paris and London by measures that fell well short of war.

Within Berlin, what Ulbricht termed 'die Moderne Grenze' – 'the modern border' – comprised a major obstacle almost thirty miles long. A hundred-mile-long barbed-wire security fence – 'The Wire' – already existed between the Western Allied sectors and the Soviet Zone of Occupation in East Germany, although prior to 13 August no such obstacle had existed between the Soviet and Western sectors within the city. But by first light on Sunday 13 August the East Germans had sealed off many of the inter-sector streets, and the process of erecting temporary barricades and obstacles continued for the rest of that day. A force of border guards and *Vopos*, equipped with four water-cannon vehicles, sealed off the Strasse des 17 Juni. They then remained stationed just to the west of the Brandenburg Gate all day, in anticipation of that site being the focus of any West Berlin demonstrations in response to the rapidly unfolding events. The Brandenburg Gate lay within the British sector of Berlin and mobile patrols of the Royal Military Police (RMP) continued to observe and monitor developments. Meanwhile, elsewhere within West Berlin, there was increasing incredulity and anger at the lack of a robust response by the Western Allies; an anger that was articulated with particular authority by the formidable mayor of West Berlin, Willy Brandt. But the East Germans had planned and conducted the operation with meticulous care, and ensured that it remained entirely within the Soviet sector of Berlin, so that there was virtually no room for the West to take any direct action.

A protest was made by the Allied Commandants to the Soviet Commandant, Colonel Andrei Solovyev, on Tuesday 15 August about the illegal deployment of NVA troops within the Soviet sector, but this was rebutted with the response that the Soviet authorities did not interfere with the internal affairs of the GDR. On the same day, the first East German border guard to defect since 13 August made a successful bid for freedom. Before his comrades realised what he intended, Conrad Schumann sprinted the few yards to a temporary barrier and leapt over the low wire entanglement adjacent to his post at the corner of Bernauer and Ruppiner Strasse, discarding his submachine-gun as he did so. By chance, his escape was recorded on camera. Schumann was but the first of 2,171 such escapees from the GDR security forces over the next eight years. As well as these, many thousands of civilian East Germans managed to circumvent the 'modern border' by ever more ingenious means between 1961 and 1989. However, 258 would-be escapers died while attempting to cross the Wall in Berlin, plus ten who drowned while trying to cross the river sections of the border. Some twenty-five border security guards also lost their lives in connection with escape attempts.

But to return to mid-August 1961, US President John F. Kennedy understood the need for quick action to bolster morale in West Berlin and allay the fears that its people were being abandoned by the Western Allies. Vice-President Lyndon B. Johnson was dispatched to the city with General Lucius Clay, the former US Commandant in Berlin during the 1948 Berlin Airlift. At the same time, 1,500 soldiers of the 18th US Infantry Regiment, a unit of the 8th 'Golden Arrow' US Infantry Division, were sent from their base in West Germany via the southern autobahn link between Berlin and West Germany to reinforce the US garrison in the beleaguered city. The British added eighteen armoured personnel carriers and eighteen light armoured cars to their garrison. These measures did much to reassure the population of West Berlin. But in East Berlin construction work on what was now known universally as 'the Wall' continued without pause. By September the eighty-eight pre-13 August 1961 crossing points available to Berliners had been reduced to thirteen, with only one rail crossing open. This was at the Friedrichstrasse S-Bahn Station. For the Western Allies, only the Friedrichstrasse crossing point was authorised, and here the US military police established an administrative post designated 'Checkpoint Charlie'.[44] Later, British RMP and French Gendarmerie joined the Americans to man this potential flashpoint jointly.

Inevitably, there were frequent incidents after 13 August; some were surreal, some were humorous and some were incredible, but all had potentially serious implications. On 22 October Mr Allan Lightner, the principal US official in Berlin, and his wife set out in their US-registered Volkswagen car to enjoy a night at the opera in East Berlin. They reached Checkpoint Charlie and proceeded to cross into the East. However, they were immediately stopped and asked to present their passports – a requirement from which the Western Allies were exempt due to the Four-Power Agreement on rights of access within the city. The matter finally resulted in the Lightners proceeding to their evening engagement in considerable style – they were escorted through the crossing into East Berlin by armed US soldiers, who were in turn covered by the guns of four M-48 Patton tanks from positions adjacent to Checkpoint Charlie.

Subsequently, several 'right of entry' crossings were carried out, of which the most significant was on Wednesday, 25 October. On this occasion two US Army officers were deliberately sent into East Berlin wearing civilian clothes and travelling in a civilian car with US Armed Forces registration plates.[45] As expected, they were stopped and turned back by the GDR border guards; but when they returned escorted by three jeeps full of armed GIs in combat clothing they were allowed into the East. However, 25 October had already been identified by General Lucius Clay and Washington as the day on which a stand was to be taken, and that on which the right of access issue was finally to be resolved.

Consequently, just half an hour after the two Americans gained access to East Berlin, ten M-48 tanks and two M-113 armoured personnel carriers arrived at Checkpoint Charlie and took up fire positions at and close by the crossing. The developing situation was recorded by a multitude of media cameras and news commentators. During the next twenty-four hours a number of entries were carried out by military personnel in civilian clothes, all of which produced an initial refusal by the East Germans, followed by acquiescence when the jeeps full of uniformed infantrymen appeared to escort these personnel. Clearly the matter was coming to a head, and on the night of Thursday 26 October events took a more sinister turn when a Soviet tank battalion of thirty-three T-54/55s appeared in the area just to the north-east of the Brandenburg Gate. Not since the uprising of 17 June 1953 had Soviet armour been seen in East Berlin. As one company of ten Soviet tanks moved off to take up fire positions in Friedrichstrasse, only 100 yards away from the ten US tanks, the world held its breath.

Despite his strong declarations of support for West Berlin, however, Kennedy was certainly not prepared to go to war over this issue. Neither was Khrushchev. Consequently, by Saturday, 28 October the crisis had been defused, with the withdrawal of the T-54/55s that morning, followed shortly thereafter by the US tanks, and a suitable compromise on the right of access issue was arrived at during the days that followed. This included Western agreement to the wearing of uniform by all military personnel entering East Berlin in the future; but with civilian personnel and the dependants of servicemen simply showing their passports, whilst not submitting them for formal examination.

During the following March the Soviets again attempted to restrict Western civilian air movement to and from Berlin. This harassment included the dangerous practices of jamming the air safety radio frequency and air traffic control radar systems. The Soviets also repeated the 1948 tactic of buzzing Western aircraft with their fighters. However, this reckless policy was quickly ended by the direct intervention of the British Foreign Secretary, Lord Home.

Meanwhile, as 1962 drew on, General Lucius Clay remained the driving force behind US actions and reactions in Berlin. Perhaps memories of his earlier successes in 1948 influenced him excessively, as some military commanders and political leaders in the West began to voice concerns that his robust and uncompromising approach risked an unnecessary escalation of the ongoing crisis, notwithstanding his great popularity with the West Berliners. In any event, by the spring of that year his task in the city was all but complete, and he departed Berlin on the conclusion of his second major contribution to the city's post-war history, and the story of the Cold War.

All the while construction of the Wall about Berlin had continued, as had the escape attempts – many were successful, but others were less so. By December 1961 twenty people had died trying to flee to West Berlin, and the GDR border guard orders to shoot would-be escapers were being applied regularly. The final phase of the Wall's development (the use of one-metre wide, smooth concrete slabs, welded together and surmounted by a round pipe arrangement that offered no handholds) was completed in the mid to late 1970s. The hundred-miles-long obstacle then consisted of concrete slabs (sixty-one miles), metal fencing (thirty miles), barbed wire (three miles) and other obstacles (six miles). These were linked into an intricate network of between two and three hundred observation posts and towers, some 136 bunkers, 160 miles of dog runs with provision for more than 200 dogs to be in place, sixty-five miles of trenches, seventy-one miles of vehicle-bearing patrol roads, sixty-three miles of anti-vehicle ditches and seventy-six miles of electrified fences, all fitted with warning devices and remotely operated firing devices. Along the whole length of the Wall on land ran a sandy strip that was originally believed to have been mined, but the purpose of which was in fact to afford the guards a clear field of fire, and to reveal by the tell-tale footprints left in the carefully raked sand where an otherwise unde-tected escape had taken place. That the border guards were expected to shoot at would-be escapers was not in doubt, as former Unteroffizier Manfred Milde of Grenzregiment Nr. 40 explained after his own escape to West Berlin on 19 December, 1966:

> After the 'border violater' has got over the first barrier of the border, which is usually an innocent-looking fence, you are to yell at him, 'Halt! Border guard! Hands up!' If the man you're yelling at doesn't raise his

hands and also doesn't stop, you are to fire a warning shot. If he still doesn't stop, you are to aim right at him, no matter how many barriers he still has to cross. If the 'border violater' is so near to the border that yelling or firing the warning shot might give him enough time to make his escape, you are to shoot to kill right away.[46]

The formidable defences were manned by a force of some 14,000 GDR security force personnel, including the border guards and the regular NVA, plus the *Vopos*.[47]

During the almost three decades that followed the Wall's construction the escapes, killings, political manoeuvrings, attempts to curtail rights of access and movement, devices to advance or decry the legitimacy of the GDR and the FRG, and all sorts of lesser crises centred directly or indirectly upon Berlin, continued on a regular basis. But the presence of the Wall was now an undeniable fact, and its existence shaped the perceptions of the forces of West and East as well as physically dividing them. After the immediate flurry of reactions and expressions of outrage over its construction in 1961 and 1962 had more or less ceased, the principal responsibility for the management and control of 'the question of Berlin' moved back quite properly from the military commanders to the political leaders of the major Cold War powers, although the full range of military options remained always available to these leaders throughout the Cold War. This political responsibility was reinforced on 26 June 1963, when President Kennedy stated his commitment and that of the West to support, sustain and if necessary defend West Berlin. During a visit to the Wall he made the famous pronouncement: 'All free men, wherever they may live, are citizens of Berlin, and therefore, as a free man, I take pride in the words: Ich bin ein Berliner.'[48]

After 1961 there was a steady flow of high-profile visits by numerous heads of state, statesmen and politicians to the Wall. From time to time the tragic deaths of would-be escapers were reported, balanced by the success of other daring escapes; and expressions of outrage and thought-provoking articles about the Wall's continued existence regularly appeared in the Western media. Certainly the very presence of the Wall symbolised the deep ideological and cultural rift that existed between East and West. But despite all this, after 1962 it was inconceivable that the city would be allowed to trigger the nuclear holocaust that the world so feared.

Over time, the ugly physical presence, solidity and permanence of the Wall acquired a prominent place in the consciousness of the international community. For the West Germans it remained a symbol of their country's division, and as such it was generally abhorred by them. For the West it was a useful reminder of the true nature of communism, if the left-wing influences within their own countries should become too powerful.

Yet within East Germany, particularly among the older generation and those in the armed forces and security forces, there were many who benefited from the existence of Ulbricht's 'modern border'. Only in recent years, however, with the continuing general decline and succession of economic crises in the former GDR, have such views been voiced openly. Meanwhile, at the time of its construction the Wall effectively curtailed a human outflow from East Germany and Eastern Europe that was rapidly assuming the proportions of an uncontrollable flood. Very many of those who were fleeing to the West were not the older members of the population, but were the young and able-bodied upon whom the post-war regeneration and economic future of Eastern Europe depended. At a stroke the Wall had halted that outflow and reduced it to a trickle. Therefore, however politically uncomfortable the hypothesis may be, a pragmatic view of the wider impact of the Wall suggests that it actually had a stabilising effect upon East–West relations at a time when those relations were otherwise anything but stable.

In practice, the constraining effect of the Wall upon the peoples of Eastern Europe extended far beyond Berlin; for just as the obstacle about the city had been created and modernised since 1961 so also had the very formidable and in many ways much more significant 'modern border' that now extended along the whole length of the Iron Curtain: from the Baltic in the north to the Austrian and Swiss borders in the south. By arresting the wholesale movement of the people of Eastern Europe to Western Europe the Wall stabilised those states that were at various stages of crisis in the early 1960s, as much of their labour force and best brains sought refuge in the West.

The Wall also affected very directly the longer-term relationship between the Soviet Union and the West. It forced the formulation of realistic and workable crisis management rules, arrangements and protocols – whether formally laid down or simply 'understood' by Moscow, Washington, Bonn, London and Paris – concerning the way in which the wider issues of Europe should be dealt with in the future. In other words, a significant result of the Wall was that it crystallised many of the ground rules for the future conduct of the Cold War in Europe.

Finally, Berlin's unique situation impacted directly upon several specific aspects of the Cold War right through to 1989. First, despite the inference and assumption that the Soviets would have preferred the withdrawal of the Western Allies from the city, their presence conferred several advantages on the Soviets and their GDR allies. The Western garrison provided a ready source of military intelligence information, as well as a range of subversive and espionage conduits to the West. Meanwhile, the Western Allies' situation in the city was patently precarious, and it was no accident that the British and Americans generally chose not to deploy their most up-to-date military hardware to West Berlin; in the event of war the Western garrisons would have been effectively sealed within a prison camp of their own making. This meant that the equivalent of an infantry division would have been unavailable to NATO for operations beyond Berlin. Indeed, when the Warsaw Pact plans for Berlin were publicised in 1994 it was revealed that, far from any Soviet intention to rerun their costly 1945 battle for Berlin, the responsibility for dealing with the Western garrison had been allocated exclusively to the NVA. 'Operation Centre' envisaged combined arms assaults by NVA formations on four main axes, preceded by a helicopter assault carried out by special purpose airborne forces. The attack was to be supported by the extensive use of psychological operations, with the aim of destroying the Western Allies' cohesion by suggesting that the French and British should 'not waste their lives defending American interests'. These plans were extensively revised in 1988 after a NVA study indicated that a force of up to 100,000 men would be needed for the task. Thereafter, the new plan called for West Berlin to be completely invested, besieged and starved into submission. While the potential success of the first plan was questionable, its 1988 successor was probably viable, albeit after a very protracted siege.[49]

Arguably, the military benefits to the Western Allies of their continued presence in West Berlin were less apparent than those for the Soviets and East Germans. However, the most significant and almost incalculable value of West Berlin to the West was its function as a prime source of intelligence, located as it was deep inside East Germany and GSFG. Through simple day-to-day observation within Berlin and on its borders, or while travelling to or from the city by road, rail or air, and through analysis of the 'take' from the sophisticated electronic monitoring equipment sited within the 'golf balls' (so called because of the large white spherical covers positioned over the equipment to protect it against the weather) antennas on the Teufelsberg hill, West Berlin provided a unique opportunity for the West to gain invaluable intelligence on all aspects of the Soviet and GDR forces. Also, Berlin enabled the British, French and US military missions to the Soviet commander-in-chief to conduct their overt but invaluable task of intelligence gathering and liaison throughout the GDR. Consequently, the strategic intelligence value of West Berlin probably justified the inevitable loss or neutralisation of the Western garrison in the event of war.

Last of all, Berlin provided a unique East–West point of contact, from which both sides benefited in diverse ways. At one extreme, the Glienicke Bridge became famous for several high-profile exchanges of spies, defectors, and others who prosecuted the generally unseen but vitally important 'shadow war' in support of the policies of East and West. Meanwhile, at the other end of the spectrum, only in Berlin could the military forces of both sides routinely view each other face-to-face. And it was entirely conceivable that the Western Allied soldiers stationed in West Berlin occasionally identified in a GDR border guard or NVA soldier manning the Berlin border, or in a Soviet soldier or officer checking documents at the road or rail checkpoint at Helmstedt, the qualities common to all who have followed the profession of arms – irrespective of the uniform that they wore. And such contacts might just have allowed them to achieve a greater mutual understanding of the surreal, volatile and potentially dangerous situations in which they found themselves during almost three decades of confrontation that followed the events of Sunday, 13 August 1961.

Czechoslovakia, 1968: The Prague Spring

As the years passed, Europe developed and moved on. In East and West alike, by the late 1960s the Soviet suppression of the Hungarian uprising had become an ever more distant memory. Within Czechoslovakia, during some twenty years of typically unimaginative and authoritarian – but generally not oppressive – communist rule, the population had become increasingly aware of the very different lifestyle enjoyed by its Western neighbours. Perhaps the lack of a permanent Soviet garrison in Czechoslovakia had bred a perception that the Czechs were sufficiently trusted and good communists for a relaxation of the traditional control that the Soviets exercised over their satellite states? Perhaps it was the fact that the Czechs had genuinely welcomed the Red Army soldiers as liberators in 1945? Or perhaps it was because the Czechs had been treated shamefully by Neville Chamberlain and others thirty years before, at Munich – so much so that surely the Kremlin would not now deny the Czechs a measure of freedom within the Warsaw Pact?

In January 1968, Alexander Dubcek was appointed First Secretary of the Communist Party of Czechoslovakia, having previously indicated that he would institute significant reforms, including the end of media censorship, a review and revamping of the political system and a reappraisal and reform of the state education system. All this was put in train by the spring of 1968, and during the heady months of what became known as the 'Prague Spring' Czechoslovakia began to enjoy freedoms that had been denied to virtually all ever since the beginning of the German occupation during the Second World War. As spring gave way to early summer, any thoughts of a Hungary-style Soviet military intervention receded. After all, had not the Czechs approached the whole matter as the civilised people that Brezhnev and the

Politburo knew them to be? There had been no armed insurrection, and in any case, with no Soviet forces stationed on Czech territory, there was no focus for such action had it even been contemplated. For Dubcek and the Czech leadership, 1968 was clearly destined to be the year that Czechoslovakia would begin to reclaim its former status, liberty and self-esteem as a sovereign nation – albeit within the Warsaw Pact.

Yet even though more than a decade had passed since Soviet tanks had rolled into Budapest, Moscow's view of the status of the Eastern bloc states had not changed. Consequently, the developments in Prague generated considerable concern in Moscow, as well as in some other Warsaw Pact capitals, during the spring of 1968.[50] There was a growing fear that the Czechs' new-found freedom would spread to other Warsaw Pact countries, which would not only weaken those regimes but might also threaten the effectiveness of the buffer of Eastern bloc states upon whom the Soviet Union relied to provide a geographical and military bulwark against Western imperialism and capitalism.

In June and July a succession of discussions and negotiations took place between the Soviets, the other Warsaw Pact governments and the Czechs. By the end of July the issue had apparently been resolved, but in reality the Soviets were already planning to deal with the Czechoslovakia problem by force of arms. The sequence of events that followed mirrored the scenario of countless Warsaw Pact and NATO training exercises whereby a mobilisation of Soviet forces would be followed by a major exercise, which was then suddenly transformed into a full-scale invasion of NATO territory. Usually these exercises depicted an early NATO incursion on to Warsaw Pact territory; this being necessary to cast NATO in the role of the aggressor, in order to justify a politically acceptable communist military response.

A command post exercise based within Czechoslovakia was conducted from 20 to 30 June. This was followed by a further exercise from 23 July to 10 August, which involved the call-up of Soviet reservists, and then continued as a command and control and air-defence operation from 11 to 20 August. The final day of this exercise was a Sunday, and at 23.00 hours that night a Soviet *Spetsnaz* battalion seized the airport that served Prague. Shortly afterwards Soviet troop transports carrying soldiers of the 103rd Guards Airborne Division began arriving at the airport. As soon as the planes landed, their occupants moved off to secure key government, communications and military sites within Prague. At the same time, a massive Warsaw Pact armoured force some 250,000 strong crossed the Czech borders. Four divisions of the Soviet 1st Guards Tank Army (the headquarters of which was normally based at Dresden), plus one NVA division, entered Czechoslovakia from the GDR and drove to the border with West Germany, where they sealed the border to prevent any possible interference from NATO. A further four Soviet divisions, of the 20th Guards Army (based normally about Eberswalde in the GDR), with another NVA division, entered Czechoslovakia from the GDR and Poland. These five divisions moved into Prague and took over responsibility for the city from the Soviet paratroopers. Meanwhile, five more Soviet divisions moved into the east from the Soviet Union and from southern Poland. Finally, two Hungarian divisions plus some Soviet units crossed into the south of Czechoslovakia, while four Polish divisions moved in from the north. The ground troops were supported by the Soviet 24th Tactical Air Army in such strength that it was able to occupy every airfield in Czechoslovakia.

As the invading Soviet divisions deployed into Czechoslovakia, the vacuum they left in the GDR and Poland was quickly filled by divisions moved west from the Soviet Union. Meanwhile, the invading divisions replaced the Czech forces stationed in the west of the country facing NATO. The sheer scale of the military force that moved into Czechoslovakia meant that armed resistance was never a realistic option, although widespread public protests did take place in Prague and elsewhere. These had little impact, and Alexander Dubcek's all too short Prague Spring came to an abrupt end within a few days. At a stroke Moscow had reasserted its direct control over its erring satellite, and had also contrived to reinforce significantly its force levels in the forward area facing NATO across the Iron Curtain. Lastly, Leonid Brezhnev had demonstrated unequivocally Moscow's view on the issue of Czechoslovakian sovereignty – an object lesson for any other Warsaw Pact state that might contemplate loosening its Soviet control in the future.

Although the West protested at the Warsaw Pact military intervention in Czechoslovakia, this was treated as little more than a formality, and the Czechs were aware that they had again been abandoned by the West. Ironically, German troops (this time of the NVA) were once again imposing their wishes upon the Czech people by force of arms – just twenty-three years after the Red Army had liberated Czechoslovakia from the German forces of the Third Reich.

Immediately following the invasion on 20 August, NATO alert states were raised to reflect the increased threat, and in West Germany many NATO units carried out the operational deployments from barracks that would normally have preceded their response to a communist attack across the IGB. But these actions were prompted more by a concern that the invasion of Czechoslovakia might be the precursor to war between the Warsaw Pact and NATO, rather than to imply military support for the Czechs. Accordingly, these units soon returned to their barracks. In any case, military intervention by NATO over Czechoslovakia was never likely – the precedent set by

Western passivity over Hungary in 1956 had illustrated this – and both Brezhnev and President Johnson (who was by then wholly preoccupied with the political and military consequences of the communist Tet 1968 offensive in South Vietnam) were very well aware of that.

Poland, 1980–1

Although Poland's relations with the Soviet Union had been difficult even before the Second World War,[51] the unrest that emerged during 1980 was rooted in the mid-1950s, when Polish leader Gomulka secured Khrushchev's agreement to some limited reforms. More unrest then occurred intermittently throughout the 1970s. The subsequent, sometimes violent, protests over economic issues and workers' rights resulted in further Soviet and Polish government concessions. Finally, in mid-1980, calls for trade union and political reform coincided with protests over food prices and a strike by 50,000 workers that August. Much of this unrest was focused on the huge Gdansk shipyard, where the ship-workers were key players in the emergence of the new 'Solidarity' union.

During the three months from January 1981 events closely followed the pattern of the Czech crisis of 1968. This in itself was a clear indication that the Soviet Union was still not prepared to tolerate any weakening of Warsaw Pact cohesion. Many ordinary Poles may not have fully appreciated the strategic importance of their country to Moscow, but Poland's geographical position between the Soviet Union and its arch-enemy of two World Wars was plain to anyone who understood the depth of anti-German feeling that still existed in the Soviet Union. Quite apart from its role as a buffer state, any Soviet attack into West Germany and beyond had to be mounted, reinforced and resupplied along the main road and rail routes that ran westward from the Soviet border, through Poland, and into East Germany. Strategically, Poland was indispensable to the success of any Warsaw Pact ground war against NATO.

Through the spring and summer of 1981, military exercises paralleled discussions and consultations, while Moscow's pressure upon the Polish leader, Stanislaw Kania, increased daily. There is little doubt that had a solution acceptable to the Kremlin leaders not been achieved, Warsaw Pact forces would have rolled into Poland and imposed a solution by force; just as they had done in East Germany, Hungary and Czechoslovakia.

On 28 October, however, the Polish Minister of National Defence, General Wojciech Jaruzelski, was appointed First Secretary of the Polish United Workers Party and thus became the new leader of Poland. He acted promptly and decisively to regain government control of the developing crisis. First, he banned all strikes for ninety days and then, on 13 December, he imposed martial law. Jaruzelski could at any stage have called upon Soviet or Warsaw Pact forces to assist him in the pacification of his country if that had been necessary; but fortunately for Poland these measures proved sufficient to obviate the need for another Warsaw Pact invasion of one of its members. Nevertheless, the imminent threat of such intervention was clearly underlined by the previously unscheduled concentration of several thousand NVA soldiers at Prora on Rügen Island during late November 1981. Indeed, the GDR leader Erich Honecker – ever faithful to his Soviet masters – had that same month enthusiastically urged a military intervention to Brezhnev. Thus the familiar indicators of an invasion in preparation were fast developing or were already in place during November, and within NATO an invasion of Poland had actually been forecast by military analysts for about 8 December. Indeed, between September 1980 and December 1981, NATO had recorded no less than fourteen Warsaw Pact major exercises involving or adjacent to Poland.

But Jaruzelski's firm actions forestalled any such action, and thus avoided a conflict which had the potential to turn into an even bloodier affair than had the 1956 Hungarian uprising, since much of the Polish army would probably have sided with its own people against any invader. Although Jaruzelski attracted much criticism in the West for his authoritarian action to deal with the unrest, there is little doubt that he was sufficiently pragmatic and man of vision to realise that taking a Dubcek or Imre Nagy approach would have invited disaster. Accordingly, and particularly in light of Poland's international progress since 1990, it may well be that history will record a kinder assessment of Jaruzelski's role in the Cold War than did most of the media and many political commentators in the 1980s.

The End of the Cold War in Europe

In the succeeding years, the Berlin Wall continued to provide a tangible and symbolic focus for the great divide between East and West. The massive Brandenburg Gate, surmounted by the famous Quadriga chariot, set squarely and inaccessibly within the East Berlin border security zone, served as a constant reminder of the meaning of Soviet domination. There was a certain irony in this, as prior to 1945 Europeans, Americans and Russians had identified the Brandenburg Gate with German imperialism in the nineteenth century, and again in 1914–18 and 1939–45. But for the forty-five years of the Cold War the Brandenburg Gate and the Wall had assumed a different mantle. Therefore, it was entirely fitting that the visible collapse of communism and the Soviet domination of Eastern Europe took place at that site.

The events immediately preceding the end of the Berlin Wall gained pace in late 1989, following (and certainly affected by) Mikhail Gorbachev's visit to

East Berlin on 7 October. The increasingly relaxed line by Moscow had already permeated the population of the GDR, and civil unrest was increasing: its momentum unconstrained by Soviet or East German security forces. The hard-line leader Erich Honecker was replaced by Egon Krenz on 18 October. Following significant demonstrations in Leipzig, Erfurt, Gera, Rostock and Dresden later that month, Krenz initiated talks with the West German leader, Helmut Kohl, about relaxing the inter-state border controls. On 4 November, one million people demonstrated peacefully in East Berlin. Then, five days later on 9 November, during a radio interview, Krenz was understood to have indicated that any GDR citizen who so wished could obtain an immediate exit visa at the border. Much of the population of East Berlin took him at his word and headed for the several official checkpoints at the Wall. Prudently, the border security guards simply opened the barriers. In an ecstatic but surreal atmosphere the human tide surged into the brightly lit streets of West Berlin, and more than three million East Germans entered West Berlin and West Germany during the weekend that followed. Krenz saw that change was inevitable and spoke of his intention to promote 'reformed socialism'. On 11 November he published plans for radical new measures, including free elections, independent courts, economic reform, a freer press, autonomous trade unions and scrutiny of the infamous state security police, the *Staatssicherheit*, or '*Stasi*'.

The communist regime, however, could not survive. Mikhail Gorbachev had already told US President George Bush that he supported the GDR decision to open its borders, and hoped that the situation would remain calm. This thinly disguised indication that the Soviet Union had no intention of intervening in East Germany, or by implication anywhere else in the Eastern bloc states, meant that the GDR's days as a sovereign state were numbered. It also signified that Soviet military domination of Eastern Europe and the need for the Warsaw Pact were at an end. Finally, it ensured that the Soviet Union itself would soon be no more than an (albeit important) entry in the history books. The Cold War conflict in Europe that began shortly after the Red Army captured Hitler's Reichstag building Berlin in May 1945 had ended at that same spot a little more than forty-four years later.

CHAPTER SIX

THE KOREAN WAR, 1950–3

A few minutes before four o'clock on the morning of Sunday, 25 June 1950, the first light of dawn was appearing in the skies above the Korean peninsula. In their border posts and bunkers along the 38th parallel – the frontier between the communist Democratic People's Republic of Korea (DPRK) to the north and the non-communist Republic of Korea (ROK) to the south – those duty personnel of the ROK paramilitary security forces not away on weekend leave viewed the seemingly deserted hills and valleys that stretched away from the border into the DPRK. Suddenly, their world was turned upside-down in a cacophony of sound, light, dust, smoke and explosions, as the shells and bombs from more than 1,600 guns and mortars rained down on their positions, before lifting their fire to engage other targets in depth. At the same time, flights of Illyushin Il-10 bombers thundered south to engage airfields and other targets that were beyond the reach of the field artillery.

Out of the dust and destruction of that devastating Soviet-style bombard-ment emerged the next horror for the ROK soldiers who had survived thus far, as columns of T-34 tanks stormed across the 38th parallel into South Korea. Behind the tanks came olive-green clad hordes of well-equipped infantry. The ROK infantry had no effective anti-armour weapons and their positions were quickly overrun, as the T-34s rumbled on virtually unscathed, the armoured spearhead of ten DPRK combined arms divisions streaming south on four main axes of advance. Surprise was absolute,[52] and in any case the 95,000 ill-trained, poorly equipped and in many cases unmotivated and inadequately led men of the ROK were no match for 135,000 well-drilled and highly motivated soldiers of the North Korean People's Army (NKPA). On the morning of 28 June, just three days after they crossed the 38th parallel, the first communist troops entered the South Korean capital, Seoul, which had been abandoned to its fate by the ROK army twenty-four hours earlier.

Opinions will always vary as to which of the several 'hot wars' that occurred during the course of the Cold War was the most significant in terms of its wider importance and impact. However, by the way it shaped the Cold War subsequently and by its influence upon world events, the war in Korea from 1950 to 1953 (and beyond, inasmuch as no peace treaty was formally signed at its end, merely an armistice) was a prime contender for that distinction. During a single conflict, many policies and guidelines were set as indicators to the way in which the two superpowers would do busi-ness for much of the next thirty years. Not least, political administrations and military leaders already familiar with waging a total war from 1939 to

1945 came to terms with the concepts and modalities for war-fighting at lower levels of intensity. Most important of all, the implications of using what was in 1950 still a very new weapon, the atom bomb, were addressed for the first time in light of the often divergent needs of military operations and political expediency.

At the same time, the position of the UN vis-à-vis the superpowers and

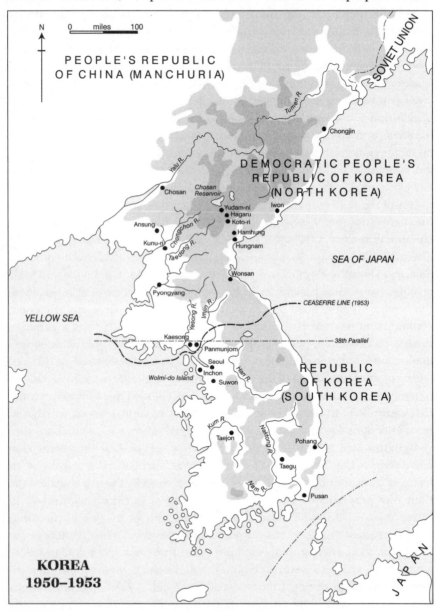

communist China was highlighted. Korea also provided a first opportunity for the PRC to enter the world stage after its long civil war, and to flex its military muscles against what it had identified as its principal ideological opponents: the capitalists and imperialists of the United States and the British Commonwealth. This military foray by the communist Chinese was carried out at the same time as somewhat less obvious Chinese support was flowing steadily south to aid the communist Viet Minh in their struggle against the other great Western imperial power, France, in Indochina.

In addition to its strategic and political significance, the Korean conflict also provided many operational lessons for those involved. During three years of fighting Korea was a catalyst that forced changes of organisation, weapons, equipment, training and tactics and signalled the end – or the beginning of the end – of the Second World War military mindset. Consequently, although some of the lessons were hard-learned (for the United States and Great Britain especially), it might be argued that Korea ensured that the West (and therefore NATO) was better prepared to conduct and win the Cold War. All this illustrated the wider importance of the three-year conflict fought on the 600-mile-long by 150-mile-wide Korean peninsula – a country virtually unnoticed by the news media and world statesmen until the final days of the Second World War.

A Land Divided: 1945–50

Unlike many of the conflicts in Asia and the Far East that began as nationalist campaigns against former colonial powers and subsequently became communist-inspired struggles, the Korean War was a direct result of various events and decisions made in the closing months of the Second World War. By early 1945 it was clear that the defeat of Japan, whose forces then occupied Korea,[53] was only a matter of months away; and it was agreed that the Soviet Union would declare war on Japan and deal with the Japanese troops in the north of Korea, while the United States would deal with those in the south. Separation of the Soviet and American operations was to be by the division of the country and of their respective areas of responsibility along the 38th parallel. However, US use of the atom bomb at Hiroshima on 6 August 1945, followed by the second at Nagasaki, pre-empted the Soviet declaration of war on 8 August. The Japanese capitulation followed shortly after the second atomic attack, and events then moved quickly as the agreed arrangements to process the Japanese surrender in Korea were implemented. US forces arrived in the south on 8 September, but found that – despite its late involvement in Korea – Red Army units had reached the demarcation line of the 38th parallel by 26 August, and had already begun to establish North Korea as a communist state in the Soviet mould.

By the time that the UN attempted, in November 1947, to introduce a process of national elections for the whole of Korea, the creation and consolidation of the Soviet-sponsored state was well advanced and a unified Korea with a single, democratically elected government was no longer achievable. Separate elections were held in the south and the north, and on 13 July 1948 the Republic of Korea was proclaimed in South Korea, headed by President Syngman Rhee. In North Korea the Democratic People's Republic of Korea was proclaimed on 8 September 1948, with Kim Il Sung as its first president. Both administrations asserted their constitutional right to govern the whole of Korea. Thus were sown the seeds of future conflict.

Arguably, given the antagonistic but nevertheless manageable relationship that then existed between the Soviets and the Western Powers in Central Europe, the continued presence of American and Soviet troops in Korea might have maintained a degree of stability, and even averted the outbreak of war. However, the UN General Assembly expressed its wish in December 1948 that all Soviet and US forces (apart from some military training advisers) should be removed from Korea. Accordingly, all of the Red Army units were withdrawn from the North by 25 December, whilst those of the United States finally departed the South in July 1949. With these troops gone, and with events in Europe and elsewhere occupying Washington much more than the future of an isolated peninsula on the southern border of China, the two Korean republics embarked upon their own campaigns of harassment and propaganda, all of which passed largely unnoticed in the West. However, Moscow and Beijing had certainly not lost interest in Korea. At the end of 1949 Stalin and the Chinese leader, Mao Tse-Tung, were busily forming their own plans for Korea – plans that would ultimately introduce the PRC into the Cold War equation and establish that country as a new and enduring threat to US interests in the region.

When the Soviets and Americans left Korea, the two indigenous armed forces that they had created were very different. In the DPRK the NKPA – 135,000 strong – had (by June 1950) seven combat-ready divisions, an armoured brigade equipped with 150 Soviet T-34 tanks, three additional reserve divisions and a motorcycle combination-equipped reconnaissance regiment. Virtually all of the NKPA's weapons and logistic support assets were of Soviet origin. The NKPA's supporting firepower included a total of 1,643 guns within ten divisional towed artillery regiments (122mm howitzers) and self-propelled gun battalions (76mm guns). Large numbers of mortars of various calibres were also available below division-level to provide direct fire support to brigades, regiments and battalions. Finally, DPRK airpower included some 200 Soviet Yak-9 fighters and Il-10 bombers.

The contrast between the NKPA and its southern counterpart could not have been more marked. The ROK army numbered 95,000 men, but it had no tanks, and possessed only 140 light anti-tank guns, a number of ex-US Army M-3 105mm howitzers, light mortars and a quantity of 2.36in anti-armour bazookas, plus a full range of late-1940s American small-arms. The ROK possessed no bombers or fighter aircraft, its airpower being limited to a number of T-6 trainers – all of which were destroyed on the ground during the first hours of the war. Once its first-line ammunition stocks were exhausted, only a further six days' reserves remained. The ROK logistic chain was decrepit. More than a third of its vehicles were unserviceable in mid-1950, with virtually no spare parts available to effect repairs. Low morale, corruption and lack of motivation of the ROK forces all reflected similar failings within the regime that they served.[54] Given the unequal nature of the two Korean national forces, it was not surprising that the communist invaders made rapid progress during those final few days of June 1950.

A Decisive Response: June to September 1950

From Washington, President Truman directed General of the Army Douglas MacArthur, commander of US forces in the Far East (which included the occupation forces in Japan) to send matériel assistance to the beleaguered ROK forces and to assess the situation in Korea. In his initial evaluation MacArthur judged that a complete collapse of the ROK forces was imminent, so Truman authorised the use of US airpower and naval units to support them, but with the proviso that such support was only to be provided south of the 38th parallel.[55] At the same time, the US 7th Fleet was ordered to the seas between Japan and Korea.

It might be wondered why – apart from the indisputable fact that North Korea was the aggressor – the United States showed such alacrity in supporting South Korea. After all, President Syngman Rhee's administration was profligate, corrupt and oppressive, and so could hardly claim to be democratic. However, Truman's decision needs to be viewed in the context of the time at which it was made. In the United States the persecution of alleged communists climaxed in 1950. This process had been instigated and pursued enthusiastically by Senator Joseph Raymond McCarthy, following his election to the Senate in 1946, and these purges had rocked all levels of American society. Anti-communist fears were also at a fever pitch following the Soviet Union's first successful atomic weapons test in 1949. Meanwhile, J. Edgar Hoover's FBI was vigorously pursuing a number of spy rings: a process that eventually revealed communist spies such as Klaus Fuchs and Julius and Ethel Rosenberg. Against this background President Truman, on the enthusiastic and obsessive advice of Attorney-General Tom Clark,[56] had allowed the anti-communist campaign in America to escalate rapidly ever since 1945. Consequently, by 1950 the question of whether or not the United States should assist what was patently an undemocratic – but crucially non-communist – regime to counter a clear act of communist military aggression was fairly easily resolved. As a result, objections to US military intervention against the communist invaders were minimal in America at the outset of the war; although this did change later on. At the strategic level, for the two major non-communist states in the region – Japan and Nationalist China, both of which were closely linked to the United States – the implications of an all-communist Korean peninsula were very evident. In light of all this, Washington's decision to support South Korea was neither surprising nor perverse.

In New York the UN was also taking action. On the day of the North Korean invasion the Security Council called for an immediate ceasefire and the withdrawal of all NKPA units south of the 38th parallel. Most significantly, the Soviet Union's representative was absent from the meeting on 25 June. Indeed, he had been absent from these meetings since 13 January, after walking out in protest over the Security Council's refusal to replace the Nationalist Chinese representative with a delegate from the PRC. Had he been present he would assuredly have supported the DPRK, and the subsequent course of history might then have been very different. However, his absence enabled the UN not only to call for a ceasefire, but also – uniquely in the history of the organisation – to identify one of the warring sides as the aggressor. Consequently, on 27 June the Security Council passed a further resolution, calling on all UN member states to provide military aid to South Korea in order to repel the invaders.

The same day, possibly without its great significance being fully appreciated, an ill-judged statement was made by President Truman to the effect that 'the occupation of Formosa by communist forces would be a direct threat to the Pacific area and to US forces performing their lawful and necessary functions in that area'. The president's words, although clearly made in the specific context of the invasion of South Korea by the NKPA, were regarded by Beijing as an unequivocal commitment by the United States to prevent a communist takeover of Formosa. Such a commitment represented a direct threat to the national interest of the PRC, not least because it provided an opening for General Chiang Kai Shek's 33,000 nationalist Chinese soldiers to enter the conflict on the UN side. This could have dire consequences for the PRC if North Korea were to be defeated and occupied, as nationalist Chinese troops might then make an appearance on the Manchurian border.

Consequently, a country that had so far only tacitly approved and indirectly supported the military actions of its North Korean neighbour now viewed events on the Korean peninsula with considerable concern. By a single ill-advised statement Truman had linked Beijing's fear of encirclement and foreign invasion with its ideological hatred of Western imperialism and its aspiration to 'liberate' Taiwan; and the international and domestic consequences of this returned time and again to haunt successive US administrations during and after the Korean War. Accordingly, Truman's pronouncement on 27 June was one of the defining moments of the Korean conflict, and of the wider Cold War as well.

Meanwhile, the fighting continued. The South Korean capital had fallen, and NKPA units were driving rapidly southward through the mountains that lined the eastern side of the Korean peninsula, while columns of T-34 tanks also rumbled along the roads south-east towards Taegu and the coastal town of Pusan, on the extreme tip of the peninsula. On 29 June General MacArthur visited Korea and made his own appreciation of the rapidly deteriorating situation. In light of what he saw and heard in Korea he recommended to Truman that US ground forces should be deployed to support South Korea, and that a failure to do this would inevitably result in the loss of Korea to the communists. The next day Truman directed the committal as necessary of the four divisions of the 8th US Army – the US Army of Occupation in Japan – to combat the invasion. General MacArthur was also appointed commander-in-chief of the UN forces in Korea. The American divisions based in Japan reacted speedily to this call to arms. The first of these (the 24th Infantry Division) began arriving at Pusan on 1 July, followed between 10 and 15 July by the 25th US Infantry Division, and by the 1st US Cavalry Division (an infantry division, despite its title) on 18 July. The three divisions were commanded by Lieutenant General Walton 'Bulldog' Walker, who had previously commanded the 20th US Corps within General Patton's 3rd US Army during the final year of the Second World War.

The initial deployment was neither an easy nor a happy experience for the troops involved. The enforced speed of deployment and lack of US political or military readiness to deal with the crisis in Korea were typified by the experience of the 24th US Infantry Division. In June 1950 the Japan-based division was enjoying the routine, comfortable and relatively uneventful life of an army of occupation, with its units based at Kyushu and Honshu, when:[57]

On 1 July 1950 [the division] was ordered to send a small delaying force [to Korea] by air (Task Force Smith), shortly followed by a full battalion. The rest of the division was to depart by sea at once. The 24th Infantry Division found itself short of over 2,000 [2,108 in fact] officers and men and quickly cannibalized other units stationed in Japan to bring itself up to full strength. Units were committed to action the second they landed, and found themselves facing a far more formidable enemy than expected. Lack of communications, intelligence and adequate weapons led to a terrible mauling of the division's units, and as a result they were forced to quickly retreat back toward Pusan. The division's [commander], General William F. Dean, was reported missing in action on 20 July, and was [one month] later captured by North Korean forces.[58]

Before Dean's headquarters in Taejon was overrun, he had already seen the collapse of successive units of his division with little or no real damage or delay inflicted upon the NKPA. Shortly after the precipitate retreat of his division's 34th US Infantry Regiment on 6 July, he had relieved the 34th's commanding officer of his command; this was but the first of a number of sackings that resulted from failures of American arms at all levels in Korea during that summer of 1950.

Although its lack of military readiness was inexcusable, there were reasons for the poor performance of the 8th US Army. In 1950 it was occupying a country that had been totally subjugated by the US forces, and which had just five years before been devastated and traumatised by the use of the first atom bombs against two of its cities. Indeed, the possession of the atom bomb by the United States had encouraged a belief that any future war would be won by the use of air-delivered atomic weapons – an over-simplistic and flawed theory that nonetheless provided a politically attractive justification for the US government to neglect or deliberately reduce the nation's defence capability. Meanwhile, the attitudes that a privileged lifestyle and soldiering in a professionally undemanding environment engendered in the troops of the 8th US Army had combined with the wider post-1945 malaise of the US armed forces to produce an army that was simply not trained, equipped or motivated to fight in Korea – or indeed anywhere else! But although the blame for the 8th US Army's lack of readiness did not lie exclusively with its commanders, it was certainly true that MacArthur himself had consistently neglected to accord combat training an appropriate priority – as opposed to the army's representative role and duties in Japan. Even the intelligence indicators were disregarded, and both the military headquarters in Tokyo and the CIA in Washington had discounted a flurry of intelligence reports in early 1950 that indicated the likelihood of an invasion of South Korea. One such CIA report on 10 March specified an invasion by North Korea scheduled for June.[59] Consequently, the North Koreans and their communist Chinese and Soviet mentors achieved near-total surprise on 25 June. At that point, however, one of the great ironies of history occurred, when (as already mentioned) the Soviet representative's absence from the crucial Security Council meeting convened in New York on 25 June 1950 enabled military action to be directed by the UN. Had he been present he would undoubtedly have used the Soviet veto, and so would have prevented the robust UN response which in turn launched a military campaign in Korea that eventually resulted in the defeat of the communists.

Despite the deployment of the three US divisions and isolated instances of successful delaying actions by some ROK and American units, these forces continued their withdrawal south-east. On 31 July they crossed the Naktong River and occupied the 130-mile perimeter of a salient based on the port of Pusan about eighty miles to the south. Initially, General Walker had some 47,000 US troops available to him, plus the residue of the ROK army of about 45,000 men, and despite several locally successful NKPA assaults on to and into the salient, the tide was about to turn. Indeed, by early August the defenders of Pusan actually outnumbered the attacking NKPA, and also commanded significantly greater firepower than did the communists.

Although all of the fighting in support of South Korea had been conducted under UN auspices since 27 June, it was really only at this stage that the forces opposing the communist onslaught could truly be identified as a UN force, with the arrival of British and British Commonwealth troops, including the 27th Commonwealth Infantry Brigade from Hong Kong, plus contingents from other nations to reinforce the ROK and US forces. The defenders of the Pusan salient were also reinforced by troops from the continental United States during early August, including the 1st US Marine Provisional Brigade. At last, the NKPA offensive slowed, and finally ground to a halt in front of the UN defences at Pusan.

Inchon and its Aftermath: September 1950

The time had come for the UN forces to take the offensive, and General MacArthur did so with an inspired strategic move that ranked as one of the historic moments of twentieth-century warfare. Yet this decision provoked an unforeseen political and military outcome that had serious short-term implications for the UN forces in Korea and, in the longer term, for the wider Cold War and the United States. It also propelled the PRC and its embryo, but potentially formidable, military capability to the front of the world stage. Paradoxically, MacArthur's triumph also marked the start of a chain of events that culminated in his removal as the UN commander in Korea.

The concept of landing a significant force on the west coast of Korea, far to the north, but still south of the politically crucial 38th parallel, had been actively considered ever since 4 July, just nine days after the North Korean invasion. The original idea for the landing at Inchon was virtually

MacArthur's alone, which demonstrated his strategic awareness as well as his audacity and acumen as a modern military commander. The aim of the operation was to sever the overstretched NKPA supply lines and force its capitulation or withdrawal. At the same time, by landing at the port of Inchon, close to Seoul, the South Korean capital could be quickly recaptured. Apart from the obvious political benefits of this, taking Seoul would also give the UN forces control of Korea's principal road and rail hub. Finally, whatever the NKPA did in response to the landing, cutting their lines of communication would allow the 8th US Army to break out from the Pusan salient and begin to push the North Koreans back to the 38th parallel.

Despite numerous delays and setbacks, and lengthy consideration of the many issues that might prejudice what was undoubtedly a risky operation (including the need to weaken the Pusan perimeter in order to support the amphibious landings), the planning for Operation Chromite proceeded apace. Many problems faced the UN forces at Inchon. The first waves of assault troops would need to use ladders to scale a 12ft-high sea wall, rather than landing over open beaches. The access channel into the port was very narrow and Inchon had extreme tidal variations, which produced almost three miles of mudflats between the harbour and the sea at low tide. Next, there were only three hours of high water, on one day per month, when the water was deep enough to allow tank landing ships (LST) to disembark the armour necessary to counter the T-34s of the NKPA. And finally, all the proposed landing sites were dominated by the hills that rose up to the east of Inchon.

Nevertheless, at a meeting at Chief of Staff level in Tokyo on 23 August, MacArthur briefed the details of the plan for some three-quarters of an hour without reference to any notes, and successfully justified the concept and his choice of the landing site at Inchon largely on the basis that its clear unsuitability would ensure that the UN forces achieved complete surprise! Final authorisation by the US Joint Chiefs of Staff was secured on 28 August, and planning for the largest amphibious operation conducted since the Second World War was completed on 4 September. D-Day was set for 15 September.

As with the best of all military schemes – whether tactical, operational or strategic – the plan for Operation Chromite was relatively simple. The principal formations involved were the 1st US Marine Division from the United States and the 7th US Infantry Division from Japan, which together formed the 10th US Corps. These two divisions were augmented by units from within the Pusan perimeter, plus some ROK army units and US marines embarked on ships of the US 6th Fleet. Some 230 ships from the United States, Great Britain, Canada, New Zealand, South Korea, Australia and France completed the task organisation. The 10th US Corps was to be commanded by

MacArthur's Chief of Staff, Major General Edward Almond, while command of the overall operation and all phases until the point at which the ground troops were safely ashore was assigned to Admiral Arthur Struble, Commander-in-Chief US 7th Fleet. In all, some 70,000 men were committed to Operation Chromite.

First, the marines would secure the island of Wolmi-do, which dominated access to Inchon from the sea. This would be followed by the main landing of the 1st US Marine Division. The marines would then push inland to capture Inchon, Kimpo airfield and Seoul, the capital being about eighteen miles distant from the coast. The NKPA strength at Inchon was assessed to be about 2,000 troops, with some additional forces at Seoul. Shortly after the initial landings, the 7th US Infantry Division would land a little to the south of the marines and push southward to Suwon. Finally, the 10th US Corps would hold its positions until the 8th US Army offensive reached it. In addition to the main assault, diversionary landings and air and naval bombardments would be carried out between 1 and 13 September all along the west coast of Korea, and against the North Korean capital, Pyongyang.

Apart from one or two minor modifications, the operation proceeded as planned and in textbook style. A preparatory landing on a small island adjacent to the seaward end of the channel into Inchon harbour was made on 31 August by a small team of personnel led by a USN lieutenant. This party provided invaluable intelligence right up to the day of the main landings, as well as target information for the naval bombardment that began on 13 September. At 06.33 hours on 15 September the 3rd Battalion of the 5th US Marine Regiment landed on Wolmi-do with the morning tide, and secured the tactically important island by 07.30 hours, sustaining only seventeen casualties wounded in the process.

With the evening tide came the main landings by the 1st and 5th US Marine Regiments. Their landing craft hit the shoreline shortly after half past five that afternoon. The US marines, easily recognisable by the distinctive green, brown and tan-mottled camouflage helmet covers used by the United States Marine Corps (USMC) ever since the early 1940s, quickly scaled the sea wall and moved inland. The 5th Regiment secured the high ground beyond Inchon by midnight, and the 1st Regiment was advancing steadily along the main road to Seoul by about half past one o'clock the next morning, when the order came to establish a perimeter six miles or so inland from the landing areas. There was some resistance by the NKPA, but it was largely ineffective and, with all their objectives secured, UN losses on D-Day amounted to only twenty men killed, 174 wounded and one missing. The following day the 7th US Infantry Division landed as planned and moved south-east towards the advancing 8th US Army, which began its breakout from the Pusan salient on 16 September. Seoul fell to the UN forces on 22 September, although the city was not finally cleared of what turned out to be 20,000 NKPA defenders until 27 September. Finally, General Almond's 10th US Corps linked up with General Walker's 8th US Army on 26 September.

Some of the heaviest fighting took place in Seoul. There, the UN forces' ready use of their devastating firepower against any remaining pockets of NKPA resistance destroyed large areas of the city. The consequences of this were all too predictable for a civilian population that had already suffered horrific atrocities committed by the North Koreans during their three-month occupation of the capital; but the nature of this fighting was but a foretaste of that which was to come. By late September 1950, Operation Chromite had achieved all that MacArthur had asked and expected of it, as the outflanked and defeated NKPA streamed back across the 38th parallel and into the relative safety of North Korea.

At that stage many on the UN side might perhaps have been forgiven for believing that the war had been won, that their task was complete, and that the various non-Korean forces involved would shortly be on their way home. However, in Washington and elsewhere, pressure to carry the battle beyond the 38th parallel and destroy the NKPA was gaining momentum. Surely, it was argued, North Korea had committed a blatant act of armed aggression, invaded another country, and almost defeated it. It had also been directly responsible for the destruction of much of South Korea and the death of thousands of its citizens. Therefore, the DPRK could not simply be permitted to revert to the status quo ante, with its communist government still in power and its armed forces a badly mauled but still effective fighting force – capable of repeating the exercise in the future. For MacArthur, the need to pursue and destroy the NKPA was a logical and essential tactical and strategic next step in order to resolve the Korean crisis satisfactorily, and it was at this point that wider issues and political considerations began to influence the war. From that which followed was born the 'limited war' concept that dominated political and strategic thinking in the West for the remaining years of the Cold War, and beyond.

The main concern now for the Americans and their allies was whether or not a UN advance would provoke a Soviet or Chinese intervention. There was also apprehension that the Security Council, with the Soviet representative again back in place, would now be unable to propose a resolution permitting an advance across the 38th parallel without inviting a Soviet veto. However, although intelligence on Chinese intentions was scant, it was evident from the steady flow of intelligence emanating from sources in Moscow that the Soviet leadership was actually seeking to distance itself from events in Korea; therefore a direct Soviet intervention was thought unlikely. But the Americans committed a serious error when they chose to discount the Chinese communist dimension – treating it as subordinate to and indivisible from that of the Soviets.

In the wake of the UN success at Inchon, however, the military imperatives were clear, and following considerable debate in Washington the Joint Chiefs of Staff (JCS) issued a new directive to MacArthur at the end of September. In summary, this set the destruction of the NKPA as a strategic objective, and authorised ground operations north of the 38th parallel to achieve this. However, such operations were not authorised where the entry of Soviet or Chinese communist forces into Korea had taken place or was anticipated. Most importantly, MacArthur was in no circumstances to allow his forces to cross the border into the Soviet Union or Manchuria, or to authorise them to carry out air or naval gunfire attacks against Soviet or PRC territory. Similarly, no non-Korean ground forces were to be permitted to operate adjacent to the northern borders. Armed with this directive, and with the knowledge that his main allies supported in principle an advance northward, MacArthur prepared the plans that he believed would complete his victory and confirm him as one of the greatest generals of the twentieth century.

Unsurprisingly, a key element of General MacArthur's plan was an amphibious landing designed to cut off the retreating NKPA. This operation involved a landing at Wonsan by General Almond's 10th US Corps, which would be extracted from Inchon and move via Pusan for the purpose. Meanwhile, General Walker's 8th US Army would continue its advance north to seize Pyongyang and the surrounding territory of North Korea. The decision to maintain a divided command (with General Almond reporting directly to MacArthur, rather than subordinated to General Walker) attracted a deal of criticism and fuelled the US debate about Walker's professional competence. However, the apparently impending end of the war probably led MacArthur to conclude that he could both weather the political storm and also avoid having to relieve Walker before the final victory was achieved. Thus the stage was set for the UN offensive.

Washington had hoped for a subtle approach to this critical new venture, which was beginning to generate some unease in London, together with appreciable concern in Beijing. But MacArthur ignored such considerations and indicated to North Korea that unless its forces surrendered forthwith, 'such military action as may be necessary' would be taken against them. The die was cast, and President Truman chose to back MacArthur; although by mid-October there were already signs of a growing rift between the president and his general.

On 28 September ROK army units advanced across the 38th parallel, and on 7 October the leading armoured units of the 8th US Army spearheaded the main UN advance northward. After a short period of intense fighting the remnants of the NKPA broke and fled, pursued by the tanks and armoured half-tracked infantry carriers of the 1st US Cavalry Division and the 24th US Infantry Division. Meanwhile, the 1st US Marine Division and 7th US Infantry Division moved towards their embarkation points in preparation for their amphibious operation at Wonsan at the end of the month.

In a whirl of optimism and growing confidence the 8th US Army and its ROK allies stormed north, meeting little resistance. On 19 October they took Pyongyang, and by late October the lead elements were approaching the area of the Yalu River – the border between North Korea and Manchuria in the PRC. Indeed, General Walker's army moved so speedily that the US marines who eventually landed at Wonsan on 25 October found to their embarrassment that two ROK divisions had already reached the town on 10 October, and that the entertainer Bob Hope had staged a USO show in Wonsan on the evening of the 24th! The 7th US Infantry Division's experience was similar, when it eventually landed and formed up at Iwon on 1 November. But although the NKPA collapse was heartening, the landings and subsequent operations of the 10th US Corps that October were by no means as straightforward as those carried out at Inchon a month earlier.

On 20 October MacArthur ordered all of his forces to prepare to advance to the border, and on 24 October he removed unilaterally all constraints on non-ROK troops moving into the border zone. He stated his intention to secure all of North Korea by military means and on 25 October the first ROK army units reached the Yalu River. Despite ever more cautionary voices in Washington and London, the political leaders failed to regain control of a military commander who was in effect running his very own war. But in late October 1950 it was a war that seemed to promise total victory, the unification of Korea under a regime sympathetic to the West, and of course the opportunity for those same politicians to bask in the reflected glory of 'their general' at the moment of his greatest achievement.

Enter the Dragon: October 1950 to March 1951

Prior to MacArthur's declaration of intent, the Korean crisis might have been resolved by a negotiated compromise. However, the twin failures of the president and the JCS not insisting upon MacArthur conforming to their directives, and (above all else) that of the Western intelligence community in not assessing correctly the communist Chinese perspective and probable response to the presence of UN forces on the banks of the Yalu River, together negated much of that which the UN forces had achieved since June. It also meant that a war which might otherwise have been concluded by the autumn of 1950 continued for almost three more years. But the future course of events had been set as soon as US ground forces crossed the 38th parallel. The very next day Chairman Mao Tse-Tung issued orders that just a week later brought the PLA into direct combat with the UN forces.

Between 13 and 25 October hundreds of thousands of Chinese soldiers moved southward by road and rail to the Yalu River. Generally, they marched by night and remained concealed by day. They provided none of the tell-tale trademarks of a modern army's deployment – radio communications, vehicle movement, concentration areas and so on – and so they crossed the Yalu River bridges unobserved, unreported and unopposed by the UN forces. They established a large bridgehead on the south side up to fifty miles deep in places, where regiments and divisions of tough little Chinese soldiers simply clothed in lightweight canvas and rubber shoes, olive drab quilted cotton uniforms with reversible camouflage smocks, with the small red star of communism emblazoned on their caps, paused briefly before moving rapidly and enthusiastically onwards to do battle with the 'imperialist aggressors' that apparently threatened their country. Many were veterans of the years of fighting against the nationalist Chinese forces.

From 14 October almost 200,000 'volunteers' of the PLA crossed the Yalu River and advanced southward along the west and centre of the peninsula. This huge force was part of the PLA's 4th Field Army. It was designated the 13th Army Group, which was made up of six armies: the 38th, 39th, 40th, 42nd, 50th and 66th. By 24 November a further PLA army group, the 9th, had also moved into North Korea, on the eastern side of the country. The PLA armies each comprised three infantry divisions (each of 10,000 men), a cavalry regiment and five regiments of artillery.

Although some early contacts occurred between the PLA and the 8th US Army in the north-west on 27 and 30 October and with the 10th US Corps to the north-east on 29 October, it was on the night of 1 November 1950 that battle was finally joined right across the front. In his account of the war, Max Hastings recorded the crisis that befell the UN over the next five days, from which a number of extracts conveyed the mixture of shock, horror, disbelief, complacency and chaos that ensued within the UN forces and the US-led high command. They also provided an insight into the nature of the forces that now opposed them:[60]

On the [25 October], the ROK 2nd Corps, driving north on the western axis of the UN advance, was strongly attacked, and in the action that followed, almost destroyed. Despite the fact that some Chinese communist soldiers, in uniform, had been captured by the ROK soldiers and clearly identified as such by General Paek Sun Yup, commanding the ROK 2nd Corps, neither General Milburn, commanding 1st US Corps, nor his immediate superior, General Walker, chose to believe the report or the assessments that were by then being revised rapidly by their intelligence staff. Walker's reasoning for the Chinese presence among or in place of the familiar NKPA forces was that 'After all, a lot of Mexicans live in Texas ...'

On 1 November near Ansung, about midway across the Korean peninsula, it was the turn of the Americans. Strong [Chinese communist] forces hit them with great determination, separating their units, then attacking them piecemeal. Batteries in transit on the roads, rifle companies on positions, found themselves under devastating fire from small-arms, mortars and katyusha rockets. The 3rd Battalion of the 8th Cavalry was effectively destroyed. The regiment's other battalions were severely mauled, and elements of the 5th Cavalry damaged.

'There was just mass hysteria on the position,' recorded Private Carl Simon of G Company, 8th US Cavalry. 'It was every man for himself. The shooting was terrific, there were Chinese shouting everywhere, I didn't know which way to go. In the end I just ran with the crowd. We just ran and ran until the [Chinese] bugles grew fainter.'

'They were unlike any enemy I had seen before,' wrote Lieutenant Colin Mitchell[61] of the Argyll & Sutherland Highlanders [of the British 27th Brigade]. 'They wore thick padded clothing, which made them look like little Michelin men. I turned one body over with my foot, and saw that he wore a peaked cap with a red star badge. These were Chinese. I turned over another and, as I looked down at him, he opened one eye and looked up at me. I shot him with my Luger, shouting to the platoon, "they're alive!" It was quickly over, and all the enemy lay dead.'

And on the Chinese communist side:

[On 1 November,] Li Hua, the propaganda officer of his company, examined his unit's first American prisoner at much the same time, and with much the same curiosity, as Eighth [US] Army were studying its captives from the PLA: 'This young American, he fell on his knees and begged for mercy. We felt very sorry for him. He obviously didn't want to fight.'

Yu Xiu [a regimental deputy political commissar] was one of the men who stormed the 8th [US] Cavalry's positions on 1 November, exulting to discover the success of their techniques of hard-hitting night assault ... He said that the overwhelming lesson the PLA learned from its first brushes with the Americans was the need for speed. 'In the Liberation War [against the nationalist Chinese], one might take days to surround a Kuomintang division, then slowly close the circle around it. With the Americans, if we took more than a few hours, they would bring up reinforcements, aircraft, artillery.'

And finally, Li Hebei, an infantry platoon commander of the 587th Regiment, while talking about conditions of service and the communist Chinese soldiers' motivation, observed:

'Life [in the PLA] was very hard, but the atmosphere was very good, because we were full of hope.' [And as Hastings observed] Most [of the PLA soldiers] were genuinely enthused by the spirit of revolution, the sense of participation in a new China that seemed to offer brighter promise than the old land of tyrannical landlordism and official corruption.

However naïve the Chinese view may seem today, it undoubtedly provided a degree of motivation and level of morale that to some extent offset the significant matériel deficiencies of the PLA and contrasted markedly with the views of some of the UN troops who found themselves in Korea in the autumn of 1950.

So, with Chinese MiG-15 jet fighters screaming overhead and a rolling tide of thousands of infantrymen pursuing or infiltrating their fragmented formations, the UN forces withdrew rapidly, and in some cases in considerable disorder, from the area of the Yalu. Nevertheless, by 6 November the superior firepower of the UN forces again began to tell and a new defensive line was established on the Chongchon River. Also, UN reinforcements were arriving in Korea in some strength, and on 12 November the 3rd US Infantry Division joined the UN order of battle. Three days later, everyday life in Seoul was reportedly returning to normal, whereas a short while previously the city's population had been on the verge of fleeing from the prospect of a second occupation by the communists. It seemed that once again the situation might be saved and that MacArthur might yet have the victory he craved. 'Home by Christmas' seemed to be a realistic aspiration for the UN troops, and Christmas was certainly drawing closer, as the damp chill of autumn gave way to the first signs of the notoriously severe Korean winter.

On 24 November the UN troops resumed their advance northward to recover the territory lost after 1 November, but just two days later the PLA launched its own offensive – on a massive scale. Only ten days earlier President Truman, in line with his limited war policy, had stated categorically that the UN forces would not in any circumstances extend their operations beyond the Chinese border. Secure in that knowledge, the PLA once again swept southward, and inflicted a slaughter and panic upon the UN forces which well exceeded that of the initial assault three weeks earlier. This new onslaught also had military and political implications that extended far beyond the Korean peninsula. As well as leading to the end of MacArthur's career it signalled to Beijing and Moscow that the United States was not prepared to wage all-out war, no matter what the repercussions might be for its soldiers and its allies. A very significant precedent had been established, and with it the parameters were set for every other major Cold War conflict involving the United States.

The UN retreat was little short of a total disaster:

In camps and vehicle concentrations along the length of the Chong-chon Valley, Americans found themselves wakened in their sleeping bags by a terrifying cacophony of bugles, drums, rattles, whistles – and gunfire. Again and again, Chinese assault groups smashed through ill-prepared perimeters, overrunning infantry positions, gunlines, rear areas … Amid individual acts of great bravery, the collective American response was feeble. From Army Command to the meanest hilltop foxhole, men seemed too shocked and appalled by the surprise that had overtaken them to respond effectively.[62]

Among the many disasters of the retreat at the end of November, that which befell the 2nd US Infantry Division at the pass of Kunu-ri was one of the worst. While the division's official history describes an action that cost the division 3,000 men and almost all of its vehicles, weapons and equipment as 'a magnificent stand', its ambush along the six-mile-long single road within the Kunu-ri pass was by no means an edifying action, the outcome of which rendered the 2nd US Infantry Division non-combat effective for many months thereafter. Soldiers of the Middlesex Regiment from the British 27th Brigade were fighting the Chinese at the south end of the pass when the unfortunate American convoy drove into it from the north. The long column of nose-to-tail vehicles immediately became embroiled in a storm of mortar and machine-gun fire from the hills that dominated the valley, when, at half-past one o'clock on the afternoon of 30 November:

Through six miles of enemy fire, vehicles sought to smash their way past the blazing wreckage of those that had gone before. Infantrymen ran among them, seeking their own salvation, and rarely finding it. A dreadful paralysis of command and discipline overtook the division. Major Walt Killalie, commanding the division's mobile anti-aircraft battalion, saw men sitting motionless in their vehicles, incapable even of rousing themselves to return the hail of Chinese fire, merely waiting for death ... Nightfall brought infantry attacks from the Chinese, ending in desperate close-quarter fighting among the shambles of vehicles and casualties on the road. Only a handful of men like Colonel James Skeldon, commanding the 2nd/38th Infantry, kept their heads and maintained their units' cohesion sufficiently to maintain an effective defence, and lead their survivors to safety.[63]

Only the arrival of American ground attack aircraft on the morning of 1 December, to attack the Chinese positions in the hills, allowed those who had survived the débâcle finally to extricate themselves and escape to the south. With the passage through of the last remnants of the 2nd US Infantry Division, the soldiers of the 27th British Brigade also headed south. Although the sheer panic, despair and breakdown of discipline evident in the American and ROK formations that November were generally not replicated in the British units or in some other national contingents, the steady flow southward must have seemed unstoppable to the UN commanders in Washington and Tokyo. Pyongyang was vacated on 5 December, with much military matériel left behind intact. General Walker's 8th US Army was in total disarray; incapable of offering other than token resistance to the Chinese advance, having lost 11,000 men dead, wounded and missing during the first few days of the PLA offensive. In early December, Colonel Paul Freeman of the 23rd US Infantry Regiment in the 2nd US Infantry Division remarked to his executive officer: 'Look around here, this is a sight that hasn't been seen for hundreds of years: the men of a whole United States Army fleeing from a battlefield, abandoning their wounded, running for their lives.'[64] As the general retreat continued, so the full force of the bitterly cold Korean winter swept down on the warring armies to add to their problems and their misery. The harsh weather and initial speed of the Chinese advance began to tell on the PLA, particularly its ability to support and supply its combat troops. Consequently the pressure on the retreating 8th US Army gradually eased as December drew on, and by Christmas 1950 the front had more or less stabilised along the familiar line of the 38th parallel.[65]

Meanwhile, well to the north-east of Korea, at the Chosin Reservoir, the effects of the arctic weather conditions were felt particularly acutely by the marines and soldiers of General Almond's 10th US Corps (which from 28 November included the British marines of 41 Independent Commando Royal Marines) who had landed at Wonsan and Iwon in late October, and were, at the end of November, preparing to continue their own push northward even as the new Chinese offensive struck them. But despite the appalling weather conditions and the increasingly acrimonious relationship between General

Almond and the commander of the 1st US Marine Division, Major General O. P. Smith,[66] as the early days of December passed, the troops of the 10th US Corps – the 1st Marine Division in particular – managed to restore some of the reputation of American arms lost by their comrades of the 8th US Army on the west side of the peninsula.

On 27 November, the 10th US Corps was centred on Wonsan, with the 7th US Infantry Division to the north-east and the 1st Marine Division to the north and west; both divisions were deployed in the general area about the Chosin Reservoir. When the Chinese offensive struck the corps that day its huge scale was very soon obvious, and General Almond ordered a withdrawal to the coast. The task of securing the main supply route that ran south from Yudam-ni, at the extreme north of the corps area, all the way to Hamhung and the port of Hungnam some fifty miles away, fell to Major General Smith's division. In simple terms, this mission also meant that (apart from a valiant stand by the 7th US Infantry Division's 32nd Regimental Combat Team to the east of the reservoir, when this unit was virtually annihilated) the American and British marines would be the rearguard for the 10th US Corps' withdrawal to the coast. On 1 December their own fighting withdrawal began, when the 5th and 7th US Marine Regiments set out along the fourteen miles from Yudam-ni to Hagaru. The battalion spearheading the column was led by a single tank, and as the force moved southward the companies and platoons leapfrogged their way from shoulder to shoulder of the hills that rose above the road, clearing the Chinese away by assault after assault. On 3 December the marines reached Hagaru. Of the 2,000 men that the lead battalion (3rd Battalion of the 5th Marine Regiment) commander, Lieutenant Colonel Robert Taplett, had mustered at Yudam-ni three days earlier, only 326 were still unwounded and fit for further combat. The last men arrived at Hagaru on the night of 4 December, and the division prepared for the next phase of the withdrawal: from Hagaru to Koto-ri, a distance of eleven miles.

This withdrawal commenced on 6 December and cost the division a further 103 men killed and 506 wounded; plus 147 of 160 Chinese prisoners of war who were shot by the marines when they attempted to escape during one of the many PLA bombardments from the surrounding hills. At Koto-ri 15,000 men and about 1,500 vehicles crowded into the marines' positions. At Koto-ri the marines also took the opportunity to bury their dead, brought with them so conscientiously all the way from Yuam-ni and Hagaru. Despite its precarious situation, this was an indication of the high morale and standard of discipline of the 1st US Marine Division.

The final part of the withdrawal (from Koto-ri to Hamhung) continued, during which the marines applied the same tactics that they had successfully employed during the earlier stages of the operation. Despite considerations such as the need to bridge a 30ft-wide chasm with bridge sections parachuted to them for the purpose, dealing with the continuing Chinese fire and occasional local attacks, and the need to separate the marines' rear-guard from some 3,000 refugees at the rear of the column by the expedient of blowing up a bridge in their faces and stranding the refugees on the north side, the first marines began to arrive in the port of Hamhung on 10 December. Although many marines and their commanders voiced their belief that a salient based on Hamhung could well have been successfully defended against the PLA, the decision to evacuate had already been taken, and the 100,000 men – marines, soldiers and ROK troops – of the 10th US Corps boarded the large fleet of amphibious landing craft that awaited them. After destroying any matériel that could not be removed, the corps sailed for Pusan, leaving the navy to bombard Hamhung on 24 December and reduce its buildings, jetties and other facilities to rubble and twisted metal. In what was otherwise a bleak period of American military history, the fighting with-drawal of the 1st US Marine Division from Chosin to Hamhung was in the best traditions of the USMC, albeit the division had sustained 4,418 casualties in combat, plus 7,313 non-battle casualties (mainly from frostbite).

Meanwhile, the PLA had lost about 37,500 men in the battle about Chosin and the fighting to the south of the reservoir, having also suffered severely from the cold. Indeed, ninety per cent of the Chinese soldiers reportedly suffered various degrees of frostbite during the winter of 1950–1, and the PLA's 27th Army suffered 10,000 non-combat casualties that winter. But despite this, and although the PLA offensive in the east had ground to a halt early in the final phase of the 10th US Corps' withdrawal to Hamhung, due to the sheer inability of its rudimentary supply chain to support the speed and tempo of its advance,[67] the Chinese had successfully forced the entire 10th US Corps to withdraw from North Korean territory. Even though the PLA lacked the strategic and logistic capability to destroy the UN forces, the implications and lessons of the PLA's successes (against the military might of the United States in particular) were not lost upon the watching Soviet leaders.

By Christmas 1950 the UN forces were more or less back where they had started, and the US military leaders were dealing with an unprecedented amount of domestic criticism of its operations and leadership, as well as from some of its allies in Korea.[68] The demoralised 8th US Army attracted particular censure, and fate took a hand in its future fortunes when, on 23 December, General Walton Walker was killed in a traffic accident. His jeep was hit by a ROK army truck that suddenly turned into its path and General Walker was thrown from the vehicle, sustaining severe head injuries from which he died while en route to the hospital.[69] His untimely demise opened the way for the very professional and widely respected former leader of the

82nd US Airborne Division and 18th US Airborne Corps in the Second World War – the fifty-six-year-old Lieutenant General Matthew Bunker Ridgway – to fill the vacant post at Headquarters 8th US Army. Ridgway arrived in Korea on 26 December 1950, very conscious of the formidable task ahead of him.

In the meantime, in parallel with the changed nature of the war in Korea since the PLA intervention, a growing political and strategic debate had surfaced in Washington. There, a military consensus now favoured bombing targets north of the Yalu River – an action long sought by MacArthur. Indeed, MacArthur was indicating publicly and not too subtly his view that the use of atomic weapons against the Chinese should be actively considered. This issue was raised again on 30 November, when Truman himself confirmed in an unguarded moment at a press conference that there had 'always been active consideration of its use', a comment that alarmed many in the British government headed by socialist Prime Minister Clement Attlee. However, despite this Truman remained adamant that there was to be no escalation of the scale or nature of the conflict, a line that reflected the wider American belief that the PRC was simply an extension of the Soviet Union, and that any direct attack on China would therefore bring the Soviets into the conflict. This view was one that the British intelligence community did not support, for its analysts believed that the differences between the two great communist states were much more significant than their American equivalents believed, and that the risk of Soviet involvement in Korea was therefore minimal; although American use of the atom bomb against China could of course change that situation considerably.

In December 1950 a key meeting took place between the US President and Attlee in Washington. Parallel meetings were held at military Chiefs of Staff level. Much was discussed, and this meeting set the future policy for the conduct of the war. Truman reassured Attlee that the United States was not actively considering the use of the atom bomb, or any expansion of the conflict.[70] However, it was also agreed that in the event of any subsequent decision to expand the war this would only be done in consultation with Britain and the other allies. Finally, the Americans conceded that their original aim of creating a unified, non-communist Korean state was now unachievable, and that a border settlement based on the old 38th parallel would be acceptable. When MacArthur and his headquarters staff in Tokyo were apprised of these decisions, their paranoia and suspicions that the political leadership in Washington was selling them out were virtually boundless. This reaction progressively diminished MacArthur's stature, as he used various ill-judged devices to persuade Washington of the need to escalate and expand the war. These ploys led to his downfall.

Meanwhile, in Korea Lieutenant General Ridgway set about retraining and revitalising the 8th US Army, and preparing viable plans for the defence of Korea rather than for an evacuation, although this contingency was still entertained by Washington. Strong defences were constructed about the former Pusan salient perimeter, just in case another withdrawal might become necessary, Ridgway was quite clear, however, that this was not an option. He was also emphatic that his mission was to wreak sufficient destruction on the communist forces for an acceptable compromise peace to be achieved. In a message issued in January 1951 to all of those under his command, Ridgway specifically addressed the question 'What are we fighting for?' – a question that had frequently been put to him by his soldiers during his early days with the 8th US Army. Ridgway's response provided an insight into the strength of his personal patriotism, values and religious faith, as well as an indication of the wider philosophy, style of leadership and view of communism of very many senior American military commanders, political leaders and ordinary citizens of the early 1950s:

To me the issues are clear. It is not a question of this or that Korean town or village. Real estate is, here, incidental. It is not restricted to the issue of freedom for our South Korean Allies, whose fidelity and valour under the severest stresses of battle we recognise; though that freedom is a symbol of the wider issues, and included among them ... The real issues are whether the power of Western civilization, as God has permitted it to flower in our own beloved lands, shall defy and defeat Communism; whether the rule of men who shoot their prisoners, enslave their citizens, and deride the dignity of man, shall displace the rule of those to whom the individual and his individual rights are sacred; whether we are to survive with God's hand to guide and lead us, or to perish in the dead existence of a Godless world ... If these be true, and to me they are beyond any possibility of challenge, then this has long ceased to be a fight for freedom for our Korean Allies alone and for their national survival. It has become, and it continues to be, a fight for our own freedom, for our own survival, in an honourable, independent national existence ... In the final analysis, the issue now joined right here in Korea is whether Communism or individual freedom shall prevail, and, make no mistake, whether [or not it] shall be checked and defeated overseas or [be] permitted, step by step, to close in on our own homeland and at some future time, however distant, to engulf our own loved ones in all its misery and despair. These are the things for which we fight.[71]

Through January, February and March 1951 a transformed 8th US Army and 10th US Corps, with their allies from the other UN nations, weathered a new Chinese attack and mounted a series of major offensives. Formations such as the 2nd and 25th US Infantry Divisions were at last able to lay the ghosts of Kunu-ri and the retreat from the Yalu River of the previous November, as a combination of improved training, appropriate tactics and effective leadership, underwritten by overwhelming firepower – notably airpower – and matériel resources boosted the self-confidence of the UN troops. 'The myth of the magical millions of Chinese in Korea has been exploded. In the last United Nations offensive, the Americans have learned how easy it is to kill the Chinese, and their morale has greatly increased thereby' – so observed British Air Vice-Marshal C. A. Bouchier in February 1951.[72] Although the war was by no means popular with many of those that he commanded, the impact of Ridgway's leadership upon the UN forces was electric, and from January to early April, despite some tactical reverses, it appeared that the UN forces would never again need to endure events such as those of the last two months of 1950.

Contingency plans were still being developed for another general advance to the Yalu and the complete removal of the North Korean communist regime. However, it had already been tacitly accepted that the conflict was moving inexorably towards some sort of compromise settlement based upon the 38th parallel. Given the operational and strategic constraints imposed by the limited war policy, neither the use of US atomic weapons nor a direct attack on the PRC with conventional weapons were acceptable strategic-political options, although by early 1951 these were probably the only means by which a speedy and decisive UN victory might yet have been won.

These political constraints were entirely contrary to the line that MacArthur was still advocating in his obsessive quest for the total victory that he had so nearly achieved at Inchon. By the end of December he was pushing hard for the use of Chiang Kai-shek's nationalist Chinese troops both in Korea and directly against the PRC. He also advocated the destruction of China's military-industrial capability by air and sea bombardment, plus a maritime blockade of China. At the same time, he was also criticising Truman's limited war policy ever more openly and publicly. Even Ridgway, whose appointment to command the 8th US Army had been MacArthur's own choice, was finding his commander's style of command increasingly difficult to cope with.[73] The outcome of all this was inevitable, and on 11 April 1951 President Truman relieved General Douglas MacArthur of his command.

Deliberations over whether or not this was the correct course of action had occupied President Truman, Secretary of Defence Marshall, Secretary of State Acheson, Chairman of the Joint Chiefs Bradley and others for many months. Indeed, MacArthur's autocratic command of the US forces occupying Japan had led to calls for his removal from that post as much as two years earlier. But from early December 1950 MacArthur's own actions and media pronouncements made the pressure for his removal irresistible. The rationale for this decision was clear from Truman's press statement on the matter: 'With deep regret I have concluded that General of the Army Douglas MacArthur is unable to give his wholehearted support to the policies of the United States government and of the United Nations in matters pertaining to his official duties.' On MacArthur's departure Ridgway was appointed Supreme Commander of the UN forces, and Lieutenant General James van Fleet replaced Ridgway as commander of the 8th US Army.

In mid-March the UN forces recaptured Seoul for a final time. By mid-April they had advanced to a new defensive line slightly to the north of the 38th parallel, with part of this line based on the range of hills by the Imjin River. But then, just as the front appeared to be stabilising, on Sunday 22 April the PLA launched its major spring offensive.

Battle on the Imjin: March to April 1951

Thus far much of the story has dealt with the US role in the fighting. Certainly, apart from the ROK forces, the Americans were the first UN troops into action and their force level – which peaked at more than 300,000 men – was always significantly greater than that of any other nation on the UN side. However, fifteen other nations had also provided contingents to the UN force. Of these, the most significant were those from Britain (two infantry brigades and one armoured regiment, plus engineers and service support, together with Royal Navy ships and Royal Air Force units), Turkey (one infantry brigade), Canada (one reinforced infantry brigade, plus naval forces and transport aircraft) and Australia (two infantry battalions, plus maritime and air assets). However, Belgium, France, Thailand, South Africa, the Philippines, New Zealand, Holland, Greece, Ethiopia and Colombia all supplied contingents of about battalion or regimental size, together with ships and aircraft in some cases. Even Luxembourg provided an infantry company, while Norway, Denmark, Italy, Sweden and India gave medical support. Although the grand total of these allied contingents never exceeded about 44,000 men, they fulfilled a vital political purpose by demonstrating that the force opposing the communists was indeed an international UN force. But, far from being merely presentational, their military contributions were significant. The Turkish, British and British Commonwealth, French and Belgian troops acquitted themselves particularly well during some of the hardest fighting of the war. Among many such examples, the Chinese spring offensive against the UN defensive line on the River Imjin led to an action that exemplified the sense of duty, stoicism, and courage that have characterised British infantry regiments of the line throughout history.

In late April the PLA's strategic intention was to smash through the UN line of defences and recapture Seoul by May Day, thereby winning a political and a military victory. The 1st US Corps had earlier advanced on the left of the UN deployment. Within this corps were the 27th Commonwealth Brigade[74] and the British 29th Infantry Brigade, the former having been sent to Korea from Hong Kong in August 1950 and the latter having arrived from the United Kingdom at the end of that year. By 22 April the focus of the fighting was at the centre of the UN defensive line, which involved the 27th Brigade in the area of Kapyong and, to the west, the 29th Brigade. The 29th Brigade's units included 1st Battalion the Gloucestershire Regiment (1 Glosters), 1st Battalion the Royal Northumberland Fusiliers (1 RNF) (also known as the '5th Fusiliers'), 1st Battalion the Royal Ulster Rifles (1 RUR), and a Belgian battalion, with the tanks of the 8th King's Royal Irish Hussars (KRIH) and the 25-pounder guns of 45 Field Regiment Royal Artillery (RA) in support. The Glosters' positions were sited on the left or west of the brigade defensive position, overlooking the various fords across the Imjin River, which meandered on its muddy way across the plain that lay between the adjacent hills. On the Glosters' left were ROK army units. Although few of the Gloucestershire soldiers manning their slit trenches and bunkers that April may have been aware of it, the positions they occupied straddled the route to Seoul that had been used successfully by invading northern armies for centuries. And the Chinese commander of the 63rd Army (which comprised the 187th, 188th and 189th Divisions, each of 9,000 men) saw no reason to deviate from the practices of his historic predecessors.

On 22 April 1951, Second Lieutenant Denys Whatmore was a platoon commander serving in D Company, 1st Battalion the Gloucestershire Regiment. His matter of fact description of the battle that the battalion fought on the Imjin in late April encapsulated the intensity and nature of the fighting, as well as the British infantryman's frequently understated but invariably professional approach to the business of war:

> There were too few UN infantry units adequately to defend the ground. The units of 29 Brigade were so spread out that they were not mutually supporting. The gap between 1 Glosters and the ROK division to the west invited penetration. Even between 1 Glosters companies there were gaps of up to 2 kilometres, making interlocking [arcs of] small-arms fire between them impossible, reliance having to be placed in this respect on the battalion's [Vickers] medium machine guns and three-inch mortars, and on artillery bombardment. No 8th Hussars

tanks were available in 1 Glosters area. The terrain was quite unsuit-able for the ponderous Centurions.[75] Only meagre supplies of barbed wire and trip flares were laid out in the forward areas. Despite all this, however, the companies, each sited on hill formations commanding the river fords and the tracks leading south from them, were quite well dug in, in the unfriendly rock.

Chinese were spotted on the north bank of the river on 22 April, but they only started to wade over what became known as 'Gloster Crossing' that night. Lieutenant Colonel Carne [the battalion's commanding officer] had placed a strong patrol covering the crossing exit at the south bank and these men, plus the artillery fire they called down, played havoc with the vulnerable Chinese infantry in and approaching the river. The patrol was withdrawn when their ammunition was exhausted, without casualties. The withdrawal was timely because the Chinese were now pouring across the river at several fordable points and pressing on into UN lines.

On the battalion front, A Company was the first to be seriously attacked. [They were] the left hand company, they occupied 'Castle Hill' closest to the river, with good fields of fire towards it. They were, however, a bit isolated and fought a long and lonely battle all night 22/23 April until, with the company commander and two platoon comman-ders dead, the third wounded, and heavy casualties, they were forced to withdraw at 0800 hours on 23 April.

Meanwhile, the Chinese had advanced against D and B Companies, and these too fought an all night and early morning battle against over-whelming numbers of Chinese infantry advancing time and again in the human wave tactics they commonly used. This was infantry fighting at its bloodiest, and the most forward platoon [commanded by Second Lieutenant Whatmore] of D Company lost two thirds of its men, dead or wounded. The D and B Company positions were held, however, until a withdrawal was ordered at about 0830 hours on 23 April. On withdrawal, D Company were ordered to join what was left of A Company on Hill 235 [which later became known as 'Gloster Hill'] immediately overlooking the vital road, where they remained until the final breakout.

B Company was sent to join the reserve company – C Company – in the foothills of Kaman San, the mountain looming over all the action, and whose lower western slopes also dominated the road from which the Chinese continued to be barred. But advanced Chinese units had already penetrated beyond the Glosters' position by other routes and encirclement was only a matter of time. Decisions were made in higher headquarters requiring 1 Glosters to continue to hold their position while UN formations in the rear were regrouped [ready] to stem any Chinese breakthrough elsewhere.

On the night 23/24 April (Monday/Tuesday), B and C Companies were heavily attacked, while probing attacks against Hill 235 also kept the night alive with the flashes and thunder of war. From 235 it was possible to watch, but not to help, the B and C Company battle across the road, and to observe [the] hours of heavy fighting, and its eventual end. In early daylight 24 April, the remnants of B Company – about twenty men led by Major Denis Harding – ran across the road far below us on 235 and were able to join what was left of the battalion. B and C Company casualties were heavy, and those who could walk, and who tried to evade the Chinese and escape to the south, were rounded up and made prisoners. The battalion was now surrounded, and in depth.

During the daylight hours of 24 April, the Chinese made sporadic attacks on Hill 235, repulsed by the determined efforts of A Company, reinforced by a miscellany of men from other subunits. Captain Farrar-Hockley, the adjutant, himself led a successful counter attack. Lieutenant Colonel Carne, with a few men, also chased away some Chinese infiltrators. The defenders of Hill 235 held the ring all that day and all that night, when Chinese attacks resumed in intensity. News soon came through that attempts to relieve 1 Glosters had failed, and [a] promised re-supply by air had hardly any success.

In early morning daylight on 25 April (Wednesday), two events heartened us all. One was a defiant reply to the Chinese and their bugle calls … by bugle calls of our own, played by Drum Major Buss on the orders of the commanding officer.[76] The other was the sudden appearance of American fighter bombers which roared in very low and strafed [the] Chinese positions with rockets, napalm and cannon fire. The effect was devastating if short lived; but it was a welcome addition to the constant and accurate support which had been provided all this time by 45 Field Regiment. 25 April was the last day of the battle. With many wounded, little water and no food, and ammunition running low, the commanding officer made it clear to brigade HQ, on his fading radio, that it was not possible to hold on much longer.

Orders were received then to break off the action and to try to break through the surrounding enemy to reach UN lines. Lieutenant Colonel Carne gave his own orders at about 1030 hours. The wounded could not be moved, and the doctor, [Captain] Bob Hickey, the padre, Sam Davies, and some medical orderlies stayed with them to await capture. What was left of A, B and C Companies and Battalion HQ personnel set off into the hills to the south and southwest, the most direct route to the UN lines. Months later, we learned that they met with overwhelming numbers of Chinese and had to surrender to avoid annihilation.

[However,] D Company commander, Captain Mike Harvey, took a different route. He led his men, now joined by sundry Support Company men, to a total number of about ninety, due north for a few hundred yards, into ground which, he guessed, would be empty of Chinese. He was dead right! Turning west and then south down a steep-sided valley, it was only after two or three miles that Chinese were encountered, hidden in the ridges covering the valley, with excellent fields of fire. The Glosters column, moving south, now ran the gauntlet. They then bumped into some American tanks, [the nervous crews of] which also fired on them. Eventually however, the survivors were taken out by those same tanks. Forty-seven of the original column of ninety men reached safety and were taken to join the rear elements of 1 Glosters which had been left out of battle. The tribulations of those who escaped were over. For those taken prisoner, however, they were just beginning, and many are the stories of heroism and endurance among the [Glosters] prisoners on the march to the prison camps in North Korea and during their two years of captivity.[77]

Of the 850 men of the Glosters who had begun the battle just three days before there were just 169 left, including those who had been 'left out of battle' with the battalion's rear echelon. These men provided the nucleus for rebuilding the 1st Battalion of the Gloucestershire Regiment. The decimated battalion had imposed such a delay upon the Chinese advance that there was time for the South Korean capital's defences to be organised, which meant that the communists' objective of capturing Seoul was denied to them. For his actions as commanding officer during the battle Lieutenant Colonel Carne was awarded the Victoria Cross.[78] Indeed, all of the officers and soldiers of the 1st Battalion of the Gloucestershire Regiment had written a new page in the long history of their regiment. The Americans also recognised the extent of the Glosters' sacrifice and feat of arms on the Imjin when they subsequently conferred the US Presidential Unit Citation on the regiment, and on the other units who had supported and fought alongside the infantry regiment that was thereafter forever known as 'The Glorious Glosters'.[79]

The widely dispersed deployment of the 29th Brigade on the Imjin – an imposed tactical layout about which the British brigade commander had been most uneasy – followed by the failure of the American higher commanders to appreciate the seriousness of the Glosters' predicament until it was too late, resulted in the destruction of a much-needed infantry battalion that could and should have been avoided. Had 29th Brigade been given the chance to conduct a fighting withdrawal to already prepared positions further south, the PLA could still have been sufficiently delayed to safeguard Seoul, and the 1st Battalion the Gloucestershire Regiment would probably have still been a viable combat unit at the end of the battle. Certainly, the 1,000 casualties sustained by the 29th Brigade had been a very high price to pay, notwithstanding estimated Chinese losses of 10,000 during their battle on the Imjin in April 1951.

One particularly positive outcome of this battle, however, was the formation of the Commonwealth Division in July 1951, under the command of Major General James Cassels. This new division finally provided a unified division-level command for the brigades, combat units and supporting arms and services that had been supplied to the UN force by Great Britain and the members of the British Commonwealth. This enabled all of these units and formations to form a cohesive and highly potent fighting formation, ending the practice of allocating them piecemeal to various US formations below the corps level of command.

Stalemate and Armistice: June 1951 to July 1953
With the front line between the UN and the communist forces more or less stabilised, with Ridgway in command, and with Washington having regained political and strategic control of the UN campaign, the war settled down to a campaign of attrition, during which the tide of battle ebbed and flowed about the hills and valleys all along the general line of the 38th parallel. As the weeks and months passed, both sides conducted tunnelling, entrenching and bunker construction on a scale not seen since the campaign on the Western Front during the First World War.

Only an occasional increase in resources, the reinforcement of an area, or some technological advance relieved the virtual stalemate that ensued once the second phase of the spring offensive had been halted in early June 1951. On 23 June Yakov Malik, the Soviet Ambassador to the UN, called for a ceasefire; this was quickly followed on 25 June by a Chinese broadcast indicating the PRC desire for a ceasefire. Thereafter, a series of largely unproductive and faltering armistice negotiations took place against a violent backdrop of military confrontation, active patrolling and occasional large-scale offensive operations by both sides.[80] Despite this form of stalemate, both sides suffered more casualties during the period from mid-1951 to mid-1953 than they had during the more intense fighting conducted in the course of the first year of the war.

They say that it was possible to walk nearly the entire distance from Korea's west coast to the east without ever leaving the trenchworks! The trenches were not simply strung out across flat land – because there is very little flat land in this part of Korea. They spanned hills and mountains; there were gaps only where some impossible terrain feature had been encountered. In front of the trenches – on higher ground wherever possible – was the network of OPs [observation posts] and listening posts which were manned day and night. The men lived in bunkers that were dug by troops who had long since left the battle zone either on rotation or because they had become battle casualties. The bunkers were strongly reinforced and when an enemy attack got really rugged the troops pulled back into their bunkers – fairly safe from anything short of a direct hit by an extra-heavy shell. From the bunkers they could call down friendly artillery fire on the Reds [communists] assaulting their trenches. The main line of resistance (MLR) consisted of the exposed trenches on the forward slope of the hills we held. The men in these trenches were in view of the enemy – and vice versa – twenty-four hours a day. They were separated at some places by as little as 50 yards of no-man's land! In some places there were 3 or 4 miles between them. The river sides were usually separated by about 1,000 yards. No-man's land was heavy with barbed wire, tin cans, and high-powered microphones designed to pick up any sounds of movement.

Almost continually, our troops were involved in an activity that is hard to explain – the battle for the 'in-between hills' – the high points that stood between the enemy lines and our own. From a military standpoint it was next to impossible to hold these exposed hill positions – but neither could Eighth [US] Army sit back and let the CCF [Chinese Communist Forces] hold them. To do the latter would be tantamount to giving the Reds a press-box seat from which they could peer right down into the trenches and positions we occupied. And so we became engaged in a campaign of bitter 'jockeying for position' and many strongpoints changed hands several times a day. In some sectors this assumed a timetable schedule: UNC [United Nations Command] troops would seize a position at nightfall and hold it until dawn. When they withdrew the enemy would return. Late in the day the Reds would pull back when our artillery started to pound them prior to our own movement toward the hill. It was monotonous, ugly, and extremely hazardous warfare.[81]

The armistice talks lasted two years. They were initially based at Kaesong, and later at Panmunjom. Throughout, a major stumbling block was the question of the repatriation of prisoners, as the communists demanded the return of all their captured troops; but very many of these soldiers had seen the lifestyle south of the 38th parallel, and understandably had no desire to return to the bleak communist world of North Korea and China. Linked to this issue, prison camp riots, the unauthorised release of North Koreans with the connivance of the South Korean government, and Western outrage over the treatment of UN soldiers while in communist hands, all contributed to the frustration of the negotiators and to the inertia of the talks.

Meanwhile, on 12 May 1952 General Mark Clark succeeded General Ridgway as the UN's Supreme Commander in Korea. Ridgway had been appointed as NATO Supreme Allied Commander in Europe (SACEUR) in succession to General Dwight D. Eisenhower, the Republican nominee to oppose Truman for the presidency in 1952 who beat Truman convincingly at the polls that November. A key element in Eisenhower's successful campaign had been a determination to 'go to Korea' himself, in order to assess the situation and, by implication, to resolve the long-running and unpopular conflict. Eisenhower visited Korea on 29 November but, to the evident disappointment of both General Clark and General Van Fleet, far from resolving the conflict by military means he seemed to be preoccupied with negotiating a viable truce and ceasefire. Therefore, despite the new administration in Washington, the war continued into 1953 still with no clear end in sight. However, some new political and strategic issues were emerging, together with an important advance in military technology, and these had various impacts upon the Korean conflict and the Cold War.

In January 1953 the Americans successfully detonated a nuclear device that could be fired from an artillery weapon, and suddenly a whole new range of tactical options was available to the UN forces. Despite President Eisenhower's best intentions, after many months of unproductive armistice negotiations, he was finally forced to threaten China and the Soviet Union that, unless an armistice was signed soon, the UN would abandon its self-imposed limited war concept, and would resume the offensive with air strikes beyond the Yalu – including the use of tactical atomic weapons against North Korea.[82] Not surprisingly perhaps, an armistice was signed at 10.00 a.m. on 27 July 1953, shortly after the issue of the US ultimatum by Secretary of State Dulles. However, Joseph Stalin, the principal architect of the Soviet Union and post-war communist empire, did not live to see this, as he had died in March that year.

In fact, Stalin's death did not have the immediate or momentous impact upon the Korean War that might reasonably have been anticipated by the West, other than perhaps emboldening Eisenhower to issue his 'sign or else' ultimatum to the Chinese and Soviet governments. There were three reasons for this. First, negotiations directed towards a ceasefire and eventual armistice had already been ongoing for some twenty months, even though both sides had continued to wage a 'hot' war across and about the 38th parallel.[83] Next, although the Soviets had certainly condoned and supported the North Korean action, they had underestimated the US response to the NKPA invasion in 1950, and had certainly never wished the conflict to result in a direct clash of arms between the United States and the PRC north of the Yalu: a situation that would have posed for Moscow the critical problem of whether or not to intervene directly. Had they done so, it would have been difficult to avoid the use of nuclear weapons, with an escalation of the war into a regional and possibly global conflict. Lastly, the fundamental fact that had eluded the American consciousness ever since June 1950 was that the principal player on the communist side was not the Soviet Union working through a communist Chinese client state, but a communist Chinese state that was its own master, with policies, national interests and a culture all very different from those of its superpower neighbour. Even the communist ideology of Beijing differed from that promoted by Moscow. Therefore, although changes in the Soviet Union after the death of Stalin probably eased the achievement of an armistice in Korea, this event was by no means as significant in Korea as it was within the Soviet bloc countries in Europe.

What then were the principal lessons or experiences that emerged from the three years of war in Korea? For the military leaders in Washington, New York and the Western capitals, as well as in Beijing and Pyongyang, it had been a salutary experience. As the UN forces had failed to secure a North Korean surrender, and South Korean President Syngman Rhee had refused to sign the armistice document, the United States was faced with the fact that it had fought a three-year war without securing a definitive victory. Although the non-communist campaign had been conducted under UN auspices, nobody was under any illusions that the vast majority of the UN forces had been American, and that the whole force had been directed, led and exten-sively resourced by the United States.[84] Certainly these forces had (eventually) repelled the NKPA and PLA invaders, but 33,629 dead and 105,785 wounded American servicemen was a high price to have paid to restore the status quo ante; and of these casualties, almost half were sustained after the start of the armistice negotiations. Meanwhile, the financial cost of the war to the United States had been more than 22 billion US dollars.

The allies on the UN side had suffered proportionate casualties, with Britain and the Commonwealth countries losing 1,263 killed and 4,817 wounded, while the other military contingents lost a total 1,800 dead and 7,000 wounded. Of these, the Turkish contingent, whose military perfor-mance and professionalism had been exemplary, sustained almost half of the casualties. But whereas the combat performance of all of the non-American contingents was by no means insignificant, the political message that the multinational UN force sent to the world was its most important contribution to the war. Although the US high command was undoubtedly frustrated by the command and control implications of alliance operations, the political advantages of having allies were clear to see in Korea. In later years, in Europe, this perception strengthened the structure and modalities of the newly formed NATO Alliance as it gained military strength and political stature.

Finally, the ROK forces, always the primary focus of every communist offensive, suffered losses of about 415,000 killed and some 429,000 wounded. The ROK government had always set its sights on winning a comprehensive military victory, with the elimination of Kim Il Sung's communist regime and the establishment of a single non-communist Korean state. But it was clear from the outset of Eisenhower's presidency that this was both undesirable and unachievable. Eisenhower understood that implicit in these objectives was a commitment to carry the war into China and, possibly, into a direct confrontation with the Soviet Union. He also understood that in all probability the use of nuclear weapons could not be avoided. Therefore, right up to the point in 1953 at which he was obliged to use the threat of the new tactical nuclear weapons to break the deadlocked armistice negotiations, he continued to support his predecessor's concept of the limited war. By so doing, both Truman and Eisenhower had drawn a dividing line between the way in which military commanders had fought in 1939–45, where there had been no real constraints on how military commanders achieved their objectives, and the new way in war, with significant political direction and control imposed upon commanders in the field.

Of course, military commanders resisted this interference, but the key difference from the situation that obtained prior to August 1945 was the fact that the atom bomb was now in the weapons inventory. And the new generation of political leaders and rising military commanders began to understand that despite its obvious military applications, the real importance of this new capability was its power as a political weapon. This understanding was further informed by the first successful Soviet atom bomb test in 1949. Although some had advocated the use of the bomb against the Soviet Union prior to 1949, and later against the Chinese in Korea and north of the Yalu, the decisions not to do so were probably well-founded. Despite the theoretical use of nuclear weapons as an adjunct to campaigns hitherto fought exclusively with conventional weapons (and military planners routinely incorporated nuclear operations in parallel with or as an extension of conventional warfare) after 1945 the gulf between the comparative effects and conceptual applications of conventional and nuclear weapons was realistically unbridgeable. Indeed, if the atom bomb had not existed, the UN forces could probably have used their immense conventional firepower to carry out MacArthur's wish to strike the PLA and other strategic targets in China with relative impunity, and certainly without risking a global nuclear conflict.

Although MacArthur was the most vociferous and high-profile advocate of carrying the war into China he was by no means alone in this view, and many senior American commanders in Korea resented the loss of life by their forces when (as they saw it) they possessed the means to avoid this. Even General Mark Clark, the former commander of the 5th US Army during the Allied invasion of Italy in 1943 and at Anzio in 1944, who had replaced General Ridgway as supreme commander in mid-1952, abhorred acceptance of anything less than a UN victory. Thus Korea was one of the earliest examples of nuclear deterrence in action, as it indirectly limited the scale of the conflict; yet at the same time it prolonged it, and finally resulted in a compromise settlement, plus the loss of significantly more UN lives than might otherwise have been the case.

But what of the losses sustained by the PLA and NKPA? Estimates of the communist losses vary, but were conservatively set at more than 500,000 for the North Koreans and about 900,000 for the Chinese. However, while North Korea had gained nothing from the war, the PRC had learned some valuable lessons from it, albeit at a huge price in human terms. First of all, in just a couple of years, communist China had emerged into the limelight from a position of relative obscurity, and one of the greatest failures of the West had been its disregard of the importance of the PRC. The presence of US forces close to the Yalu in 1950 could not have been viewed by the People's Republic other than as a direct threat to its national interests and territorial integrity and its armed response to the situation was therefore quite predictable. Remarkably, although 1950s China was militarily and industrially far behind the West and its Soviet neighbour, it nonetheless chose to confront the most powerful post-1945 nation in the world and, initially, overcame its military forces decisively.

Nevertheless, the early successes of the seemingly inexhaustible supplies of manpower that were flung against the ill-prepared UN forces did not last, and (even though Mao Tse-Tung continued to advocate the ideological view that low-technology massed forces would always overcome those of a non-communist Western power) the Korean War prompted the eventual modernisation and industrialisation of China and its armed forces, albeit that many of the PLA generals who identified and implemented these changes were then purged by Mao in later years. But the main lessons learned by Beijing were political, and these informed and extended their understanding of the nature of the West.

In Korea, the Chinese learnt that howsoever an armed intervention might be described – as nationalism, as counter-colonialism, as a war of liberation or whatever – it should never again allow itself to be identified as the aggressor or supporter of an aggressor. Just as importantly, the Chinese also recognised the fundamental difference between the Western perception of time and their own. In the West politicians and their national armed forces became increasingly wary of any conflict that was open-ended or in which there was no certain prospect of winning an unequivocal victory. In parallel with this, there was a growing reluctance by Western politicians to accept that casualties are an inescapable consequence of war. In later years, particularly since 1990, this trend became even more marked. The Chinese judged, quite correctly, that in any future conflict with the non-communist West they could use human attrition and time to offset the technological imbalance between the two sides. But for this strategy to work, the general population of the enemy Western state had to be kept constantly aware of the losses sustained by their forces: the so-called 'body bag factor' which was so vividly, diligently (but often inaccurately and unhelpfully) reported by the television news agencies and photo-journalists throughout the post-1950s era, particularly in Vietnam. Accordingly, Korea spawned a concept of media reporting that dominated later conflicts, and also alerted those on both sides of the Iron Curtain (or 'Bamboo Curtain' in Asia and the Far East) to the almost infinite possibilities presented by the manipulation of the media to support their divergent political and military aims. Thus what later became known as the 'CNN factor' was born and this, together with the many other military and political lessons learned by Beijing in Korea, were soon utilised against the French in Indochina, and subsequently to even more telling effect against the Americans in Vietnam.

For their part, the United States and its allies had also learned important military lessons from the Korean experience. That Western technology and firepower had eventually triumphed over the huge but technologically inferior PLA was not in doubt. But the politically attractive deduction that superior technology would therefore invariably prevail over such forces in the future was naïve, and this flawed appreciation was an important contributor to the American failure in Vietnam twenty years later. While the British did not make the same mistake in Malaya between 1948 and 1960, their access to high-technology military assets could never have remotely approached that of the United States in any case, given the national indebtedness and economic crises that afflicted successive post-1945 British governments.

Nevertheless, for the United States and Great Britain, Korea provided a timely warning, and varying levels of rearmament, an extension of conscription and improvements to all manner of military training and equipment followed the conflict. All of this had important spin-offs for their NATO forces in Europe, and sweeping improvements were made in the wake of what had been in a number of respects an unsatisfactory campaign. Sadly, the United States subsequently ignored or forgot the lessons of Korea by the time of their next South-east Asian conflict, so that a senior American veteran of Korea and Vietnam commented after 1975: 'We went into Korea with a very poor army, and [consequent upon the lessons learned from that experience] came out with a pretty good one. We went into Vietnam with a pretty good army, and came out with a terrible one.'[85]

Once the Korean conflict had reached a stalemate in 1951, it became an increasingly forgotten and unpopular war, while civil rights and anti-war movements gained more and more support in America and elsewhere in the West as the months of static warfare dragged on. Although on a much lesser scale than that seen during the Vietnam War in the late 1960s and early 1970s, the disregard and sometimes open hostility displayed by some (but by no means all) US communities and citizens to the returning Korean veterans in 1952 and 1953 was a sad comment upon the changing attitudes in America. Similar reactions were also encountered by certain other UN force contributors, but the scale of this was insignificant compared with that experienced by the returning American soldiers and repatriated prisoners of war in parts of the United States.

Meanwhile, the seeds of discord and disillusion had also been sown within the US armed forces early in the piece by inequities in the mobilisation system and drafting of personnel to fight in Korea. Subsequent attempts to provide a fair system of rotation and tour length through a points system actually reduced combat effectiveness. After the first eight months of the war, moreover, the morale and motivation of many US servicemen was also adversely affected by a perception that they were being required to fight and possibly die in a war 'whose purpose was not clear, which they were not supposed to win, and which just seemed to go on and on'.[86]

Another such issue within the American forces was the fact that in 1950 the army, the navy and the marines were still generally segregated into white and non-white units. The inequities of this situation attracted increasing attention in Korea, and from 1954 desegregation of the US armed forces moved on apace, although the legacy of segregation and the bitterness that it engendered persisted long after that.

In the United Kingdom the call-up of reservists for Korea was also mishandled in many hundreds of cases. Men who had been classified medically unfit were recalled to active duty, and hundreds of ex-prisoners of war of the Japanese and Germans in the Second World War found themselves once again in uniform, just as they were beginning to rebuild their post-war lives.[87] Indeed, the thoughts of those men who had recently suffered years of captivity as prisoners of the Japanese can only be imagined, as their imminent capture by another oriental foe became a distinct possibility. However, just as had been the case from 1939–45, the British soldier's attitude to the war was generally less political than that of his American counterpart, and the concept of fighting for his country, his regiment, or simply for his comrades more often than not superseded any abstract notions of conducting an ideological struggle or crusade against communism in Korea.

So it was that the Korean War took its place in the history of the Cold War as the first direct armed conflict between a major communist power and non-communist powers. This, together with the crucial military-political policy decisions taken in Washington, New York, London, Beijing and Moscow which flowed from the crucial debates over the expansion of the war and options for the use of nuclear weapons, conferred particular significance upon an unpleasant and generally inglorious war. But perhaps the single most important matter to emerge from the Korean conflict was the adoption by the United States of the concept of the limited war as its war-fighting solution for any future campaigns to contain the communist threat. For better or worse, the United States had shown the PRC and the Soviet Union just how far it was prepared to go in its use of armed force in regions that lay beyond its areas of vital interest. It had also provided its own military leaders with an unequivocal signal that, other than in a general war, they could not henceforth expect to exercise the almost total control of their forces in the field that their predecessors had enjoyed during the Second World War. Korea heralded new ways of using armed force, but not all the political and military leaders necessarily understood, or were prepared to accept, the changes this implied at what was still an early stage of the Cold War.

Meanwhile, as the fighting on the Korean peninsula flowed back and forth, the British had been involved in their own separate war against another communist threat in South-east Asia ever since 1948. Here also Chinese involvement was an important factor. Unlike the compromise settlement that ended the war in Korea, however, the outcome of the Malayan Emergency was a clear military and political victory for the armed forces of Britain and Malaya.

CHAPTER SEVEN

MALAYA, 1948–60

Origins of an Insurgency

The conquest of Malaya by the Japanese during the Second World War and the post-war communist victory in China together enabled and encouraged the growth, from 1948, of a communist insurgency in the British colony of Malaya. During the pre-war years large numbers of workers had emigrated from China to the various European colonies that had been established and developed in South-east Asia during the previous two centuries. In the 1930s and 1940s these immigrants inevitably included many communists, including those with ambitions to export the form of communism that was then being advocated by Mao Tse Tung and his followers in their struggle against Chiang Kai-shek's nationalists in the post-1945 period. Although the pre-war effectiveness of the embryo communist movement in Malaya was limited, the war actually enabled the communists to acquire the means to prosecute an armed struggle. They were sufficiently organised to constitute the main core of the resistance movement following the Japanese invasion of the Malayan peninsula, and consequently they gained popular support within the country as well as formal recognition and matériel support from the Allied forces combating the invaders throughout the region.

The armed element of the Malayan Communist Party (MCP) was equipped with weapons discarded during the 1942 fighting and with new weapons air-dropped into their jungle bases. Yet despite their combat potential, the communist fighters were not employed against the Japanese on a large scale or in set-piece battles. Rather, they remained as a guerrilla force in waiting – one that was already planning for the post-war era. To that end, when the Japanese defeat came in 1945 the MCP accepted the disarmament of its units and a return to the political arena. Many of its weapons, however, remained hidden in the jungle, while in the populated areas the MCP had over time established its members in key positions within several Malayan institutions, notably in the trade unions, schools and throughout the sizeable population of landless Chinese workers. Also, in a foretaste of what was to come, while it was still in open possession of its arms the MCP utilised the months between the defeat of the Japanese and the return of the British administration to eliminate a number of Malays who opposed their objective of a communist Malaya.

In 1945 the main MCP power base lay within the Chinese Malay population. For that reason it never achieved the blend of communist and nationalist appeal and support that occurred (for example) in its near neighbour

Indochina. It was viewed as an ethnically Chinese – and therefore 'foreign' –
organisation by a great majority of Malays, not least by the powerful nationalist United Malayan National Organisation (UMNO), which opposed the
British intention to set up a Malay Union (the future Malaysia). Had the MCP
and UMNO united, events might have taken a different course. However, the
influence of the two great motivators and separators since time immemorial
– race and ideology – virtually guaranteed that the MCP would be forced to
pursue its campaign independently. Also, an early British declaration of
intent to grant Malaya its independence (the British had, by 1948, already left
the Indian subcontinent and Burma) largely undercut any opposition cause
based on freedom and independence. In light of this, it was perhaps remarkable that the communist campaign was subsequently conducted on the scale
that it was. But it did illustrate the potential for political exploitation, instability and violence that exists where a large ethnically different and – in this
case – economically disadvantaged and politically unrepresented immigrant
population was allowed to establish itself within a country.

In mid-1948 this potential was translated into reality when, probably at
the instigation of Moscow, simultaneous communist uprisings began in
Burma, Indonesia, the Philippines and Malaya. For Britain, by then
embroiled in the Greek civil war, the prospect of having to deal with a guerrilla campaign in the Far East was less than welcome; and it had also been
watching the deteriorating situation in French Indochina with a mixture of
concern and a degree of empathy. Meanwhile, in Malaya Chin Peng led the
MCP and its former armed element into the jungle, where they recovered
their long-concealed weapons and formed the emotively titled Malayan
Races Liberation Army (MRLA). The title, however, was inaccurate, as the
MRLA cause was more about domination than liberation, and at least ninety
per cent of the organisation was ethnically Chinese. The Labour government in London and the British authorities in Kuala Lumpur, headed by Sir
Henry Gurney the High Commissioner, braced themselves for the coming
conflict. By late 1948 the MRLA numbered about 4,500 (including 1,200 guerrillas who had formerly fought against the Japanese), while the Malayan
security forces were about 21,000 strong.

The scene of the impending struggle comprised very varied terrain, some
eighty per cent of which was primary jungle and almost impenetrable tropical swampland, the whole crowned by a dense canopy of soaring trees that
routinely rose 200 feet into the sky. Primary jungle covered most of the
central area of Malaya and was criss-crossed throughout by thousands of
streams and rivers, some navigable by canoe, but most of them simply
cascading down to the coastal plain, where they joined the country's main
waterways. Most of these torrents rose among the chain of mountains –

some of them 7,000ft high – that formed the central spine of the Malayan peninsula. Adjacent to the main populated areas (almost all of which were on or close to the coastal plain), vast areas had been cultivated for the production of rubber, creating large plantations served by well-established roads and tracks. To the north lay Thailand, while off the southern tip of the Malayan peninsula was the British colony of Singapore, with its important naval and military bases.

Shortly after the communists took to the jungle the first blow fell in Perak province, when three young Chinese men bicycled into the Elphil Estate and calmly shot dead Arthur Walker, a fifty-year-old British planter. Meanwhile, a few miles away Ian Christian, an estate owner, and his manager Mr J. Alison were seized by terrorists, tied to chairs and summarily shot. Britain responded by declaring a State of Emergency, a measure imposed country-wide by the end of July. Further terrorist attacks took place over the next three years as the communist campaign gained momentum. By March 1950 the terrorists had killed 863 civilians, 323 police officers and 154 soldiers, although 1,138 terrorists had been killed, plus 645 captured and 359 surrendered. But, despite the escalating violence, Malaya's established systems for the administration of justice – based largely on the principles of British law – stood the test well during the early years of the Emergency. Nevertheless, the normal arrangements were supplemented by the extensive use of detention without trial, and at one stage some 10,000 suspects were being held. This measure was generally accepted by the population as entirely necessary, and in any case a system of tribunals to review all cases of detention was in place (albeit that the final decision in these matters rested with the authorities).

A Plan of Campaign: 1948–51

The military campaign against the terrorists was headed by Lieutenant General Sir Harold Briggs, the Director of Operations, who had a wealth of experience in the region, having formerly been General Officer Commanding Burma, as well as the commander of the 4th Indian Division. The organisation and arrangements that Briggs put in place to deal with the growing conflict addressed and countered most of the key elements[88] expounded by Mao Tse Tung as essential to the success of a revolutionary war, and Briggs established many counter-guerrilla principles, practices and procedures that are still valid today. Yet while other states recognised the particular merits of the British operations in Malaya and sought to emulate them elsewhere, they sometimes failed to repeat the British success. This was often due to a failure to adapt the Malayan solution to the particular geography, ethnicity and motivating influences that affected their own guerrilla operations, all too often simply applying an unmodified Malayan campaign model to such situations.

Briggs appreciated the vital importance of securing the government bases, forces and population centres. Once this had been achieved the security forces could expand their operations into the rural areas and finally dominate all parts of the country. A counter-revolutionary campaign usually poses the dilemma of whether to prioritise in favour of securing the main centres of population and production and the military bases, or whether (under political pressure to deliver an early victory) to sally forth and confront the guerrillas in battle. Invariably, the latter is unachievable until the former has been accomplished, and Mao specifically counselled against engaging government forces in formal battle unless and until a guerrilla victory was certain. Both Gurney and Briggs in Kuala Lumpur, and the British government in London, understood that there could be no quick victory in Malaya and that a secure and legally based organisation and administration, together with secure strategic and operational bases, were indispensable to the success of their campaign. But at the same time it was still necessary to deny the communists the opportunity to establish their own support infrastructure and bases.

First of all, the elimination of the latent threat posed by the Chinese embedded within the main urban areas was paramount. The very professional Malayan Special Branch dealt effectively with this particular threat, and subsequently did so in the rural areas as well. At all levels, Briggs ensured that three key elements – police, military and civil administration – were invariably represented in all decision-making committees, so that security, political, resource and economic issues were always dealt with together, not as discrete functions. Thus the Malayan government machine was founded on an organisation that was both efficient and pragmatic, and which was seen to be so by the population as a whole. At the same time, Briggs ensured that the destruction of the MCP's political infrastructure (the Min Yuen) was accorded the highest priority, even at the expense of time and resources deployed against the more visible armed terrorist groups.

Mao Tse-Tung had emphasised the need to mobilise the masses if a revolutionary conflict was to succeed. Potentially, the half-million Chinese squatters scattered throughout the Malayan peninsula were a ready source of political and matériel support. However, by resettling these people into new villages the authorities removed them from those areas in which the MRLA sought their co-operation and assistance. At the same time, because the new village policy was implemented logically and sympathetically, it provided the relocated villagers with a better standard of living and an economic stake in Malaya that fostered reconciliation and encouraged their positive support for the government. This process was assisted on the one hand by the continued success of the Malayan police and its Special Branch, and on the other by a most effective military psychological operations campaign. These activities were set against a backdrop of increasingly successful conventional and special forces military operations against the terrorists in the jungle, the latter actions conducted primarily by the 22nd Special Air Service Regiment (22 SAS), often assisted by native trackers.

The new village strategy was a masterpiece of planning and organisation. It sought to relocate some 500,000 people into 410 new villages, the sites for which were secure and also entirely habitable. Indeed, in addition to its dwellings, each new village had a school, shops and a medical clinic, plus a fresh-water supply. As a minimum standard, each dwelling area had sufficient space for the subsistence level of livestock management and cultivation that the relocated family had practised in their old village. So-called dormitory villages were also built to cater for those who needed to live securely, but travelled away to their regular work at the local rubber plantation or mine, while agricultural villages provided accommodation appropriate to those who earned a living by farming. Each relocated family was given the materials with which to build their new house – the typical Malayan house was constructed of bamboo poles, timber and palm leaves – plus one hundred dollars in cash. Most importantly for the former squatters, the inhabitants of the new villages received a legal title of ownership for their allotted piece of land, and in later years the traditional Malay dwellings were increasingly replaced with brick-built houses.

As well as the physical defences of wire, ditches, watchtowers and anti-intruder devices, each village (or 'kampong'), was protected by an on-site police post, the officers for which were later supplemented by locally raised village Home Guard or militia units. Eventually, each new village was run by its own locally elected village committee, the success of which indicated the progress of the government campaign and also confirmed Britain's clear intention for Malaya to have free elections and independence. The whole process of setting up and implementing the new village programme was supported by an effective intelligence and civil affairs operation, which also built on the government's more immediate military successes, and so it was both self-perpetuating and self-enhancing. Finally, the government's information (or perception management) operation was overlaid upon the more conventional military and police campaign.

Mao had also declared that a revolutionary campaign must enjoy international support. In the Malayan Emergency, the co-operation of the PRC might have been assumed, with all that that implied. However, although political support and some matériel were forthcoming, until 1949 the communists in China were primarily preoccupied with defeating the nationalists – followed almost immediately by the war in Korea. In fact, the Korean War provided a dramatic increase in Malayan government revenues, as its principal exports – rubber and tin – greatly increased in price; and this enabled the Malayan government to fund the entire costs of the campaign, with the British government simply paying the normal operating costs of its own military forces. Also, because Malaya was a peninsula and had no common land border with China, the considerable power of the Royal Navy (just as had been the case with the USN in Korea) prevented any large-scale support from the PRC by sea. Consequently, support for the MRLA from Beijing and Moscow mainly took the form of expressions of political backing rather than the provision of quantities of manpower and equipment.

Hearts, Minds and Independence: October 1951 to July 1960

Despite the steady but inevitably slow progress made by the government forces, the communists waged their guerrilla campaign with increasing ferocity during the first three years of the conflict. In addition to the wholesale destruction of rubber plantations and other commercial targets, more than 2,000 civilians were murdered by the terrorists as they concentrated their attention on the rural areas, and on the road and rail links. By cutting these they sought to isolate and dominate the villages from which they drew their support, or which they had terrorised into providing.

These acts of terror – usually through assassinations and by ambushing the security forces on their main lines of communication and resupply – culminated in the murder of Sir Henry Gurney on 7 October 1951. This was the high-water mark of the communist insurgency. When the new High Commissioner and Director of Operations, General Sir Gerald Templer, arrived in Malaya in early January 1952, he had at his disposal some 60,000 police and 30,000 military personnel, whereas although the MRLA had increased in size since 1948, the guerrillas numbered no more than about 10,000 at that stage. Templer immediately set about building on the work begun by Briggs and Gurney, while at the same time applying his own special talents as a brilliant military commander and diplomat. He also brought to the task a particular awareness of the political and human perspectives, which led directly to the further development of 'hearts and minds' as a vital concept for counter-revolutionary warfare. After making an initial assessment of the situation, Templer expressed the view:

Any idea that the business of normal civil Government and the business of the Emergency are two separate entities must be killed for good and all. The two activities are completely and utterly inter-related ...

The answer lies not in pouring more men into the jungle, but in winning the hearts and minds of the people.

The practical application of that philosophy throughout the remaining eight years of the campaign was the key to the British military success in Malaya.

A vital element of Templer's operational concept was the further refinement of the military psychological operations (psyops) campaign. This operation was a model of its kind, particularly during the first half of the 1950s.

In Malaya, the Security Forces' aim was to bring the armed struggle against the Malayan Communist Party (MCP) to a victorious conclusion, so that a reasonably peaceful political and military climate could be established to permit democratic elections to take place prior to the granting of Malayan independence. From this strategic aim two clear psyops campaign objectives were identified: to induce the members of the communist terrorist organisation to surrender with their arms, and to help win the hearts and minds of the uncommitted members of the Malayan population. [This] translated into the traditional psyops activities of persuading, informing and reassuring: in order to weaken the will of the enemy, strengthen the resolve of the loyal and gain the support of the uncommitted. In the Malayan campaign, the importance of the fundamental and immutable principle that UK military psyops had to be founded at all times on the truth was well demonstrated. By [its] absolute adherence to that basic tenet the psyops organisation in Malaya maintained the credibility upon which it depended for its effectiveness in support of the overall operational plan. The psyops campaign in Malaya was based on a firm foundation of intelligence support, research and analysis, evaluation and expert advice (both military and civilian). The full range of psyops dissemination assets were used to support the campaign. These included handbills, films, playlets, the use of key communicators, the press, newssheets, radio and loudspeaker broadcasts. An innovation was the successful use of aircraft for leaflet distribution and voice broadcasts to the communist terrorists hiding deep in the Malayan jungle. The surrender of large numbers of communist terrorists, the collapse of the terrorist movement and the achievement of a politically stable, democratic election campaign were testimony to the success of the Malayan campaign, and to the major role played by psyops within it.[89]

Although such activities may seem crude, archaic even, in the modern technological age, the British psychological operations campaign in 1950s

Malaya was state of the art for its time; and even in the modern age there is little point in addressing psychological operations messages via sophisticated media where the target audience is so artless that it lacks the technology to receive the message. Consequently, British military psychological operations in Malaya were conducted at precisely the correct level of sophistication for the target audience, whilst using to best advantage the latest technology then available.

Under Templer's leadership the government's political and military campaigns progressed rapidly. Typical of the high-profile joint police/army operations conducted near the main centres of population was Operation Hive, which was carried out, over a two-month period in late 1952, around the town of Seremban in Negri Sembilan province by two battalions of the 7th Gurkha Rifles, D Company of the 1st Fijian Infantry Regiment and two SAS squadrons, plus a large force of police.

> Op 'Hive' was designed to saturate a selected area with troops so that the terrorists' mode of life would be completely disrupted. A concentrated programme of police checks on roads and New Villages was planned in detail with the aim of driving the bandits back on to their jungle food dumps where they would be forced to eat up valuable reserves. Then the military units would move into specific areas where it was hoped, by intensive ambushes and patrols, to force out the terrorists once more into the open or into the many 'stop' (ambush) positions, established on recorded and likely tracks in the jungle surrounding Seramban.[90]

As Malaya's political stability and future prosperity became ever more assured, support for the MRLA waned, while an increasing number of intelligence-based ambushes by the security forces continued to deplete the communists' fighting strength. This led to disillusionment within the terrorist groups in the jungle, which produced a steady stream of surrenders and defections. Despite their involvement in the armed struggle and terrorism, those Chinese who surrendered were generally well treated, which led to even more surrenders when this fact was communicated (by leaflets and aircraft-mounted loudspeaker broadcasts for example) to those terrorists still in their jungle bases.

Throughout the campaign, a vulnerability that affected the communists and the security forces alike was the need to move and deploy along the relatively limited number of easily negotiable routes. For the terrorists, these were usually no more than jungle trails, while the government forces utilised the road and rail routes essential for the speedy movement of rapid reaction forces, major troop deployments and resupply. Consequently, although the jungle provided near-perfect concealment to the static forces of both sides, it tended to favour the small bands of terrorists. Accordingly, these jungle trails were the main focus of security force ambush operations. These ambushes demanded an enormous amount of patience, and one esti-mate indicated that 1,800 man-hours were necessary to produce a single contact, with an even greater number of man-hours required to produce a confirmed kill.

The ambush tactics used by the security forces were many and varied, and were refined and developed as the Emergency drew on. For the army, whilst all the infantry ambush patrols deployed into the jungle enjoyed varying degrees of success, and were often assisted by local guides and Iban trackers from Borneo, the real experts in long-duration, long-range patrols were the Gurkhas (notably the 1/10th Gurkha Rifles) and 22 SAS. Rather than wasting time and risking detection by a ground approach to the ambush area, the SAS patrols were parachuted into the jungle by a technique titled 'tree jumping'. This was a fairly risky manoeuvre:

Typical of the operations from 1954 onward, when the enemy was becoming concentrated in certain identifiable areas of wilderness, was Operation 'Termite'. It lasted from July to November, and began with a heavy bombing of the jungle by RAF Lincolns [bombers] – an indis-criminate use of air power which was as likely to kill [the indigenous] aborigines[91] as communist guerrillas, and one which the SAS regarded as counter-productive. Two SAS squadrons, a total of 177 men, then parachuted into jungle clearings created by the bombs. That clearings had to be made in this way attests to the number of casualties suffered by the [22 SAS] Regiment in its attempts to perfect 'tree-jumping'. Even then, the drop generated four casualties. Such casualties were occur-ring not just as a result of the unpredictable behaviour of parachutes as they were 'bounced' by the thermal effect of air above the trees: the technique of abseiling out of the trees was also proving defective. In theory, the soldier detached himself from his parachute, lashed a long webbing strap to a branch, and descended safely to the ground. The webbing bulged at intervals, where it had been stitched, and therefore snagged at high speed as it travelled through D-rings on the soldier's harness. As a result, three men were killed and one seriously injured taking part in Operation 'Sword' in January 1954, one of the deaths occurring after a soldier in great pain had cut away from the harness and fallen 150 feet. In addition to the SAS, four infantry battalions took part in Operation 'Termite'.[92]

The operation resulted in the death, capture or surrender of fifteen rebels – an indication of the scale of action necessary to achieve what some might regard as a limited success.

Meanwhile, on the political front, Templer engineered the establishment of the Alliance Party, led by Tunku Abdul Rahman. This multi-ethnic, multi-culture and broad-based political coalition of the Malayan Chinese Association, the Malayan Indian Congress and the UMNO undercut the MCP cause entirely; by the time Templer departed in 1954[93] both the MCP and the MRLA were spent forces. Free elections were scheduled for the following year, when the Alliance Party were elected to power with a sizeable majority. This in turn allowed Tunku Abdul Rahman to offer the members of the MCP and MRLA an amnesty, but not a return to normal politics. The MCP refused this option, and so the campaign against the terrorists in the jungle resumed, with the security forces systematically hunting them down during a five-year war of attrition. The eventual outcome was inevitable, and after the communists admitted defeat and withdrew to the Thai border region their strength had dwindled from 10,000 in 1951 to a mere 500. Meanwhile, the country's political stability enabled Britain to declare Malayan independence on 31 August 1957, and three years later, on 12 July 1960, the Malayan Emergency was officially declared at an end.

Nevertheless, independence had come at a price. 1,346 policemen and 519 soldiers had been killed during the campaign, while some 2,473 civilians had lost their lives at the hands of the terrorists, with a further 810 civilians missing and never accounted for. Meanwhile, 6,711 Chinese communist guerrillas had been killed, 1,289 captured and 2,704 surrendered during the twelve years of the insurgency. But in the final analysis the total defeat of the Chinese communist guerrillas and the orderly achievement of Malayan independence were universally acclaimed as a significant British success, and a clear defeat for the forces of communism.

With the possible exception of Great Britain (if the civil disturbances that attended its planned and progressive policy of withdrawal from its former colonies, such as Aden in 1967, and its great imperial possessions, such as India in 1947, are discounted), each of the great powers – the United States, the Soviet Union, Great Britain, France and the PRC – of the Cold War era was destined to suffer at least one major military or military/political reverse in the years prior to 1990. For the Soviet Union that defeat did not come until the final decade of the Cold War, in the barren mountains of Afghanistan. For France, it came in the jungles and on the plains of Indochina, as well as in the rocky hills and teeming kasbahs of North Africa. France and Great Britain also sustained jointly a defeat at Suez in 1956, when the successful operation to seize the Suez Canal was subsequently aborted following the exertion of US pressure. China's defeat was in Korea, albeit that the UN forces perceived the stalemate of mid-1953 to be something less than a victory. As for the United States, it was in South-east Asia that it suffered its major defeat. Yet the eventual abandonment of the Republic of Vietnam in March 1973 and the final ignominious flight of the last American advisers and diplomats from the roof of the US Embassy in Saigon April 1975 were more the result of failed political leadership and policies than the failure of its forces in combat.

Nevertheless, as events in Europe post-1945 and in Korea between 1950 and 1953 illustrated, in the wars and conflicts of the Cold War era, combat was indivisible from politics, and therefore wars could no longer be waged in isolation. And in 1954, while the British government was reaping the benefits of the success of General Templer's work in Malaya, the French were suffering their greatest battlefield defeat since 1940 – in a muddy and shell-pocked complex of trenches, bunkers and debris close to the border between Tonkin and Laos, in French Indochina.

NDOCHINA AND VIETNAM, 1946–54

Colonialism, Communism and Empire

A very great deal has been written about the long, bitter struggle of the peoples of French Indochina and (since 1954) of Vietnam, Laos and Cambodia to shape their future. The war carried on by the communists against the French from 1946 to 1954 is often dealt with as a separate conflict from that which took place from 1954 against the South Vietnamese government and, soon thereafter, against the United States and its allies. Yet a constant thread that ran from 1946 through to 1975 was the nature and motivation of the indigenous communist enemy and its political and military leaders. The movement began fairly inauspiciously with the founding of a Communist Party of Indochina in 1930. However, from the 1940s Ho Chi Minh and his military commander Vo Nguyen Giap transformed the old states and kingdoms of Indochina – Cochin China, Tonkin, Annam (which together comprised Vietnam), Cambodia and Laos – from their 1893 status as a part of the French colonial empire, into three communist-dominated sovereign states in 1975.

Throughout the Cold War the principal focus of this epic struggle was always the jungles, plains and mountains of Vietnam, and the villages and cities of a country and region that became a battleground for three decades. Indeed, in terms of actual combat, much of the Cold War was in fact fought in South-east Asia – in French Indochina, in the Republic of Korea, in Malaya and in the Republic of South Vietnam. And all of these conflicts were to varying degrees instrumental in shaping the fortunes and future strategic policies of Britain, France and the United States of America, the latter two countries in particular.

After 1945 Britain's pragmatic policies for the transformation of the British Empire into the British Commonwealth pre-empted the usual arguments advanced by nationalist and liberation movements in many other European protectorates and colonies. Malaya was a prime example of this. Similarly, the view of communism that prevailed in Britain throughout the immediate post-Second World War years was much less ideological than that in the United States, where anti-communism was rapidly assuming the status of a crusade. Even allowing for its specific context, the strength of the American view of communism was exemplified by General Ridgway's 'Why We Are Here' message to his forces in Korea in January 1951.

The view of its empire by France, however, was somewhat different from that held by Britain. Many of its possessions, in Indochina especially, were relatively recent acquisitions – gained between 1862 and 1893 – and France derived considerable economic, trade and strategic benefits from them – just as many individual diplomatic, military and civil service careers also profited enormously from service in French Indochina. Furthermore, over a hundred-year period, much blood had been shed by the military forces of France (by the French Foreign Legion in particular) to secure its possessions in South-east Asia and North Africa. Meanwhile, in the liberated Paris of 1945 there was a popular perception that France was once again a great power, and that the pre-1940 world would now be restored. Therefore, the French government was not minded to give up to any indigenous adminis-tration – whether communist or nationalist – the French territory in Indochina that had been temporarily stolen by the Japanese in 1941. The resultant decision to maintain total control of French Indochina eventually resulted in 75,000 dead servicemen, including 11,260 legionnaires and 27,000 members of the Vietnamese national army. It also indirectly paved the way for France's subsequent defeat in Algeria, and the crisis that occurred in the French army in 1961.

Apart from signalling the end of France as a great military and imperial power, however, the great significance of the events that took place in Indochina from 1945 to 1954 was the way in which, imperceptibly at first and then with increasing inevitability, Vietnam changed from a French colo-nial battlefield to one on which the United States subsequently chose to make its stand against what Ridgway had in Korea called the 'dead existence of a Godless world' and the 'misery and despair' of communism. Arguably, the scar that this left on the United States from 1975 was even greater than the crushing blow that France suffered in 1954. So how did this chain of events come about?

The French military collapse at the hands of the Germans in 1940 provided a clear indication that its fortunes were truly in decline, and this fact was lost neither upon the Japanese, who proceeded to seize the French, British and Dutch territories in the Far East from 1941, nor upon the several nationalist organisations within those territories who assessed that the time for action had at last arrived. In French Indochina one such organisation was the League for the Independence of Vietnam ('Viet Nam Doc Lap Dong Minh Hoi', or 'Viet Minh'), headed by communist Ho Chi Minh. He was a native of Annam, which ran almost the full length of the country from Cochin China in the south to Tonkin (and the Chinese border) in the north, and was the main province of Vietnam, bordering both Cambodia and Laos along most of its length. To the east of Annam lay the coast, and beyond it was the South China Sea.

Under the guidance of its military leader, Giap, the Viet Minh carried out an effective guerrilla campaign against the French Vichy administration and

Japanese occupation forces in the northern part of Indochina, while co-ordinating its activities with other nationalist movements in the country. In March 1945 the Japanese took savage military action against the small French garrisons (manned primarily by legionnaires of the 5th Regiment of Infantry (5 REI) of the French Foreign Legion) that were scattered about the country. This act of treachery removed the token Vichy French administration headed by 'a corrupt minority of pro-Japanese collaborators'[94] and enabled the Viet Minh to concentrate all its efforts against the Japanese. In turn, this produced increased military support from the United States, which now viewed the Viet Minh as the principal counter-Japanese force in the country. Apart from this, President Roosevelt had already made his position on Indochina clear on 24 January 1944, when he stated that 'France has milked it for one hundred years. The people of Indochina are entitled to something better than that.'[95] Thus, when the atomic bombs dropped on Hiroshima and Nagasaki brought about an unexpectedly abrupt end to the war in the region, the communists were sufficiently well armed and in control of events to establish the Democratic Republic of Vietnam, with its capital at Hanoi.

The new republic was declared on 2 September 1945. In July of that year, however, the Allies had decided at Potsdam that France would regain its Indochinese possessions. But France was in no position to do so in August 1945, and next month British and nationalist Chinese forces respectively occupied the south and north of the country. The size of their task was such that by October the British had found it necessary to rearm some of the surrendered Japanese units in order for them to act as a paramilitary police force in the south of the country. The British force comprised the 26,000 men of Major General D. Gracey's battle-hardened 20th Indian Division, plus air force and additional artillery support. But whereas the Chinese were content to deal with the Japanese without affecting the new regime in Hanoi, the British were firmly committed to return Indochina to French control. Accordingly, on 5 October 1945 a French Expeditionary Corps, 21,500 strong and led by General Leclerc, entered Saigon and began the process of relieving the British forces, who handed over their temporary stewardship of southern Indochina to the French four days later. In the months prior to and after the British withdrawal there was much political manoeuvring, while several violent confrontations between the communists, nationalists, French forces, French colonists, Gaullists, former Vichy supporters and other disparate groups also occurred. During this turbulent period various potentially workable compromises emerged, although none were acceptable to Paris.[96]

The situation degenerated with each passing month as two diametrically opposed philosophies and forces moved towards open conflict in early 1946.

First of all there were the French, determined to retain control of French Indochina at all costs. Second, there were the communists, inspired by a charismatic leader committed to establish an independent, communist-dominated Vietnamese republic. Although the motivation used by Ho Chi Minh was initially anti-colonialist, then nationalist, there is little doubt that a communist state was always his ultimate goal throughout the war that was about to commence.

A major amphibious landing had been carried out by the French at Haiphong in the Red River Delta on 6 March 1946, and the always uneasy relationship between the French and the newly established government in Hanoi deteriorated rapidly, against a backdrop of small-scale armed clashes. The landing by major elements of the French Expeditionary Corps added thousands of men to the 150,000 nationalist Chinese troops and Viet Minh forces already in the Red River Delta area. For the local population the significance of this was dramatic, as the 1945 rice harvest had been very poor, and even before the arrival of these armies they were literally starving. Consequently, the Red River Delta was particularly receptive to any action that might expel the French and Chinese occupiers.

On 19 December the Viet Minh struck French positions all about Hanoi with artillery, mortar and small-arms fire, which severed the city's electricity and water supplies. Shortly afterwards the guerrillas withdrew to their bases in the swamps and mountains of Tonkin and the area of the Chinese border. There they prepared to conduct a classic revolutionary war in accordance with the principles expounded by Mao Tse Tung, whose own campaign was then proceeding successfully against the nationalist Chinese armies to the north.

Over the next three years the Viet Minh carried out numerous ambushes of French supply columns and attacks on isolated forts, as well as various acts of terrorism. Although the French forces (following the pattern of their colonial strategy of former times) were dispersed throughout the country, the main area of conflict was to the north, in Tonkin. During those first years after the French return, the Legion bore the brunt of the attacks, and it continued to do so throughout France's post-1945 involvement with Indochina.

On the night of 25 July [1948] the fort at Phu Tong Hoa astride the strategically sensitive road linking Hanoi and the Chinese border came under accurate mortar attack which breached the perimeter fence. Inside, a company of 3 REI [3e Régiment Étranger d'Infanterie], heavily outnumbered, fought on even after more than half their base was overrun, until they were relieved three days later. By then, twenty-one legionnaires, including the two most senior officers, were dead. The forty survivors, wearing their best Number Ones [uniforms], presented arms as reinforcements drove through the gate.[97]

Such incidents were typical both of the nature of the Legion and of the war that it was required to fight for France in Indochina. Meanwhile, in an ill-disguised attempt to placate the nationalists in particular, but also the communists, while at the same time installing a ruler who would be entirely under French control, in April 1948 Paris had established the discredited former Emperor Bao Dai as emperor of an independent Vietnam. Not surprisingly the Viet Minh were unimpressed, and in February 1950, following a successful attack on the French outpost at Lao Kai on the Red River close to the Chinese border (an event which coincided with Mao's victory in China and the prospect of significant quantities of Chinese aid for the Viet Minh in the future), Giap and Ho felt sufficiently confident to move their guerrilla campaign into the counter-offensive phase.

In early 1950 Giap had at his disposal two infantry divisions, plus heavy mortars and anti-aircraft guns; but by the end of that year he had increased the strength of his regular forces to three divisions. Throughout the war, the French underestimated the Viet Minh capability, but two other important factors also affected French hopes and perceptions. First, the post-Roosevelt administration of President Truman, fuelled by McCarthyism and anti-communist sentiments in the United States – much reinforced by the North Korean invasion of South Korea in June 1950 – all indicated the possibility of American military support for the French cause. Second, the French government hoped that the National Assembly in Paris would authorise the deployment of conscripts to Indochina, which would alleviate the chronic shortage of French troops and the consequent reliance upon regular units, the Legion and volunteers to serve there. However, although America's eventual post-1954 military involvement in Vietnam was massive, it was never used to assist the French. Similarly, the use of conscripts to fight beyond metropolitan France was never sanctioned by the National Assembly – a decision much influenced by a disaster that was just about to befall the French forces in Tonkin in the early autumn of 1950.

On 16 September, just six weeks before the PLA launched its devastating offensive against the UN forces in Korea, Giap struck the French forces in north-east Tonkin. The Viet Minh operations began with a series of assaults against French positions on the Cao Bang-Lang Son ridge.

Disaster at Cao Bang: 16 September to 17 October 1950

Dong Khe was a forward outpost of the Legion, set high in the jungle-clad, mist-shrouded hills that lay along Tonkin's border with China. The position was manned by some 260 men, comprising two companies of the 3 REI. The communist attack began with a heavy and accurate mortar barrage, followed during the next two days by further mortar bombardments interspersed with human wave attacks by more than 2,000 infantrymen. Time and again the attackers overwhelmed the perimeter defences and engaged in savage close combat with the legionnaires. Time and again they were forced to withdraw. But the outcome of the battle was never in doubt, and at the end of the second day the few surviving legionnaires managed to escape from the shattered outpost. But the significance of this battle extended well beyond the loss of a single outpost.

The fort at Dong Khe had previously been designated as the rendezvous point for a French column that was already moving towards it from the small town of Cao Bang, about fifteen miles away. The column's mission was to evacuate and escort the anti-communist civilian population of Cao Bang to safety; and in view of what transpired Giap must have already been aware of the particular significance of Dong Khe. Indeed, the outpost was critical to the safety of the French column, and 1 BEP (1er Bataillon Étranger de Parachutistes) plus a large body of Moroccan troops – a total of some 5,000 men – tried unsuccessfully to recapture it. However, this force was ambushed in the Coc Xa valley by as many as 30,000 Viet Minh guerrillas. Despite the gallantry and discipline of the legionnaires during a battle that lasted for more than two weeks, the force was gradually overwhelmed and, with the Moroccans' morale on the verge of collapse, on 9 October the order came to break out of the valley. Only a handful of legionnaires and a number of terrified Moroccan soldiers managed to escape from the horrific few hours of fighting that ensued. The disaster was compounded shortly afterwards when the fleeing Moroccans encountered the approaching column from Cao Bang, where their fear speedily infected the Moroccan troops of that unit.

At that moment the Viet Minh attacked the main column. The result was a massacre on a grand scale, one of the worst military defeats in French colonial history. By 17 October the Viet Minh were left in undisputed control of the border region and the principal supply routes into Tonkin from China. In the fighting about and between Dong Khe and Cao Bang the French lost about 7,000 men dead or as prisoners. The force had originally numbered about 10,000 in all. The recently formed 1 BEP was almost annihilated, and only about a dozen of its paratroopers survived. These men eventually reached the safety of the main French positions to the south, led by the battalion's adjutant, Captain Pierre Jeanpierre.[98]

Quite apart from the huge number of French casualties, the weapons and equipment lost were quickly turned against their former owners. The Viet

Minh haul included thirteen artillery pieces, 125 mortars, more than 900 machine guns, 1,200 automatic rifles, 8,000 rifles and about 450 trucks. In Paris and throughout France the government and people were appalled by the disaster. Without hesitation a law was passed to prevent the hundreds of young Frenchmen conscripted for military service each year from being sent to areas in which military operations were taking place, or to take part in them other than in time of war. This new law provided the communists with an important propaganda weapon, as they were able to cite the French government's disregard for the lives of its North African colonial troops and those of the Foreign Legion as opposed to those of true European Frenchman. As 1950 drew to a close, the morale of the population in France and its supporters in Indochina reached its lowest point since the return of French troops to Indochina.

An Expanding Conflict: January 1951 to November 1953

Giap's resounding victory in north-east Tonkin nevertheless bred a degree of over-confidence and incaution on the part of the communists, as the Viet Minh decided to advance their strategic campaign and engage the French on conventional battlefields. This decision coincided with the arrival of General Jean de Lattre de Tassigny as the French High Commissioner and Commander-in-Chief in Indochina. He was a highly capable commander who concentrated his forces – even at the expense of security in the southern parts of Vietnam in Annam and Cochin China. From January to June 1951 he used the superior French technology, firepower and control of the air to inflict significant losses on the Viet Minh during their new offensive in the Red River Delta. De Tassigny devised a strategy of creating fortified bases deep within Viet Minh territory, which Giap was then forced to attack. This brought the Viet Minh into killing areas for French artillery and air power, where the communists incurred substantial losses at little or no cost to the French garrisons. However, this modern form of attrition warfare demanded large commitments of manpower – by the communists to replace their casualties and by the French to maintain the momentum of their strategy. And whereas Giap more or less managed to make good his losses, the manpower requirements that de Tassigny passed back to Paris were hardly addressed, and only a fraction of the reinforcements he needed actually arrived in Indochina. Nevertheless, the operational concept developed by de Tassigny continued to appeal to the French high command, and its later application in 1953 precipitated the major battle that finally ended the French presence in Indochina.

On the first occasion that Giap's forces clashed with de Tassigny's, at Vinh Yen from 13 to 17 January 1951, two communist divisions lost up to 9,000 dead, 8,000 wounded, with 600 men taken prisoner. They had been opposed by only 8,000 French soldiers, but these troops were supported by a generous allocation of air power, and the liberal use of napalm destroyed the concentrated Viet Minh units. Subsequently, the communists also suffered serious defeats at Mao Khe in March, where Giap lost 3,000 casualties in three days, and at the Day River (or Phat Diem) in June, where they sustained a further 11,000 casualties. Meanwhile, General de Tassigny protected the Tonkinese capital, Hanoi, with a chain of forts (the de Lattre Line) and maintained a formidable mobile reserve, comprised of paratroops, armoured and amphibious units and vehicle-borne infantry, to deal with any attack against the French outposts.

However, de Tassigny's successes and improving morale likewise bred over-confidence on the French side. In mid-November 1951, a major operation began, designed to seize the initiative from the communists and gradually destroy their bases and infrastructure; but this was abandoned the following February, when a garrison of paratroops and other units at the newly established base of Hoa Binh was forced to withdraw in the face of a strong Viet Minh force which had cut off the base. By then, however, General Raoul Salan had replaced de Tassigny as French commander in Indochina, and it soon became obvious that the lessons of Cao Bang-Lang Son and Hoa Binh – the dangers of over-extended lines of communication, isolated garrisons, inadequate reserves, a dependence upon air support and (above all else) underestimating the enemy – had not been well learned.

The next blow came as soon as the 1952 monsoon ended in October. It fell on the French positions at the Nghia Lo ridge, astride the ground between the Red River and the Black River to the north-west of Hanoi. Here, the communist 308th, 312th and 316th Divisions sought to destroy the French outposts at Nghia Lo and Gia Hoi, prior to a major assault on the strategically vital Red River Delta. First, the 308th Division overwhelmed the Nghia Lo garrison, from which onslaught only a few survivors escaped, covered by a near-suicidal – but nonetheless effective – parachute assault. Giap's forces enjoyed similar successes elsewhere, and by 17 October they controlled the important Nghia Lo ridge.

An attempt by General Salan to turn the communist gains to his advantage failed, when a counter-offensive (Operation Lorraine) by some 30,000 soldiers in armoured, amphibious, engineer and parachute units, became over-extended. Giap managed to draw the French ever further into the jungle and despite the capture by the French of considerable quantities of Viet Minh matériel – including a number of Soviet-supplied trucks – the French high command ordered a withdrawal on 14 November. A familiar pattern then emerged as the French suffered some 1,200 casualties between 17 and 24

November, during their withdrawal along roads and tracks constantly ambushed from the dense jungle and hills that surrounded them. Salan's Operation Lorraine proved to be a costly venture for the French and there was a real need for a new strategic initiative.

Throughout the war, despite the French military presence along the length and breadth of Indochina, the main focus of conflict was always in Tonkin and northern Vietnam, specifically in the border areas and the Red River Delta to the south of Hanoi. In late 1952 the French achieved a success reminiscent of those of early 1951, when a well-defended base at Na San, close to the border with Laos, not only defeated all of Giap's attempts to overrun it, but also compelled the Viet Minh to concentrate their forces and so made them vulnerable to air attack.[99] The communists suffered enormous losses, and there was an immediate revival of interest in the concept of forcing a conventional battle on ground of French choosing, so that the full weight of French fire and air power could be brought to bear.

Coincidentally, the whole focus of the French campaign had moved towards the Vietnam–Laos border during the early months of 1953, when the Viet Minh invaded Laos that April. By May the French had deployed soldiers to new forward bases within Laos at Luang Prabang, Muong Khoua and on the Plaine des Jarres, with the task of interdicting the invading Viet Minh units. In fact, Giap's intentions were to seize the Laotian opium crop and to tie in his operations with those of the communist Pathet Lao guerrillas in furtherance of his long-term strategy; but in practice it was the French response to this invasion that initiated the chain of events which decided the outcome of the war just a year later.

Soon after Giap's incursion into Laos, General Henri Navarre replaced Salan as French commander in Indochina. Despite having 190,000 men at his disposal, and a potentially useful Vietnamese national army in embryo, General Navarre's forces, with their countrywide security remit, were overstretched even before their deployment into Laos and they were now more thinly spread than ever. As 1953 drew on, General Navarre reviewed his options for the future conduct of the campaign. His considerations were driven by four imperatives. There was the need to create and maintain a viable mobile reserve, the need to isolate the Viet Minh forces in Laos, the need to maintain control of the Red River Delta – the key to Hanoi and the vital port of Haiphong – and finally the need to reduce the overall level or scale of French static commitments throughout Indochina. The last of these was dependent upon compelling the Viet Minh to concentrate their forces into fewer areas. This in turn meant that the French had to seize the operational initiative in order to drive strategic events. Navarre was also under constant political pressure from Paris to create 'military conditions favourable to a resolution of the conflict' and so end what had become, within France, an unpopular foreign war. Central to these considerations was the fact of the Viet Minh presence in Laos, and their consequent need to move regularly between Tonkin and Laos.

Inevitably, therefore, General Navarre's eyes were drawn towards the main Viet Minh transit route into Laos: from Tam Giao in Tonkin to the Nam Ou valley in Laos. This was the route that the communist 312th Division had followed during its invasion of Laos in April. It had crossed into Laos just after passing through a large village and airstrip sited in the middle of a wide, flat valley surrounded by the jungle-clad hills of the T'ai mountains. The name of this otherwise unremarkable village was soon destined to be as familiar to the citizens of France as that of Paris, Calais or Marseilles. It was called Dien Bien Phu.[100]

Dien Bien Phu: November 1953 to May 1954

With the recent success at Na San firmly in mind, Navarre decided to commit twelve (subsequently reinforced to seventeen) battalions – the bulk of the French Union forces in Tonkin, more than 15,000 men – to a two-phase oper- ation that would initially enable the evacuation of the isolated French-led T'ai garrison at Lai Chau to the north of Dien Bien Phu. Then, once the evacuees had successfully reached the base at Dien Bien Phu, this base would provide a pivot about which French patrols would interdict Viet Minh movement into and from Laos. Ultimately, it was reasoned, General Giap would be induced to attack Dien Bien Phu, and at that stage the full power of the French air force and artillery would be deployed against the Viet Minh. The evacuation of Lai Chau was titled Operation Pollux, while that to seize and hold Dien Bien Phu was called Operation Castor. The operation depended upon a correct French assessment of Viet Minh military capability and intentions, as well as the unin- terrupted availability of French air power.

Between Friday, 20 and Sunday, 22 November 1953 six French Union parachute battalions jumped into the valley of Dien Bien Phu. After a brief but intense battle with a force of Viet Minh regular troops of People's Army Inde- pendent Regiment No 148, which had been undergoing training in the broad valley, the Dien Bien Phu base was secured.

The Dien Bien Phu valley was some twelve miles long and eight miles wide, and it was about 150 miles from Hanoi by air. In addition to the main village of Muong Thanh at its centre, a few smaller hamlets and isolated dwellings were scattered along it. Although the village straddled one of the main east–west road routes into Laos, Dien Bien Phu's road links south to Hanoi and the Red River Delta were tortuous, and in many cases virtually non-exis- tent. Much of the valley, which was well served by the meandering river Nam Youm, was extensively cultivated with rice paddies and other subsistence farming supporting the indigenous population. Finally, there was a military airstrip at Dien Bien Phu, adjacent to the village of Muong Thanh. Ground suitable for improvement as a second airstrip lay further to the south.

Having gained control of the main valley, the paratroops quickly extended their security perimeter by dispatching patrols into the surrounding hills. They then set about fortifying the new base, as well as preparing the main airstrip for extensive use. Thus far, all was going more or less according to plan. But in late November Giap reacted: he moved the 312th – already very familiar with that area – and 308th Divisions towards Dien Bien Phu. Then, a month later, the withdrawal of the T'ai units from Lai Chau to Dien Bien Phu – the success of which was critical to the plan for the future use of the base – turned into a catastrophe when, soon after setting out, the retreating columns were ambushed and destroyed. This defeat negated the original concept of Operations Castor and Pollux and (with two Viet Minh divisions closing on Dien Bien Phu) General Navarre made the historic but controversial decision that this was the time and place at which to fight the defining battle of the war. The ground was of his choice and (in the view of the high command) French technology and the superior fighting qualities of the French Union soldiers would quickly triumph over what was after all only a guerrilla army.

Thereafter, despite a very significant lack of engineer stores for the task, work to fortify the base proceeded apace, while at the same time the original garrison was reinforced by airlifts of thousands of troops. As 1953 drew to a close, the French dug ever deeper into their trenches, bunkers, underground hospital, command posts, gun and mortar emplacements, stores and a host of other constructions – all covered, wherever possible, by tons of earth and reinforced with logs. However, although the French were able to push patrols into the surrounding hills that overlooked the base on all sides, they still had neither the matériel nor the manpower to occupy and fortify these vantage points on a permanent basis. Also, the Viet Minh presence[101] about Dien Bien Phu was growing rapidly, and their ability to counter the French sorties was becoming ever more effective. Consequently, by mid-February 1954 the French had lost control of the hills that dominated their valley fortress. Nevertheless, within their trenches and bunkers, and under the protective umbrella of their warplanes, they remained confident. Even the fall of a first salvo of communist artillery shells on to their positions that month failed to dissuade the French that theirs would be the final victory. Neither the fact that the communists could bring down indirect artillery fire on to the airfield nor the garrison's increasingly troglodyte existence affected either the resolve of the commanders or of those they commanded.

Meanwhile, Giap had spent the weeks to mid-March achieving what the French intelligence assessments had considered impossible. Using the labour of some 75,000 pioneers he had moved more than 200 artillery guns – mainly 105mm calibre – into positions in the hills about Dien Bien Phu. These guns, together with storage for stocks of ammunition, were dug deep into the hillsides and were elaborately concealed from aerial view. Their lengthy journey to the valley under cover of darkness, along scarcely navigable jungle trails, had been carried out just as carefully. The key targets on which these guns were now ranged were the French command and control facilities and the two airstrips. To protect the communist artillery, a mass of anti-aircraft guns (many of which were operated by regular Chinese troops, who were by then no longer engaged in Korea), ringed the valley and protected the artillery emplacements. The core of the Viet Minh air defence artillery was the 367th Flak Regiment, which was equipped with thirty-six 37mm guns and a number of .50in calibre heavy machine-guns.

Indeed, direct aid to the Viet Minh from the PRC during 1953 included more than 700 artillery pieces and mortars of various types and calibres, 416 machine-guns, more than 6,000 small-arms, plus some eight million rounds of ammunition. The Chinese also provided the Viet Minh with landmines, explosives, and a wide range of support equipment, fuel, vehicles, uniforms and medical supplies. Aid also came from the Soviet Union, and in the final days of the siege of Dien Bien Phu a number of Soviet-made multi-barrel rocket launchers were added to the Viet Minh artillery.[102]

By the first week of March the French garrison was about 10,800 men strong. It included two parachute battalions,[103] three Algerian battalions, one Moroccan battalion, four legion battalions and two T'ai battalions. Its combat support included an engineer battalion, seven artillery batteries with a total of twenty-four 105mm guns, plus four 155 mm guns, a tank company with ten M-24 tanks, and a transport company. A squadron of six Bearcat fighter-bombers, plus a small number of artillery observation aircraft, were based at the main airstrip. This entire force was commanded by Colonel Christian de Castries, a former cavalry officer, who allegedly[104] named the several strong-points that comprised the Dien Bien Phu complex after his various mistresses. The main command post was based at the main village of Dien Bien Phu (or Muong Thanh), with Claudine to the south of it, Eliane to the east, Dominique to the north-east and Huguette to the west. Further away lay Anne-Marie, to the north-west of Huguette; Beatrice, a mile to the north-east; Gabrielle, two miles away to the north; and finally Isabelle, four miles to the south, at the second airstrip.

On 13 March a heavy, prolonged and very accurate artillery barrage descended upon Dien Bien Phu, as the Viet Minh began their battle to destroy the French garrison. The effects of this barrage were devastating and prepared the way for a series of concerted attacks. In just six days Beatrice and

Gabrielle were overwhelmed by massed infantry assaults and Anne-Marie was abandoned when the battalion of locally recruited troops based thereon deserted and melted away into the surrounding hills and jungle – victims of a most effective communist propaganda campaign. Two French Union battalions (one Foreign Legion and one Algerian) were virtually annihilated while a third had literally disappeared. Most significantly, however, the loss of this high ground so close to the main position at Dien Bien Phu enabled the Viet Minh to bring accurate artillery fire to bear on the main airstrip virtually at any time. The runway was forced to close, although a last evacuation of casualties by air was achieved by a single transport aircraft on 27 March. The garrison's six fighter-bombers were all destroyed on the ground. Thereafter, the only way into Dien Bien Phu was by parachute, and the only way out was through the hills controlled by more than 40,000 Viet Minh troops. The French situation was precarious.

In spite of this, Giap's forces had also suffered heavy losses during the opening days of the battle, and after the fall of Anne-Marie no more major ground assaults were launched for almost two weeks. But the artillery fire was incessant; three days after the airstrip closed the main transit road within Dien Bien Phu also became unusable. Meanwhile, the air force was unable to locate and strike the communist artillery positions; nor was the French artillery able to engage these guns. In fact, during the whole period of the siege, sixty-two aircraft were destroyed and 167 badly damaged by anti-aircraft fire. On 15 March the French artillery commander, Colonel Charles Piroth, who had confidently predicted before the battle that no communist artillery shells would hit Dien Bien Phu, went to his bunker and killed himself with a hand grenade.

On 29 March the first monsoon rains began to fall, accompanied by low cloud that further disrupted the already problematical parachute supply drops. Much of the matériel (probably about thirty per cent in total) that was dispatched fell well outside the defensive perimeter, directly into the hands of the Viet Minh. Meanwhile, floods of water swept into the underground passages, bunkers and trenches of the French defenders, making their existence one of continuous danger from the shellfire above ground and of unrelieved misery underground, due to the sea of red mud in which they now lived. During the second half of March three more parachute battalions were dropped into Dien Bien Phu, which raised the garrison's strength almost to its final total of just over 15,000.

On 30 March the Viet Minh resumed their assault with a full-scale attack on Isabelle, which was defended desperately by Algerian troops. Subsequent attacks were launched against Huguette on 1 April and against Isabelle and Eliane on 3 April. Despite wave after wave of assaults, the French positions held, and cost the communists some 2,500 casualties. Even the Viet Minh could not absorb casualties on this scale, and so – supported by more than three hundred 105mm guns – the Viet Minh adopted the siege tactics of an earlier age by digging oblique trenches and tunnels towards the French strongpoints, until an assault could be launched with minimal exposure to French fire in the open. Giap also took the time to reinforce his divisions. Indeed, in several Viet Minh units, their enormous casualties had affected the morale and confidence of even the most committed communist soldiers and there was even some talk of mutiny. But by the end of April these losses had been made up, and the encircling Viet Minh at that stage numbered more than 50,000 men.

On 9 and 10 April 2 BEP jumped into Dien Bien Phu to join its sister battalion, which had been in the valley since the very beginning of Operation Castor on 21 November. The paratroops were initially used as a general reserve force, although as the perimeter contracted and the separate strong-points became ever more isolated, these soldiers were increasingly tied into the static defence, and detailed to carry out counter-attacks at specific locations. In addition to the legion paratroops, hundreds of volunteers from 3 REI, 5 REI and a number of other French units not committed to the battle, parachuted in to reinforce their comrades. For many of these volunteers it was their first parachute jump. Among those items that were successfully dropped into the garrison on 15 April was an authorisation for the promotion of several of its principal commanders, including that of Colonel de Castries to brigadier-general ('one star') rank.[105]

Despite the futility of the defence of Dien Bien Phu, it nevertheless demonstrated the courage, tenacious fighting ability and dedication of these regular French soldiers and their North African comrades. Many later observed that these gallant men had deserved neither the inadequate political leadership in Paris nor the less than professional military leadership in Hanoi that had sent them to Dien Bien Phu.

On 22 April the full force of the tropical monsoon deluged the valley, when many of the already waterlogged emplacements were completely flooded.

For almost six months, apart from some recent moves to convene an international conference in Geneva to resolve the conflict, the events at Dien Bien Phu had thus far been an exclusively French affair (apart from some supply aircraft reportedly flown by American civilian pilots). However, on 23 April the French Under-Secretary of State André Bougenot, in the presence of Premier Laniel, approached Washington to seek US air support against the communist forces. Somewhat bizarrely, he suggested that the United States 'could commit its naval aircraft to the battle of Dien Bien Phu without risking American prestige or committing an act of belligerency by placing such aircraft, painted with French insignia and construed as part of the French Foreign Legion, under nominal French command for an isolated action consisting of air strikes lasting two or three days'.

The proposed attack was named Operation Vulture, and it received serious consideration in Washington, notwithstanding an assessment that it would provoke direct armed intervention by the PRC, which would in turn necessitate the direct air attack of targets in China, to include the use of atomic weapons. The US navy and air force both favoured intervention, whilst the army did not. However, although the concept was developed by an Anglo-US planning team, the insistence of the US Congress that Britain would have to participate fully in the operation and that France would subsequently be required to grant Indochina full independence, were conditions unacceptable to the British and French governments. In addition, British Prime Minister Winston Churchill expressed his concern that, by reason of the Sino-Soviet pact, a war with China would inevitably involve the Soviet Union. This in turn could result in a Soviet nuclear attack on US air bases in Britain. It was a view that echoed many of those expressed during the recently ended Korean conflict, and added substance to the argument that communism should be contained by carefully controlled limited wars, rather than attempting its defeat by waging total war. In any event, as the Operation Vulture conditions imposed by the US Congress could not be agreed, President Eisenhower ruled against US military support for the French, and the fate of the garrison at Dien Bien Phu was sealed, together with that of French Indochina.[106]

Despite a final drop by a French parachute battalion on 2 May – into the midst of Giap's main assault, which had begun the previous day – the end of the battle was by then imminent. The 308th Division closed in from the west, the 312th from the east and the 316th from the south-east. To the south, the 304th Division attacked the long-isolated strongpoint at Isabelle. During seven days of almost indescribably bitter and desperate fighting one after another of the French strongpoints succumbed to the human tide that swept up to and over them. In most cases the French had exhausted their ammunition, and there was no possibility of further replenishment. On 7 May Huguette, Eliane and the central area of the devastated fortress fell, and at 17.30 hours General de Castries ordered a ceasefire and emerged from his command bunker to surrender his beleaguered command to soldiers of the Viet Minh 308th Division who had fought their way to the very entrance of the bunker. The next day, 8 May 1954, the defenders of Isabelle submitted to the 304th Division and the surrender of Dien Bien Phu was complete. The ceasefire declared at Dien Bien Phu was extended throughout Indochina by General Navarre.

The destruction at Dien Bien Phu of some of the best infantry and parachute units of the French army cost General Giap's divisions in the order of 23,000 casualties, many from his best-trained regular units. However, France had already lost 2,293 dead and 5,134 men wounded over the six months since November 1953, and now the 11,000 men who had survived and surrendered on 8 May began a march of several hundred kilometres to the Viet Minh prison camps. For most, repatriation came many months later, following the agreement signed at Geneva on 21 July which ended the war and French imperial aspirations in Indochina for ever. In accordance with this agreement, the last French troops in Indochina departed Hanoi on 9 October 1954. However, of the several thousand French soldiers – many with severe wounds – who set out on the punishing march northward after Dien Bien Phu, very many had already died of their wounds, illness, malnutrition or ill-treatment en route to the camps or once they reached them, and so never returned home from Indochina.

End of an Empire

In France the political consequences of the war were traumatic, and Laniel's administration did not long survive. In 1958 the French Fourth Republic also fell, albeit that Indochina was but one of the several contributory issues and failures that led to this.

But while governments may come and go, and defeated or discredited politicians regularly reinvent themselves to fight (metaphorically) another day, this option was not available to the almost 82,000 French, French Foreign Legion, North and West African and Vietnamese national army soldiers who had died during nine years of fighting in Indochina. Although the communists emerged as the victors they too had paid a very heavy price for their success; some estimated their dead as high as 150,000 over the same period. Nevertheless, Ho and Giap could still be well satisfied. Laos, Cambodia and North and South Vietnam were now independent states, with the boundary between communist North Vietnam and the non-communist Republic of South Vietnam set by the Geneva conference at the 17th parallel. Apart from the fact that part of Vietnam was still under non-communist control, the two leaders and their supporters in Beijing and Moscow could reflect with considerable satisfaction on the campaign that the Viet Minh had conducted since the defeat of the Japanese in 1945.

So why was the French defeat in Indochina so comprehensive and – for many French political and military leaders – so unexpected? The reasons for the catastrophe of 1954 were political and military. At the outset, the French government of 1945 had faced the formidable task of healing a divided nation following the Vichy years and restoring the former power and glory of France. Part of this process involved the reacquisition and retention of the pre-1940

French empire overseas. However, France was no longer a great power, and its leaders seriously misjudged the mood of the post-war world – that of the United States in particular – with regard to European imperialism and colonialism. Many Americans would argue that these 'isms' of the pre-1939 world had already drawn the United States into two world wars. If France had declared in 1945 an intention simply to stabilise its possessions in Indochina prior to granting them full independence, Paris might have undercut the communist and nationalist coalition and weakened the nationalist cause, while even attracting the latter's active co-operation. Such a policy could also have been looked upon favourably by the United States if and when France had requested American support to achieve it.

But in post-invasion, post-Vichy, post-occupation and post-war France, popular attitudes were such that nothing short of a return to the status quo ante bellum was acceptable. Therefore, the government of the Fourth Republic was determined to restore French dominance in Indochina, rather than to follow the traditional republican ideals of *liberté*, *égalité*, *fraternité*. It followed that the so-called independence talks conducted from 1947 to 1950, based upon the return of the Emperor Bao Dai as a puppet ruler, were no more than a rather transparent device to maintain French dominance of the region.

The adoption of a more enlightened French policy for Indochina might well have produced a satisfactory settlement before 1953; thereby pre-empting the significant support provided to the Viet Minh by China after the armistice in Korea. In such circumstances, it is also less likely that the Soviets would have chosen to embrace Ho Chi Minh's cause so wholeheartedly, especially if the war had ended before the Soviet Union's successful atom bomb test on 23 September 1949, when Stalin's attention was also focused primarily upon Europe.

After the Cao Bang disaster, however, the French people viewed the war in Indochina with an ambivalence that combined concern with something amounting to denial. While there were increasingly strident protests and calls from the left for an end to the war and for France to grant Indochina its independence, there was never a readily identifiable mass protest movement against hostilities. Part of the reason for this was that much of the war was being fought for France by foreigners. These included the French Foreign Legion, units of the Armeé d'Afrique (the Algerians and Moroccans) and the pro-French Vietnamese national army, plus various Indochinese indigenous tribes. Also, only regular French soldiers and volunteers were permitted to serve in Indochina. Meanwhile, had the French catastrophe at Cao Bang not happened, with the consequent block on ordinary French conscripts serving in Indochina, the views and reactions of the French public to the war might have been very different. But, with a conflict that was taking place far away, being fought exclusively by professional soldiers and foreigners, the French people allowed themselves the luxury of hoping for a victory and the restoration of French glory, while simultaneously distancing themselves from the actualities of the war; and in some cases even indicating an abhorrence of it and those who fought it on their behalf. This last was exemplified by the fact that 'none of the casualties from Indochina could be taken across Paris because of possible left-wing demonstrations' and a decision had also been taken 'when blood was being donated, to specify that it would not be used for the casualties of Indochina'.[107]

The conscription decision denied the high command in Hanoi the manpower they needed to conduct a successful counter-revolutionary campaign. As a result, the French commanders in Indochina received only a fraction of the men and matériel that they required to accomplish their mission, and this was a deciding factor in what became a war of attrition. Giap fully appreciated that this was so when he stated in late 1950: 'The enemy will pass slowly from the offensive to the defensive. The blitzkrieg will transform itself into a war of long duration. Thus, the enemy will be caught in a dilemma: he has to drag out the war in order to win it and does not possess, on the other hand, the psychological and political means to fight a long drawn-out war.'[108] Giap's words later proved just as prophetic during the next conflict in South-east Asia.

Even if they had received the necessary resources, however, the conduct of the French military campaign still left a great deal to be desired. The history of France and her empire is littered with the divergence between the valiant efforts of her soldiers and the professional shortcomings of those who commanded them at the highest level. In Indochina much of the potentially formidable French combat capability was once again often misdirected or squandered by political and military ineptitude at the operational and strategic levels.

From the very beginning, the French made the fundamental error of assessing incorrectly the nature and capability of the Viet Minh. Consequently, they applied traditional concepts of conventional war-fighting – where the destruction of the enemy was the overriding priority – to deal with the much more complex nature of a revolutionary war. This initial misconception was symptomatic of the overall failure of French strategic intelligence in South-east Asia throughout the conflict.

Stemming from such a major error, it was perhaps no surprise that there was such a lack of intelligence, or of the correct interpretation of the intelligence that was available, prior to and during the battle of Dien Bien Phu.[109]

The failure of the artillery assessment and the totally inadequate level of combat engineer support were striking examples of this, and they were major contributors to the French defeat. At the same time, the correlation between events on the battlefield and the political and information management perspectives were not understood. Therefore, the French military campaign was conducted more or less in isolation from these complementary activities. It followed that the French never really addressed, and so could not reasonably have hoped to win, the 'hearts and minds' campaign in Indochina. However, Ho Chi Minh and Giap understood very well the vital importance of these adjuncts to the military campaign.

Throughout the war, the communists sought and generally gained (either by reward or by coercion) the support of the people of northern Indochina. They were therefore able to live and operate within the civilian community, whereas the French were constrained to operate from their bases, and thus were never able to reverse the support of the people for the Viet Minh. If de Tassigny had been given the resources to do so, he might have been able to adopt a similar scheme of 'new villages' to that which Briggs and Templer were using in Malaya at about the same time. However, in Malaya the aim of this concept was to remove and so deny support to the Chinese terrorists, whereas the French approach was to create locations at or from which the Viet Minh could be destroyed. It would be wrong, therefore, to infer close parallels between the new villages of Malaya and new forts of Indochina. The latter, with the implied expectation of combat, also required considerable amounts of manpower both at the fort and to reinforce it when the attack came. It was therefore an inappropriate strategy for a force that always suffered from severe manpower constraints throughout the war. Moreover, when reaction forces or reinforcements did move to assist a beleaguered fort, they usually travelled either by vehicle on the relatively few roads or (when the boats or amphibious vehicles were available) by river, thereby falling prey to Viet Minh ambushes.

Finally, the French relied heavily upon the ready availability of air power to support the ground forces. Their several successes against the Viet Minh in 1951 and at the end of 1952 encouraged the view that this was the panacea that would win the war. Nowhere was the fallacy of this more evident than at Dien Bien Phu, by which time Giap had correctly assessed the danger posed to his forces from the air, and had accordingly developed the necessary anti-aircraft defence to counter this threat.[110]

The ordinary French Union soldiers, including their comrades of the Vietnamese national army, the Foreign Legion and the Armeé d'Afrique, deserved a better cause to fight for and better leadership in Indochina. Yet in spite of that, their conduct during the conflict was remarkable, and their fighting abilities at unit level were almost without exception in the best traditions of the great days of the old French army. Although the war in Indochina was an inglorious period in terms of French political and international history, for many of the regiments that fought there it provided an opportunity to build upon their already proud history and record of selfless dedication to France. But in Indochina many of these men found that once again their destiny was being determined by a government and political agenda that did not measure up to the standards of honour, duty and discipline of an army that became increasingly decoupled from Paris – both geographically and philosophically. In Algeria, in 1961, a revolt by some of the most illustrious units of the French army was to demonstrate the true extent of this deteriorating situation.

By the close of 1954, however, the French struggle in Vietnam, Laos and Cambodia was at an end, while at Geneva the foundations for what is often termed the 'Second Indochina War' were already being laid. For Ho Chi Minh and General Giap this new conflict was merely the next phase in their struggle to impose communism upon the whole of Vietnam.

Geneva, 1954: The Seeds of Future Conflict

The settlement that was agreed at Geneva bears special mention, as it set the stage for the impending US involvement in Vietnam, which in turn had wider implications for the development of the Cold War.

In addition to the representatives of the Indochinese nations involved, all of the principal Cold War players attended the Geneva Conference: the United States, the Soviet Union, Great Britain and France, together with the PRC. The Geneva Agreement established a ceasefire line along the 17th parallel, and a three hundred-day period during which free movement was to take place across what subsequently became the border and demilitarised zone. Canada, Poland and India provided members for an International Supervisory Commission to oversee the ceasefire, and the Viet Minh forces still in Laos and Cambodia were required to leave those countries. Finally, free elections to reunite North and South Vietnam were scheduled for 1956. Much of the package was strikingly similar in concept to that applied in Korea the previous year. Given the clear ideological split between North Vietnam and South Vietnam, underlined by the movement of some 900,000 civilians to the South and almost 100,000 Viet Minh and communist supporters and sympathisers to the North during the free movement period, the idea of early reunification was somewhat optimistic. During the years that followed, an alignment of the United States with South Vietnam and of communist China and the Soviet Union with North Vietnam took place. Meanwhile, some 1,000 Viet Minh soldiers remained in South Vietnam, in flagrant contravention of the Geneva Agreement.

In the North, with its population already several millions greater than that of the South, Ho Chi Minh's newly legitimised regime received extensive aid from the communist bloc states, although Ho shunned total reliance upon this assistance and strove for an independent, self-sufficient country, with a primarily agricultural economy sustained by a basic but effective industrial base. The programme of land reform that this policy involved was badly mismanaged at first, but Ho's leadership and skills as a politician, propagandist and organiser enabled him to create a viable state within a few years.

Meanwhile, in South Vietnam, Ngo Dinh Diem, a genuinely independent nationalist and potentially a strong leader for the new country, was selected by Emperor Bao Dai as premier. Although he enjoyed, in theory, total authority over all the apparatus of government and the military, Diem found himself at the head of a divided and disparate country, in which the legacies of the recent war were disunity, discord and corruption – together with an influx of 900,000 landless immigrants and a focus for future armed resistance in the form of 1,000 Viet Minh guerrillas. The military forces and groups within the country were neither under a unified national command nor had they a single political and ideological vision for South Vietnam. As early as 1955 it was clear that the way ahead for Vietnam would not be easy.

In the North the Geneva settlement had afforded Ho Chi Minh and Giap time to consolidate and regroup their forces, and events in the South indicated to the Hanoi leadership that the next part of their war should begin soon. Despite many months of political turbulence and some violence in South Vietnam, in 1955 Diem achieved Emperor Bao Dai's approval to establish the Republic of Vietnam, with Diem as its first president. To his credit he had already managed to suppress the main areas of dissent and to stabilise and generally pacify South Vietnam. In parallel with this, aid and military support – including military advisers – for the armed forces poured into what was rapidly becoming a prosperous and modern industrialised country. The new republic was recognised by Western governments, but Cold War imperatives prevented separate UN membership of the UN for North and South Vietnam, due to the demise of a similar proposal for West and East Germany.

With some irony, it was another German issue that subsequently enabled Diem to forgo a requirement to conduct elections in 1956. On that occasion (despite its backing for the Hanoi regime, and the fact that the greater population in the North would probably have enabled a communist-dominated, reunified Vietnam) the Soviet Union refused to permit these to take place, as free elections in Vietnam would have provided a precedent for free elections in both East Germany and Korea, neither of which were acceptable to Moscow or Beijing at that time.

INDOCHINA AND VIETNAM, 1954-75

America's War: Origins, Nature and Perceptions

Modern wars are fought on many levels, with a multiplicity of elements. Apart from the more easily discerned conventional military operations, the Cold War conflicts increasingly included aspects of political, psychological, moral, propaganda, civil affairs, nation-building, humanitarian and media operations as adjuncts to the primary business of war-fighting. Indeed, since the end of the Cold War, Western military commanders might be forgiven for thinking that their main raison d'être – the destruction of the enemy – had been almost entirely supplanted by the imperative to place humanitarian needs, the observance of peacetime legal niceties and the presentation of a favourable image to the international media, at the top of their list of priorities. The transition from the way of war in 1939–45 to that which today's armed forces are constrained to conduct was not sudden, and Korea marked the start point of this process.

It is in the West, due to its open and democratic nature, that the impact of this change has been most marked. For the United States, the process began in Korea and continued throughout America's subsequent lengthy involvement in Vietnam, where the intense fighting in South-east Asia was conducted against a backdrop of massive social change and new attitudes to patriotism, war and national identity both in America and in Europe. These changes were fundamental and intensely painful, not least because they were often ill-directed and blatantly, but most cleverly, exploited by communist propagandists. They were considerably assisted – whether unwittingly or not – by a technologically sophisticated and commercially competitive Western media that, with the burgeoning emphasis on photo-journalism and television reporting of the 1960s and 1970s, was particularly susceptible to editorial pressures to provide spectacular, striking and violent visual images of the war.

In 1954, with the eyes of the world upon it, France lost its war in Indochina and suffered the political consequences. Nevertheless, the American leadership in Washington were confident that – if the United States were to become involved in Vietnam – it would not experience a similar defeat. In fact, that assessment of the late 1950s was generally accurate, for the United States did indeed win its military campaign (but not the war) in Vietnam. However, America's long and bitter struggle was never simply about victory on the battlefield. It was about public perceptions of military success and failure. It was about the way in which those politicians who had

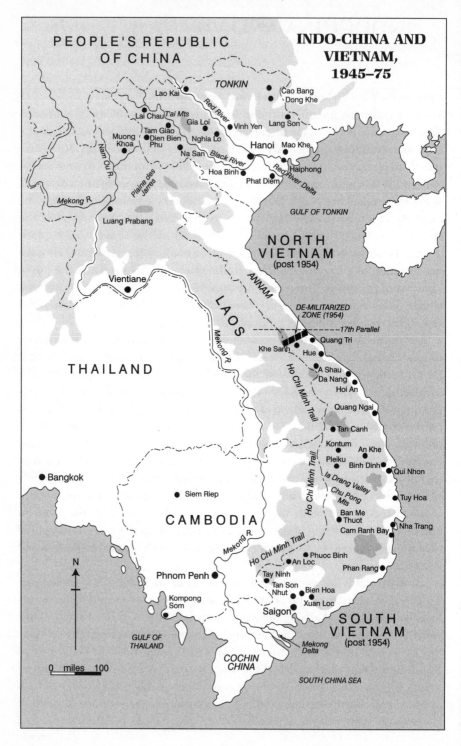

INDO-CHINA AND
VIETNAM,
1945–75

PEOPLE'S REPUBLIC
OF CHINA

TONKIN

Lao Kai

Cao Bang
Dong Khe

Lai Chau *Tai Mts*
Gia Loi
Vinh Yen
Lang Son

Tam Giao
Muong
Khoa
Dien Bien
Phu
Nghia Lo

Red River

Hanoi
Mao Khe

Na San
Black River

Nam Ou R.

Hoa Binh
Haiphong

Red River Delta

Phat Diem

*Plaine des
Jarres*

Mekong R.

GULF OF TONKIN

Luang Prabang

NORTH
VIETNAM
(post 1954)

Vientiane

ANNAM

LAOS

DE-MILITARIZED
ZONE (1954)

17th Parallel

THAILAND

Mekong R.

Quang Tri

Khe Sanh
Hue

Ho Chi Minh Trail

A Shau
Da Nang
Hoi An

Quang Ngai

Tan Canh

Kontum
An Khe
Pleiku
Binh Dinh
Qui Nhon

Bangkok

Ia Drang Valley

Siem Riep

Chu Pong
Mts

Tuy Hoa

CAMBODIA

Ho Chi Minh Trail

Ban Me
Thuot
Nha Trang

Cam Ranh Bay

Mekong R.

N

Ho Chi Minh Trail

Phuoc Binh
An Loc

Phan Rang

Tay Ninh

Phnom Penh

Tan Son
Nhut
Bien Hoa

Kompong
Som

Xuan Loc

Saigon

SOUTH
VIETNAM
(post 1954)

0   miles   100

GULF OF
THAILAND

*Mekong
Delta*

COCHIN
CHINA

SOUTH CHINA SEA

committed the troops to the war subsequently constrained the military commanders charged with conducting it. But above all, it was about the presentation and visual impact of the Vietnam War on several million American television screens each day. Vietnam was truly the first of the media wars and the power of the CNN factor could not be ignored by military commanders and politicians alike.

An unconstrained Western media enjoyed the freedom to photograph and report in every detail such incidents as the massacre of some 347 civilians by a platoon of young soldiers from C Company, 1st Battalion 20th US Infantry Regiment – a unit of the 23rd US Infantry Division ('Americal'), at the hamlet of My Lai near Quang Ngai on 16 March 1968. However, it failed (and would in any case have been prevented by the communists) similarly to report many of the acts of mass-murder carried out by the Viet Cong and North Vietnamese Army (NVA): the murder of more than 5,000 civilians at Hue in 1968 was but one such example of this. All wars are invariably unpleasant, usually horrific, and inevitably involve acts by both sides that cannot and should not be judged under the normal standards of peacetime behaviour. In any event, by its scale and inhumanity, the violence inflicted on non-combatants by the communists as a planned part of their ideological and terror campaigns far surpassed the extent of death and destruction that the US forces visited incidentally upon the civilian population of Vietnam and Indochina. In Vietnam, a Western media that might have believed it was reporting the war independently, in practice provided a powerful weapon for the communists. The increasing disenchantment of the American public during the Korean War had been duly noted in Hanoi, Beijing and Moscow, and the resultant communist information campaign during the Vietnam War ultimately proved to be a much more potent weapon than any of the less subtle weaponry deployed by either side.

Thus it was that even at the moment of one of their greatest military successes – the defeat of the communist 1968 Tet offensive, when the Viet Cong were finally destroyed as a fighting force – misreporting by the Western media transformed an operational victory into a strategic defeat, and thus paved the way for the United States to abandon South Vietnam. This in turn condemned that country to oblivion and its people to a precarious future under an oppressive communist regime.

So how did the United States become embroiled in this conflict? And why did this war divide the American nation and change the foreign policy of America for ever; as well as dealing the US armed forces – the army in particular – a blow to their prestige and morale from which America has still not entirely recovered, even though it is almost thirty years since the last US combat soldier left the former Republic of South Vietnam?

When Ho Chi Minh accepted under the terms of the Geneva Agreement that the border between North and South Vietnam should be set at the 17th parallel he did so confident in his belief that the South would soon implode and enable him to achieve his final goal of a communist-dominated Vietnam. He knew that this would necessarily mean the enforced subjugation of the South, as the centres of communism in Indochina – Tonkin and northern Annam – were regarded as foreign countries by the peoples of central and southern Annam and Cochin China. However, as the Diem regime in Saigon presided over an increasingly prosperous Republic of South Vietnam, Ho Chi Minh realised that he would after all need to resume the armed struggle in order to destabilise and subdue the South. Although this might bring the North Vietnamese into direct conflict with the United States, Ho and Giap understood the vulnerabilities of the Western nations only too well. They knew that neither significant casualties nor the prospect of a potentially open-ended war would have an effect upon the population of North Vietnam that even began to equal that in the United States. Accordingly, in 1959 the former Viet Minh – now called the Viet Cong (VC), or 'Vietnamese communists' – were recalled to arms (many were already in place in South Vietnam) and resumed the conflict that had paused briefly in 1954.

Apart from the difficulties imposed by long lines of communication and supply, the terrain and geography of South Vietnam suited guerrilla warfare particularly well. A chain of mountains and dense jungle ran the length of the country from the border almost all the way to Saigon, parallel to the border with Laos and Cambodia, before it swept into the southern plain, with the swamps and waterways of the Mekong delta to the south-west of Saigon. The western land border with Cambodia and Laos extended for about 600 miles, while to the east, beyond the coastal plain, lay the South China Sea. In the late 1950s, the regime in Hanoi enjoyed a considerable amount of active support within Cambodia from its ruler Prince Norodum Sihanouk and the Khmer Rouge, and in the border regions of Laos from the communist Pathet Lao. For any commander seeking to defend South Vietnam, these separate states of the former French Indochina posed major political, strategic and tactical problems. Most of the geopolitical advantages that the UN in Korea and the British in Malaya had enjoyed were not available to the South Vietnamese and their US ally.

First, for all practical purposes, the 600-mile land border was entirely porous, with two states on its other side that were either pro-Hanoi or at the very least pretended to neutrality. This allowed the communists to overcome their line of communication difficulties by the establishment of the 'Ho Chi Minh Trail' – a network of roads, tracks and trails that ran from Hanoi into Laos well to the north of the 17th parallel, and on into Cambodia, where it connected to the Sihanouk Trail north-west of Saigon. The Ho Chi Minh Trail followed the line of the border and had an infinite number of offshoots into South Vietnam. It began in the 1950s as a jungle trail via which – on foot or bicycles – most of the former Viet Minh were reinserted into South Vietnam. But by the end of America's involvement in the war in 1973 the trail had become a multi-lane road, with oil refuelling pipelines, metalled sections and substantial bridges. In Korea and Malaya respectively, the UN and the British had benefited from the maritime border about the land they were seeking to defend. Malaya did not flank a hostile power, and in Korea the only land boundary was that with North Korea, albeit by extension with communist China. The rationale behind General Matthew B. Ridgway's advice to the JCS in Washington in 1954, that US ground forces would encounter significant difficulties if they were committed in Vietnam, was understandable.

Meanwhile, US influence, based on its recent experience in Korea, was all too evident in the organisation and equipment of the armed forces of South Vietnam. After the French withdrawal, the United States built up the ARVN – the Army of the Republic of Vietnam – as a conventional force, supported by a small navy and air force. A formidable capability to deal with a conventional invasion had been developed, but not one suited to conducting a counter-revolutionary or counter-guerrilla war. In 1954 the defence forces of South Vietnam comprised an army of about 135,000 men, plus a polyglot organisation of civil guards, local village and hamlet defence units, and a national paramilitary police force: a grand total that exceeded 170,000. The bulk of the ARVN was organised into 10,000-man infantry divisions, equipped with the current range of US small-arms, infantry support weapons and field artillery. Consequently, by 1959 South Vietnam was well prepared to fight another Korea-style war, to defend the South against a conventional invasion, or even to stage another Dien Bien Phu; but it was ill prepared for the type of campaign that General Giap launched against it.

During 1957 the communists re-established their infrastructure in South Vietnam and carried out low-level operations and terrorism, characterised by assassinations, abductions, acts of sabotage, murders and the ambush of police and armed forces on the main roads. By the end of 1958 some 2,000 Viet Cong, organised in units of from fifty to 200 men, were attacking ARVN units of company size. Despite the growing tempo of communist activity the commander of the US Military Assistance and Advisory Group in Vietnam (MAAG-V),[111] Lieutenant General Samuel Williams, still maintained the policy of keeping the ARVN as a conventional force, while the police and local defence units dealt with the Viet Cong. While the American experience in Korea no doubt influenced this decision, the French involvement in

Indochina should have prompted its modification. For the remainder of the decade the Viet Cong operations continued, while their organisation in the South grew, and terrorism became part of everyday life for the people of South Vietnam. Despite the country's prosperity the security situation was clearly deteriorating, and in 1961 General Maxwell Taylor advised President John F. Kennedy that American military aid should be increased substantially. Kennedy, very conscious of the global Cold War threats – the Berlin Wall had appeared in August that year, and in Cuba the ill-fated US-supported Bay of Pigs invasion by Cuban exiles had taken place in April – was very receptive to this assessment, and on 11 December 1961 direct US military aid began to reach South Vietnam, with the arrival of two support helicopter companies at Saigon.

There is little doubt that Kennedy viewed US involvement in Vietnam as a natural extension of America's post-1945 crusade to defeat communism. But in any case this intervention in Vietnam was almost inevitable, given America's prominent position within the South-East Asia Treaty Organisation (SEATO), the presence of US military personnel in the country since 1953, and the belief in Washington that if South Vietnam fell it would have a 'domino effect' on the neighbouring states of the region. This last view was given added impetus by the existence already of active communist movements in Laos and Cambodia. Indeed, in light of the deteriorating circumstances in Laos, a brigade of US marines had been deployed to northern Thailand earlier in 1961, with the mission to enhance the security of the American air bases sited there under SEATO arrangements. The situation was exacerbated by a later agreement in Geneva in May 1961 which accorded Laos neutral status, thereby allowing the communists virtually unrestricted movement along the Ho Chi Minh trail. Understanding this fact only too well, President Diem in Saigon refused to sign the agreement. His decision, however, did not sit well with Washington, and this was but the first of several issues that within three years would lead to Diem's downfall.

With the Ho Chi Minh trail in full flow, the tempo of the Viet Cong campaign increased, although the South Vietnamese and the Americans still managed more or less to contain the growing threat – a process assisted from 1962 by the establishment of so-called strategic hamlets in the rural areas on lines that resembled the new villages set up by the British in Malaya during the 1950s. However, these strategic hamlets were set up primarily for defensive and military purposes rather than for the long-term development of new communities, and the French experience of less than a decade previously was disregarded.

Growing disquiet in Washington in respect of its protégé's intransigence over the Laos issue was further aggravated when Diem pursued an active campaign of harassment against the Buddhist community, while favouring the Roman Catholics. He was heavily influenced in this policy by his sister-in-law, Madame Ngo Dinh Nhu. The anti-Buddhist campaign was exemplified by a photograph that appeared time and again in the West, when Associated Press reporter Malcolm Browne captured on film the ritual suicide of a Buddhist monk by self-immolation in central Saigon on 5 October 1963. The picture of the burning monk wreathed in the flames that were rapidly consuming his petrol-soaked robes was speedily published worldwide; together with accounts of the Buddhist protest against their treatment by the Diem regime. In America the image shocked a population that was very susceptible to any graphic image of violence that did not accord with their own concept of normality. It was but the first of several historic and opinion-forming images that emerged from America's war in South-east Asia.

The Buddhist issue was only one of many matters causing concern to President Kennedy's administration. Government corruption, media censorship, nepotism, increasing unrest among the officers of the Vietnamese armed forces, the failure of the ARVN to deal effectively with the Viet Cong, and the South Vietnamese president's refusal to carry out reforms, all signalled that Diem's days were numbered. Continued US support for Diem eventually became impossible. Although Washington maintained an outward show of co-operation with Diem and his brother Nhu, it secretly indicated to the generals opposing him that a change of government in Saigon would not automatically result in the withdrawal of American assistance, provided that a new regime enjoyed popular support and could conduct an effective war against the communists. Consequently, on 1 November 1963 units of the ARVN surrounded the presidential palace in Saigon and compelled the surrender of the forces loyal to Diem. The two brothers escaped from the palace into the city via a secret tunnel, but were captured the next day. While in captivity and en route to the headquarters of those who had staged the coup both Diem and Nhu were murdered. The coup leader, General Duong Van Minh, assumed the presidency.

These events, however, failed to achieve stability. Strikes, protests and riots in the cities were matched by a significant upsurge in Viet Cong activity across South Vietnam. A second coup on 30 January 1964 resulted in Major General Nguyen Kanh occupying the presidential palace, and these coups set a recurring pattern for changes of government in South Vietnam throughout the next decade. In hindsight, Diem's personal failings notwithstanding, it would probably have been better had the full weight of US and SEATO support been thrown behind his regime, but conditional upon Diem carrying out significant internal reforms, including the removal of his brother Ngo Dinh Nhu from the government. However, in autumn 1963 the

US Ambassador Henry Cabot Lodge had advised Kennedy that Diem was unlikely ever to accede to Washington's demands. Consequently, despite counter-arguments from General Paul D. Harkins, commander of the US MAAG-V, President Kennedy opted for US non-involvement in the coup, whilst still undertaking to support an acceptable follow-on regime.

But political murder was not solely the preserve of war-torn South-east Asia. Just three weeks after Diem's death in Saigon, President John F. Kennedy was shot by an assassin while travelling with his wife in a motorcade in Dallas, Texas. News of the assassination reverberated around the world, and still attracts speculation and controversy more than forty years on. Shortly after Kennedy's death in the emergency room of a Dallas hospital, Vice-President Lyndon B. Johnson was sworn-in as president. Johnson – or 'LBJ' – was destined to lead America and its people during some of the most traumatic years of what had begun as Kennedy's crusade against communism. At the outset of Johnson's time in office the situation in Vietnam was worsening rapidly, although he had no mandate to increase the level of US involvement. Fate, however, intervened to assist Johnson: the place was the Gulf of Tonkin, and the date was 2 August – a defining moment of America's war in Vietnam.

On that day, the USS *Maddox* had just completed an intelligence-gathering mission off the North Vietnam coast. The destroyer was crossing the Gulf of Tonkin beyond the international twelve-mile limit when three North Vietnamese patrol boats approached at high speed. Armed with torpedoes, they posed a clear threat to the US warship, and when warning shots from the *Maddox* failed to deter these craft, the destroyer engaged them with its 5in guns. Two boats were hit, one being severely disabled. Nevertheless, they were able to fire two torpedoes before aircraft from the carrier USS *Ticonderoga* arrived to support the *Maddox*. Neither of the torpedoes hit the *Maddox*, and no American casualties were sustained. Nevertheless, in Washington President Johnson indicated that 'North Vietnam will be under no misapprehension as to the grave consequences which would inevitably result from any further unprovoked military action against United States forces.' He also ordered that the Gulf of Tonkin patrol should be strengthened. Accordingly, the destroyer USS *C. Turner Joy* joined the *Maddox* on 3 August. And there the matter might have ended, had not a further attack by five North Vietnamese patrol boats been reported and repelled by these two destroyers on the evening of 4 August.[112]

Johnson decided that action was necessary both to back up his statement on the first attack and to demonstrate US resolve in the region. Consequently, on 5 August aircraft from the carriers USS *Ticonderoga* and USS *Constellation* struck North Vietnamese naval bases and oil-storage facilities.

The attack was devastating: twenty-five torpedo boats were destroyed, together with almost the whole of the oil-storage facility. Two American aircraft were downed by anti-aircraft fire and a further two were damaged. In the United States, support for Johnson's action was enthusiastic and widespread, and on 7 August the US Congress approved the president's intention 'to take all necessary steps including the use of armed force to assist any member or protocol state' of SEATO. Spurred on by public opinion, Johnson signed the South-east Asia (Gulf of Tonkin) Resolution on 11 August. This had the effect of giving the president the authority to take any military action he deemed necessary in defence of US forces and to support South Vietnam. Meanwhile, by avoiding labelling North Vietnam as the aggressor and by not declaring war on the North, the likelihood of the direct involvement of the PRC or of the Soviet Union was much reduced. But the 11 August resolution did commit America to an open-ended conflict in Vietnam.

Although the resolution bolstered public confidence in the South, the government of Major General Nguyen Kanh (who formally proclaimed himself president on 16 August in the wake of the Tonkin incidents) was decidedly shaky; it was even displaying some of the characteristics of the old Diem regime, much to the concern of the United States. In Washington it was becoming ever clearer that, rather than merely supporting a joint US–South Vietnamese military campaign, the way forward would probably need to be American-led, in order to underwrite South Vietnamese resolve and influence the Saigon regime directly.

In the United States 1964 was an election year, and between August and October the conflict in Vietnam, the Gulf of Tonkin incidents, public opinion, the nature of the Saigon government, and the pressure on Johnson to carry the war into the North became inextricably enmeshed. The Joint Chiefs of Staff (JCS) even proposed that North Vietnam should be provoked into attacking US naval forces in order to enable and legitimise a bombing campaign against the North.[113] Johnson did not acquiesce to this proposal, although various clandestine and maritime operations continued against the communists. Even after a Viet Cong attack on Bien Hoa airbase on 2 November – which left five Americans dead, seventy-six wounded and six bombers destroyed – Johnson did not authorise retaliatory air strikes. Perhaps his caution was justified, as on 4 November he defeated the Republican Senator Barry Goldwater at the polls and was re-elected president in his own right, with a clear majority. But although he had won the election, by late 1964 there were increasing signs of public unease in America over his conduct of the war. By then about 23,000 US servicemen were already involved in the conflict. Meanwhile, in South Vietnam entire ARVN units were suffering defeats at Viet Cong hands, and in February 1965 the guerrillas launched direct assaults, sabotage and terrorist attacks against American bases, installations and off-duty facilities in South Vietnam. At the same time, the Hanoi government ordered the regular soldiers of the NVA to infiltrate along the Ho Chi Minh trail into the South.

The Die is Cast: 1965

With an awareness that the West had already failed to stem or contain the communist tide in the region three times before – with Chiang Kai-shek's defeat in China in 1949, the stalemate in Korea in 1953, and the French defeat in Indochina in 1954 – Johnson (armed with the 11 August resolution) was determined that his government would act decisively in Vietnam. Accordingly, on 7 February 1965 the US air force (USAF) and its South Vietnamese allies began bombing targets in North Vietnam. A month later, on 8 March, a USMC battalion arrived at Da Nang as the lead element of the 9th Marine Expeditionary Brigade. The heavily laden marines conducted a symbolic landing unopposed but 'wet footed' from amphibious assault craft across the South Vietnam beaches, and were greeted by a group of official representatives and a number of young girls equipped with the floral *leis* used for traditional Vietnamese welcomes. This somewhat surreal occasion was faithfully recorded by banks of cameras and a host of journalists pre-positioned on the beach. With Lyndon B. Johnson in the White House, Robert McNamara as Secretary of State for Defence, and the appointment in June 1965 of General William C. Westmoreland as the commander of Military Assistance Command Vietnam (MACV) (which had absorbed MAAG-V the previous month), the principal political and military leaders who would direct the US role in the war were all in place.[114] Meanwhile, as the American build-up of forces proceeded rapidly, the familiar political turmoil continued within South Vietnam, and on 19 June Air Vice-Marshal Nguyen Cao Ky became premier of South Vietnam. The scene was set for what quickly developed into a war of attrition.

From the outset, the East-versus-West and communist-versus-capitalist battle lines were clearly drawn. While the United States and some of its SEATO allies sent troops, matériel and supplies to South Vietnam, communist China poured support into North Vietnam. Concurrently, the communist bloc states led by the Soviet Union shipped equipment to the North, mainly through Haiphong; and despite often intense USAF bombing, the North's ability to generate and maintain its industrial and war support base remained viable throughout the war. The Ho Chi Minh trail also remained operational, and the flow of communist forces into Laos and down the trail, before they broke away along the network of trails that took them east or south into the heart of South Vietnam, was virtually uninterrupted.

Giap used the NVA to combat the US forces as far from the main centres of population as possible, while in the urban areas the Viet Cong attacked the ARVN and US rear area logistic facilities, and prosecuted their campaign of political indoctrination, sabotage, subversion and terrorism. One of the first major battles between the US ground forces and the NVA occurred at the valley of Ia Drang in November 1965.[115] Its particular significance was the fact that it saw the first large-scale use of the newly created 1st US Cavalry Division (Airmobile),[116] with its huge complement of integral helicopter gunships, utility helicopters, and supply and specialist helicopters. Next, many aspects of the operation that took place at Ia Drang were typical of the airmobile operations that the Americans conducted from mid-1965 until the end of their involvement in the war. Finally, it was the helicopter more than any other single item of equipment that symbolised and drove the American war in Vietnam. Consequently, an explanation of the organisation of the 1st US Cavalry Division (Airmobile) and of the key elements of an air assault are essential prerequisites for understanding the events that took place in the Ia Drang Valley in Pleiku Province during the six days following 14 November 1965, at the conclusion of the division's Operation Silver Bayonet, as well as assisting a comprehension of the overall nature of the war to which America was now committed.

Airmobile and Air Assault: 1965-8

Formed originally from the 11th Air Assault Division (Test), the 1st US Cavalry Division (Airmobile) was a brand-new organisation that had adopted a wholly novel concept of war-fighting – the concept of 'air envelopment' – by its routine use of the air as a third operating dimension from and in which its troopers fought their battles. Airmobility was a core aspect of US operations in Vietnam, which subsequently impacted directly upon the development of the tactics, organisation and equipment of American ground forces worldwide, including situations where they faced the Warsaw Pact forces in Central Europe.

The fighting element of the 1st US Cavalry division comprised nine airmobile infantry battalions (1st and 2nd Battalions, 5th Cavalry; 1st, 2nd and 5th Battalions, 7th Cavalry; 1st and 2nd Battalions, 8th Cavalry; 1st and 2nd Battalions, 12th Cavalry). But these troops could only fight once they were on the ground, and in order to place them there the division was supported by the 11th Aviation Group, with three assault helicopter battalions and three specialist aviation companies. These utility and transport helicopters (all of which were armed to varying degrees) were completely integrated within the division. However, once landed, the airmobile infantry troopers needed the sort of fire support normally provided to non-airmobile or armoured forces by artillery and fixed-wing attack aircraft. Clearly, the air assault concept often precluded such support, whether temporarily or for a whole operation. Therefore, the division had its own 'aerial artillery' in the form of the helicopter gunships that are today a familiar part of modern warfare, but which in the mid-1960s were still a real innovation. These gunships initially included the proven and ubiquitous UH-1C 'Huey' armed helicopters within the division's aerial weapons companies, although the UH-1Cs were progressively replaced by the even more potent AH-1G Cobra attack helicopters after September 1967. The Cobras had originally been designed for a war in Central Europe, but found another very appropriate role in Vietnam. In addition, as part of its own artillery support, the division fielded an aerial rocket artillery battalion, with some thirty-nine or more helicopters armed with 2.75in aerial rockets. Typically, this battalion would substitute for the fire support of the division's 105mm artillery battalions when necessary.

As well as a wide range of airmobile command and control assets, combat service support, medical, intelligence, military police units and so on, the 1st US Cavalry Division included on a permanent or temporary basis two mechanised infantry battalions, three armoured cavalry squadrons, and a specialist reconnaissance and long-range patrol force, plus the considerable firepower of four 105mm and one 155mm artillery battalions. When the 1st Cavalry shipped out of the United States on 28 July 1965, 'six passenger ships, eleven cargo vessels, and four aircraft carriers were required to move its more than 15,000 soldiers, 3,100 vehicles, 470 aircraft, and 19,000 tons of cargo to Vietnam'.[117] To these assets were added the various specialist and reinforcing units that made the division the most potent and combat-capable US division in Vietnam; and central to the division's ability to take the war to the enemy were its operational concepts of airmobility and air assault.

Unlike their parachute- and glider-borne forebears of the 1940s and mid-1950s, enormous advances in rotary wing technology had enabled the 1st US Cavalry Division to develop a true 'air assault' concept, in which the airmobile force was able to engage or suppress the enemy from the moment of first contact, throughout the air transit and landing, and until accomplishment of the capture or destruction of the objective. This concept relied upon a combination of well-practised procedures and sophisticated command and control arrangements, together with the almost infinite flexibility of all the commanders and troops involved.

The helicopter component of US Army airmobile units was organised into four functional teams: RED, WHITE, PINK and BLUE Teams. A RED Team comprised two gunships: the direct fire support for an airmobile force. The WHITE Team comprised two helicopters whose primary mission was reconnaissance. The PINK Team consisted of at least one gunship and one reconnaissance helicopter utilizing direct fire, or indirect artillery fire called in from firebases, to engage opportunity or pre-planned targets. The BLUE Team could be of any size and included the troop transport helicopters: the UH-1Ds, or Hueys. The number of Hueys in this Team depended upon the size of force to be lifted. The four teams were the principal component parts of an air assault force. In overall command of an air assault would be a single force commander: utilizing a UH-1D fitted with additional communications to turn the Huey into an airborne command post. The use of a single commander [as opposed to separate ground force and helicopter force commanders] is significant and was based on the hard-learned lessons of combat. The commander was provided with a minimum of three secure UHF/VHF voice links: this communications fit was also the direct result of operational experience. The supporting staff in this Huey included an operations officer, an air liaison officer (to control and direct offensive air support (OAS), but not to deal with air movement) and an artillery officer, responsible for coordinating the indirect fire in support of an assault. The only additional personnel in the command Huey normally would be aircrew and signallers.[118]

That then was the basic tactical organisation of an air cavalry or airmobile infantry assault force in 1965. The sequence of actions for an air assault into territory assessed under enemy control and with a presence in the area of the intended landing zone (LZ) then followed a common pattern:

First, a PINK Team would conduct a confirmatory reconnaissance of the LZ; this might be preceded by indirect fire or bombing of the area. At this time the assault force probably would be airborne in transit to the LZ. During close reconnaissance by a Huey or OH-6 Cayuse light helicopter, the accompanying gunship (a Huey or (from 1967) a Bell AH-1G Huey Cobra) would orbit well above the LZ area: protecting the reconnaissance helicopter below, providing suppressive fire if required and relaying updating information on the LZ to the fast-approaching force commander. Minutes before the arrival of the assault troops, RED Teams would saturate the LZ area with fire. Simultaneously, the PINK Team would re-deploy to observe other locations from which subsequent threats might develop; calling for artillery and other fire support as necessary.

In ideal circumstances, within a minute of the RED Team ceasing its engagement of the LZ area and its departure to seek other targets, the troop-carrying UH-1D Hueys (commonly termed 'slicks') would begin landing. [The Hueys would fly in a stacked or stepped formation, rather like a descending staircase. The number of separate landing points (LP) within the LZ would depend upon the overall size of the latter.] The aim was for the maximum number of 'slicks' to land simultaneously in the first and subsequent assault waves. As the first wave landed, the door gunners would engage the edges of the LZ with prophylactic machine-gun fire. In one of the Hueys of the first wave would be the LZ control party in radio contact with the force commander and the PINK Team. If casualties had been sustained on the LZ they would be evacuated by the Hueys of the second and following waves once the combat troops had disembarked. Although medevac UH-1H helicopters were in common use, the ad hoc usage of utility helicopters for this purpose revolutionized life-saving in Vietnam and was a significant morale factor.[119] The first battle of the [opposed] air assault was invariably that for the LZ, for through it would flow the remainder of the force to achieve its ground combat mission. Throughout this battle and then for as long as the situation demanded, the force commander would remain airborne in his UH-1D command and control helicopter. From this aircraft he could orchestrate the deployment and any modification of it, utilise his birds-eye view of the battlefield to direct the ground action, intercept enemy counter-moves by fire or direct combat and maintain tight overall control of the fire support allocated to the operation. Whilst airborne he continued to enjoy access to the superior communications fitted to his Huey UH-1D.

Once the air assault had been completed successfully and the LZ secured, the support and other medium helicopters, such as the CH-47 Chinooks and CH-54 Sky Cranes, would lift heavy stores, artillery and additional personnel in support of the subsequent or follow-up phases of the operation. These helicopters would also recover any helicopters downed in the first part of the action. From this point the operation would develop to match the mission requirements. The assault force might continue to secure the LZ for follow-up troops; it might move out to seize depth objectives or it might be reinforced, relieved in place or withdrawn. Where an assault was launched into a 'hot' (enemy-held) LZ the initial waves of troops might well have sustained casualties in numbers sufficient to limit their subsequent ground re-deployment.[120]

Such was the nature of the airmobile operation in which the 3rd Brigade of the 1st Cavalry Division was engaged in the Ia Drang Valley in November 1965, when its 1st Battalion, 7th Cavalry Regiment (1/7th) arrived at LZ X-RAY, close to the Chu Pong Mountains, at 10.50 hours on the morning of 14 November 1965. This formed part of the continuing operations against the NVA on the Cambodian border in the Ia Drang Valley, which lay some thirty miles south-west of Pleiku.

The commanders of the 1/7th were aware of an enemy presence in the area from an important haul of maps and battle plans made by soldiers of the 1st Brigade during the previous week, but not that the enemy presence close to LZ X-RAY consisted of some 4,000 troops of the 33rd and 66th NVA Regiments. The NVA soldiers were dispersed in camps, bunkers and under-ground tunnels in the hills surrounding the LZ. They had just completed a period of refurbishment and retraining prior to resuming their own offensive operations when B Company 1/7th and the battalion's command element landed in the middle of the area. The battalion's commanding officer was Lieutenant Colonel Harold G. Moore and the officer commanding B Company was Captain John Herren.

The usual hosing-down of the LZ perimeter by the door machine-gunners had taken place, but there was no return fire. Clutching their new 5.56mm M-16 assault rifles,[121] M-60 machine guns, M-79 grenade launchers, and all the other paraphernalia of war, the troopers leapt from the Hueys and moved quickly from the LPs through the long grass, around the 6ft-high anthills on the LZ, and into the cover provided by the trees and foliage at its perimeter.

Contact with the communists was not immediate, but occurred as soon as the US soldiers moved off the LZ to the east. Lieutenant Al Deveny's 1st Platoon came under heavy small-arms fire from two NVA companies just after it crossed a dried-up river bed. Lieutenant Henry Herrick's 2nd Platoon attempted to reinforce 1st Platoon, but was suddenly overwhelmed by a storm of fire. Hand-to-hand fighting ensued. Dead and wounded troopers lay everywhere. The platoon commander and his platoon sergeant were among the dead, and Sergeant Clyde E. Savage assumed command of the seven unwounded survivors of what had been a twenty-seven-man platoon just twenty minutes before. The outnumbered Americans were forced to withdraw back to the LZ, although the remnants of 2nd Platoon were cut off from the rest of B Company.

Simultaneously, the LZ began to receive rocket, mortar and some artillery fire, as Lieutenant Deal was ordered to take his 3rd Platoon – previously held in reserve – to try to reach the embattled 1st and 2nd Platoons. Meanwhile, Lieutenant Colonel Moore had set up his command post by the medical aid post beside a large anthill at the centre of the LZ. Although this provided him with a good view and control of the escalating situation – and most importantly to maintain a clear link with the helicopters that were still flying in and out of the LZ – even here the command post was receiving direct fire from NVA machine-gunners. Despite this, Captain Robert H. Edward's C Company landed more or less intact, thereby doubling the number of US infantrymen on the ground within a mere five minutes. Although the 1/7th's A Company, commanded by Captain Ramon A. Nadal, was also able to land complete, plus a few helicopters of Captain Louis R. 'Ray' Lefebvre's D Company (including the company commander), the weight of fire on to and about LZ X-RAY forced Moore to wave off any further landings at that stage. All of the troops that had landed successfully came into immediate contact with attacking NVA units at the south-west of the LZ and eventually formed a defensive perimeter along the line of a waist-deep river bed. C Company, reinforced by the few D Company troopers who had landed, held the southern side of the LZ against a series of concerted NVA attacks. During mid-afternoon, Moore was able to land the remainder of his battalion, including its medium mortars, although two helicopters were lost in the process.

At 16.20 hours A and B Companies staged a counter-attack in an attempt to reach Sergeant Savage's 2nd Platoon survivors, but they were stopped by NVA troops dug into well-concealed weapons pits with numerous machine-gun positions. During this attack Lieutenant Walter J. 'Joe' Marm Jr won the 1st Cavalry Division's first Congressional Medal of Honor in Vietnam for destroying NVA machine-gun positions with grenades, while leading his platoon. Marm was critically wounded during this attack, which had stalled and was faltering, until Lieutenant Colonel Moore called down white phosphorus artillery fire on to his own positions in order to enable a break-clean. As a veteran of the war in Korea, Moore had learned the value of this admittedly risky technique for dealing with massed infantry attacks. It worked again at LZ X-RAY. The isolated remnants of Sergeant Savage's 2nd Platoon, although under constant assault, also continued to call in artillery fire on the NVA forces that were moving all about them en route to attack the main 1/7th positions.

Meanwhile, the 1/7th were steadily sustaining casualties. They were surrounded by superior numbers of communist regular soldiers, and their only source of more manpower and matériel – LZ X-RAY – was under heavy fire.

Away from the scene of the main fighting, helicopter observers adjusted supporting artillery fire from fire-bases, and from the guns redeployed as underslung loads to new positions from which to engage the enemy. Meanwhile, the 3rd Brigade's commander, Colonel Thomas W. Brown, was desperately building new reserves and reinforcements for the 1/7th from the other units within the brigade, all of which were already involved in other tasks and missions.

The NVA fire continued intermittently throughout the night 14/15 November, and then at dawn a major assault was launched by wave after wave of NVA infantry, the leading units attacking through the final rounds of their own supporting artillery fire. Bayonet-tipped AK-47 assault rifles clashed with M-16s as hand-to-hand fighting broke out once more and the human tide of NVA soldiers threatened at last to overwhelm the 1/7th. At this point, Moore (whose command post had already endured the near-disastrous consequences of one misdropped napalm strike from an A-1E Skyraider) ordered USAF F4C Phantoms and F-100 fighter-bombers to drop bombs and napalm virtually on top of LZ X-RAY.

The result was decisive. The mass of NVA infantrymen, caught in the open, disappeared in a storm of fire, oily smoke, flying metal and explosions. The NVA offensive was finally broken shortly after 08.00 hours on 15 November, although the dawn attack resulted in heavy casualties to both sides. However, more US troops were being lifted into LZ X-RAY and the surrounding area, and one of Colonel Brown's reinforcing battalions was also moving to LZ X-RAY from a new LZ (LZ VICTOR) just one and a half miles away. This force arrived at X-RAY at noon, when the NVA began to pull back the troops that still faced the 1/7th. In the lull that followed the early morning attack on 15 November the troopers of the 1/7th secured the LZ perimeter and soon afterwards they began pushing out of their positions to link up with the survivors of the 2nd Platoon.

Meanwhile, the rate of force generation by the Americans at X-RAY could not be matched by the NVA, and so the communists began to withdraw from the Ia Drang. By the next day the residual fighting within the valley had become sporadic and it ended that day. No pursuit of the NVA into the Chu Pong Mountains was carried out, as B-52 bomber strikes were planned against the deeply dug emplacements identified there. At last the troopers of the 1/7th Cavalry Regiment departed LZ X-RAY and were flown to Pleiku. The battleground was temporarily occupied by two relieving battalions for one more night; it was then abandoned on 17 November, as its long-term occupation was never intended and it had by then served its purpose as the temporary focus of an air assault operation.[122]

So what was the real operational significance of the clash at the Ia Drang Valley? First and foremost, it was the first genuine test of the airmobile or air assault concept in combat, and of the largely untried troops who were pitted against experienced NVA fighters in their first real battle. The efficacy of the airmobile tactics and the airmobile troopers alike might be measured by the more than 600 NVA troops killed between 14 and 16 November, albeit that the 1/7th also sustained seventy-nine fatal casualties. However, in the context of the Vietnam War as a whole, the 1/7th proved in the Ia Drang Valley clash that the airmobile tactics they had previously developed and practised in the United States did work in combat. They showed that, despite certain constraints, helicopters could operate into a LZ in the face of hostile indirect fire. They demonstrated the ability to generate forces faster by air than could the NVA on the ground. Also, each helicopter that landed added to the American strength while simultaneously removing their casualties, together with their burden of medical care on the battlefield. Finally, the force commander was able to move and concentrate troops to counter NVA attacks, as well as lifting and delivering troops well beyond the LZ to cut the NVA lines of communication and resupply during the battle, and finally to ambush the NVA formations as they withdrew after 15 November.

Although the fighting on 14/15 November was undoubtedly the most intense combat of Operation Silver Bayonet, the battle at LZ X-RAY was but the last part of an action that had lasted a month. During the twenty-nine-days' operation only four helicopters were downed (with three recovered later). 1,771 NVA soldiers were killed, while the US units involved lost more than 240 dead. Meanwhile, the three NVA regiments (the 32nd, 33rd and 66th) engaged by the 1st Cavalry Division (Airmobile) during the period 23 October to 20 November 1965 were rendered non-combat effective until the late spring of the following year. However, General Giap and his NVA and Viet Cong commanders were quick to recognise the new threat posed by the air cavalry formations, and Ia Drang underlined the previously urgent but now essential requirement for the NVA to acquire effective low-level air defence systems to counter the helicopters.

For the Americans, although the airmobile concept was certainly validated, these early battles spawned an escalating reliance upon the helicopter that placed it at the centre of US tactical doctrine in Vietnam. Assuredly, the helicopter was a vital military tool – nowhere more so than in countering a guerrilla army in South-east Asia. But the degree of American dependence upon what was ultimately a finite resource risked the development of single-option tactics that relied absolutely upon helicopter availability. This, even more riskily, prompted the development of an overarching military strategy driven by the helicopter rather than supported by it. The statistics indicated the scale of US helicopter usage in Vietnam, and the total number of sorties rose from 2,993 in 1966 to 5,516 in 1967, 7,418 in 1968, and peaked with 8,441 in 1969.[123]

Meanwhile, the first year of full US involvement saw some 184,310 American troops committed in Vietnam. In 1966 that figure rose to 385,300, as the

Above: Here united as allies, but their decisions sowed the seeds of future East-West conflict: Churchill, Truman and Stalin at Potsdam, July 1945.

Right: Watched by a crowd of West Berliners, a US C-54 Skymaster transport aircraft completes yet another supply run into Tempelhof airport during the Berlin Airlift, June 1948 to May 1949.

Left: US marines scale the sea wall during the successful amphibious landing carried out at Inchon, Korea, 15 September, 1950.

Left: Enter the Dragon. A column of troops of the Chinese People's Liberation Army crosses the River Yalu, Korea, in October 1950 prior to joining the North Koreans in battle against the UN forces.

Left: Steep hills, trenches, bunkers, snow and sub-zero temperatures characterised much of the war in Korea. Infantrymen of Company E, 179th US Infantry Regiment in front-line positions, Korea, January 1952.

Above: Early indications of dissent and repression east of the Iron Curtain at Potsdamer Platz, Berlin, where Soviet T-34 tanks quickly suppressed the 1953 uprising in East Berlin.

Below: Towards the end of what was an ill-judged venture, desperate street fighting took place in Budapest during the Hungarian uprising in November 1956. It was comprehensively crushed by Soviet armoured forces.

Above: The end of the 'Prague Spring' of 1968. A Soviet T-54A tank in Wenceslas Square, August 1968, ensures that there is no recurrence of the earlier popular uprising.

Left: The attempt by France to retain control of its pre-1945 territories proved very costly. Here, French paratroopers provide first aid to battle casualties in Tonkin, French Indochina, late 1953.

Top right: An unexpectedly formidable enemy. Communist Viet Minh forces moving to reinforce the People's Army of Vietnam divisions at the Dien Bien Phu valley, early 1954.

Right: End of a colonial empire. French paratroopers man their defensive positions during the six-month long battle of Dien Bien Phu.

Below: British paratroopers of A Company, 3rd Battalion the Parachute Regiment consolidate their positions on 5 November 1956, after clearing the airport buildings at El Gamil Airfield, Port Said, during the airborne assault phase of the Anglo-French operation at Suez.

Bottom: A military success but a political failure. French troops of the Anglo-French force deployed to seize the Suez Canal surge ashore on 6 November 1956; but their relatively easy victory was short-lived.

Right: A recipe for counter-insurgency success: intelligence-led operations, hearts and minds, and sound tactics. Here a British Army patrol seeks out communist terrorists during the final years of the Malayan Emergency 1948–60.

Right: The violent, divisive and frustrating war in Algeria. Here, French Foreign Legion paratroopers of the 2 REP question an ALN insurgent captured during a cordon and search operation in the winter of 1956–57.

Right: On the brink of Armageddon. US air-reconnaissance photograph showing Soviet medium-range missile facilities in Cuba, October 1962.

Left: Harbingers of the 'new order' in Africa. Guerrillas of the 'National Liberation Forces' in Portuguese Angola, 1968.

Left: Fighting an ever more difficult and disheartening campaign, despite many tactical successes. Here, Portuguese infantry – most of whom were conscripts – in action against guerrilla forces in Angola, late 1960s.

Left: Spearhead of the Soviet threat against NATO in Europe. T-62 tanks of the Guards Tank Regiment 'Suche Bator', an armoured unit of the elite Group of Soviet Forces Germany.

Right: Epicentre of the Cold War: the Brandenburg Gate, Berlin, 1969.

Below: Truly an 'Iron Curtain': the Berlin Wall at Bernauer Strasse, Berlin, 1969.

Left: The Soviet military monolith: a May Day parade in Moscow, mid-1970s.

Centre left: Soldiers serving an unequal alliance: members of the Polish, Soviet and East German armies during Warsaw Pact Exercise Waffenbrüderschaft 80, in East Germany, September 1980.

Below: Although it was designed for general war, and had entered service in 1955 as the principal strategic bomber of the USAF, the B-52 (here a B-52F) saw extensive service supporting US conventional warfare operations throughout the war in Vietnam.

Right: Peril from the deep: a Soviet Typhoon-class SLBM-armed nuclear submarine, post-1980. The NATO nuclear powers and the Soviet Union alike relied heavily upon SLBMs as a key element of their strategic deterrent forces.

Below: A classic image of US and Soviet Cold War confrontation and strategic power projection. This 1971 photo shows the USS *Kitty Hawk* (CV-63) aircraft carrier being overflown by one of the mainstays of Soviet strategic air power throughout the Cold War, a Soviet Tu-95 Bear D bomber. The Tu-95 is in turn being closely monitored by two USN F-4J Phantom fighters. The USS *Kitty Hawk* can carry a complement of more than eighty aircraft.

Above: Many believed that the time of the battleship had finally ended in 1945; but several USN battleships (here BB-61, the USS *Iowa*) were subsequently updated and provided sterling service throughout the Cold War – including use of their 16-inch guns to provide naval gunfire support to US ground forces throughout the Vietnam war during the late 1960s and early 1970s.

Above right: The epitome of Cold War strategic deterrence: the ICBM. Both superpowers maintained large stocks of ICBMs, and here a US Minuteman 2 of Strategic Air Command carries out a successful test launch in the late-1960s.

Below: NATO, an alliance of equals. One example of this was the successful STANAVFORLANT (standing naval force Atlantic): in which the ships of six different NATO navies operated within a single maritime task group.

Right: A superpower in waiting? Other than in Korea 1950–53 and by its support for communist insurgencies and conflicts in Indochina and elsewhere, the People's Republic of China remained largely uninvolved in the Cold War. However, it may well realise its enormous military and economic potential during the twenty-first century, and might eventually fill the power vacuum left by the demise of the Soviet Union.

Below: Desert victory: Israeli M-3 half-track armoured carriers advance past truckloads of Arab prisoners during the Six-Day War, June 1967.

Left: Yom Kippur 1973. A column of Egyptian armoured carriers crosses the Suez Canal following their well-planned and successful assault crossing on 6 October.

Left: Counter-stroke: an Israeli M-48 tank crosses the Suez Canal after 17 October 1973, during the IDF move to outflank the Egyptian 2nd and 3rd Armies once the Egyptians had over-extended their forces.

Left: Airmobile! Troopers of the US 173rd Airborne Brigade – the 'Sky Soldiers' – leap from their UH-1 Huey helicopters during an air assault in South Vietnam, 1966.

Above: Jungle warfare. US marines of Company G, 2nd Battalion, 4th Marine Regiment in action against Viet Cong forces near Phu Bai, South Vietnam, August 1967.

Above right and below: North Vietnamese communist troops moving along the Ho Chi Minh trail in the late 1960s. Their war against the US forces in Vietnam from 1965 was merely a continuation of the earlier post-1945 struggle against the French.

Above: Fighters in a war with unforeseen long-term global consequences: Muslim Mujahideen guerrilla fighters with captured Soviet weapons in Afghanistan, early 1980s.

Below: An indispensable source of Soviet firepower during what was later characterised as 'Moscow's Vietnam War': a Hind-D Mi-24 helicopter gunship on a combat air patrol in the mountains of Afghanistan, early 1980s.

war intensified and the further bombing of the North, this time by B-52 bombers, was authorised in April. During that year 5,008 US servicemen died in combat in Vietnam, plus a further 1,045 from non-hostile incidents. In 1967 – with 485,600 US servicemen in Vietnam – these casualty figures rose to 9,378 and 1,680 respectively.[124] Although the main weight of the fighting fell upon the US and South Vietnam forces, by the mid-1960s there were also Australian, New Zealand, Philippines, South Korean (one division) and Thailand (three brigades) units and formations serving alongside the US and South Vietnamese forces.

In the United States, the involvement of many ordinary American families with the war became more immediate as the programme of conscription – the draft – was expanded in order to accommodate the increased force levels required and the rotation system which provided for individuals to complete a one-year tour of duty in Vietnam. In the early years of the Vietnam War draftees were wherever possible posted throughout the world to replace regular servicemen – in order to release the latter for duty in South-east Asia. By 1966, however, as the manpower bill for Vietnam rose inexorably, the policy of not sending draftees into the combat zone was abandoned and substantial numbers were committed to the war. For a variety of reasons, the draft system tended to produce a large number of infantry recruits from the lower socio-economic and ethnic minority groups. As ever, the infantry bore the brunt of the combat and therefore sustained most of the battle casualties – a fact that was readily exploited by the communists and by other groups in the United States.

Yet despite the rising number of casualties and the growing disquiet at home, the US forces were defeating the communists on the battlefield in every major clash of arms and, although they had enjoyed some successes against the South Vietnamese security forces in the interior, the NVA and Viet Cong were sustaining huge losses wherever they met the Americans in battle. Between 1 January and 31 December 1967 the US forces and their allies mounted no less than thirty-one formation-level operations, each of which resulted in at least 500 enemy personnel killed in action. Some of the longer campaigns led to the death of many thousands of NVA and Viet Cong fighters. Operation Junction City from February to May produced 2,728 enemy dead, Operation Buffalo in July resulted in 1,281, while the enemy killed in action during the 1st Cavalry Division's twelve-months' Operation Pershing I and II, begun in February 1967, finally numbered 5,401.

But, unlike some of the American field commanders who had from the outset followed a rather simplistic and primarily military approach to the defeat of the communists, for Ho Chi Minh and Giap the military campaign was always complementary to their objective of creating a united Vietnam under communist domination. For Hanoi a war of attrition was acceptable, and whilst regrettable, the high casualties were the unavoidable price of that political prize – even though the heavily censored communist media did not report the North's casualty figures accurately. In any case, an already high birth-rate in the North meant that, just as Ho had planned, the regeneration of the Vietnamese population would be sustained in the long term. Meanwhile, despite the US bombing, supplies of war matériel from China, the Soviet Union and other communist bloc countries continued to flow largely unabated into North Vietnam. This matériel was then moved onward via the Ho Chi Minh trail to the Viet Cong and North Vietnamese units fighting in the South.

Incredibly, after only two and a half years of full US military involvement, a massive and technologically very sophisticated military machine that was undefeated on the battlefield was nevertheless losing the war. Ho Chi Minh and Giap were very aware of this and of the paramount importance of the presentational, information management and propaganda campaigns to their eventual victory.

General William Westmoreland was all too aware of these indirect threats to his campaign in Vietnam. In an address to the Associated Press in New York during a brief visit to the United States in April 1967, he highlighted the global support that the communists had managed to generate for their cause 'through a clever combination of psychological and political warfare, which gives him hope that he can win politically that which he cannot accomplish militarily'. These remarks, together with Westmoreland's accurate if unquantifiable assertion that media criticism of American involvement in Vietnam was encouraging the enemy and costing American lives, attracted a storm of protest from a still-small but vociferous and growing anti-war movement within the United States. The American university campus was a particular source of protest, where effigies of political and military leaders were regularly burnt, along with the American flag that they served. Such events received extensive media coverage, and the insidious effect of this home-based campaign on the discipline and morale of the US armed forces was increasingly evident.

Westmoreland's visit to the United States in 1967 was one of the key political-strategic events of the war, as it was then that he briefed President Johnson, Secretary of State Rusk, Secretary of Defence McNamara, Chairman of the JCS General Wheeler and the members of a high-level planning and policy group on his vision of the way ahead for the US war in Vietnam. He described a 'minimum essential force' of 550,000 with which he could end the war successfully within about five years. However, with an 'optimum force' of 670,000 men he would be able to do so in about three years. During May and June 1967 the American leadership considered its options. These included an invasion of North Vietnam, Laos or Cambodia, although the risk of Chinese intervention subsequently excluded it, and thus Truman's 1950s limited war doctrine still obtained.

In order, however, to achieve Westmoreland's optimum 670,000 force level in Vietnam it would have been necessary to mobilise the US reserve forces and place America's economy on a war footing, which would inevitably be at the expense of domestic policies. The already unpopular and (as viewed by some) inequitable draft selection criteria would become unsustainable and the reaction of the anti-war movement to such an increase could easily be imagined – as could the public reaction to cut-backs in social programmes. With a presidential election due in 1968 it was perhaps unsurprising that Johnson did not approve the optimum force increase; but neither did he support his commander in the field by authorising the minimum 550,000 men he had requested. After much deliberation, Johnson eventually advised Westmoreland in July that the manpower increase agreed for 1968 would be 47,000, producing a total ceiling of 525,000 for that year (which did in fact rise to about 536,000 in practice, but still 14,000 short of the minimum strength Westmoreland needed). Even this lesser increase produced a storm of protest in America, which culminated in a major protest by 35,000 anti-war activists in October, one that reached the steps of the Pentagon.

There was yet another change of president in South Vietnam in 1967, when General Nguyen Van Thieu was democratically elected to office on 3 September. At that point Westmoreland and the US Ambassador in Saigon, Ellsworth Bunker, assessed that the United States and its South Vietnamese ally were overall making satisfactory progress against the communists and (linked to Johnson's impending campaign for re-election) both men were prevailed upon to repeat their positive view of the situation to the US media. This process included a speech made by Westmoreland to the Press Club in Washington on 21 November when he stated: 'We have reached an important point when the end begins to come into view', and noted that the ARVN, then the subject of a major capability enhancement, would soon be able increasingly to take on the burden of the combat role, so that within two years or less some withdrawals of US forces from Vietnam might begin. President Thieu's election provided the hope that the political turmoil in the South might at last be at an end.

Although Westmoreland's assessment was accurate in military terms, it produced a dangerously optimistic 'feel good factor', which raised the level of public reassurance and complacency about the war, which was construed by many as being as good as won, or at least imminently passed over to the South Vietnamese. This perception played directly into the hands of Ho Chi Minh, whose forces were even then preparing a major operation: one that would result in the annihilation of the Viet Cong and the defeat of the NVA in battle, but which would nevertheless lead to an otherwise militarily undefeated United States subsequently losing the war.

As 1967 drew to a close, in Hanoi, Saigon and Washington the political and military leaders and the nations they led had very different hopes, ambitions and intentions for 1968. In Vietnam the upcoming Lunar New Year holiday period was known as 'Tet'.

A Defining Moment: The Tet Offensive, 1968

Hanoi's 1968 Tet offensive was one of the defining moments of the Vietnam War. It was also one of the most misunderstood and misrepresented military actions of the post-Second World War period. At the same time, it demonstrated the linkage of military action, politics and political expediency, propaganda and the media in the Vietnam conflict. Finally, it said a great deal about the very different natures of communist and Western society; which extended well beyond their more obvious ideological differences.

In mid-1967 the communists were losing the war on the battlefield and were sustaining huge numbers of casualties. However, the mounting toll of American and South Vietnamese casualties was causing increasing concern in the White House, and in Hanoi Ho Chi Minh and Giap planned to create a situation that would force the United States to disengage from Vietnam. They decided to change their strategy of using the NVA to fight the Americans primarily in the border regions, while the Viet Cong engaged the South Vietnamese further inland, to a new strategy involving a full-scale attack on the South. This would include direct assaults on key cities by the NVA – targets previously left to the Viet Cong – while at the same time the in-place communist infrastructure in the South would rise up and topple the South Vietnamese government on a wave of popular support for the communists. Although this popular uprising was presented to the Hanoi leadership and military commanders by Ho as a realistic aspiration, it is doubtful that he actually believed in its feasibility. Nevertheless, Ho and Giap knew that the effect of such a dramatic military operation on South Vietnam itself was entirely secondary to the effect that it would have on the Americans. And Ho's target audience in this new endeavour was not primarily the US combat troops in South Vietnam, but their wives, children, parents and political leaders in America. But in order to achieve Ho's political and strategic objectives, General Giap had to achieve one thing above all others: he had to gain surprise, and thereby traumatise an American nation that was convinced that a US victory in Vietnam was clearly in sight.

In the late summer of 1967 Ho and Giap had selected the Lunar New Year holiday period, 29 to 31 January 1968, for the great new offensive, and had set about preparing for it with a comprehensive programme of political and military action. Surprise, security, deception and the neutralisation of American air supremacy were all vital prerequisites for success, and here the communists used politics to achieve their military needs.

In the knowledge that Washington would seize upon any chance to start peace talks, in order to placate its domestic critics, Hanoi let it be known that a halt to the bombing of the North would result in such talks being held. Obligingly, the Americans indicated that they would cease bombing in the area of Hanoi, and in consideration of the religious and cultural significance of Tet, an informal but fairly general ceasefire was in any case anticipated from 29 to 31 January. As Rick Atkinson, a staff writer for the *Washington Post*, noted:

> The Year of the Monkey began on Tuesday, January 30, 1968, the first and holiest day of Tet. To Americans, the week-long Vietnamese celebration of the lunar new year seemed to combine Christmas, Easter, Halloween, the Fourth of July, and New Year's Eve into one huge holiday. To celebrate, both sides had agreed to a thirty-six hour ceasefire.[125]

This observation by an American confirmed the wisdom of Ho's choice of date for the offensive. Nevertheless, conscious of the importance of Tet to its own people in North Vietnam, the Hanoi regime declared that the day of the 1968 Tet holiday would be 29 not 30 January. This allowed the North to celebrate Tet (which would in practice begin on the evening of 28 January) before the new offensive began.

Next, Giap needed a suitable diversion to keep US forces away from the imminent battles in the cities, and to imply that there was no change from the former policy of engaging the Americans primarily in the border regions. To that end, on 21 January the NVA initiated what developed into an eleven-week siege of the US marines' base close to the North–South border at Khe Sanh. This siege soon assumed a mystique similar to that of Dien Bien Phu fourteen years earlier.

Although the in-country support available to General Westmoreland was such that Khe Sanh was never seriously at risk, there were indeed some similarities between the two situations. This was not lost on the countless journalists who flew in, took the required photographs, and then flew back to their hotels in Saigon and elsewhere to write and file their stories, many of which predicted the eventual collapse of the base, thereby fuelling the pressure on Washington for it to be held. Meanwhile, three NVA divisions (the 304th, 323rd, 325th) surrounded Khe Sanh and began an almost incessant artillery bombardment, with a daily rate of fire that often had as many as 1,000 rounds falling on the base. One of the American arguments for holding the base was that the surrounding concentrations of NVA troops offered excellent targets for B-52 strikes. Indeed, by the end of the siege, 100,000 tons of bombs had been dropped on and about Khe Sanh, which made it the most heavily bombed single target in the history of warfare up to that date. However, despite a number of assaults, several of which culminated in bitter hand-to-hand fighting, no serious attempt was made to overrun it, and some commentators suggested that its capture (together with the 6,000 US marines of the garrison) might actually have been counterproductive to Hanoi's international campaign of political propaganda. The communist failure to deny the garrison its air resupply, or to cut off or pollute the natural water supply into the base – both of which measures were within their capability – were evidence for this, and so the parallels with the French predicament at Dien Bien Phu were fairly tenuous.

In practice, Giap's operational strategy at Khe Sanh proved very sound, as the US high command in Saigon – in accordance with explicit direction from Washington – was forced to hold a number of divisions in readiness to support or relieve Khe Sanh if necessary. These troops were therefore unavailable for operations elsewhere, including the blocking of the southward movement of other NVA formations, particularly towards the old city of Hue. Once the main communist offensive began, the preoccupation of the US administration with what was in practice the largely symbolic importance of Khe Sanh meant that these US divisions were still held in readiness to support the marine garrison – a garrison that might itself have been better employed other than at Khe Sanh.

However, there are two sides to any assessment, and (notwithstanding that the decision to besiege the base was made by the communists) it was also true that the 6,000 troops at Khe Sanh, proportionally only one-sixtieth of the total American and South Vietnamese combat forces, were themselves occupying the attention of some 20,000 NVA troops that Giap could have employed on other tasks had they not been deployed there. In any event, Giap was able to turn to considerable advantage the determination of the Americans – and especially that of senior USMC commanders – to hold at all costs a base that was in reality of ever-diminishing operational importance to the US high command. Consequently, the NVA diversionary operation at Khe Sanh was permitted to run its full course, from 21 January to 14 April.

The various events that together comprised the main Tet offensive fell generally into three parts. First was the North's preparatory action – political, psychological and military. This included an intensification of the border campaign at the end of 1967, to ensure a continued American focus away from the cities. Then there was the main offensive by the Viet Cong and NVA. The storm broke across the whole country but (apart from the diversionary action in progress at Khe Sanh) the most significant actions were at Saigon, Hue and in the Mekong Delta. Finally, there was the outcome of Tet 1968. The elements of this outcome were military and political, internal and external, and together provided the real reason for the significance of Tet 1968 to the Vietnam War. But perhaps the most important fall-out from Tet was the media reaction to it, for this marked the real beginning of the end of America's war in Vietnam.

Although Giap had taken great pains to ensure surprise, the South Vietnamese and Americans had sensed that some sort of major event was due to take place that January. Therefore, although the South Vietnamese troops were by and large permitted to stand down for the holiday, a number of commanders denied their men the leave period, or maintained an increased level of readiness by those personnel who were in any case on duty. Notwithstanding his 1967 assessment of the progress of the war, General Westmoreland was especially concerned that an attack was imminent, and persuaded a reluctant President Thieu to cancel the informal ceasefire in the northern operational sector and reduce it from thirty-six to twenty-four hours elsewhere. Thieu also agreed to retain some 366,000 ARVN troops – half the ARVN total strength – on duty over Tet.

The numerous intelligence indicators of a communist build-up and impending offensive action were indeed confirmed when Viet Cong attacks were launched prematurely against eight population centres in the Central Highlands and on the coastal plain some twenty-four hours before the Tet holiday. Among the places hit by battalion attacks, mortars, rockets and sabotage raids were Pleiku, Qui Nhon, Da Nang, Nha Trang, Hoi An and Ban Me Thuot. This resulted in the immediate cancellation of the Tet ceasefire on 30 January, and all US and ARVN units in the South were alerted. Nevertheless, whereas the Viet Cong had completed their deployments and infiltrations by the 30th, many thousands of ARVN soldiers were still considerable distances away from their places of duty. Even President Thieu was at his family home at My Tho, in the Mekong Delta south-west of Saigon.

Just before dawn on 31 January the full force of the offensive struck in Saigon. The historian and former infantry commander Charles B. Macdonald described the first attacks carried out by a party of fifteen Viet Cong sappers (experts in the use of explosives, sabotage and terrorism) against the US embassy in Saigon, close to the presidential palace, even though the embassy was one of the best protected of such sites in South Vietnam:

Before daylight on 31 January, sappers in civilian clothing blew a hole in the wall. Two [US] military police guards killed the first two VC [Viet Cong] to enter the grounds of the embassy but were themselves killed in the exchange of gunfire. Two more military policemen in a jeep patrol responding to a call for help also died, as did a US marine who climbed atop a nearby building to fire into the compound. Another military policeman closed the heavy doors of the chancery so that no VC were able to enter the building. Under fire from a helicopter and, soon after daylight, from a platoon of American airborne troops heli-lifted to the chancery roof, all the VC were killed within about six hours.[126]

At the same time, Viet Cong sappers and fighters launched multiple attacks against military, government and other key installations across the capital. In many respects the emergence of the Viet Cong to engage in open combat was just what the US and South Vietnamese commanders had been trying to bring about since 1965, and the demise of the fifteen sappers on the first day of Tet was but one of very many clashes in which the Viet Cong were system-atically annihilated. However, the shock of that first attack and its target impacted significantly and disproportionately upon the whole future course of the war.

Most of the scores of civilian journalists based in South Vietnam were accommodated in what had been until 31 January the relative security of the many hotels in downtown Saigon. In the pre-dawn confusion of the attack on the US embassy an incorrect report sent by one of these journalists stated that the chancery had been penetrated by the Viet Cong. This erroneous report was blazoned across newspapers and television news programmes throughout the world. Despite an early denial and correction of the story by General Westmoreland, reporters quoted 'other sources' and continued to maintain its accuracy while at the same time accusing Westmoreland of concealing the truth of the affair. Meanwhile, an American public and US Congress that was in any case becoming more and more wary of govern-ment pronouncements, saw the early photographs and television film footage of Viet Cong within the embassy compound (but not inside the chancery), and drew their own conclusions. The psychological effect of this could not have been more favourable to Hanoi had Ho and Giap drafted the erroneous report themselves. The enormous danger inherent in television and photo-journalists shaping public opinion prematurely or incorrectly by their inaccurate reporting of modern wars was exemplified by an American account of one US-based political commentator's reaction to the news of the embassy attack:

The shock was tremendous. 'What the hell is going on here?' Walter Kronkite is alleged to have exclaimed when the news came over the teletype. 'I thought we were supposed to be winning this war,' a reaction surely shared by many of his countrymen.[127]

Many of the in-country correspondents had no personal military combat experience, and in their comfortable hotel environment, lulled by Westmoreland's recent optimistic assessment of the progress of the war, they were profoundly shocked by the immediacy, scale and ferocity of the Viet Cong's initial attacks. In a frenzy of panicked reporting they communicated their own fears to the wider world via news agencies, television stations and sponsors worldwide. In the course of producing these reports, ever-conscious of their news deadlines and determined to be first with the news of what they interpreted as an imminent American defeat, many correspondents focused only on the Viet Cong's relatively few early successes. Consequently, much unsubstantiated, sensationalised and factually incorrect material was transmitted, including a great deal of inaccurate interpretation and speculation. Given the general confusion and pace of events at the start of the communist offensive, many of these reports remained uncorrected, and therefore the media's presentation of the events of the end of January and early February 1968 differed quite significantly from that which had actually happened.

In fact, despite some fighting about the presidential palace, two more substantial actions at Tan Son Nhut airport and at the ARVN Joint General Staff Headquarters, plus the elimination of a further five attacks by groups of Viet Cong sappers, the South Vietnamese capital was virtually clear of Viet Cong by 5 February. Elsewhere, right across South Vietnam some 84,000 communist troops launched their attacks. In the north these were mainly carried out by NVA regulars, but the vast majority of the communist forces engaged were Viet Cong. These guerrilla fighters died in their thousands – some 32,000 in the first two weeks of the offensive, plus 5,800 captured – as the US and South Vietnamese forces quickly restored the situation. But the sheer number and dispersion of the attacks notwithstanding – five major cities, thirty-six provincial capitals, sixty-four district capitals and fifty hamlets were all struck on or shortly after 31 January – the communist attacks were neutralised within a few days. Only in Saigon and the ancient city of Hue, where three battalions of US marines took twenty-five days to clear the city, did the fighting continue.

There was no popular uprising in support of the communists, and wherever the ARVN and the South Vietnamese militia units were engaged, their soldiers generally fought bravely and effectively. As the US marines dealt with the last pockets of Viet Cong in the rubble of Hue, where the Viet Cong had tortured and murdered several thousands of its citizens during the brief communist occupation, the American high command and South Vietnamese leadership derived considerable satisfaction from a military victory that had resulted in more than 45,000 dead communists, with the capture of almost 7,000 more, plus a considerable amount of Viet Cong and NVA weapons and equipment. Indeed, the Viet Cong had been destroyed as a viable fighting force, and the South Vietnamese militia units speedily occupied the vacuum that their defeat had created in the rural areas.

Paradoxically, the destruction of the Viet Cong may not have been entirely an error of judgement by Ho Chi Minh. Their deliberate and extensive committal to the Tet offensive provided Ho with the political and psychological victory he sought, while at the same time neutralising an ethnically South Vietnamese power base which might have challenged the authority of Hanoi in the future. At the same time, the non-use of the NVA reserve divisions once the early attacks slowed, with no popular uprising in evidence, preserved largely intact the regular troops Ho and Giap knew would be needed as the core of a future invasion force.

Meanwhile, the United States and its non-South Vietnamese allies had suffered 1,536 dead, 7,764 wounded and eleven soldiers missing; while the ARVN had lost 2,788 dead, 8,299 wounded and 587 missing. Also, some 14,000 civilians had been killed, plus 24,000 wounded, with almost a further 700,000 made refugees by the communist offensive. But despite the human cost Tet was a decisive military victory for the forces of the United States and South Vietnam.

In the months that followed, two further communist attacks were suppressed with ease. These resulted in defections and desertions from the North Vietnamese forces, while the South's rural pacification and reconstruction programmes were reinvigorated and gained a new momentum. US military aid for the ARVN and the militia increased significantly, while the recruitment and morale of the triumphant South Vietnamese forces which had borne the brunt of the Tet offensive soared. Public support for President Thieu and his government was never higher.

Yet this victory was presented by the Western media as a significant defeat for American arms. Therefore, in the press handling of the Vietnam War – the reporting of Tet 1968 in particular – lie important lessons for Western democracies concerning the management of information and public perceptions in modern wars. A few examples highlighted by Charles B. MacDonald in his 1979 study of the Tet offensive served to illustrate the point:

> To [the journalists and commentators] the Tet offensive was an incredible shock, an unmitigated disaster, a clear American and South Vietnamese

defeat. None of them thought to draw parallels with other wars in which a losing side had staged a grand surprise assault ... Confirmed in their long-held scepticism, they were determined to expose the subterfuge and chicanery they saw behind the Johnson administration's claims of progress ... Television cameras focusing on one badly damaged block could give the impression of an entire city in ruins ... the culprits who wrought such devastation were never the communists, who had brought the war into the cities, but the Americans and South Vietnamese with their artillery and airpower. The [figures for] civilian casualties and refugees made the headlines – not the 5,000 or more civilians systemati-cally tortured and executed by the communists in Hue and elsewhere ... Reporters claimed that the imperial palace in Hue was totally destroyed: damage was, in fact, superficial. Saigon, most of which suffered only light damage, was shown to American television audiences as a smouldering ruin ... Newsmen countered official claims of a communist defeat by saying that even if it were true (which they refused to accept, as they did the official account of enemy losses), the communists had achieved a psychological victory.[128]

The misrepresentation of the actual situation in Vietnam impacted at the highest level:

Many civilian officials reacted like the [US] presidential special assistant who noted that whenever he read the official cables from Saigon, he found them 'almost hallucinatory' in view of what he had seen on tele-vision the night before. There the story, told in gruesome pictures and doleful words, was presented so convincingly that he believed the reporters rather than the officials.[129]

One more 'gruesome picture' of the Vietnam War joined the images of the self-immolation of the Buddhist monk in 1963, of the little girl burned and fleeing down a road following a napalm attack on her village, and of the villagers massacred by a platoon of C Company, 1st/20th US Infantry in March 1968. Now a photo-journalist captured for posterity the summary execution of a Viet Cong officer captured in civilian clothes in Saigon during the Tet offensive. The photograph showed Brigadier Nguyen Ngoc Loan, the Saigon police chief, shooting the captive in the head with a pistol.

The impact of such powerful images, often taken completely out of context, served the communist cause very well in the civilised Western world. However, it is a matter of record that the greatest media impact in the

United States was that on the array of politicians, bureaucrats and liberal intellectuals, rather than upon the general population. In fact, immediately after Tet the people looked to President Johnson to take even more decisive military action to deal with the communists once and for all. Consequently, General Wheeler, the Chairman of the JCS, together with General Westmoreland, saw an opportunity to increase the overall US force level by 206,000 men, with 103,000 for South Vietnam and 103,000 to reconstitute the country's strategic reserve for potential tasks worldwide (by early 1968 that reserve force stood at just one division). Two studies into this proposal were carried out, both of which advised against it. But before the White House could indicate this, the *New York Times* reported incorrectly that the administration was considering dispatching a further 206,000 personnel to Vietnam. The wider media reaction was predictable, and fuelled the activities of the growing anti-Vietnam War movement – although a poor result for the Democrats in the New Hampshire primary a few days later was in fact due more to voter concerns over Johnson's lack of a robust response to Tet, rather than to any renewed protest against the war.

Yet the damage had been done. On 1 November President Johnson declared a halt to the bombing of the North (constraints had already been placed on the bombing campaign on 31 March) in a bid to bring Hanoi to the negotiating table. He also declared his withdrawal from the 1968 presidential contest, and was succeeded by the Republican candidate, Richard Nixon, at the end of the year. Meanwhile, in July General Creighton W. Abrams, deputy to General Westmoreland, had succeeded his chief as US commander in South Vietnam, when Westmoreland was appointed US Army Chief of Staff. This change had been decided by Johnson in mid-January, by which time Westmoreland had been in his post in South Vietnam for almost four and a half years. However, although all these changes were occasioned by routine administrative and (for Johnson) personal considerations, the anti-war movement presented them as the removal of a flawed and inadequate president and a less than competent military commander, following a communist success at Tet 1968. This perception was strengthened when Hanoi agreed to participate in peace talks. Accordingly, on 25 January 1969 formal negotiations with a view to achieving a truce began in Paris.

In reality, however, this was evidence of the enormous blow that had been inflicted upon the communist forces just a year earlier at Tet. But although he had lost on the battlefield, Giap had secured a significant political and psychological victory, and he now needed time to regroup, re-equip and prepare the NVA for future operations, including an invasion of the South. Indeed, the destruction of the Viet Cong during Tet 1968 meant that any resumption of the guerrilla war was no longer viable. For North Vietnam, if not for Ho Chi Minh (then in his seventy-ninth year), time was again on the communist side. By the pretence of engaging in negotiations, Hanoi appeared to have gained the moral high ground, it could set an agenda that would control the future course of the war, and it was within sight of its goal of removing the United States from direct military involvement in South Vietnam.

So, as 1968 drew to a close, General Giap's longer-term plans for his army to sweep south in due course were progressing well. At the same time Hanoi knew that an increasingly war-weary American public were now led by a new president who was very aware of the fate that had attended his predecessor. He would therefore be favourably disposed to the 'Vietnamisation' of the war, and he would maintain the bombing halt against the North, while at the same time seeking ways to effect a US military withdrawal and continuing negotiations with the communists.

All this confirmed that Tet 1968 was the catalyst for America's disengagement from Vietnam in 1973, which also foreshadowed the defeat of the South in 1975. The start of the Vietnamese Year of the Monkey at Tet 1968 was assuredly the defining moment of the Vietnam War.

The Beginning of the End: 1970–2

Ironically, the three years that followed the end of the 1968 Tet offensive were probably the best for South Vietnam since the ejection of the French in 1954. Even its arch-enemy, Ho Chi Minh, died in 1969, although no dramatic change in North Vietnamese policy and aspirations followed the death of the man who had inspired and motivated the communist movement in Indochina ever since the end of the Second World War. Ho Chi Minh had been a dynamic and talented political leader of his people, and the debate as to whether he was a true communist, or simply a nationalist posing as a communist in order to use the Soviets and Chinese to further his nationalist aims, will no doubt continue. Because he died before the North finally overwhelmed the South in 1975, it is a question that can never be finally resolved, but his communist credentials were certainly adequate to satisfy his sponsors in Beijing and Moscow. In any event, there is little if any contra-evidence that Ho Chi Minh would have accepted an end-state that fell short of a united Vietnam governed by Hanoi, and implicit in this solution was domination by a communist political system. Whatever history's final verdict upon Ho Chi Minh may be, it should never be forgotten that he was responsible for the deaths of many hundreds of thousands of his Vietnamese countrymen, and indirectly for the deaths of many thousands more in Laos and Cambodia. Although Ho's passing produced no obvious change of strategic policy or objectives in Hanoi, it was nonetheless true that in 1969 the first formal peace talks (both publicly and privately) began in Paris, albeit with little or no progress made until 1972.

Although US bombing against the North (but not of Laos, Cambodia or along the Ho Chi Minh trail) had been curtailed by Johnson's parting declaration and by Nixon's commitment to pursue negotiations with Hanoi, the pacification of the hinterland and reinvigoration of the ARVN were very successful, so that the other two of Nixon's policy pillars – Vietnamisation of the war and a progressive reduction of American forces – now appeared to be achievable. The in-country military and political leadership of General Abrams and US Ambassador Ellsworth Bunker was particularly effective, and together they implemented joint security policies that were closely coordinated with the needs of the Saigon government. This advanced the Vietnamisation programme rapidly.

With the Viet Cong neutralised, military operations were conducted successfully throughout the South, where confidence in a stable and secure future grew with each week and month that passed. A limited expedition by US forces into Cambodia in April 1970 followed the overthrow of pro-Hanoi Prince Sihanouk by Prince Sirik Matak and General Lon Nol, the prime minister, on 18 March. Apart from boosting (albeit for only a few years) the new Republic of Cambodia's security and severing the Sihanouk Trail, the destruction inflicted upon the four divisions of NVA troops stationed there delayed implementation of Giap's invasion plans by two years.

The American incursion, however, was reported by the media as an expansion of the war, which attracted a storm of criticism, and this in turn gave rise to violent anti-war protests. The strength of domestic feeling about the conflict in general and the Cambodian operation in particular was highlighted on 4 May, when a student protest at Kent State University in Ohio was dispersed by State National Guardsmen, with four student protestors shot dead. Despite such incidents, however, opinion polls and surveys conducted in 1972 indicated that fifty-eight per cent of the population as a whole still supported US action in Vietnam; with fifty-two per cent support from the key eighteen to twenty-nine age group.[130] Yet majorities of just over fifty per cent fell well short of an unequivocal mandate for continued US military involvement in Vietnam, other than in the short term.

During June and July 1970 the US forces still deployed in Cambodia withdrew back into South Vietnam. Meanwhile, a similar operation into Laos, Operation Lam Son 719, was conducted predominantly by the ARVN from 30 January to 6 April 1971 and resulted in the deaths of some 19,360 communist fighters, mainly NVA troops. Although elements of the 101st US Airborne Division (Airmobile) and 5th US Infantry Division (Mechanised) were also involved with Operation Lam Son 719, and carried out combat missions to support it within South Vietnam, the sheer scale of the communist casualties, together with the destruction of the NVA lines of communication within central Laos, indicated the new confidence and fighting ability of the ARVN since Tet 1968.

If South Vietnam had continued to enjoy the support of US airpower, its defence and long-term existence as a sovereign state remained perfectly feasible at the close of the 1960s. However, on 31 December 1970, just a month before the start of the operation in Laos, the US Congress had repealed the South-east Asia (Gulf of Tonkin) Resolution. This was the key document signed by President Johnson on 11 August 1964 which had provided the political and legal justification for the president to take any action he deemed necessary to prosecute the war in Vietnam. The repeal of this resolution, primarily to satisfy American domestic concerns, signalled to Hanoi and Saigon that future US military support for South Vietnam would be at best very limited. Thus the US Congress enabled General Giap to plan his invasion of the South in the certain knowledge that the NVA would in the main be confronted by the ARVN alone. It also signalled Washington's eventual intention to renege on its obligations to its South-east Asian ally – a policy change that was duly noted elsewhere, on both sides of the Iron Curtain.

On 31 January 1969 US troop strengths had peaked at about 536,000, but on 8 July the first part of the phased withdrawal began, and by the end of 1971 they stood at just 158,120. Despite this downsizing, November 1969 and May 1970 nevertheless witnessed yet more extensive protests and demonstrations by the anti-war movement right across the United States, and there was an irresistible pressure on the government to move the withdrawal ahead even more speedily. Consequently, by the end of 1972, there were just 24,000 US personnel in South Vietnam. But another factor that heavily influenced Washington was the presence of numbers of American prisoners, including many pilots who had been shot down over North Vietnam, then being held in often appalling conditions in communist prison camps. In addition to 591 known prisoners in January 1973 there were also 1,380 missing in action and a further 1,929 US servicemen unaccounted for.

Meanwhile, the many and various pressures imposed by the war as it moved into the new decade were also beginning to affect the increasingly fragile, unsure and sometimes ambiguous situation of the US forces in Vietnam. The *Washington Post* staff writer Rick Atkinson observed:

As New Year's slipped past and a new decade [the 1970s] began, there were ominous signs of an American Army coming apart at the seams. Yet few military men cared to recognize the portents of disaster, given both their native American optimism and the relative success of the 1969 campaigns. Viet Cong strength had been broken by staggering losses in Tet of 1968, and Saigon now completely controlled 70 per cent of the country's villages and enjoyed reasonable security in another 20 per cent. Highways were safer than they had been since 1956. US intelligence analysts estimated that Viet Cong manpower in the [Mekong] delta had plummeted to about two thousand troops.

But those were tactical triumphs. Strategically, the war was slipping away. The nation's will to win the conflict was evaporating and the Army was crumbling from within. Considering that the Army fielded in 1966 and 1967 was, in the estimation of some historians, the finest ever assembled by the United States, the collapse happened with remarkable speed. Desertion and AWOL [absence without leave] rates began to soar, as did heroin addiction. In the next two years, the Army would suffer hundreds of fraggings.[131] In an effort to caulk morale, the military began distributing medals so promiscuously that they became known derisively as gongs. In 1970 alone, more than half a million decorations were handed out, twice the number of US personnel remaining in-country.

As they had from the beginning, lieutenants and captains bore the brunt of the casualties within the officer corps. (In eleven years of combat, only eight colonels and three generals would be killed; the number of lieutenants killed was seventeen hundred.) In part, this was because platoons and companies served as the basic fighting units of a mobile war against an elusive enemy. The changing style of combat leadership was also a factor, as senior officers gradually migrated to the rear in modern conflicts. In the [American] Civil War, by contrast, the chance of a general being killed was 50 per cent higher than that of a private; among both Confederate and Union forces, the proportion of all officers killed was 15 per cent higher than dead enlisted troops.[132]

Relating this situation to his account of the West Point graduates of 1966 Atkinson added:

Among the West Pointers from the class of 1966, the death toll [had] continued to rise with monotonous consistency. Soon it proportionately exceeded even the Korean War losses of the class of 1950, a group widely regarded [within the United States] as having been mauled in combat. The chance of being killed in Vietnam was about one in twenty among the '66ers; the chance of being wounded was about one in six.

Hollow Victory: The Defeat of the Communist Invasion, 1972

With US strengths reduced to levels not seen since the mid-1960s, and South Vietnam's industry, commerce and even agriculture booming, Hanoi could delay its invasion no longer. The ARVN was also gaining in strength and professionalism by the month. Forgoing the option of mounting another offensive at Tet, the date selected was March 1972. This would allow the NVA to complete its new campaign before the monsoon rains arrived in May to hamper armoured movement and favour the forces defending South Vietnam. The fact that a US presidential election was once again in the offing was a bonus, but not entirely coincidental.

In 1971, Le Duan, formerly the senior Viet Minh leader in South Vietnam, had visited Moscow and secured Soviet approval of a conventional invasion of the South, plus an agreement to provide the necessary matériel and equipment to carry it out. As many hundreds of tons of armaments (including T-34, PT-76 and T-54/55 tanks, 122mm and 130mm artillery pieces and SA-2 and SA-7 surface-to-air missile (SAM) systems) and supplies flowed into North Vietnam, the USAF and South Vietnamese air force resumed their bombing of targets below the 20th parallel; but they still stopped short of strategic strikes against Hanoi and Haiphong, or at the PRC–North Vietnam border. Where they did attack the NVA build-up, these air strikes were generally very effective, but political constraints limited the extent of the USAF missions. With their bombing accuracy and techniques the Americans could almost certainly have stopped the impending invasion in its tracks; but all too familiar political pressures in Washington, a US fear of being labelled as aggressors, and the evidence of direct Soviet support for the North, all combined to inhibit the commanders in the field.

At 02.00 hours on 30 March thousands of shells, rockets and mortar rounds fell on South Vietnamese positions along the demilitarised zone (DMZ). This tremendous bombardment neutralised the ARVN fire support bases and was followed shortly afterwards by the rumble of tank tracks as the NVA 304th and 308th Divisions stormed across the border. The NVA attack was spearheaded by the newly acquired T-54/55 main battle tanks. Simultaneously the NVA 324th Division broke across the western border from Laos and drove eastward from the A Shau Valley towards Hue. Some 40,000 NVA troops swept into Quang Tri province, and within six days they had penetrated ten miles into the South. Eventually, a total of six NVA divisions were committed in the area of South Vietnam designated Military Region I (MR I). Despite early gains of territory and the collapse of the ARVN 3rd Division, with the subsequent loss of Quang Tri city on 1 May, the South Vietnamese held Hue successfully. By mid-May they had stabilised the whole front, due in no small measure to the competence of General Ngo Quang

Truong, the ARVN commander. Following some redeployments and reinforcement during June, they launched a counter-offensive against the NVA in Quang Tri province on 28 June. During two months of severe fighting the ARVN recaptured virtually all of the territory it had lost in April and May, and Quang Tri city was finally recaptured by the élite South Vietnamese Marine Division on 16 September. Within Quang Tri province, six NVA divisions had suffered a resounding defeat at the hands of just three ARVN divisions.

Giap's invasion, however, had been launched on three separate fronts, and on 23 April another massive artillery bombardment had fallen on the network of ARVN bunkers and emplacements astride Route 14 in the Central Highlands – the key road route to the cities of Tan Canh, Kontum and Pleiku. This bombardment preceded a thrust from Laos by two NVA divisions (the 2nd and 320th) and some Viet Cong units eastward into MR II the next morning. Despite the initial collapse of a few ARVN units (notably the 22nd Division at Tan Canh) in the face of this armoured onslaught, spirited counter-attacks, the sound use of air support – including the unorthodox but highly effective employment of B-52 bombers in a tactical role – and the resolute defence of Kontum city by the ARVN 23rd Division, together resulted in the communist threat to MR II being stalled by the end of May. A subsidiary attack towards the coast and Binh Dinh province while Kontum was under siege was also neutralised, primarily by the use of air power. Despite the fact that some ARVN units had certainly performed much better than others, and that outbreaks of fighting still occurred sporadically during the next few months, the communist attack in the Central Highlands had been defeated.

Giap's third attack of the 1972 invasion was launched against Military Regions III and IV to the south, within which lay Saigon, Tay Ninh, An Loc and the important Mekong Delta. It involved a total of five divisions and was mounted from Cambodia. The assault commenced on 2 April and by 6 April two ARVN fire support bases, plus the ARVN garrison of Loc Ninh to the north of Tay Ninh city, had been overrun. However, this action was a diversionary attack, and the main objective – Saigon apart – was An Loc; by 13 April that city was under siege by the NVA 9th Division, reinforced soon thereafter by the 5th and 7th Divisions. From 13 April to 10 May some 1,000 artillery rounds fell on An Loc and its 4,000 defenders each day. But here again the American B-52s proved decisive. They were instrumental in preventing the fall of the city in mid-April and then, on 10, 11 and 12 May, they struck the massed NVA armour and infantry of the seven regiments engaged in a final attack to capture the city. The combination of US and South Vietnamese air power and the gallantry and resolute action of the ARVN garrison shattered all of these assaults, and by 15 May the NVA, apart from some stay-behind units, had withdrawn. The ARVN set about dealing with the latter in short order and on 18 June the siege of An Loc was declared officially ended.

The 1972 invasion, conducted on three separate fronts by fourteen infantry divisions with significant armour and artillery support, was the high-water mark of NVA offensive action on such a scale and – just as at Tet 1968 – the communist forces had been found wanting. By late June the communists had incurred about 120,000 casualties, many NVA infantry battalions had been reduced to less than fifty men, while desertions, indiscipline and open dissent by some commanders had reached unprecedented levels. For every ARVN casualty the NVA had lost four or five men, and retreating NVA units were even seen to be abandoning serviceable equipment, weapons and ammunition – something virtually unheard of during the earlier years of the conflict. A great deal has been said about indiscipline, low morale and drug abuse in the US forces at this time, but the equivalent situation in the armed forces of North Vietnam after Tet 1968 and then following the defeat of Giap's 1972 invasion attracted relatively little media attention or comment. This was not surprising, given the strict censorship in the North and the mood of the time in America; but it has tended to unbalance perceptions of the war by later generations and by those who were not directly involved in it.

In practice, by the end of June 1972, if the United States had maintained indefinitely its original commitment to support the South, the Hanoi regime would have faced total defeat and the end of the late Ho Chi Minh's dream of a united, communist, Vietnam. Indeed, such a commitment might even have led to a complete reversal of the North–South political situation, with the stability, prosperity and security of the South eventually prompting a popular anti-communist revolution in the North – although such a development would no doubt have been balked by the PRC and the Soviet Union.

The reasons for the North's defeat in 1972 were several. First and foremost Giap's army was unready to fight the sort of conventional all-arms campaign upon which it had embarked on 30 March. Certainly it had the necessary equipment and firepower, but it lacked experience in this sort of warfare, especially as it was deployed against South Vietnamese forces that had always been more comfortable with this type of combat. Failures of battlefield communications (also evident during Tet 1968), breakdowns of the logistic system (the provision of fuel for the tanks in particular), the misuse of armour in close country and built-up areas, and the over-concentration of armoured forces (presenting them as targets for air strikes) were all symptomatic of a former guerrilla or Third World army that was ill-prepared to fight a conventional European-style war. Strategically, Giap did not display the awareness and tactical acumen that he had shown at the operational level against the French at Dien Bien Phu almost two decades earlier. Although the southern thrusts towards An Loc and Saigon were probably his intended points of main effort, this was unclear. Consequently, his failure to reinforce the NVA's early successes in that area, and then to use the mobility and shock effect of his armoured units to bypass An Loc and strike towards Saigon – which would undoubtedly have caused considerable panic in the capital, as well as providing a significant psychological impact – was an important strategic omission.

At the political-military level the invasion had far-reaching consequences. First, while the South Vietnamese could have neutralised the NVA once and for all and – with some justification – could even have carried the ground war into the North, the leadership in Saigon was still dependent upon US support, especially air power. But President Nixon was constrained by domestic pressure to end US involvement and to secure the release of those Americans held prisoner by the North, which meant that a ceasefire had to be achieved; and this could not happen if the ground war were to be carried into North Vietnam. Therefore, the war remained limited and inextricably bound up with American national interests, which meant that South Vietnam was denied the opportunity to complete the defeat of its communist enemy and so change the future history of South-east Asia.

At the same time, the reverses suffered by Hanoi in 1972 confirmed that its political aspirations would always be frustrated if any US military support for Saigon was still available. Consequently, as a matter of policy, no further invasion of the South was planned to take place until any possibility of American involvement had been removed. Accordingly, Hanoi now concentrated on the negotiating table rather than the battlefield, with the overriding aim of entirely decoupling America from South Vietnam.

The support provided to the ARVN in 1972 was the last direct involvement of US forces on a large scale, although air strikes continued at various levels of intensity after the invasion, as well as during the ongoing negotiations with the North Vietnamese representatives in Paris. Military targets were the main focus of the bombing, but the use of new precision-bombing technology now enabled supply depots, bridges, highways, railways and military-related power plants and industrial complexes to be attacked. The mining of Haiphong and six other North Vietnam harbours was also carried out from 8 May. This could and should have been done much earlier in the war; when it would have had a much greater impact upon North Vietnam's ability to receive Soviet matériel and thus develop its conventional war-fighting capability. Indeed, by late 1972, US bombing of the North had become a central negotiating issue at the peace talks, and even though an

American withdrawal was plainly taking place, the B-52 bombing missions against the North (resumed in April) had from the outset attracted another storm of protest in the United States, and prompted accusations that America was escalating the conflict.

Although these air strikes were undeniably among the heaviest of the war, this view was somewhat misplaced in light of the North Vietnamese aggression in March. However, by 1972 both the political and the presentational wars had been lost by the United States, as the new administration in Washington sought to end US involvement in South Vietnam with all due dispatch, hand the conflict over to Thieu's government in Saigon, and (for many Americans the highest priority of all) bring the prisoners of war home to America. All the while US force levels were dropping. On 31 March there were still 96,000 US personnel in South Vietnam; a mere six months later there were 32,000 and by the end of 1972 the figure had fallen to just 24,000.

The Great Betrayal: 1973–5

On 23 January 1973 Le Duc Tho, the North Vietnamese chief negotiator in Paris, and Henry Kissinger initialled the ceasefire document, which was formally signed on 27 January. In that same year both men received jointly a rather premature award of a Nobel Peace Prize for their efforts. Hanoi's change of policy, with the new emphasis on negotiation, had finally provided the communists with exactly what they wanted. US bombing had already ceased on 30 December 1972, arrangements for the repatriation of prisoners of war were agreed, and the way was open for a total withdrawal of American combat support for Saigon. The ceasefire also implicitly legitimised the continued presence of NVA soldiers in South Vietnam, where a number of units had held on to some of the tenuous gains made earlier the previous year. This concession was understandably of particular concern to President Thieu. However, he felt able to accept the less than ideal ceasefire arrangements following receipt of a written undertaking from President Nixon stating: 'You have my absolute assurance that if Hanoi fails to abide by the terms of this agreement it is my intention to take swift and severe retaliatory action.'[133] But this was an undertaking that Nixon must have known he could not honour. Thus on 27 January 1973 the fate of the Republic of South Vietnam was sealed, and the United States prepared finally to abandon its long-standing South-east Asian ally. In Hanoi intensive military planning resumed for another invasion of the South, one that would this time assuredly achieve the overthrow of the Saigon regime.

For the American servicemen in Vietnam the accelerating pace of the ceasefire negotiations after 1969, together with the rundown of force levels, had a predictable effect. Morale and indiscipline problems increased, while an obsessive preoccupation with tour lengths and days in combat pervaded. Nobody wanted to be the last man to die in a war that was just about to end. The earlier problems of selection for the draft had been exacerbated from 1971, when many of the professional school course and college deferments ended. This resulted in large numbers of well-educated and politically aware draftees arriving as reinforcements for combat units in Vietnam. These highly politicised ex-students were often better educated than the officers who commanded them, and many had experienced at first-hand the anti-war dissent and campus demonstrations in America before being drafted. Some also regarded the war in South-east Asia as symptomatic of a wider socio-political malaise of capitalist Western society.

Meanwhile, Richard Nixon had fought a successful presidential election campaign during 1972, which produced a clear victory and his re-election in November. But, some months earlier, in Washington DC on 17 June, one James McCord, the chief of security of the Committee for the Re-election of the President, together with four other men, had been arrested while attempting to plant eavesdropping devices inside the Democratic Party national headquarters at the Watergate Hotel. The fall-out from this bizarre incident was dramatic. Following Nixon's landslide victory in November, a steady stream of accusations of corruption, dishonesty, illegal surveillance, burglary, fraud, extortion, illegal use of campaign funds, conspiracy and so on was levelled against the administration. These resulted in the disgrace and in some cases the criminal conviction of various aides, officials and others directly connected with the White House, although Nixon denied any personal knowledge or involvement. The burgeoning crisis deepened significantly in October 1973, with the resignation of Vice-President Spiro T. Agnew, who was then faced with criminal charges concerned with his former position as governor of Maryland.

Still Nixon held on, but he was already a lame-duck president, which meant that America's international power and influence were significantly diminished. On 5 August 1974 the final act in this sordid political scandal took place, with the release of secret White House tapes which provided clear evidence of Nixon's involvement, and of his deliberate intention to cover up the original surveillance operation at the Watergate Hotel. Impeachment was inevitable, and he resigned on 8 August. He was succeeded the next day by Vice-President Gerald R. Ford. With the decline and fall of Nixon, many of those who had opposed the war in Vietnam proclaimed a total vindication of their long-held belief that successive administrations and officials in Washington had misled the American people over the conduct of the war ever since the early 1960s. Whatever the truth of the matter, the scars of Watergate ran very deep.

Following the bitter anti-war protests of the Johnson era and then the revelations about US policy in South-east Asia contained in the so-called Pentagon Papers leaked by the *New York Times* in June 1971,[134] Watergate finally destroyed the trust of many ordinary Americans in their leaders, their political system and their very claim to be the champions of democracy in the Free World. While it was all of these matters together, not only the Vietnam War, which shook the American people and their armed forces for many years to come, the common factor in this crisis of confidence was American military involvement in South-east Asia.

Just as the United States was reverberating from these political traumas, the war moved into its final phase. Despite the ceasefire, the North had continued to carry out limited attacks into and within South Vietnam: the first of these came on the very morning after the ceasefire document was signed in Paris. If there was ever a belief in North Vietnamese good faith, then surely such acts now dispelled it utterly. Hanoi reinforced and refurbished the NVA in preparation for a new invasion, while quite openly continuing to violate the ceasefire agreement by infiltrating quantities of men, matériel and heavy equipment into the South. Nevertheless, the American rundown continued, and on 29 March 1973 the last US troops had left South Vietnam. On the same day, a final repatriation of American prisoners of war held by the North Vietnamese had taken place.[135]

The security situation deteriorated rapidly during the next two years as the NVA escalated their renewed campaign within South Vietnam. With Nixon's resignation on 8 August 1974 went any realistic hope for President Thieu that the undertaking given by the disgraced president in January 1973 would be honoured. Meanwhile, by early 1975 the North Vietnamese had received huge quantities of Soviet equipment and, with some 225,000 NVA troops and 40,000 guerrillas already in the South or just over its borders, they were almost ready to launch a new assault on the South. In addition to a total of about 375,000 personnel organised into twenty divisions, the NVA was supported by more than 600 tanks and armoured personnel carriers, plus almost 350 aircraft and a comprehensive air defence organisation, which included anti-aircraft artillery and SAM regiments. With the American air threat eliminated, no NVA forces needed to be allocated to the defence of the North. Finally, sufficient combat supplies to sustain an intensive campaign over twelve months had been amassed. Overall command of this new venture lay with General Van Tien Dung.

Decline and Fall: 1975

The first domino toppled when Cambodia fell under communist control in late March, as the Khmer Rouge, boosted by thousands of NVA and Viet

Cong troops, overthrew Lon Nol. This campaign had begun in January, and directly complemented the impending invasion of South Vietnam. In Cambodia the anti-communist government had also depended upon US military assistance and air power, and (apart from airlifts of food, fuel and ammunition) this was no longer forthcoming. On 12 April the last Americans were evacuated from Phnom Penh by USMC helicopters and, when the last government units succumbed five days later, the way was opened for the genocide of Pol Pot's nightmare regime in the renamed Kampuchea. The campaign in Cambodia had provided Hanoi with unrestricted access across South Vietnam's eastern and south-eastern borders since late January 1975 and this continued with the Kampuchean communists now in power.

By 1975 the South Vietnamese forces, starved of US military and financial aid, were about 100,000 weaker than they had been during the 1972 invasion. In early 1975 the ARVN was about 180,600 strong, with some 350 tanks and 880 armoured personnel carriers, while the regional and popular forces numbered 289,000 and 193,000 respectively. Although this provided a fighting strength of 662,600, these forces were spread thinly throughout the South in a vain attempt to counter any of an infinite number of NVA threats. The South Vietnamese air force still had 1,673 aircraft available, but this number was considerably less than it had been able to call upon when the United States had provided its supporting air power. Furthermore, the reduced American aid meant that the ARVN no longer had sufficient fuel stocks or ammunition to combat a full-scale invasion. The NVA high command was fully aware of the significantly weakened state of the South's armed forces and in January 1975, in parallel with its operations in Cambodia, it initiated a chain of events intended to precipitate the military and political collapse of South Vietnam.

The first blow fell upon Phuoc Long province to the north-east of Saigon, with the capture of the provincial capital, Phuoc Binh city, on 7 January. This placed the NVA 9th Division less than 100 miles from Saigon and so prevented the defenders of the nation's capital from being deployed elsewhere. On 11 March, Ban Me Thuot in the Central Highlands fell to General Dung's forces, following diversionary moves towards Pleiku and Kontum. President Thieu authorised the local commander, General Pham Van Phu, to evacuate Pleiku and Kontum and withdraw to the coast. Chaos ensued as the communists attacked the retreating columns of troops and refugees, causing great suffering and large numbers of casualties. Further north, the communists advanced southward from Quang Tri and towards Hue, from which President Thieu had already ordered the élite South Vietnamese Airborne Division to redeploy to the Saigon area to provide a strategic reserve. This caused considerable civilian panic throughout MR I, and at Hue in particular. To the south of Hue, the South Vietnamese marines – another very sound and professional formation – held Da Nang, which soon became a Mecca for thousands of refugees from MR I. The airbase was overwhelmed by the human tide seeking to escape the advancing communists, and from Da Nang they tried every way to flee South Vietnam by air, sea and land. On 29 March a last Boeing 727 transport aircraft took off from Da Nang with about 300 people on board, the majority of whom were soldiers who had forced their way aboard. Hue and Da Nang soon fell to the communists, and Nha Trang, Tuy Hoa and Cam Ranh Bay were all in communist hands by early April. Although Hanoi had originally anticipated a lengthy campaign, Giap and Dung sensed – quite correctly – that it was now time to modify their original invasion plan and strike directly at Saigon. Building on the hard-learned lessons of 1972, the NVA air defence and logistics organisations switched their focus to support the concerted drive on Saigon, while some thirteen NVA divisions advanced towards Saigon. Truckloads of supplies thundered south, and further reinforcements and matériel were leapfrogged forward by sea and air to the major ports and airbases that were now firmly under communist control.

Despite President Ford's desire to provide funding support to Saigon and to Phnom Penh, Congress vehemently opposed any further involvement in the region; and although the communists continued to watch anxiously for any signs of US combat aircraft or bombers moving towards Vietnam from Thailand, no such direct military intervention was ever contemplated. Nevertheless, on 3 April the Americans did begin a major air evacuation using large numbers of military cargo aircraft. On 21 April President Thieu resigned. At the same time, he made public Nixon's original undertaking to support the South if Hanoi reneged on the Paris agreements and bitterly denounced the US abandonment of South Vietnam. The vice-president, General Duong Van Minh (the former president who had led the 1963 coup against Diem), was appointed president; and in Saigon the air force commander, General Nguyen Cao Ky, proposed an all-out defence of the capital street-by-street and building-by-building. Meanwhile the American C-141 and C-130 transport aircraft continued to fly into the few remaining usable airstrips and took off with their human cargo of American civilian personnel, government officials and refugees.

Although they were still fighting, many of the ARVN's best units engaged at Xuan Loc were by now entirely cut off from the capital thirty miles away. At Xuan Loc the ARVN 18th Division fought valiantly for almost three days against overwhelming numbers in a vain attempt to halt the NVA advance on the capital from the north and east. Meanwhile, Bien Hoa air base was under heavy attack and virtually unusable other than by C-130s, and by dawn on 30 April the artillery fire against Saigon's Tan Son Nhut airbase rendered further landings by fixed-wing aircraft impossible. The evacuation of Saigon continued, using helicopters. Clearly the end was fast approaching.

The final helicopter evacuation was titled Operation Frequent Wind. It lasted for about eighteen hours through the night 29/30 April and was conducted in the main by the USMC and USAF H-53 and H-46 helicopters, plus a number of CIA-sponsored Air America UH-1 Hueys. The operation was mounted from the fleet of US warships by then lying off the south coast of Vietnam. In a last surge of helicopter activity, 1,373 Americans, 6,422 non-Americans and 989 US marines were successfully evacuated, with no aircraft lost. But by 29 April public order was virtually non-existent, and many of the vehicle convoys moving evacuees to landing points at the US embassy or Tan Son Nhut were attacked by armed ARVN deserters and civilian mobs. Meanwhile, US F-4 Phantom Wild Weasel fighters circled above the helicopters ready to destroy any SAM sites that sought to engage the vulnerable craft. One of the very last combat actions by US forces in Vietnam took place when two Phantoms destroyed a 57mm anti-aircraft gun about ten miles north-east of Saigon on the late afternoon of the 29th. Ambassador Graham Martin was officially ordered to quit the embassy and was one of the final evacuees. However, the last Americans to leave were eleven US marines who had continued to protect the embassy until the very end. As they waited on the roof, a rampaging mob of looters and desperate refugees had already occupied the lower floors of the building and were even then trying to break through a locked door and a shattered window to reach the rooftop helipad.

At 7.49 on the morning of April 30, 1975, specks appeared in the south-eastern sky. Before 7.51, they were identifiable as one Chinook [C]-46 escorted by six nimble Cobra gunships, which looked and manoeuvred as much like dragonflies as any machine man had ever devised. And then the eleven Marines left on the roof of what had been the American Embassy in Saigon unloaded canister after canister of teargas grenades over the front, back and sides of the building on to the heads of the Vietnamese below. Over the back, from which came the major threat, they put a hand-grenade in a box of teargas canisters. They did it for their own protection. But they forgot that a settling helicopter sucks up air. So the last official Americans out of Vietnam – the eleven Marines and the crew of the CH-46, including the pilot – all flew blind out of Saigon.[136]

Thus ended the residual US presence in South Vietnam.[137] The hurried, chaotic and ignominious final exit from the embassy roof contrasted markedly with the heady self-confidence that had attended events such as the arrival of the 1st Cavalry Division (Airmobile) at Qui Nhon and An Khe in the late-summer of 1965, and that of the US marines at Da Nang on 8 March the same year; or indeed the decisive military defeats of the NVA and Viet Cong in 1968 and 1972. Australian photo-journalist Neil Davis witnessed the moment of North Vietnam's final victory:

> The tank was turning the corner to approach the main gate [of the presidential palace]. Through a break in the trees, Davis now could see it clearly, and there was no question as to what it was: a Russian T-54 tank [with turret number 844] with a soldier sitting on its nose waving the biggest Viet Cong flag Davis had ever seen ... Tank 844 was quickly joined by others from its column, which had proceeded up Thuong Nhut Boulevard past the American Embassy and around the basilica ... The tanks formed a semicircle facing the [presidential] palace, and for a moment Davis thought they were going to blow it away. The lawn was filling with infantry as well as tank crews. And then, as both the man from tank 844 and a second soldier with a Viet Cong flag appeared simultaneously on the balcony of the palace, the air was filled with the sound of hundreds of weapons being fired into the sky. The two figures waved the flags so they crisscrossed, as if they were flashing a semaphore signal of the end of the war.[138]

Although the West's thirty-year war against communism in French Indochina and then in Cambodia, Laos and Vietnam had finally come to an end, the fall-out from the conflict resulted in many more years of suffering for the peoples of Indochina at the hands of their new masters. It precipitated mass movements of refugees (such as the so-called Vietnamese boat people) who were in many cases seeking relief from communist oppression, whilst hoping to find a better life and economic opportunity in the non-communist world. But its effects, albeit very different in nature but nonetheless pronounced, were also deeply engraved upon the American consciousness and that of its armed forces for decades to come. This most significant Cold War conflict had indeed been little short of disastrous for that superpower.

From 1961 to 1973, about nine and a half million Americans were called up for military service; of these, almost three million served in Vietnam. Compared with its Free World force allies, the US military commitment to support South Vietnam was enormous. Between 1 January 1961 and 31

December 1976, 46,558 Americans died in action in Vietnam, plus 10,390 from other causes (including 354 suicides and 199 murders). Diseases claimed 454 and strokes and heart attacks 208. A further 695 were, and (as at 1976) remained, missing or captured and unaccounted for. In the army, 208,576 personnel were wounded, and of these 3,521 later died of their wounds.[139]

Since the departure of the French in 1954 the communists had lost well over one million NVA and Viet Cong troops killed, while the South had lost about 400,000. Although the more than 47,000 American lives lost in South-east Asia was by no means insignificant, a rough comparison with the fatal casualties incurred by its immediate ally – about nine South Vietnamese servicemen for every one American – did demonstrate the different values placed upon human life and political commitment in the Western world. The contrast with the human losses that Hanoi was prepared to suffer in order to guarantee success was even more extreme.

Having committed the United States to championing the cause of freedom in South Vietnam, perhaps the American people should have been prepared to accept significantly greater numbers of casualties in order to achieve an overall victory, and so make worthwhile the sacrifice of all those who had died. However, the lesson here is one primarily for the politicians. It is that every war is potentially open-ended, and its progress will always be unpredictable – therefore, the decision to commit a nation and its armed forces to any conflict must be well-judged, resolute and wholehearted, with a clear end-state (whether it be victory or some other more limited objective) clearly predetermined. But once such a commitment has been correctly made by a democratically elected leadership, it should be the business of the whole nation to support the cause unreservedly. Arguably, the Kennedy administration's original decision to engage in South-east Asia was flawed, but that unsatisfactory situation could probably have been retrieved had successive US administrations and the American people – albeit ill-informed by an often inaccurate and generally over-politicised media – not lost the will to win in South Vietnam.

The outfall and lessons of Vietnam went straight to the heart of the Cold War relationship between the United States and the Soviet Union, and that of the latter with the PRC. It also showed very clearly the changes in the superpower balance of power that had occurred since the Korean War.

While the Viet Minh's victory at Dien Bien Phu in 1954 had been won by a guerrilla army, North Vietnam's victory in 1975 was the result of a conventional campaign. This was something that it had signally failed to achieve in 1968 and 1972, but by 1975 the level of Soviet military assistance to Hanoi had increased enormously. Although Washington was very aware of this, it no longer had the total freedom of action that it had enjoyed (but chosen not to exercise) in Korea, as the Soviet Union had so expanded its ICBM holdings by the mid-1960s that an approximate strategic parity with the United States had been achieved. Meanwhile, as the Soviet Union's ideological relationship with China worsened through the 1960s, its interest in maintaining an ally on China's southern border, together with the use of the massive naval base at Cam Ranh Bay by the Soviet Far East Fleet, became ever more important. Consequently, the North Vietnamese victory in April 1975 was also a major Cold War victory for Moscow, as it simultaneously secured part of the Soviet Union's southern flank and enabled an enhancement of Soviet maritime power. It might also have facilitated a military operation against the PRC by a Vietnamese-led coalition of Indochinese forces, if ever Sino–Soviet relations should have deteriorated to that extent.

In any event, it ensured that some fifteen Chinese divisions which could have been deployed to the Sino–Soviet border region were, in the late 1970s, deployed instead to the Vietnam border. During the further conflict that took place in Kampuchea during 1978 and 1979, the Vietnamese army (by then about 600,000 strong and still extensively backed by the Soviet Union) consolidated its control of Laos and Kampuchea and so became the dominant power in the region. It had taken more than three decades, but by the early 1980s both Hanoi and Moscow could look back with considerable satisfaction upon all that had been achieved in Indochina.

For the United States the process of self-analysis and assessment of its greatest war of the Cold War period had begun long before April 1975. The loss of the psychological and information war have already been highlighted, but the impact of this and of media misrepresentation and unbalanced reporting of the war cannot be overstated. The former occurred both through genuine error and through deliberate action. The latter was sometimes indicative of political bias, but was often simply a case of editorial pressure to produce sensational and controversial pictures and copy. The reporting imbalance also reflected North Vietnam's very effective media censorship. On the other hand, had Washington handled the whole business of information warfare better, it could certainly have limited much of the damage inflicted upon the nation and the morale of its armed forces by its domestic media. That said, the increasing evidence of corruption, misuse of power, high-level cover-ups and misinformation carried out by politicians and officials in Washington, which eventually culminated in the Watergate scandal and the downfall of Nixon, destroyed the integrity of the US government and the office of president. Indeed, although an American domestic issue, Watergate sealed the fate of South Vietnam, as it effectively prevented

Nixon from fulfilling his commitment to President Thieu concerning the Paris ceasefire agreement.

For better or worse, the suspicions of the American people about many of the activities of those elected to govern them still persist almost thirty years after Vietnam. This atmosphere of suspicion and scepticism has since extended well beyond the United States, and many Western politicians, political organisations and officials are today probably more mistrusted, and held generally in lower esteem by the people they seek to govern, than at any other time since 1945.

But it was in the US armed forces – the army in particular – that the impact of the Vietnam War was most felt and this had implications for the Western democracies and NATO Alliance, both of which depended upon the continued effectiveness of the US forces to limit, deter and counter the global threat posed by the Soviet Union.

Vietnam showed that the lessons of Korea had not been well learned by the Pentagon, where many of the attitudes and concepts that had directed America's Second World War campaigns in north-west Europe and the Pacific persisted into the 1960s. Much of the military leadership was still of the opinion that offensive action, devastating firepower and superior technology were the essential and exclusive elements that guaranteed military success, and that the only measure of success was the total defeat of the enemy. It is a truism that a beaten army learns the lessons of its defeat far more readily than does the victor acknowledge, analyse and learn from the less satisfactory aspects of his victory.

As late as 1964, the Chairman of the JCS, General Earle Wheeler, stated: 'It is fashionable in some quarters to say that the problems in South-east Asia are primarily political and economic rather than military. I do not agree. The essence of the problem is military.'[140] This illustrated the American military's attitude to war at the highest level, and implied an ongoing unease with Truman's doctrine of the limited war. Prior to 1968 the war was still being waged primarily by the Viet Cong guerrillas, but the search-and-destroy strategy adopted by General Westmoreland, together with McNamara's preoccupation with body counts as a measure of success, denied South Vietnam other options to deal with the communists before they became capable of fighting a conventional war. This was partly because the US military actually relished the chance to move to that higher level of conflict, where it was able to bring its tactical doctrine and particular strengths to bear. However, had the real consequences of Tet 1968 been foreseen, it might have been more disposed to adopt a lower-profile military-political-economic campaign – possibly more like the British counter-revolutionary campaign in Malaya.

Ironically, the change in tempo to conventional war did indeed allow the United States to employ its air power to devastating effect which, together with an ARVN that was well prepared to fight a conventional war, resulted in the communist defeats of 1968 and 1972. At the same time, however, these very defeats were perversely translated into communist successes through their wider perception beyond Vietnam. If Nixon had still been able to abide by his 1973 pledge to President Thieu and deploy the full weight of US air power in Cambodia in late 1974 and against the advancing NVA divisions in March and April 1975, the communist invasion would not have succeeded. But by then it was quite clear that American assistance would not be forthcoming, and that the United States had – for the whole world to see – chosen to desert its Indochinese allies.

The US abandonment of South Vietnam was not lost upon its NATO and SEATO allies, or upon the political leaders in Moscow and Beijing. Neither was it lost upon certain political and religious leaders in the Middle East. There, America's unfailing support for the state of Israel, the West's insatiable appetite for oil, plus its intervention, interference and commercial involvement in the region, and the rapidly accelerating growth of Islamic fundamentalism, were already sowing the seeds of an entirely new and potent threat. That threat finally emerged in all its uncontrolled and mindless horror on 11 September 2001, and it may yet prove to be a greater global menace to democracy and the nations of the Free World than communism ever was, even during the darkest days of the Cold War.

CHAPTER TEN

TOWARDS ARMAGEDDON:
THE MIDDLE EAST, 1947–90

A Matter of Conscience: Palestine, Israel and the Arabs, 1945–50

The strategic significance of the Middle East stemmed primarily from its geographical position, the importance of the Suez Canal, and the vast oilfields that lay beneath the desert sands. A permanent backdrop to anything that took place in the Middle East was the multiplicity of religious sites and religions – Christianity, Judaism, Islam and many variations of all these – that existed in close proximity in Palestine, and which had always made the Middle East a uniquely volatile and unstable region. After 1945, however, other factors emerged to compound the already complex politics of the Middle East. Foremost of these were the new impetus of Zionism, the dramatic increase in Jewish immigration to Palestine and the establishment of the state of Israel. These activities all ran directly contrary to the traditional aspirations and expectations of the Palestinian Arabs, and the postwar Jewish-Palestinian conflict was virtually inevitable.

To a greater or lesser extent, all wars carry the seeds of future wars. This is usually because they breed victors and vanquished, and the latter (unless entirely annihilated) are usually dissatisfied with the peace terms imposed by the former. Sometimes the imposition of an unsatisfactory closure of a conflict may stem from a well-meant intention by the victors to right a great wrong or to divert and correct the course of history. Reluctant though they may be to admit it, in most cases human beings – in the guise of international statesmen – are rarely able to achieve that which they intended without unbalancing the equilibrium of international relations in other ways, thus inviting new conflicts. The whole story of Judea, Palestine and ultimately Israel is just such an instance. The small state that finally emerged – almost literally – from the concentration camps of the Holocaust has provided the focus for an escalating level of violence, tension, international terrorism and global instability for more than half a century. The state of Israel that was imposed upon the state of Palestine in 1947 reversed the long distant action of the Romans in about AD135, when they decreed that the land of Judea should henceforth be called Palestine, so favouring the Jews' arch-enemies of biblical times – the Philistines. Thereafter, Palestine was dominated first by the Arab nations and then by the Ottoman Turks, who governed the country into the First World War. During the final decades of the nineteenth century the Zionist movement emerged following the 1895 publication of Herzl's *Jewish State*, a prime aim of which was to establish (or re-establish?) a permanent Jewish homeland in Palestine.

In 1917 the Balfour Declaration indicated British support for a national home in Palestine for the Jews, and after the 1918 peace settlement the League of Nations provided the mandate under which Britain governed and administered the country. Between the two world wars, Jewish immigration to the British Mandate of Palestine was continuous but more or less manageable. Despite ongoing tensions and some friction, the British government of the day stated that while it 'favoured a national home for the Jews in Palestine', it was quite clear that 'nothing shall be done which may prejudice the civil and religious rights of existing non-Jewish communities'. Accordingly, the relatively harmonious co-existence of Arabs and Jews in a land administered by Britain seemed destined to continue into the foreseeable future.

But then came the 1930s and the emergence and meteoric rise to power of the Nazi Party in Germany. This was swiftly followed by the Second World War, by the end of which the names of Belsen, Ravensbrück, Auschwitz, Dachau, Treblinka and a hundred other concentration camps and extermination camps were etched indelibly upon the consciousness and conscience of the Western world. The whole international approach to what the Nazis termed 'the Jewish question' had changed forever, and from 1945 the would-be mass immigration of Jews to Palestine proceeded apace. It did so in parallel with the determination of the West (of the United States in particular)[141] to enable a viable Jewish homeland in Palestine, and the rapidly growing fear of the Palestinian Arabs that a country which had been an Arab state for the previous sixteen centuries was about to be overrun and stolen from them by hundreds of thousands of European and Russian Jews. These fears led to a number of uprisings and direct acts against the existing Jewish communities. To compound the situation, from 1944 an increasingly active anti-British terrorist campaign – one of the most bitter such conflicts of its time – was mounted by Jewish insurgents seeking to establish a new Jewish state in Palestine.

The UN resolution of 29 November 1947 had provided the international legality for the creation of the new Jewish state, and on 14 May 1948 the existence of Israel was proclaimed. This resolution allocated fifty-five per cent of the territory of the new state to the Jews and forty-five per cent to the Arabs. With Israel formally established, the British mandate ended. On the same day, the five Arab states that surrounded Israel – Egypt, Syria, Transjordan, Lebanon and Iraq – and the Palestinian Arabs within, attacked the embryo Jewish state. Remarkably, by the time a ceasefire was declared in June, the Israelis possessed sufficient Arab territory to be able to negotiate with their enemies from a position of strength, although sporadic fighting continued into 1949. Finally, Israel was adjudged the overall victor, and among its signif-

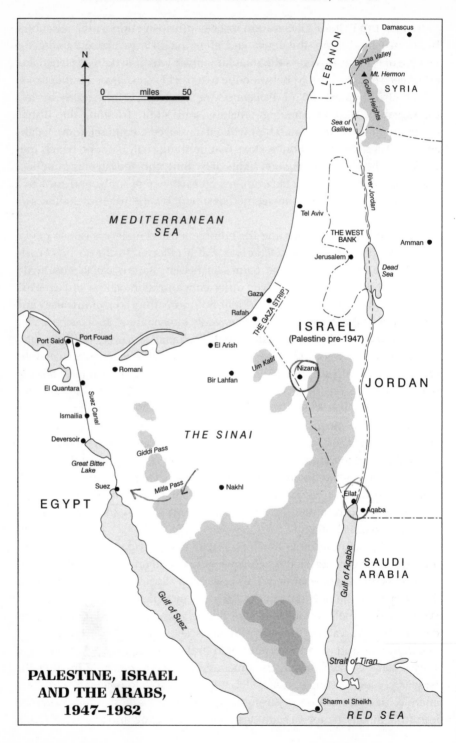

PALESTINE, ISRAEL
AND THE ARABS,
1947–1982

icant gains was a secure access route to Arab-held Jerusalem. But most importantly, it had firmly established its international existence as a sovereign state. Yet although the new state was generally better placed than it had been at the start of the war, Israel's borders were by no means secure, and it was fairly clear that what had been in some respects an inconclusive clash of arms was but the first of other wars to come.

From the outset Israel enjoyed the unqualified support of the United States. This was exemplified by President Truman's insistence in 1945 that 100,000 European Jews should be admitted into Palestine forthwith. Understandably, this potentially destabilising human influx was favoured by neither the Arabs nor the British at the time. Despite a few aberrations during the 1939–45 conflict, the Arabs had generally been regarded as supportive of Britain during the two World Wars, and (unlike the USA, with its national oil deposits) Western Europe depended upon Middle Eastern oil. Also, Britain needed the Suez Canal, which lay within Egyptian territory, for commercial and strategic movement to and from its imperial territories in India and the Far East. Thus, from its very birth, the fate and future of Israel were bound up inextricably with the interests, policies and actions of the great powers – the United States, Great Britain and France, as well as with the implacably hostile and formidable array of Arab states that surrounded it. Meanwhile, as the Soviet Union generally supported the Arab cause and was in any case already engaged in the Cold War against the Western Powers, Moscow was also involved from the outset. Finally, the post-1947 Middle East situation spawned the PLO and the Islamic extremism and terrorism that have in modern times touched the lives and peoples of virtually every nation in the world.

Even today, Israel still struggles to survive. Its several wars punctuated the history of the Cold War in 1956, 1967, 1973 and 1982, and the Palestinian *intifada* that commenced in 1987 has continued beyond the end of the Cold War, with a beleaguered Israel forced to adopt ever more controversial and extreme military solutions to counter the enemy within its borders. But in the pre-1990 era what was of particular significance was its profound impact upon the policies and actions of the superpowers, and upon so many aspects of international security in the Cold War world.

After its military successes in 1948 and 1949, the Israeli Defence Forces (IDF) developed their motorised or mechanised infantry and light armoured forces. This matched the need for highly mobile forces that could be deployed speedily to any of Israel's vulnerable land borders. Demographic considerations meant that the IDF could only maintain a small standing regular army, with the bulk of the IDF being reservists. This in turn compelled the IDF to maintain a viable mobilisation plan and also sustain a comprehensive military and civil defence training programme that involved virtually every Israeli citizen. After 1948 the IDF set out to organise itself with all this in mind, although progress was at first relatively slow. But in 1956, by which time it had dealt with a succession of cross-border raids and attacks by its Arab neighbours, Israel faced its next major challenge.

Sinai and the Anglo-French Suez Campaign, 1956

During 1955 the attacks emanating from Egypt had been a particular problem and matters were clearly coming to a head. Meanwhile, in the cause of Arab nationalism, on 26 July 1956 President Gamal Abdel Nasser of Egypt nationalised the Suez Canal. Nasser enjoyed the support of Moscow, and the Egyptian armed forces of the time had been well provided with modern equipment from the Soviet Union and other communist bloc countries – a matter of considerable concern to the Israeli leaders in Tel Aviv.

Britain's interests (including control of the strategically important Suez Canal) and influence in Egypt stemmed from the mid-nineteenth century, and Nasser's action was therefore a serious blow to British prestige and standing in the Middle East. France also had extensive interests in North Africa, and Cairo's support for the accelerating Arab nationalist insurgency against France in Algeria provided Paris with a motive to topple Nasser. Militarily and politically, if Britain and France had acted immediately the outcome at Suez might have been different, but neither nation had the military capability to do so. However, although an Anglo-French response was clearly some weeks away, it was clear that an assault on Egypt would take place, and the Israelis saw an opportunity to capitalise on this situation by launching their own pre-emptive attack against Egypt, co-ordinated with the separate Anglo-French assault. Tel Aviv's justification for this was reinforced by an announcement on 24 October that Jordan, Syria and Egypt had decided to place all of their forces under the overall authority of the Egyptian ministry of defence and its high command.

Meanwhile, as summer turned to autumn, France and Britain at last mobilised and deployed their forces to the Mediterranean. This was a ponderous process, which necessarily included the retraining of many British paratroops who had been employed out of the parachute role. Although any joint planning between Israel and France and Britain has always been denied by the governments concerned, it would indeed be remarkable if this had not occurred. Also, the extensive upgrading and re-equipping of the IDF by France that took place from mid-1956 was unlikely to have been mere coincidence.

In any event, at last light on 29 October paratroopers of the IDF's 202nd Parachute Brigade – commanded by one Colonel Ariel Sharon – dropped on to the Mitla Pass, the gateway through the hills of the Sinai to Suez town, where the south end of the canal joined the Gulf of Suez. Simultaneously, the Second World War-vintage Sherman tanks and armoured half-tracks of the Israeli 7th and 27th Armoured Brigades and 9th Infantry Brigade rolled east and south across the Sinai, towards the canal. Despite some initial reverses and delays in the Um Katif area, and at Rafah and the Mitla Pass, the IDF generally overcame the Egyptian forces wherever they were encountered. At 18.00 hours, ostensibly using the Israeli attack and consequent threat to the security of the canal as an excuse, Britain and France issued an ultimatum to both Egypt and Israel to withdraw their forces ten miles from the canal. Egypt ignored the ultimatum, but Israel was content to comply as this requirement did not affect the attack plans of General Moshe Dayan, the IDF Chief of Staff. Consequently, on 31 October British and French aircraft began to bomb Egyptian airbases, and at dawn on 5 November a drop of Anglo-French parachute units preceded seaborne landings carried out at daybreak the next day. Meanwhile, on 1 November the Egyptian forces opposing the Israelis in the Sinai had been withdrawn to meet the impending Anglo-French invasion force at the north end of the canal. Operation Musketeer, the Anglo-French airborne and seaborne landings, was carried out more or less successfully and Port Said and Port Fouad fell by the afternoon of 6 November. However, strongly influenced by US pressure and the UN, the international response forced an early ceasefire, together with the establishment of a UN monitoring and security force at the canal and in the Sinai.

For France and Britain the Suez operation was an expensive and ignominious event that did little credit to the political leaders involved and at the same time illustrated the extent of the post-war decline of both countries. Israel's victory in the Sinai cost it only 181 dead and about 600 wounded against some 1,500 Egyptian dead. It provided a secure buffer zone on Israel's western border (even though it was subsequently forced to give up a number of its territorial gains following the Anglo-French withdrawal) and enhanced considerably the confidence and morale of its victorious forces. But it also produced some false lessons. Notably, the post-1 November fighting (when the Egyptians were withdrawing from the Sinai in any case) created a myth that the tank was the weapon system upon which the IDF should base its future organisation and tactical doctrine, at the implied expense of balanced infantry, artillery and armoured forces. Most importantly, General Moshe Dayan, who had been the architect of the Israeli success, was a major supporter of tank-focused concepts. This view drove

IDF future tactics and strategy; it also bore directly upon an ongoing debate about the IDF command and control philosophy, which centred upon whether its commanders should continue to be accorded an almost unprecedented degree of latitude for intuitive, instinctive decision-making, or should be required to follow a more rigid and traditional concept of military command.

Although Israel had gained overall, for Britain and France the Suez operation had been little short of disastrous. When Nasser announced the nationalisation of the Suez Canal the international standing of France and Britain had been considerable. These were two of the four great powers that had together vanquished the military might of Germany, Japan and Italy just a decade earlier. Both countries, as well as being key members of the newly formed NATO Alliance, still possessed extensive overseas territories, including a number of colonies. The French army, despite the disaster at Dien Bien Phu in 1954, was still a formidable fighting force. Britain not only possessed a sizeable maritime, air and (albeit by 1956 declining) ground force capability, but was also one of only three atomic powers in the world. Both countries were trusted allies of the United States, with which they provided the bulwark against the spread of communism and the extension of Soviet or Chinese power and influence. But if that was the world's perception of Britain and France prior to Operation Musketeer, the Suez campaign exposed a different truth.

Militarily, the planning and organisation of the operation had been disjointed, was subjected to many last-minute changes, and over four months had become insecure. This denied the assaulting troops the element of surprise. Furthermore, many of the aircraft and much of the equipment were inappropriate for the task. Finally, although the British troops performed as well as the ill-planned preparations allowed, the airborne assault techniques and subsequent tactics of the paratroopers of the French and French Foreign Legion units (which included many veterans of the recent war in Indochina) proved to be more effective than those of their British comparators of the 3rd Battalion of the Parachute Regiment. The marines of the British 3rd Commando Brigade fared somewhat better with their amphibious and helicopter-borne landings, although here also the debilitating effects of the post-1945 downsizing of Britain's armed forces were plain to see.

Even before the landings President Dwight D. Eisenhower had made it abundantly clear to Paris and London that Egypt was not worth the danger of destabilising the Middle East, and that the proposed invasion did not therefore enjoy US support or approval. Whereas access to Middle East oil and overseas territories were major concerns to Europe, the

American administration chose to overlook this fact. At the same time, the policy set by former President Truman for the United States to safeguard Israel was such that Washington could not accept the need for Israel to go to war. A flurry of meetings of the UN Security Council and General Assembly took place in late October, which highlighted the real extent of British and French isolation. Even within Britain there was substantial opposition to the attack against Egypt. Eventually, a combination of international and domestic political and financial pressure forced Anglo-French acceptance of a ceasefire. This effectively turned an Anglo-French military success into a setback, as Egypt, a third-rate Middle Eastern power, announced to the world, and especially to its Arab neighbours, the fact that it had stood alone and fought successfully against Britain, France and Israel.

With a growing Soviet threat, the Warsaw Pact in place, the spread of communism in South-east Asia, and a real need for a visible demonstration of Western solidarity, the Anglo-French adventure did irreparable harm to the wider credibility of Britain in particular, and to France within her North African territories, as well as damaging Anglo-French relations with the United States. Therefore, the consequences of the Suez adventure on Britain and France were long-lasting, as the vulnerabilities and impotence of these two once-great imperial powers were clear for every nationalist and anti-colonialist to see. France paid particularly dearly for this in Algeria during the next five years, while the level of mistrust between the French army and its political leaders, already at an unprecedented low following the war in Indochina, suffered a further decisive blow. Meanwhile, in Britain, Suez ended the political life of Prime Minister Sir Anthony Eden, who was forced to resign early in 1957.

The Suez campaign cost twenty-two British and ten French lives, plus ninety-seven British and thirty-three French wounded. Some 90,000 Anglo-French troops were involved, plus 500 aircraft and 130 warships (including seven aircraft carriers). In addition to those Egyptians killed by the Israelis in the Sinai, a considerable number of Egyptian military personnel and civilians died at British and French hands. Meanwhile, the canal remained blocked by forty-seven concrete-filled ships sunk by the Egyptians. In Tel Aviv, the Israeli leaders duly noted that Israel's principal support in the future would come from the United States, not Europe. And in Europe, on the day before the Anglo-French paratroopers jumped on to their Suez drop zones, the Soviet ambassador to Hungary, one Yuri Andropov, had ordered Red Army tanks to suppress the popular uprising in Budapest – confident that neither France nor Britain would be in a position to intervene, to protest, or possibly even to notice.

The Six-Day War, 1967

Despite the wars that it had already fought in 1948 and in 1956, Israel had not improved its tenuous security situation significantly by the mid-1960s. If anything, it had increased Arab hostility to the Jewish state by emphasising its existence and its determination to survive at all costs. Consequently, during the decade from 1956 Arab attitudes hardened and not one of the states that bordered Israel recognised its existence. During the two years prior to June 1967 there were 113 raids by Syrian-trained insurgents into northern Israel, causing about seventy-three Israeli deaths; one such incursion on 7 April 1967 escalated into the most extensive border fighting since 1956. Indeed, Israel's borders were in reality no more than ceasefire lines. Even if these had been internationally recognised borders, Israel's location and geography meant that it could not be defended by a conventional strategy.

Along much of the neck of land that was flanked on the west by the Mediterranean Sea and to the east by the hills of Judea, the state of Israel was no more than about thirteen to sixteen miles wide. The capital, Tel Aviv, lay in this coastal region and was therefore vulnerable to a determined armoured attack from the east – an attack that would also cut Israel in two. The area of the elongated state was only 14,000 square miles, but its long, illogical and almost accidental frontiers could not physically be defended throughout their length. This meant that, in any future clash with Israel's Arab neighbours, surprise, offensive action and concentration of strength would be paramount. It followed that the IDF had to be capable of concentrating its armoured forces sequentially at various points across the country, and the IDF high command knew that this could only be achieved so long as the Israeli air force (IAF) enjoyed air superiority.

On 16 May 1967 Egypt demanded the withdrawal of the UN force that had been in place in the Sinai since the 1956 conflict. It then proceeded to occupy the Sinai with five infantry divisions and a number of armoured units, plus forces of the Palestine Liberation Army (which was closely associated with the more than 750,000 Palestinian refugees then living just over the border in the Gaza Strip). At a stroke, the former UN buffer zone on Israel's western border was filled by the Soviet-equipped forces of Israel's principal enemy, Egypt. Israel was faced with a major and immediate threat to its very survival, and by 20 May its forces had completed their mobilisation. But Tel Aviv was then faced with a problem: either it had to go to war within two weeks, or else it had no option but to stand down the many thousands of reservists in order to return them to their economically essential civilian employment. Fortuitously, the decision was made for Israel by Egypt's Arab allies, whose actions made a war in June 1967 inevitable.

During the last weeks of May, Egypt, Jordan and Syria closed the Strait of Tiran to Israeli shipping, announced the establishment of a unified Arab military command, and demanded that Israel give up Eilat and Nizana. They did all this confident that Moscow approved their actions and that Western military intervention to support Israel was highly unlikely. While the Arabs were also confident of their ability to defeat Israel in battle, these several actions meant that war was unavoidable, and so the strategic initiative passed to Israel.

Quite apart from the nominal alignment of Israel with the West and of the Arabs with the Soviet bloc, the 'Holy War' or 'Six-Day War' of June 1967 attracted the particular attention of Cold War military analysts. This was due to the extensive use of Soviet equipment by the Arabs, and of British, French and American equipment by the IDF. Of particular interest was the performance of the Israeli Mark 5 and 7 Centurion (British) tanks against the Arab T-54/55 (Soviet) tanks, plus that of the Israeli Mirage IIIC (French) fighters against the Arabs' Soviet-supplied MiG-21s. Here was a war that could test the effectiveness of many weapons originally destined for an East–West war in Europe, but which had thus far remained untested in major combat. A further bonus for NATO and Warsaw Pact analysts was that since 1956 Egypt had trained extensively in the use of Soviet 'sword and shield' tactical doctrine and would now apply this concept in battle.

Thus, on 3 June, with Arab forces of (potentially)[142] more than half a million men, two and a half thousand tanks and almost a thousand aircraft ranged against the IDF's 264,000 men, 800 tanks and 350 aircraft, the Israeli cabinet voted to go to war for the third time in the state's short history.

Although none of the principal protagonists of the Cold War were directly involved in what followed, aspects of the conduct and outcome of the Six-Day War directly shaped tactical doctrine and equipment design on both sides of the Iron Curtain for decades thereafter. The war also produced the enlarged Israel that has continued, albeit unsought, to be the principal focus and excuse for conflict, terrorism and discord in the Middle East right up to the present day.

Israel anticipated that the recently declared Arab unified command would not be operational for some time, and so decided to deal with its enemies separately, before they could launch a co-ordinated attack. The main threat was that posed by Egypt, with its 450 combat aircraft. Accordingly, at 08.45 hours on 5 June waves of IAF fighter-bombers screamed into Egyptian airspace west from the Sinai, southward from the Red Sea and south from the Mediterranean, to strike all seventeen of Egypt's main airbases. About 300 aircraft were destroyed that day, virtually all on the ground. Once the bulk of the Egyptian air force had ceased to exist, the IAF destroyed Jordan's twenty-nine combat aircraft and sixty of Syria's aircraft, plus a further seventeen Arab aircraft on Iraqi territory. Over six days the IAF claimed to have destroyed 418 Arab aircraft and lost just twenty-seven of their own.

The IAF air campaign was a near-perfect operation. Its key features included timing the initial attacks to ensure maximum surprise, deliberately not attacking certain air defence radars in order both to enhance the deception plan and to allow the 'scrambled' air defence fighters to warm up their engines just in time for showers of French-manufactured Nord AS-30 infra-red heat-homing missiles to strike them, and maintaining a rate of air strikes and aircraft turn-around that ensured IAF aircraft were attacking the Arab airbases almost without pause. The main ground attack weapon employed by the IAF was the 30mm cannon, although new technology weapons also used included various cratering and delayed action bombs, which denied the Arabs the future use of their airbases. The whole air operation was a vindication of the maxim that offence is the best form of defence: a principle exemplified by IDF operations to the present day. However, anything less than total success on 5 June was simply not an option. Had the IAF not achieved total air superiority on that first day, the subsequent IDF ground campaign would have been impossible, and the state of Israel would almost certainly have been overwhelmed. The vital need to achieve and maintain air dominance against an opponent with superior quantities of mobile armoured forces was duly noted by NATO and Warsaw Pact observers alike.

Meanwhile, as the IAF dominated the skies, the IDF ground forces launched their attacks. They dealt first with the Egyptians in the Sinai from 5 to 8 June, with a concurrent offensive against Jordan in the West Bank between 5 and 7 June. The Syrians they left until 9 and 10 June.

In the Sinai on 5 June Generals Ariel Sharon, Abraham Yoffe and Abraham Tal drove forward with three divisions. The principal focus of the breakthrough battle was the main routes that ran through the passes adjacent to Um Katif, where an all-arms force was supported by a massive artillery barrage. Despite a comprehensive network of Soviet-style defensive positions, the Centurion tanks proved more than a match for the T-34, JS-3 and T-54/55 tanks, and by 8 June the Egyptian forces had collapsed. Airborne, armoured and amphibious forces under the command of Generals Sharon and Tal attacked their flanks and deep into their rear areas, preventing their redeployment, while Yoffe's armour raced for Bir Lahfan and so cut the enemy forces in two – denying each part the opportunity to support the other. This envelopment also severed the Egyptian lines of communication, denying the forward units command, control and resupply. Meanwhile, the Egyptian reserve armour – the 'sword' element of the 'sword and shield' concept – was quickly isolated and unable to support the main defensive positions. The Israeli tanks pushed deeper into the Sinai and reached the concentrations of Egyptian armour, when they were able to use the superior power and range of the Centurion's 105mm gun to destroy most of the Egyptian T-54/55s in place. Even before their engagement by the IDF ground forces, the IAF had more or less neutralised these armoured reserves by denying them the ability to manoeuvre, and numbers of tanks had already been dug-in in a generally vain effort to protect them from the IAF air attacks.

By the end of the battle on 8 June the Egyptians had sustained casualties of some 10,000 killed and 20,000 wounded. They had lost all but about 100 tanks, as well as the seven Sinai-based divisions that had been totally written off by the Israeli assault. Yet whereas the effectiveness of the Israeli tank units (admittedly with no air threat to worry about) was undeniable, there was also considerable evidence that the Israeli armour had outrun its supporting infantry and artillery units on numerous occasions. Also, the sheer tempo of the attacks across the Sinai meant that if the Egyptians had been able to hold their positions longer or to reinforce them, the IDF's finite quantities of men and matériel might not have been able to exploit the advantages conferred upon them by the IAF success on the first day – a situation that might have laid Israel open to a new attack from other Arab nations.

Indeed, despite the modern equipment that the IDF front-line units deployed, a news report by Murray Sayle of *The Sunday Times*, travelling behind the leading formations of the IDF in the Sinai, captured the very essence of the Israeli citizen soldiers and the precarious support measures they were constrained to use in 1967:

They move in an extraordinary way. Some of them wear uniforms and helmets, while others have odds and ends of civilian clothing with Jewish skull-caps. Many sport luxurious [luxuriant?] beards. There are no salutes and few badges of rank. Half the transport is improvised. Officers drive their own civil cars, smeared with mud to make a crude but effective camouflage. The men drive Tel Aviv buses covered with signs like 'The Cairo Express' – and the same buses bring the prisoners back. Ammunition and stores come up in farm carts pulled by tractors, in contractors' lorries, and in vans with the names of the Tel Aviv firms still visible under the mud. Dispatch-riders travel on motor-scooters. The trucks from the *kibbutzim* go up to the front loaded with crates of Jaffa oranges, which serve as effective combat rations. The officers and men are all on first-name terms – they have been training together for years. One officer told me: 'Everyone in this country is in the army – but we get eleven months' leave a year in peace-time.' The combat infantry are all men, but the girls are close up to the front all right. They are acting as drivers, military police and cooks. It is quite like a guerrilla army in a way, but with highly professional leadership. Almost all the officers appear to be European Jews, no doubt because of their superior education. Orders are given in Hebrew, but the troops talk together in German, Yiddish, French, Rumanian, Polish and just about every language of Europe.[143]

Meanwhile, on their eastern border, the Israelis had hoped that Jordan would not commit its forces to the conflict, and in many respects the geographical limits of the West Bank area held by Jordan made it indefensible. However, King Hussein – a man of integrity and honour – remained loyal to his Arab allies and committed his small country to the war in the east on 5 June. The core of the Jordanian armed forces was the well-disciplined and (originally) British-trained Arab Legion, some 50,000 strong, but these troops proved to be no match for the IDF and IAF which first destroyed Jordan's few combat aircraft on the ground and then proceeded to neutralise Jordan's artillery and armour support wherever it appeared.

Although the fighting against the Jordanians was hard, the IDF was unstoppable. The Israelis were fighting not only for the West Bank, but for the ancient city of Jerusalem and for their holiest of holies, the Wailing Wall. Photo-journalist Donald McCullin was with the infantry soldiers of the 1st Battalion of the Jerusalem Regiment as they fought their way into the alleyways and ancient buildings of the Old City, moving ever closer to their final objective:

We came through the gate at a rush. Really spewed through. The minute we got into the city we were hit by light machine gun fire, heavy machine guns, rifles and sub-machine guns. We all fanned out to escape ricochets ... there seemed to be snipers everywhere. In the first 100 yards inside the gate, we had casualties all the way. The guys had charged in, thinking they'd run to the Wailing Wall, and they were being pinned down by this fire. They knew roughly where the wall was, because it is part of the Mosque of Omar, and they could see the dome of the mosque above the buildings, so they all headed in that direction. Now they were among little stone houses and in very narrow streets, some of them not much more than a yard wide ... we moved just a few yards down the little street when heavy firing broke out. The men were moving quickly, eager to get to the wall, when the man in the lead was

shot dead. Then the next man was shot through the chest and fell ...
And then a man behind me was killed by a sniper firing from a wall
about five feet high. The men were trying to fire back, but they didn't
know where to aim. Then they put the last dead man on a stretcher
and ran off with him. He had a handkerchief over his face to show that
he was dead. All through this I could hear the sounds of a tank battle
going on outside the walls. The Jordanians, when they saw the Israelis
moving in, took their tanks up on the heights outside the city, and the
tanks started to pour shells into the city. All the time you could hear
bazooka and rocket shells exploding, and the sound of the tanks' guns
... At last, we reached the Wailing Wall. The soldiers kept coming up to
me and saying the same thing: 'You've seen the most historical event
you will ever see. We've waited a thousand years for this.' They were
hugging and kissing each other, and lifting each other off the ground.
They were doing all this while the snipers were still firing, and every
now and again a bullet would ricochet off the wall itself.[144]

In the short campaign for the West Bank and Jerusalem, the Jordanians lost
about 1,000 killed and 5,000 wounded. The Israelis suffered losses of 299
killed and 1,457 wounded, of whom 195 died and 1,131 were wounded in the
battle for the Old City of Jerusalem alone. The result of King Hussein's decision to deny Israel the West Bank was the end of Jordan as a significant
Middle East military power. Although Israel had originally hoped that it
would not need to fight Jordan in 1967, its decisive defeat removed one of
Israel's principal Arab enemies for the foreseeable future.

With Egypt and Jordan neutralised, on 9 June the Israelis turned their
attention to Syria and its forces on Mount Hermon and the Golan Heights –
features that dominated most of northern Israel and the area of the Sea of
Galilee. Here also the IDF defeated a Syrian defence based upon Soviet-style
tactical doctrine. But this success was all the more significant in that it was
achieved during almost three days of non-stop and particularly bitter
fighting against Syrian troops in extremely strong, well-supported defences
situated on high ground. These defences had been prepared over a period
of years, so even the power of the IAF's weapons was mitigated where they
were deployed against the deep bunkers and strongpoints. However, the
superior quality of the Israeli troops finally decided the battle, and thirty-six
hours after the first IDF ground attacks against the Golan, Syrian resistance
collapsed, leaving the Israelis in possession of what was undoubtedly the
most important strategic feature in the operational area: the Golan Heights
and part of Mount Hermon. The Golan battle cost Israel 115 dead and 306
wounded, while the Syrians lost about 2,500 dead and 5,000 wounded, plus

almost half of their 250 tanks and 200 of the 260 artillery pieces that had been positioned on the Golan Heights. But due to a fairly early decision to withdraw its forces to safety, the Syrian army preserved much of its manpower and matériel and thus avoided the level of destruction that Egypt and Jordan had suffered.

At the end of the Six-Day War Israel's achievements had been remarkable. Most importantly, the small state had gained strategically viable frontiers. It had the Suez Canal in the west, the River Jordan in the east and the Golan Heights to the north. It had also decisively removed what had been, just a week earlier, a potentially irresistible Arab threat to its very existence. It was assessed in Tel Aviv that Egypt and Syria would be unable to pose a further threat for up to about ten years, while Jordan had probably been neutralised for even longer. Israel had also gained substantial amounts of territory, which added about two-thirds to its size.

Nevertheless, it was still a relatively small state with a Jewish population of only about two and a half million people, entirely surrounded by a hostile Arab population that totalled more than one hundred million. And Israel's 1967 territorial gains later created very serious problems for it in the post-Cold War era, when an ill-advised and insensitive programme of Jewish settlement of the so-called occupied territories provoked an escalating level of Arab terrorism. The extreme disquiet of one and a half million Arabs who suddenly found themselves living in a state that they did not recognise and which had, in their view, compounded the original theft of Palestine in 1948 by further military conquests in 1967, was understandable, and their fears and frustrations fuelled the accelerating campaign of terrorist violence against Israel by the PLO and other groups from 1967.

The Six-Day War jarred many in Washington and Moscow, and it had shown that America's control of Israel was much weaker than had previously been assumed. Soviet President Kosygin was in close contact with President Johnson throughout, but by mid-1967 Johnson was more focused upon events in South-east Asia than on the Middle East crisis. However, as the Syrian positions on the Golan collapsed, with Israeli tanks poised to drive all the way to Damascus, President Kosygin indicated that the war now had the potential to escalate into a superpower conflict. Henry Kissinger flew to Moscow and a ceasefire was negotiated with Soviet and US agreement and acquiescence. Meanwhile, Johnson was not best pleased by a conflict that had clearly demonstrated the extent of Israel's autonomy and independence of action from US control.

The Israelis were justifiably self-confident after their stunning military victory, but they then allowed this to cloud their awareness of the realities of international relations and Middle East politics. No peace treaty was signed at the conclusion of hostilities, so for the Arabs a dormant state of war persisted between them and the state of Israel. This unsatisfactory situation provided a rationale for much of the cross-border terrorism directed against Israel, its citizens and institutions, and against Jews worldwide, in the years that followed. The Arab policy towards Israel post-1967 continued to be no recognition, no negotiation and no peace. The Six-Day War also aggravated an already significant – but formerly only Palestinian – refugee problem in the region, and so provided an almost inexhaustible source of young Arab guerrilla fighters and terrorists for the future.

Meanwhile, the IDF took the opportunity to re-equip itself at the expense of its defeated enemies. Some 300 tanks, 600 guns and 10,000 vehicles had been captured intact, together with vast amounts of partly damaged vehicles, ammunition, small-arms and other matériel. The IDF had again vindicated its doctrine of a massive pre-emptive air strike, followed by a ground attack spearheaded by armoured units. Yet the IDF commitment to the tank as a war-winner proved costly when it next went to war with its Arab neighbours. And that new conflict was inevitable; for without a workable political solution or accommodation with its Arab neighbours, and with the almost two million disaffected Arabs resident within its borders, the future existence of the state of Israel remained problematical. Despite Israel's decisive military victory in June 1967, it was only six years before this was demonstrated all too clearly.

The Yom Kippur War, 1973

An uneasy ceasefire persisted during the three years following the Six-Day War. In fact, 'ceasefire' was something of a misnomer, as from March 1969 to August 1970 the intermittent cross-border fighting that followed the June 1967 conflict reached a new intensity on Israel's western front, with both sides conducting large-scale raids and artillery duels across the Suez Canal. Eventually, the IAF carried out a series of air strikes against military, industrial and commercial targets deep within Egypt. These attacks destroyed the Egyptian air defence system – including its SAM sites – and gave rise to a progressive destabilisation of the country, so that in August 1970 the Egyptians agreed to adhere to the ceasefire.

In the meantime, however, President Nasser had managed to reconstitute and reform his armed forces by a three-phase plan. First, there was 'defensive rehabilitation', which proceeded from the June 1967 defeat to September 1968; when the organisation, training and equipment of the Egyptian forces were fundamentally analysed, overhauled and upgraded by the widespread use of Soviet advisers. Particular attention was paid to the selection and professional training of the officers, many of whom had not performed well in 1967. Next came the 'offensive defence' phase that included the cross-border attacks in the period up to August 1970. Notwithstanding the damage inflicted upon Egypt by the raids and air attacks, this border warfare – a war of attrition in all but name – permitted the Egyptian forces to rebuild their morale and offensive spirit and experiment with new tactics and equipment, while all the time draining Israel of the resources necessary to maintain strong defences east of the canal. Having set in train and overseen many of the measures necessary to restore Egyptian military strength, on 28 September 1970 Gamal Abdel Nasser died. He was succeeded as president by Anwar Sadat.

Sadat hoped to avoid yet another potentially disastrous war with Israel by lobbying America and the Soviet Union, so that they would pressurise each other and consequently Israel into agreeing to a peace settlement that would involve Israel giving up some or all of its captured territory. But despite a potentially productive summit meeting in 1972, neither President Nixon nor President Brezhnev was inclined to bring about these changes. That year, the Watergate crisis had broken in Washington, the North had invaded the South in Vietnam, and international terrorism was growing apace. That year, the Japanese Red Army had murdered twenty-six people in Tel Aviv and Black September terrorists had carried out a murderous attack on Israeli athletes at the Olympic Games in Munich, Germany. Meanwhile, both America and the Soviet Union were deeply involved in the global Cold War. Consequently, while the Soviets continued to provide military advice and support to its candidate states of Egypt and Syria, the United States armed and equipped Israel.

No doubt Moscow and Washington each hoped that a suitable balance of military power between the Israelis and the Arabs could be achieved, and that by this the United States and the Soviet Union would ensure stability in the Middle East. But Sadat knew that the superpowers would not assist his laudable aim of achieving an acceptable peace settlement, and therefore yet another war with Israel was inevitable. But how could the Arabs – even with their improved forces and equipment – defeat the IDF in battle? In order to do this the Arabs carefully analysed the Israeli strengths and weaknesses, and then laid their plans accordingly. The key to success was undoubtedly surprise – a lesson that the Arabs had learned to their cost in 1967. This meant that the Arabs had to strike first, before Israel had mobilised. Another lesson from 1967 was the absolute need for the Arabs to conduct co-ordinated and simultaneous attacks, so that Israel's limited manpower and resources could not be concentrated sequentially to deal with a series of separate threats. Lastly, it was paramount for the Arabs to neutralise the IAF at the outset.

What became known as the Yom Kippur War was in many respects more significant for the Cold War than either the 1956 Arab–Israeli war or the 1967 Six-Day War. This was for three reasons. First, the impending Egyptian and Syrian offensive displayed many of the tactical and operational procedures that NATO anticipated the Soviet and Warsaw Pact forces would use against the West in the event of a war in Europe. This was understandable in light of the quantity of Soviet advice and aid that Egypt in particular had received since 1967.

Next, the degree of strategic surprise that the Arabs achieved against the Israelis was remarkable. This was especially so given the earlier performance of the Israeli intelligence organisation to provide early warning of the Arab moves in 1967. There were lessons here for the NATO planners who depended upon accurate and early identification of a forthcoming Warsaw Pact attack, in order to provide enough time for the appropriate mobilisation, warning and reporting, and readiness alert actions to be completed (especially those activities that related to NATO nuclear forces).

Finally, the 1973 war utilised several aspects of new military technology, techniques and equipment that had until then only been combat-tested in Vietnam – an encounter clearly untypical of a NATO–Warsaw Pact conflict in the Central Region of Europe. In 1973, anti-armour guided missiles and radar-guided air defence SAM and gun systems, were all used extensively. They showed the new vulnerability of the tank and the need for electronic counter-measures (ECM) for aircraft operating in an entirely new electronic and radar-dominated air environment. Soviet obstacle-crossing equipment was used by the Egyptians to cross the Suez Canal, which provided an invaluable insight into the capabilities of this specialist engineer equipment. NATO and Soviet observers alike watched these water-obstacle crossings with great interest, as a successful Warsaw Pact attack into Western Germany would certainly have required the communist forces to cross the Rivers Elbe, Leine, Mittelland Kanal, Weser and Rhine in considerable strength, without delay, and with these crossings occurring in rapid succession.

By late 1972 Sadat was convinced that another war with Israel was unavoidable. He knew that he needed a strategy that would provide an early Arab victory on the battlefield, followed by a campaign of attrition, in order to allow the Arabs with their much greater resources to grind down the IDF. However, Sadat also needed to bring about superpower involvement at the political level before the IDF recovered sufficiently to defeat the Arabs yet again. Despite extensive improvements in all aspects of the Egyptian forces since 1967, Sadat could hardly fail to acknowledge the probable outcome of a war that continued long enough to permit the Israelis to recover and respond. In any case, the risk of a wider conflict might also threaten the vital flow of oil to the West – a matter that would certainly attract close European attention, not to mention that of the United States.

As at late summer of 1973 the IDF's 275,000 men, 1,700 tanks and 432 aircraft faced Egypt's 285,000 men, 2,000 tanks and 600 aircraft in the west. And concentrated on the north-eastern border were the 100,000 men, 1,200 tanks and 210 aircraft of the Syrian armed forces. Although Jordan's army was also taken fully into account by the Israelis in their worst-case defence planning, it was not to be directly involved in the 1973 war – apart from conducting a concurrent mobilisation exercise, which constrained the IDF to maintain forces in the Jordan valley just in case the Jordanians did subsequently enter the war.

The unified Arab command finalised its plans. Following their 1967 experience, there was to be a simultaneous and massive attack on a broad front. This would be launched by Egypt across the Suez Canal into the Sinai, while the Syrians attacked the now very strong Israeli positions on the Golan Heights. Jordan's mobilisation deception would proceed in parallel with the Egyptian and Syrian assaults. Once their initial attacks across the canal had succeeded, the Egyptians would revert to a defensive posture, and use their considerable firepower to destroy the counter-attacking Israeli armoured formations. All that remained was to decide on the date for the Arab attack.

The month selected was October, when the tidal flow in the Suez Canal was most propitious for the Egyptian bridging operation and before winter rain and snow on the Golan Heights affected the Syrian use of massed armour to recapture the ground lost in 1967. The time of the attack was set at 14.00 hours. This was a compromise, since Egypt wanted to strike in the evening when the setting sun would have been behind its forces, whilst in the east the Syrians had for the same reason favoured a dawn assault. Only the choice of date remained, and that selected was 6 October: the Jewish Day of Atonement – Yom Kippur – as well as the tenth day of Ramadan. This was a day on which the Israelis might be less alert than usual, and on which they would in any case certainly not expect the predominantly Muslim Arab forces to start a war.

The Arabs ensured absolute secrecy by exposing the details of the date and plan only at the very highest levels of the government and military high command. Although their preparatory activities could not be entirely concealed, the Egyptians managed to deceive the Israelis concerning the build-up of forces on the west bank of the canal. They repeatedly staged exercise manoeuvres, which were likely to be assessed either as routine training procedures or (as had occurred in April) devices to drain Israeli resources by prompting unnecessary mobilisations. It should also be said that a legacy of 1956 and 1967 was a firm conviction within Israel that even if another Arab attack did come, the IDF would deal with it just as expeditiously as it had on the previous two occasions. Indeed, the dramatic upsurge of Palestinian and other Arab-based terrorism against Israel in the 1970s was probably believed at that time to be a much more immediate threat than a conventional attack. Even though Israeli military intelligence had acquired the broad details of the Arab offensive plan some time before 6 October, the high command had underestimated the capability of their enemies (or, more accurately, overestimated that of the IDF) and dismissed it more or less out of hand. However, by mid-morning on 6 October the Arab preparations and intentions were plain to see, and at 10.00 hours Israel once again began a full-scale mobilisation of its reservists. But less than three hours later Egypt and Syria attacked.

At 14.00 hours, following a one-hour artillery and air bombardment of the positions held by the single Israeli division based along the east bank of the canal and in depth in the Sinai, five Egyptian divisions and a number of independent brigades, supported by about 800 tanks, launched their assault across the Suez Canal. At the same time three divisions of infantry, two armoured divisions and a number of independent brigades – the whole force spearheaded and supported by some 1,200 tanks and safeguarded from air attack by thirty-two batteries of SAM systems – surged towards the two IDF brigades with 180 tanks that occupied a thirty-mile frontage on the Golan Heights.

The Egyptian crossing of the canal was a masterpiece of planning and execution. Water jets blasted away the huge sandbanks that ran alongside the canal in order to clear the path for the Soviet amphibious bridging and ferry vehicles, which soon began to cross the waterway. Shortly afterwards pontoon bridge and ferry sites were in place to support the crossings, and ten such bridges were operational by 8 October. The troops of two Egyptian armies surged across and quickly overcame the Israeli defences. By 8 October five major bridgeheads were firmly established, and all attempts by the IDF to displace them had failed. This was due in part to the strength of the Egyptian positions, but also to a lack of co-ordination by the Israelis.

A particular reason for the failure of Israeli counter-attacks was the Egyptian use of man-portable anti-armour weapons in great numbers. These included the Soviet AT-3 Sagger anti-tank guided missiles (ATGM) and the older but still potent RPG-7 rocket-propelled grenade launchers. The image of hundreds of Egyptian infantrymen carrying suitcase-like Sagger ATGM launchers, scurrying to their temporary fire positions in the desert sands, then engaging and stopping successive tank attacks by the Israelis before hurrying back to the main defensive position, was the subject of several eyewitness reports. The wire-guided Saggers – whether fired by dismounted infantrymen or from launchers mounted on Soviet BMP armoured personnel carriers – exacted a heavy toll on the Israeli armour.

By 10 October, the Egyptian 2nd and 3rd Armies had more than 75,000 men and 800 tanks across the canal, in a narrow bridgehead that ran virtually the whole length of the waterway to the Gulf of Suez. The Egyptian 4th and 21st Armoured Divisions and 23rd Mechanised Division stood poised to reinforce or exploit the bridgeheads that the 2nd, 7th, 16th, 18th and 19th Infantry Divisions had won and held so successfully between 6 and 8 October. Ever mindful of the threat posed by the IAF, the two armies operated under a comprehensive air defence umbrella that combined the different capabilities and characteristics of the Soviet SA-2 Guideline, SA-3 Goa, SA-6 Gainful and man-portable SA-7 Grail SAM systems with those of radar-guided air defence guns such as the ZSU-23-4, and the optically aimed ZU-23 and ZPU-4 anti-aircraft guns, to form a single virtually impenetrable shield.[145] The air defence organisation included at least fifty batteries of SAM systems alone; and its plan to protect the crossings and bridgeheads also incorporated thousands of vehicle-mounted medium and heavy machine guns. Across both fronts the Israelis possibly lost as many as 200 aircraft during the ten days of the Yom Kippur War.

In the wake of this success, pressure began to build for the Egyptians to forsake their original plan and carry the battle into Israel itself; but at the same time Israel's belated mobilisation was at last beginning to generate the forces necessary to deal with the attackers. Simultaneously, the IDF was demonstrating its traditional flexibility by speedily adapting its tactics to cope with the changed nature of the threat that it faced in the Sinai.

Meanwhile, the battle was also raging on the Golan, where the immediate threat to Israel itself was actually much greater than that in the Sinai. The Syrian attack plan was in the classic Soviet doctrinal mould: three infantry divisions were required to achieve a break-in which would then be exploited by two armoured divisions. This was the form of attack that NATO forces stationed in West Germany had awaited throughout the Cold War. But the mountainous and exposed landscape of the Golan bore no resemblance to the gently undulating wooded countryside of the North German Plain. Neither did the formidable bunker complexes, strongpoints and dug-in, concreted, artillery and tank positions that the Israelis had developed on the Golan during the previous six years replicate the somewhat hastily prepared forward positions that NATO would have defended in West Germany had Soviet and Warsaw Pact forces ever crossed the IGB. Consequently, although they sustained huge numbers of casualties, the two Israeli brigades managed not only to hold against the Syrian onslaught throughout 6 and 7 October, but they also inflicted such enormous casualties that by the time the attackers achieved limited penetrations of the Israeli line they had no reserves left for exploitation. Where certain Syrian units did manage to outflank the Golan positions, they were themselves outflanked by fresh Israeli armoured units driving with all possible speed towards the beleaguered IDF brigades on the Golan Heights.

By 8 October Israeli reserve units were arriving in strength, and began pushing the Syrians back towards Damascus. Among the many hundreds of wrecked Syrian vehicles and artillery guns that littered the battlefield were 867 of the 1,200 tanks that had been involved in the initial attack two days earlier. By 9 October the battle in the east was virtually at an end, as the Syrians broke contact all along the front and withdrew, leaving the Israelis in possession of even more territory than that which they had held prior to the war. Overall, more than 1,400 Syrian tanks had been lost, against Israeli tank losses of 250. When a ceasefire was eventually declared, the leading Israeli armour was less than eighteen miles from the gates of the Syrian capital.

Prompted partly by the early success of their plans and partly by the perceived need to compensate in some way for the Syrian defeat, the Egyptian forces in the Sinai finally abandoned their original plan simply to absorb Israeli counter-attacks while awaiting a superpower or UN-imposed closure of the war. On the morning of 14 October their armour broke out of the bridgeheads and advanced east on four main axes. The intention was to secure the northern coastal route eastward and to seize the three strategically vital passes through the high ridgeline that ran north–south across the Sinai. But as they moved beyond their comprehensive air defence umbrella and into the type of manoeuvre warfare at which the Israelis excelled, the Egyptian forces realised their mistake. Even their ATGM capability was now degraded by the IDF tactic of using heavy indirect fire to prevent and disrupt the effective control of the wire-guided missiles (which required the operator to maintain sight of the missile and target throughout an engagement). At the same time, the Israelis had learned at considerable cost the error of counter-attacking with unsupported armour, and were already fielding newly consti- tuted but effective combined arms groupings of infantry, armour and artillery.

As well as adapting their tactics, the Israelis had acquired, in very short order, quantities of the American TOW (tube-launched, optically tracked, wire-guided) anti-armour missile system. This enabled the IDF to deal even more efficiently with the Egyptian tanks than had the Sagger-equipped Egyptian infantrymen which had engaged the Israeli armour earlier in the war. The powerful TOW system could be vehicle, helicopter or ground mounted. It was the US forces' main ATGM system during the final two decades of the Cold War; and until the advent of certain forms of advanced armour and the use of reactive armour protection, it could destroy any in-service Soviet or Warsaw Pact tank at ranges of up to 3,280 yards. Finally, the IAF speedily adapted its existing procedures and equipment (primarily its ECM defences) and its precision-guided ground-attack weaponry in order both to overcome the Arab air defence shield and to establish its traditional level of support for the IDF ground forces.

The outcome was predictable. About 260 of the 800 Egyptian tanks that began the breakout were destroyed by the night of the 14th. The IDF had lost about twenty tanks, and on the night of the 15th the Israelis judged the time was right to strike directly across the canal into Egypt. This attack was launched at Deversoir to the north of the Great Bitter Lake. Despite forty-eight hours of very hard fighting about the breach – made on the boundary between the Egyptian 2nd and 3rd Armies – the Israelis eventually established a substantial bridgehead. They struck south through and behind the rear of the 3rd Army and then on towards Suez. With the imminent collapse of the Egyptian forces at hand, Saudi Arabia halted Western oil exports on 20 October, and two days later a ceasefire was declared. However, it was not until 22 October that US pressure on Israel ended the fighting. The war's conclusion on 24 October, with direct superpower involvement, was precisely that for which Sadat had originally planned; but events had certainly not gone as he had intended, and the price paid by the Arabs in lost men, matériel and territory was cripplingly high.

For Israel the Yom Kippur War was an overdue but still timely reminder of its potential vulnerabilities and of the dangers of complacency. Despite this, Israel had yet again overcome the quantitatively superior forces of its two traditional enemies, albeit at no little cost to itself.

If the Yom Kippur War was a defining moment for Israel in military terms, it was no less so politically and psychologically. During one short conflict it had recognised that, in certain circumstances, Arab soldiers could not only fight and die bravely but that they could also defeat Israeli troops on the battlefield. Despite the eventual result of Yom Kippur, the Arab self-confidence and self-esteem that had been shattered in 1967 were largely restored by the events of October 1973. The same nationalistic and Islamic commitment and pride were also discernible in several of the terrorist groups that conducted an ever more violent campaign against Israel from 1973, and which were in many cases sponsored and provided with secure bases by neighbouring Arab nations, notably Syria.

Following the Saudi intervention in the conflict at an international level on 20 October, the Arab leaders began to understand, too, the true global significance of the power that, through an accident of geography and creation, they possessed. More effective and politically acceptable than any nuclear weapon was the commodity that lay in vast quantities under the desert. By the mid-1970s, the Western world and an increasingly energy-greedy United States depended upon this commodity, and it was a means by which the Arabs could, within certain parameters, directly influence future US policy towards the state of Israel. The power in question stemmed of course from oil, which from 1973 became a form of weapon in its own right.

The Lebanon, 1982

The confrontation between Israel and its Arab neighbours continued well beyond the end of the Cold War; but in addition to routine border incursions and terrorist operations, one further major clash of arms took place between Israel and Syria before 1990. This was the full-scale invasion of the southern Lebanon launched by Israel on 6 June 1982, to deal with the intolerable level of attacks then being mounted by the Palestinian forces and their Syrian sponsors from bases in that troubled country.

During the Lebanese civil war, with an almost total collapse of the country's infrastructure and the complete breakdown of law and order, the government had become incapable of asserting control over its own territory, while interference in the Lebanon from its neighbours had escalated. In parallel, the number of Palestinian refugees in the Lebanon had increased dramatically, and their several large refugee camps in the country had become little more than military training camps. These camps provided safe sanctuaries for the terrorists who regularly crossed into Israel to raid and murder, as well as for those carrying out terrorist attacks against Israeli, Western and Jewish targets worldwide. Many of the Palestinian bases lay close to the Syrian border in the Beqaa Valley, between Mount Hermon in the south-east and the high ground of the Jebel Barouk to the north-west. Ostensibly, the Israeli Operation 'Peace for Galilee' (which was in fact designated Operation 'Snowball' by the IDF) was intended to push the Palestinians and their artillery beyond the range at which they could engage Israeli positions in northern Galilee; although many of the journalists who reported the war from Beirut, and were able for the first time to provide a completely uncensored view of one of Israel's wars, subsequently came to the conclusion that the Israeli government's intentions for the Lebanon and the thousands of Palestinians who lived there were rather more far-reaching than those declared to the news media.[146]

In mid-1982 the Palestinian regular forces in Lebanon numbered about 15,000 men. The Syrians had some 30,000 troops within or able to deploy into the Lebanon. These forces were supported by up to 700 tanks, many of which were the new Soviet T-72 model. The T-72 had been developed primarily for selective export and use by the Warsaw Pact countries and other states that enjoyed Soviet support and sponsorship. The Syrians also had some thirty SAM batteries to provide the obligatory air defence shield, plus the Syrian air force. Meanwhile, the IDF had 3,000 tanks available for the operation, many of which were the new Israeli-developed and produced Merkava, plus about 600 aircraft of the IAF.

Beyond the more immediate objectives of the campaign, the Israeli invasion presented an opportunity to validate the many technological and doctrinal changes made by the IDF after the Yom Kippur War. It also afforded NATO and the Soviet Union yet another chance to assess indirectly the combat effectiveness of the military equipment that they had supplied to the main protagonists since 1973. During the intervening years the principal advances in military technology had been in the fields of enhanced protective armour (by the use of laminated and reactive armour), aircraft ECM packages, improvements to terminally guided and precision munitions and to all types of guided missiles. Following the hard lesson of 6 October 1973, the Israelis had also developed an extensive strategic and operational early warning system based on an airborne warning and control system (AWACS), airborne early warning (AEW) aircraft, and (for operational-level intelligence gathering) the use of remotely piloted vehicles. There had also been numerous technological upgrades to Israel's signals intelligence (SIGINT) capability.

A most important IDF tactical advance was the introduction of significant numbers of helicopter gunships armed with ATGM and other weapons, which reflected the tactical doctrine and practice of the US forces of the time. Thus the traditional pre-eminence of the tank in the IDF was finally ended, as it was relegated to a position of equal status with the other main combat arms: the infantry, artillery and engineers, plus the armed helicopter units.

The Israeli invasion was launched. Over the next six days the IDF's new all-arms units and formations stormed northward, and by 12 June they were in Beirut. A bitter and bloody siege then ensued until August, during which much of the Lebanese capital was reduced to rubble. By the declared end of the Israeli invasion in August, at least 12,000 Lebanese and Palestinians had died, with at least a further 20,000 wounded, the vast majority civilians. However, although the formal invasion had concluded, the IDF remained as an occupying force to ensure that the Palestinians could not regain their former pre-eminence in the country. But despite the Israeli presence, lawlessness and civil war prevailed in Beirut and elsewhere, as the Lebanese Christian militias – the Phalangists – conducted their own ruthlessly violent campaign to achieve overall power in the Lebanon. As their prime target was the Palestinians, the Phalangists enjoyed the often uneasy, but nevertheless undoubted, support of the occupying Israeli forces. Amid the semi-licensed chaos that ensued, a series of accusations and counter-accusations of atrocities attracted the attention of the international media, which considerably diminished the military success and stature of the IDF campaign. Unquestionably the most infamous of these atrocities were the massacres carried out at the Palestinian refugee camps of Sabra and Chatila in West Beirut between 16 and 18 September. Here, although some Palestinian fighters were certainly among those killed, the Phalangists systematically murdered a total of between one and two thousand men, women and children. Although this slaughter was not carried out by the IDF (despite Palestinian claims to the contrary), it was nonetheless conducted with its knowledge and passive compliance, and therefore with its implied approval.[147]

Indeed, while the IDF validated the effectiveness of the military hardware it deployed into the Lebanon, that campaign also signified the high-water mark of international support and approval for Israel that had lasted for some three decades. However contrived they may have been, the images of Palestinian freedom fighters armed only with AK-47s, rocks and petrol bombs confronting the Merkava tanks and M-113 armoured personnel carriers of the IDF, blazed across the world's media; and just as the US forces lost the media war in Vietnam in 1968, so Israel lost the same battle among the ruins of Beirut and the Lebanon in the fall-out from the 1982 invasion.

Sadly for Israel, with the continuation of the *intifada* which began in 1987, the Israeli government and the IDF failed to redress the psychological defeat that they both experienced back in 1982; and this situation has since been perpetuated by the nature and conduct of many of the internal security operations against the Palestinians within Israel's current borders.

Yet despite this, in its last major offensive during the Cold War years Israel did manage to remain generally aloof from the internal strife that the Lebanon had largely brought upon itself, although that very aloofness invited accusations of complicity in the mayhem that followed. Nevertheless, in purely military-strategic terms, it had unquestionably achieved its aims in the Lebanon and, just as importantly, had demonstrated that the IDF and the IAF were the same resolute, flexible and formidable military forces that they had been in 1948, 1956, 1967 and 1973. And it is probably inescapable that Israel's armed forces and people must always remain so, for genuine peace may be both illusory and unattainable for the Jewish state. Even half a century after its formation the very existence of Israel remains unacceptable to a majority of the principal Arab nations, and disaffected groups such as the Palestinians, while certain of Israel's more extreme expansionist and internal policies have continued to attract censure from much of the wider international community. It is therefore an uncomfortable but possibly unavoidable fact that the price of Israel's future survival and the continuation of a Jewish national state may well be an acceptance by its citizens that they and their heirs and successors can exist only if they are prepared to live in an environment of perpetual conflict.

CHAPTER ELEVEN

DARK DEEDS IN THE DARK CONTINENT: AFRICA 1952–90

During the Cold War more individual conflicts took place in Africa – from Algeria, Tunisia and Morocco in the north, to Rhodesia, Mozambique and South Africa in the south – than in any other geographical region, and the sheer savagery of many of these conflicts regularly exceeded that seen anywhere else during that period. Thus the 'Dark Continent' sobriquet coined in an earlier age proved just as appropriate in the second half of the twentieth century. The majority of these wars, uprisings and insurgencies were primarily nationalist, feudal or tribal in nature, and so were not direct contributors to or consequences of the Cold War. For Great Britain the Mau Mau terror campaign in Kenya from 1952 to 1960 exemplified this. Certainly it was one of the most violent post-1945 conflicts in which British forces were involved, and during eight years some 2,000 civilians and 600 members of the security forces were killed by the terrorists, with about 11,500 Mau Mau killed in action and 2,500 captured.[148] But this campaign was essentially a tribal dispute with little or no Cold War significance. Indeed, the sheer scale and savagery of the atrocities committed by the Mau Mau soon alienated most of the civilised world, and any initial Eastern bloc interest in supporting the terrorist campaign quickly dissipated.

Nevertheless, where these campaigns were directed against existing or former colonial or imperial powers – usually Great Britain, Portugal, Belgium or France – the Soviets and their allies regularly provided advice and assistance to the 'freedom fighters' involved. This policy was both predictable and logical, as it offered low-risk opportunities for the Soviets to extend their power and influence in Africa while simultaneously diminishing that of several key nations within the newly formed NATO Alliance. Furthermore, any West European troops needed to maintain law and order in Africa could not readily be deployed against the Warsaw Pact in continental Europe. Accordingly, support for 'liberation movements' was firmly enshrined in Soviet ideological and political doctrine, and was applied worldwide. Consequently, the 'dark deeds in the Dark Continent' during the troubled decades after the Second World War provided yet another, often unedifying, perspective to the Cold War.

Algeria, 1954–62

Just as the British security forces were starting to deal effectively with the Mau Mau problem in Kenya, a potentially much more serious conflict was developing far to the north, in French-owned Algeria. Only six months after its crushing defeat at Dien Bien Phu, France was confronted in Algeria by a nationalist and Muslim-inspired uprising seeking independence for a country that had since 1848 enjoyed a somewhat anachronistic status as an integral part of metropolitan France, rather than as a colony. The insurgent movement was the Front de Libération Nationale (FLN), which followed communist principles for the organisation and conduct of a revolutionary campaign, but remained ideologically a Muslim-based movement. The Algerian Communist Party and other anti-French groups were progressively absorbed into the FLN, and by mid-1956 it had evolved into an ideologically broad-based nationalist organisation. The French authorities, however, continued to represent it primarily as a communist-inspired movement. Meanwhile, the FLN received considerable assistance from the neighbouring countries of Tunisia and Morocco and elsewhere in the Arab world. This meant that the Soviet Union and communist bloc states had numerous conduits through which they could provide support to the FLN, and thereby divert, dissipate and degrade the military capability of an important NATO country.

Two issues influenced the insurgent cause throughout the conflict. First, there was the absolute intransigence of the French colonial settlers (*pieds noirs*) who had administered and generally exploited Algeria ever since the mid-nineteenth century. Second, there were the cultural and religious aspirations of a huge Muslim population. The Algerians had seen neighbouring Tunisia and Morocco gain independence and were not prepared for their own national destiny to be limited by an outdated legal contrivance patently designed to perpetuate French control.

In 1956 a more extreme guerrilla organisation, the Armée de Libération Nationale (ALN) succeeded the FLN. The war against the ALN ranged through the mountains of the Aures, Kabylie, Hodna and Ouarsenis. It was fought in the desert close to the Tunisian, Moroccan and Libyan borders, and in the densely populated towns and cities – such as Philippeville and Oran. Finally it spilled on to the streets of Algiers itself.

The conflict was bitter and divisive. It scarred France and its armed forces for many years after Algeria finally won its independence in 1962; historically and emotionally it was in some respects the French equivalent of the American experience in Vietnam and that of the Soviets in Afghanistan. Vehement accusations that the Algerian conflict had been won on the battlefield but lost by the Paris politicians were voiced by many French military leaders, which eventually threw elements of the French army into a direct confrontation with the government. There was also a much greater public awareness of the war in Algeria than had been so during the war in Indochina. Whereas conscripts were not permitted to serve overseas in South-east Asia, Algeria was categorised as a part of metropolitan France;

thus there were no constraints on the use of conscripts to fight – and in many cases to die – in the campaign. Eventually, public opinion was an important contributor to ending the conflict.

Although the French forces – 37,000 strong – dealt effectively with the FLN's initial attempts to start the rebellion in November 1954, the guerrilla campaign was rejuvenated the following August, when the FLN attacked and murdered 123 *pied noir* settlers near Philippeville on the coast. The excessively robust French response resulted in some 12,000 Algerian Muslims being killed, which not unexpectedly produced a surge of support for the FLN and assisted its development into the ALN – by then up to 20,000 strong.

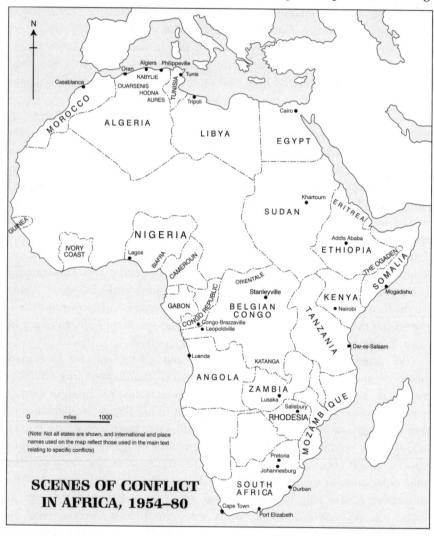

SCENES OF CONFLICT IN AFRICA, 1954–80

(Note: Not all states are shown, and international and place names used on the map reflect those used in the main text relating to specific conflicts)

The guerrilla war ran on, while the catalogue of ambushes, shootings, bombings, atrocities and reprisals grew, and the toll of casualties on both sides increased steadily. On Algeria's borders with Morocco and Tunisia formidable obstacles of wire, mines and electrified fences had been erected in 1957. These defences ran from the Mediterranean coast southward into the desert and were complemented by air and ground patrols. The border barriers effectively cut off the ALN's external support, and by 1958 the French had largely contained its military threat.

The previous year, the French high command had responded to the rapidly escalating terrorist bombing and shooting campaign in Algiers by passing total responsibility for the city to the army. On 7 January the élite 10th Parachute Division, commanded by General Jacques Massu, was ordered by Governor-General Robert Lacoste to take control of the city and restore order 'by every available means'. It did so with alacrity, and by the end of the year the ALN organisation in Algiers had been comprehensively smashed; law and order were restored to the city, and Massu's paratroops were administering Algiers with considerably greater efficiency than had the former civil authorities. In military terms the 10th Parachute Division had done exactly that which had been asked of it, and had conducted a model internal security operation. However, it had done so at a price. In order to gain the vital intelligence necessary to halt the terror campaign, the paratroops had employed torture on a wide scale during the interrogation of terrorist suspects and supporters. This fact – together with the unexplained death or disappearance of some 3,000 ALN members and suspects held in military detention – offended the delicate sensibilities of the French socialist politicians in Paris. It also provided the ALN with much material for its international propaganda campaign.

Consequently, in spring 1958 events reached crisis point. Political indecision was rampant in Paris, the *pieds noirs* in Algiers were threatening to seize control of the country, the French army in Algeria was convinced that the politicians were failing to support their war, and its commanders were openly contemplating armed action in France. Finally, the discredited government of President Coty's French Fourth Republic collapsed. In the midst of this chaos, General Charles de Gaulle became President of France and announced a five-year plan to industrialise Algeria and at the same time to destroy the ALN. Meanwhile, an FLN provisional government of Algeria had been established in Tunis. This body immediately set about gaining the direct support of the communist world for its cause; concurrently, the ALN began committing terrorist acts in mainland France.

Although the French army commanded by General Maurice Challe controlled the whole of Algeria by early 1959, de Gaulle indicated in

September of that year that Algeria's future would now be resolved by its self determination. This policy was anathema to the *pieds noirs* and the army, but found considerable political favour within a France that was by then thoroughly weary of the Algerian problem. Despite a huge protest by the *pieds noirs* and disaffected French troops in Algiers in 1960, the end was inevitable. Some months later the French began direct negotiations with representatives of the Algerian provisional government.

A coup launched by Generals Challe, Salan, Jouhard and Zeller in Algiers in April 1961 was supported by the mutiny of a small number of French army parachute and Foreign Legion units, which briefly threatened to usurp the direct authority of Paris. But the coup failed, and five generals and about 200 other officers were arrested. The 1st Foreign Legion Parachute Regiment (1 REP), which had borne the brunt of the fighting both in Algeria and before that in Indochina, had been a prime focus for the army unrest and the regiment was disbanded.

The last act in the war in Algeria took place between a new terrorist organisation – the Organisation Armée Secrète (OAS) – and the ALN. The OAS numbered *pieds noirs* and many colonists, former legionnaires and paratroopers among its ranks. It was violently anti-Muslim and sought first of all to keep Algeria French, but then (when independence became inevitable) to destroy as much as possible of the country's infrastructure and its Muslim population. The OAS terror campaign lasted until early 1962, and Algeria finally achieved its independence from France in March that year. By then more than one million Arab Muslims had died, together with 2,788 *pieds noirs* and 17,456 French soldiers. Understandably, the legacy of bitterness ran deep. On 5 July 1962, some 2,000 *pied noir* settlers arrived at Oran en route to safety in mainland France, having abandoned their homes and many of their possessions in the newly independent Algeria. At Oran they were promptly set upon by Arab Muslims and massacred. Although several tens of thousands of French soldiers were still stationed in Algeria they were ordered not to intervene to halt the carnage.[149] This massacre provided an all too appropriate epitaph for the war in Algeria.

So what was the significance of the Algerian conflict for the Cold War? The loss of Algeria marked the nadir of French global fortunes and ambitions. First Indochina had gone, then North Africa, and now the once-great French empire was no more. In 1956, furthermore, both the United States and the Soviet Union had been forthright in condemning the Anglo-French Suez operation; and in any case de Gaulle's irritation with American interference in European matters – while refusing US assistance to the beleaguered Dien Bien Phu garrison in 1954 – pre-dated Suez. Little wonder then that a period of introspection followed, one symptom of which was de

Gaulle's decision to withdraw France from the integrated command structure of NATO in 1966. Another outcome was France's determination to avoid a dependence upon others (especially the United States) for its defence in the future.

Accordingly, with its first successful atomic test completed on 2 March 1960, de Gaulle directed that France would develop its own independent strategic nuclear capability and deterrent. Such a goal was achieved when a squadron of thirty-six specially converted nuclear-capable Mirage IVA bombers became operational on 1 October 1964. This was followed in 1971 by a ground-based ICBM capability, and, in January 1972, by its submarine-launched counterpart. Although the French nuclear capability remained exclusively under French control, its weapons were nonetheless targeted only on the Soviet Union throughout the Cold War, and so still contributed significantly to the business of Western nuclear deterrence. It also provided an element of uncertainty for the Kremlin, as French military reactions and intentions would not automatically be the same as those of NATO.

Despite its socialist leanings, its motto of *liberté, égalité, fraternité*, and its history of violent revolution, the French had suffered directly from the consequences of communism during the final years of the Second World War and the first decades of the Cold War. Therefore, it had readily perceived the FLN campaign to be an extension of the communist struggle to isolate and destroy capitalism worldwide. But there was a peculiar linkage and interaction between the war in Algeria, the French perception of the communist threat of the time, the correct role of France and its army in the Cold War, and the French view of the very un-European philosophy and values of post-Second World War America. These often conflicting considerations created a difficult dilemma for many in the French army, which was clear from a comment on the Algerian conflict recorded by General Massu's Chief of Staff, Colonel Antoine Argoud, in 1960. This was two years after Massu's 10th Parachute Division had conducted their effective but controversial operation in Algiers, one year after de Gaulle had declared his policy of self-determination for Algeria, and the same year that Massu was recalled to France after daring to criticise de Gaulle's Algerian policy in a newspaper interview. Colonel Argoud remarked: 'We want to halt the decadence of the West and the march of communism. That is the duty of the army ... That is why we must win the war in Algeria.'[150]

Sadly, France's war in Algeria was politically unwinnable, and despite its military victory against the FLN and ALN, its most significant casualties were the honour and integrity of the French army, and its relationship with the people and leaders of the nation it served. It was noteworthy, however, that the unrest which bedevilled the army in Algeria did not spread to the main

French forces. But this was perhaps not surprising, as the core of the army in Algeria was the French Foreign Legion, whose overseas missions since 1831, together with its uniquely close affinity with North Africa, influenced its often subjective approach to the campaign.

The Congo, 1960–5

Just as the Algerian conflict was drawing to a close, the foundations of a new crisis were being laid in what had been, until 30 June 1960, the Belgian Congo. There, the Soviet leader Nikita Khrushchev decided that the chaos which followed Belgium's precipitate declaration of the Congo's independence provided an opportunity for the Soviet Union to gain a foothold in one of the largest and potentially richest countries of Central Africa.

At the heart of the strife was the dispute between the Congo's nominal head of state, Patrice Lumumba, and the local head of Katanga province, Moise Tshombe, who wanted mineral-rich Katanga to be independent from the Congo. Indeed, the huge territory of the Congo should probably have been divided into three or more separate tribally based regions at independence, as the indigenous infrastructure left by the Belgians was entirely inadequate to administer or control the entire country. But with most of the Congo's mineral wealth concentrated in Katanga, any solution that cut off this wealth from the rest of the Congo would undoubtedly have resulted in discord. In mid-1960, with all-out civil war imminent, the Congolese army mutinying, and thousands of white Belgian refugees trying to flee the country, a UN force flew in to restore order and safeguard the evacuation. Most importantly, it also pre-empted Soviet military intervention.

This had become a real possibility when Lumumba – who had always enjoyed a close relationship with Moscow – used the arrival of a battalion of Belgian paratroops in Katanga on 10 July to assist the Belgian evacuation as an excuse to seek Soviet military aid 'against Belgium'. However, the unusually speedy UN military response forestalled any large-scale Soviet intervention, although some military transport aircraft and vehicles were received by Lumumba's forces, and a number of Soviet and Czech military personnel were accredited to the Congolese forces as advisers.

Meanwhile, the issue of Katanga's would-be secession remained unresolved. At the time, the West was little interested in Africa, and even the United States merely expressed its disapproval of the Soviet attempt to create a military presence in Central Africa. Then, in September 1960, Lumumba was deposed in a military coup led by Joseph Mobutu, who promptly expelled the Soviet, Czech and other communist bloc representatives and personnel from the country. But peace continued to elude the Congo. Early in 1961, with support for the now imprisoned Lumumba growing in the eastern provinces, the former head of state was transferred to Katanga – where Tshombe ordered him to be shot on arrival. This summary execution provoked widespread international condemnation and considerably strengthened Antoine Gizenga, who now led Lumumba's supporters. Gizenga formed a government at Stanleyville in the northernmost province of Orientale, and on 14 February 1961 this body was recognised by the Soviet Union and Egypt. East Germany, Yugoslavia and Ghana added their recognition shortly thereafter. At the same time, the Soviet Union and India expressed severe criticism of the continuing UN operation in the Congo. Thus began Khrushchev's next bid to establish a Soviet power base in Africa.

Gizenga, with his forces in control of about half of the country and boosted by the level of Eastern bloc support for his government (he had in any case expelled the representatives of all those states that had not recognised his regime), allied himself with Cyrille Adoula to form a central government. Gizenga believed that he would be the dominant power in the partnership, and that the two forces united could end Katanga's secession and regain control of its enormous mineral wealth.

The alliance, however, did not last long and within three months Gizenga had returned to his northern stronghold at Stanleyville. In the succeeding months his followers fought the central government and the UN forces in an increasingly savage conflict typical of the tribal warfare that had blighted the Dark Continent for centuries. By January 1962 Gizenga was defeated and under arrest. With Gizenga's demise Moscow's second chance to gain influence in Africa appeared to have failed – although with the Cuban missile crisis less than nine months away, a new president in the White House, and the Berlin Wall only recently in place, Khrushchev no doubt had other priorities in early 1962. Yet while the unrest and regular periods of fighting, punctuated by frequent atrocities, continued, the communist influence in Stanleyville persisted; and in 1964 a new leader, Pierre Mulele, emerged, supported by the PRC. Meanwhile, Katanga had benefited from the conflict between the Leopoldville and Stanleyville regimes and had become the principal power in the Congo, while Tshombe basked in the support of Belgium and the United States, both of which had vested interests in the future of the Congo's mineral deposits. With the West's position quite clear, the battle lines were drawn.

On 7 September 1964 the communist-supported rebel government of Pierre Mulele, Christophe Gbenye and Nicholas Olenga declared itself as the Congolese People's Republic, and announced its implacable opposition to Tshombe's central government. Within two months Tshombe's forces embarked upon a major campaign against the rebels.

Apart from the decisive defeat of the latter, this operation was noteworthy for several reasons. First, the government forces made extensive use of white mercenaries – mostly French, Belgian and British ex-servicemen, plus a number of South Africans and Americans – to lead the often unreliable and professionally inept Congolese soldiers. Although the use of mercenaries in later wars and campaigns in Africa and elsewhere attracted criticism, there is no doubt that their use during the 1964 operation contributed significantly to the rebel defeat and saved the lives of many white hostages, although more than 200 of them were still murdered by Mulele's rebels. Next, despite the fact that Belgium had officially washed its hands of the Congo in 1960, it had retained extensive mining interests in Katanga and would undoubtedly have been pleased to see that province achieve its separate independence in the early 1960s. The unilateral deployment of a battalion of the Belgian parachute commando regiment in support of Tshombe's attack on Stanleyville on 24 November (to save white hostages held there by the rebels) illustrated Belgium's continuing interest in the country. The Soviets, while avoiding direct involvement, did provide financial and airlift support, expedited jointly by Algeria and Egypt, to the rebels. Indeed, given Tshombe's Belgian and American backing, Moscow probably had little choice but to aid the rebels in 1964, although this assistance diminished and all but ended with the flight of the rebel government to the Sudan in 1965. Finally, there was the role of the UN, which not only attracted Western annoyance over its opposition to Katanga's secession but later also incurred the wrath of Moscow and Peking by its hostility to the communist-backed rebels in Stanleyville.

Although Tshombe had defeated the rebels and consolidated his government's position, the vast territory continued to suffer frequent outbreaks of violent conflict. The development of what eventually became Zaire thus continued to be characterised by power struggles, military coups, conspiracies, murders and summary executions. Consequently, from 1965 both superpower and European interest in the Congo waned, as leaders on either side of the Iron Curtain increasingly despaired of the unending cycle of violence, tribalism and political turmoil.

By then, however, following their unsuccessful attempts to gain a foothold in the Congo, the Soviets were already looking elsewhere in Africa for other opportunities to gain or maintain a strategic foothold. They focused on Angola, together with Guinea on the north-west coast and Mozambique on Africa's eastern seaboard. Each of these Portuguese territories offered port facilities that could benefit the Soviet maritime capability. And by the 1970s this capability was already expanding apace, in accordance with Moscow's aspiration to counter the formidable sea power of the United States, Great Britain and France, following Khrushchev's climb-down over the 1962 Cuba crisis.

Angola, Mozambique and Guinea

The conflicts that preceded the end of Portugal's African empire were not extensively covered by the world media and so – with the possible exception of the later stages of the war in Angola – they took place largely out of sight and unreported beyond Portugal and the African territories affected. This was partly because the media generally ranked Portugal and its African colonies well below the more newsworthy events that occurred in Europe, the United States and South-east Asia during the 1960s and early 1970s. Nevertheless, the counter-insurgency campaign that the Portuguese army – some 150,000 strong in Africa by 1970 – conducted in Guinea, Mozambique and Angola was important. First, this was because the Portuguese army successfully applied the lessons learned from Britain's experience in Malaya and that of America in Vietnam. Second, in all of the insurgencies except that in Guinea, there was clear evidence of Soviet involvement.

In Angola, after the Portuguese departed, Moscow used Cuban troops to win overall control of the country for the communist-inspired MPLA. In all three campaigns, the guerrillas or liberation movements – the PAIGC in Guinea, FRELIMO in Mozambique and the FNLA, UNITA and MPLA in Angola[151] – were mainly tribally based and all benefited from their access to supportive neighbouring or other African states. These were Senegal and the Congo Republic for the PAIGC; Zaire, Zambia and the Congo Republic for the Angolan guerrilla forces; and Tanzania for FRELIMO. Although these organisations were geographically widely separated and differed in composition, philosophy and approach, their campaigns stemmed from a common grievance. This was the way in which, since 1933, the Portuguese regulations for its African colonies made it extremely difficult for non-white Africans to achieve a legal status broadly comparable to Portuguese citizenship. Portugal was little different from many other European colonial powers in having failed to accept that the pre-1939 era of the great European empires had finally come to an end, or to understand that the former colonial powers would best be served by encouraging an orderly, amicable and equitable transition of their overseas territories to independence.

Consequently, during the final years of the 1950s, despite mounting discontent and unrest, the Portuguese government failed to act until a major disturbance in northern Angola on 15 March 1961 left hundreds of whites and over 7,000 Africans dead. As many as 50,000 more Africans may have died in Lisbon's subsequent military response, which relied primarily on the use of air power. In parallel with this action the government sought to retrieve the political situation by correcting a number of long-standing grievances. It also introduced measures that made its Africans' legal status equivalent to that of Portuguese Europeans. However, it was too little too late, and by 1964 both the FRELIMO and the PAIGC insurgencies were under way, while in Angola the FNLA, UNITA and MPLA conducted their separate campaigns against the Portuguese throughout the 1960s.

During the first five or six years the guerrillas made some significant gains in all the Portuguese territories; but contrary both to the guerrillas' aspirations and the views of certain senior Portuguese commanders, neither an outright victory by the insurgents nor their total defeat by the Portuguese were achievable in practice. By 1973, the 60,000 Portuguese troops in Mozambique had successfully contained the 8,000 or so FRELIMO guerrillas (who infiltrated into the country from Zambia and Tanzania) within the border region. In Guinea 27,000 troops commanded by General Antonio de Spinola had reversed the PAIGC gains made during the 1960s and halted the insurgency in its tracks. Meanwhile, in Angola 55,000 Portuguese troops had successfully contained that uprising and stabilised the country. Yet despite these successes Lisbon could not continue such operations indefinitely, and an eventual Portuguese withdrawal was inevitable.

Lisbon drew extensively upon the US experience in Vietnam, and many Portuguese paratroops, marines and commandos attended courses at the special warfare training centres in America. This expertise was reflected in the generally sound use of offensive air power, and napalm proved to be a particularly efficient weapon throughout the campaign. The Portuguese also used defoliants and herbicides to good effect against the jungle bases, villages and crop fields that supported the guerrillas. The commander in Guinea, General Spinola, had also noted the British use of 'hearts and minds' in Malaya, and he oversaw the construction of some 15,000 houses, forty hospitals, 164 schools and 163 fire stations between 1968 and 1973. With military and military-civil-political successes such as these, surely Lisbon might have been able to reverse the post-1945 trend and retain control of its African colonies? But it was the very nature of the post-1945 Cold War world in which these campaigns were being fought that finally militated against this.

At an early stage, it was clear that the support provided to the guerrillas by other African states meant that Portugal was in effect committed to an open-ended war. With 150,000 soldiers – including many conscripts – involved in counter-insurgency operations in Africa by 1970, these clashes were financially crippling, and the manpower and resources required could not be sustained indefinitely. Given more than 10,000 military fatal casualties by the early 1970s, the African conflicts were also becoming increasingly unpopular, and domestic and international criticism of Lisbon's policies was growing. In Portugal this disquiet was not only confined to the civilian population, and during the early 1970s a so-called Armed Forces Movement was formed, which sought a total Portuguese withdrawal. Unlike the French experience in Algeria, relations between the Portuguese army and the white colonists whose existence they were attempting to preserve were not good. The Portuguese soldier's view of the African territories was quite different from that of his French counterpart in Algeria during the 1950s and early 1960s. Consequently, by 1970 these conflicts were in danger of inflicting real damage to the morale and structure of the Portuguese army – an important force within NATO. Matters came to a head in April 1974, when a military coup initiated by the Armed Forces Movement was staged in Lisbon, and General Spinola (who had earlier been dismissed by the government for criticising its policies) was appointed president.

With the new government in place in Lisbon, independence for Guinea and Mozambique soon followed, in September 1974 and June 1975 respectively. Independence for Angola was scheduled for 11 November 1975. However, in Angola the three disparate factions – the FNLA and UNITA, and the MPLA – had already begun fighting one another in anticipation of independence. During this final phase of the Angolan conflict Moscow sought to maintain a foothold in Africa, while South Africa attempted to stem what it identified as the southward spread of communism.

Throughout, FRELIMO had variously enjoyed the support of Algeria, China and the Soviet Union, whereas the FNLA had received both Chinese and US backing. FRELIMO and the FNLA (initially) were both supported by the OAU (Organisation of African Unity), as was the PAIGC. Meanwhile, the MPLA had been funded by the Soviet Union, Algeria, Bulgaria and Czechoslovakia (plus the OAU from 1968). When a South African-supported FNLA and UNITA force appeared in October 1975 to be on the verge of seizing overall control of Angola following the Portuguese withdrawal, the Soviets arranged for a large number of Cuban troops equipped with armour and artillery to intervene on the MPLA side. These proxy forces arrived by sea and air, and quickly destroyed the FNLA in the north. Then, following a South African withdrawal, Cuban T-34 and T-54/55 tanks, supported by 122mm multiple rocket launchers, mortars and large quantities of support weapons and resources, inflicted a decisive defeat on the FNLA and UNITA forces in the south during January of the following year. This victory was decisive, and next month the MPLA formed the new government of an independent Angola, ensuring that the Soviets had at last secured an important strategic foothold on the west coast of Africa.

Portugal's withdrawal from Angola and Mozambique also had important repercussions for the British territory of Rhodesia, where black nationalists were resisting the country's white-dominated government. With the Portuguese removed from their former territories, the Soviets – together with the East Germans, Cubans, Czechs and Bulgarians – used Mozambique and Angola to provide extensive support to the Zimbabwe African National Union (ZANU) and the Zimbabwe African People's Union (ZAPU) guerrilla campaigns in Rhodesia. Consequently, by the end of the 1970s there were about 19,500 Cubans, plus some 1,400 Soviets and almost 7,000 East Germans based in the former Portuguese colonies. The support and training provided by these communist soldiers – together with modern weapons such as SAM-7, medium mortars, small-arms, ammunition and explosives – proved decisive, and were therefore major contributors to Robert Mugabe achieving power as leader of the new state of Zimbabwe from March 1980.

Elsewhere in Africa the Soviets had also been busy in the former British colony of Nigeria, on the west coast. In this case, an indecisive Labour government in Britain and a largely apathetic government in Washington had by default allowed the Soviet Union to sustain a Nigerian government patently not attuned ideologically to communism, but which nonetheless needed the assistance that only a major European power or a superpower could provide. The existence of substantial oil deposits in eastern Nigeria was another factor that Moscow no doubt took fully into account when it decided to intervene in what became known as the Nigerian Civil War.

Nigeria, 1967–70

The Nigerian conflict was again primarily tribal in nature. It was fought between the Ibos, led by Colonel Chukwuemeka Ojukwo and based in the oil-rich province of Biafra, and the federal forces led by General Yakabu Gowon from the national capital, Lagos. The situation of an African province – in this case Biafra – that was the source of much of the parent nation's wealth seeking to secede from that nation, was similar to that of mineral-rich Katanga within the Congo during the 1960s. The Nigerian conflict was notorious for the massacres and atrocities committed by both sides, and for the appalling starvation suffered by the civilian population of Biafra, reported extensively by the television news media. However, it was also an example of the sort of attitudes and sideshow politics that the West's preoccupation with Cold War issues elsewhere produced in respect of its dealings with Africa.

The Nigerian government's response to Ojukwo's declaration of Biafran independence on 30 May 1967 was predictable, as was the course of the two and a half years of war that followed from July. Biafra was supported by neighbouring Cameroon and was recognised by the African states of Ivory Coast, Gabon, Zambia and Tanzania. It also received moral backing from France (which, in a quaint throwback to the old days of Anglo-French colonial rivalry, sought to limit British influence in Central Africa), South Africa,

Rhodesia, Portugal (already embroiled in its own African war) and the Vatican. Many of the professional officers of the Nigerian army were Ibo and joined the Biafran forces; indeed, the Ibos were among the most intelligent of African tribes. However, Ojukwo was still unable to generate forces large enough to take on and defeat the Nigerian federal army, and his 6,000 troops were soon far outnumbered by the 80,000-strong army (albeit poorly trained) that General Gowon raised to deal with them. The federal forces were also superior in artillery and armoured vehicles.

This situation was exacerbated by British government sensitivity over further association with its former colony. The involvement of the former colonial power might have been decisive, but Britain's hesitant approach resulted in its agreement only to provide the government forces with defensive weapons, such as anti-aircraft guns (the Biafrans had used an old B-26 bomber to attack Lagos during the first few months of the war), small-arms and ammunition, but not with the combat aircraft that Lagos needed to bring the war to an early conclusion. Meanwhile, Belgium and Spain provided some matériel to Biafra. Moscow, however, was delighted to fill the void created by British reticence and American neutrality (which effectively obviated the risk of a superpower confrontation), and the Nigerian federal government received ten Delfin jet fighters from Czechoslovakia and fifteen MiG-17s from the Soviet Union. Egyptian, European and South African pilots flew these aircraft. They did so to good effect, and on 12 January 1970 a ceasefire was declared, followed on 15 June by the official end of the Biafran secession. Colonel Ojukwo had already left Nigeria.

Although General Gowon's military government was by no means communist or even socialist in nature, Soviet support for the victorious federal government meant that Moscow gained another foothold in Africa, together with access for the Red Fleet's warships to the Nigerian ports on the Atlantic seaboard. In order to maximise their influence in Africa and their wider strategic advantage, the Soviets still needed maritime facilities adjacent to the Indian Ocean and the vitally important Persian Gulf region on Africa's Red Sea coast. But just as the Soviet-backed MPLA and its Cuban troops were consolidating their 1975 victory in Angola, so a new opportunity for the Soviet Union to expand its presence in Africa was developing on the littoral, in Ethiopia.

Ethiopia, Somalia and Eritrea, 1974-91

On 12 September 1974 the long-running dynasty of Emperor Haile Selassie of Ethiopia collapsed in the face of a popular revolution that followed years of maladministration by the government of what was then one of the poorest countries in the world. This situation had been aggravated by years of severe drought, along with a war against Eritrean rebels that had already lasted some fourteen years. Two weeks later the new government was itself overthrown by a military coup, in which one of the principal leaders was Mengistu Haile Mariam. This coup was accompanied by an immediate flurry of executions followed by a period of civil unrest, violent factional fighting, murder and intimidation that continued through to February 1977, by which time Mengistu had eliminated his former colleagues of the 1974 coup, and had entirely suppressed all other actual or potential opposition. On 3 February 1977 he was proclaimed president of the People's Democratic Republic of Ethiopia, at the head of a state firmly founded on the principles of Marxist-Leninism. Indeed, Mengistu had assiduously cultivated the Soviets from the outset of his bid for power a little more than two years earlier.

The United States, which had maintained a military presence in Ethiopia during Haile Selassie's rule, was forced to withdraw its people, and the last Americans left in April 1977. Meanwhile, Cuba and the Soviet Union endorsed Mengistu's regime, and from that point there was never any doubt that this new communist state, situated at the strategically important Horn of Africa, would receive the backing of the Soviet Union and other communist bloc nations – in return for maritime facilities and a permanent Soviet military presence in Ethiopia. All this was acceptable to Mengistu, as he needed Soviet support not only to reinforce his own power base but also to counter a Somali invasion into the Ogaden region of south-east Ethiopia in May 1977.

Somalia had long maintained a claim to that territory, and in May a protracted period of guerrilla warfare was converted into a well-planned military campaign. However, a treaty of friendship existed between the Soviet Union and Somalia, and Moscow had already established a number of maritime, air and communications facilities in the country. It therefore found itself in the embarrassing position of supporting, arming and supplying both parties. By September 1977, with heavy casualties on both sides, the Somali forces had made significant gains. But soon afterwards Moscow decided – even at the cost of losing its existing facilities in Somalia – that its longer-term strategic interests would be best served by backing Ethiopia, and so the Soviets left Somalia, somewhat precipitately, in November. Mengistu's earlier courting of Moscow was then well repaid by the provision of Soviet heavy artillery, multi-barrel rocket launchers, T-54/55 and T-62 tanks. In addition, the Soviets supplied Ethiopia with a number of MiG-21 fighter aircraft. Finally, some 500 of the increasingly ubiquitous Cubans arrived to train the Ethiopian forces. The Ethiopian counter-offensive began in January 1978, and by its successful end in mid-March, when the Somalis withdrew back to their own territory, there were some 11,000 Cubans and 1,500 Soviet personnel directly involved in the fighting on the Ethiopian side.

The West had limited its involvement in the fighting to the provision of defensive weapons to Somalia, and although Ethiopia dealt decisively with the Somali threat in 1978, Somalia's violent and turbulent history continued through the rest of the Cold War, and beyond. Indeed, in 1993 US forces intervened directly in Somalia in a bid to oust the warlord Mohammed Adid. The failure of this ill-conceived operation indicated yet again the risks inherent in what President George W. Bush in 2002 would term 'regime change' in countries historically, culturally and geographically far removed from the West and Washington.

With the Somali threat contained, Mengistu turned his attention to the escalating problem of the Eritrean secessionists who had made a number of territorial gains, including the capture of several coastal towns. On 17 July 1978, the Marxist-Leninist government of Ethiopia launched some 300 T-54/55 and T-62 tanks, plus four divisions with air support, against the Eritrean forces, whose political philosophy was also that of Marx. The Soviets threw their weight into the Ethiopian campaign from the sea and in the air, and its success forced the Eritreans once again to revert to a guerrilla campaign. Although this was a major setback for the rebels, they were by no means defeated, and Eritrean units later played a key role in the overthrow of the military regime in Addis Ababa in 1991. Eritrea finally achieved its independence in 1993, by which time Soviet global military power was no longer a factor.

Although the Horn of Africa continued to be troubled by widespread poverty, starvation and violence, the Soviet Union had, at an important stage in the Cold War, gained admission to the Red Sea ports that it needed. It had also successfully replaced the Western influence and presence in a strategically vital region of the world, close to the sea routes that provided access to the Middle East oilfields.

So it was that in Ethiopia, just as in Angola, Mozambique, Guinea, Nigeria and the Congo, the old European colonial and imperial powers had to varying degrees been replaced by the Soviets or by those they sponsored. And if Africa was no more than a peripheral battleground, it was nonetheless one on which the communists had in virtually every case triumphed over the United States and the West, mainly by default. Certainly many of the dark deeds that were carried out in the Dark Continent from 1945 to 1990 were by no means exclusively the preserve of the indigenous African population. In many instances the savagery involved in the new scramble for Africa from 1945 to 1990 was facilitated by the ill-judged involvement or abrogation of their responsibilities by the United States and the Western European powers. Nevertheless, the greatest external influence was undoubtedly Moscow's pro-active and expansionist African policy during the 1960s and 1970s.

THE SOVIET WAR IN AFGHANISTAN, 1979–89

The Soviet invasion of Afghanistan was one of the three most significant conflicts of the Cold War era, the others being the Korean War in the 1950s and the wars in Indochina and Vietnam from 1945 to 1975. Indeed, in many respects Afghanistan eventually became the Soviet equivalent of America's Vietnam War. It was also the only Cold War conflict in which Soviet forces were directly engaged in full-scale combat outside – or at best on the periphery of – what was generally acknowledged to be the Soviet sphere of interest. The impact of Afghanistan upon the Soviet Union, its armed forces – the army in particular – and the outcome of the Cold War was significant. Indeed, the eventual withdrawal of the Soviet forces from Afghanistan in 1989 coincided with the year that is generally considered to be that in which the Cold War ended. But as events since 1989 have demonstrated all too clearly, another importance of the Soviet adventure against its southern neighbour in 1980 was the way in which it unwittingly aggravated the Islamic extremism that was already growing in strength throughout the region. This led not only to later security problems in the former Soviet Union's predominantly Muslim southern republics, but also enabled Islamic radicalism, and the excesses and terrorism from which it is inseparable, to flourish virtually unimpeded in Afghanistan post-1989. The evidence of this eventually manifested itself in the terrorist attack at New York on 11 September 2001.

There was a certain irony in this, as US military support for the guerrillas who fought the Soviet invaders was a decisive factor in the mujahedin victory. Had Washington better understood the new threat then incubating in Asia and the Middle East, whilst at the same time appreciating that the more familiar threat posed by communism was in decline, it might have modified its attitude and response to the Soviet invasion. All that it required was for the United States to do nothing – politically, economically or militarily – when, on 27 December 1979, the Soviet Union embarked upon its ten-year attempt to subdue Afghanistan.

The main invasion began when groups of BMD[152] armoured personnel carriers filled with Soviet paratroopers of the 105th Guards Airborne Division raced to secure key points and installations in Kabul. At the same time long columns of armoured vehicles of the Soviet 66th, 201st, 357th and 360th Motor Rifle Divisions rumbled into Afghanistan at Kushka and Termez on the country's north-west and northern borders. Although the Western intelligence community had some warning of the Soviet action, the early news agency pictures of northern Afghanistan's few metalled roads clogged with columns of sand-and olive drab-coloured trucks, armoured personnel carriers, self-propelled artillery and tanks on transporters, all heading south, had an almost surreal quality. The Red Army was apparently going to war and much of its progress would be closely followed on television screens across the world, as well as through a mass of analysis and journalistic comment.

So how and why did the Kremlin leadership judge that it was necessary to invade and occupy the mountainous, inhospitable and barely civilised land that had already proved more than a match for the armed forces of the greatest empire of the previous century?

Afghanistan had been of considerable strategic importance during the nineteenth century, lying as it did between Russia and what were then the northern states of British India. The intrigues, border conflicts and wars that attended Anglo-Russian relations were then termed the 'Great Game', in which the two major imperial powers in the region each sought to dominate the area. Britain had a clear interest in maintaining the security of the northern border region of India, although in the 1880s it was clear that Russia did not intend to occupy Afghanistan, and so Britain accorded it neutral status. After 1919 Afghanistan at first enjoyed good relations with the new Bolshevik government in Moscow, but this situation deteriorated during the 1920s and 1930s, when Moscow's operations against the Soviet Central Asian provinces spilled over the border into Afghanistan, given the natural affinity the Afghans felt for their fellow Muslims.

Following Britain's withdrawal from India in 1947, with the creation of Pakistan in what had been northern India, Soviet interest in Afghanistan again intensified, and large quantities of economic aid and military assistance poured into the country in response to requests made by the Afghan Prime Minister, Prince Mohammad Daoud. He had taken power in 1953, and hoped to solicit aid from both East and West, modernising the country while simultaneously maintaining its neutrality. The United States also provided aid during the 1950s, primarily in a bid to match that from the Soviet Union. But by the 1960s, with the war in Vietnam occupying more and more American attention and resources, Washington decided that Afghanistan was of little strategic importance and so by default left the country to the Soviet Union. Daoud resigned in 1963, but was later to make a comeback.

From the 1960s, the Afghan army was organised, trained and equipped on Soviet lines, and many Soviet military and political advisers and officials were stationed in Afghanistan. During that decade, two separate Afghan communist parties emerged, and these groups were instrumental in supporting Daoud's return to power in a coup on 17 July 1973, which ended the traditional Afghan monarchy, with King Mohammed Zahir going into exile. However, once in power, Daoud's administration attempted to steer Afghanistan back towards neutrality. This was not what the communists and their Soviet supporters wanted, and on 24 April 1978 a further coup resulted in 2,000 deaths including the murder of Daoud. The *Khalq* party – one of the two original communist parties – assumed power, and the Soviets provided extensive support for the new head of state, Nur Mohammed Taraki, who proceeded to adapt every aspect of Afghan life to the Marxist-Leninist communist model.

The Soviet desire to have a friendly state on its southern border and to stem the destabilising Muslim influence adjacent to its Asian provinces was understandable; but its misjudgement of the true nature of the Afghan people was fatal, and this was demonstrated in the way in which Taraki was permitted to take forward his programme of reforms.

First, there was a major redistribution of land – a central feature of many communist programmes in Third World countries worldwide. This failed, and resulted in the collapse of the already frail and rudimentary Afghan rural economy. In parallel with major economic changes that went to the very heart of Afghan life, Taraki instituted a number of reforms to emancipate Afghan women. Laudable and humanitarian though many of these reforms were, they offended fundamental tenets of the Islamic faith that the Afghans had followed for centuries and which had guaranteed the undisputed superiority and authority of Afghan men over their women. In an ill-educated, tribal and predominantly peasant society that adhered faithfully to the teachings of the Prophet Mohammed and the rules and guidance laid down in the Koran, Taraki's attempt to transform Afghanistan into a modern, communist (and therefore, by implication, atheistic) state was doomed to failure. Only in the cities, such as Kabul and Kandahar, did the new regime achieve some success. Elsewhere, the mountain tribesmen viewed the government in Kabul in exactly the same way they had viewed all the other foreign powers, unbelievers and reformers they had overcome in the past. Meanwhile, the Soviet Union's failure to manage and modify the process of reform in Afghanistan under Mohammed Taraki made its future direct intervention a near certainty.

In the mountains, villages and provincial towns of Afghanistan, the fiercely independent mujahedin resistance fighters – united and driven both by their Islamic faith and by their historic mistrust of foreigners – began an armed struggle against the Kabul regime and its Soviet backers. This was a land whose fifteen million people were primarily tribal and essentially feudal in nature. About half were Pushtun, with the balance divided almost equally between Nooristanis, Uzbeks, Tajiks, Turkomans, Hazaras and Hiratis. These close-knit groups lived in a predominantly barren, mountainous and windswept land of some 160 million acres. Only about twelve per cent of that area was cultivatable, and only half of that was irrigated. In 1978 the average annual income per head was a mere 157 US dollars. There were no hospitals beyond the main towns and there was only one doctor for every 16,000 people; fifty per cent of children born in Afghanistan died before the age of five. Three-quarters of the population were illiterate, but followed devoutly their Muslim principles and observed absolutely the lifestyle requirements of Islam. In many respects the Afghans were not and are not a single nation – something that the Soviets in 1979 and Britain and others in the previous century failed to take adequately into account. This fact may still be insufficiently understood by those seeking to create a united Afghan nation in the wake of the disastrous Taliban regime at the beginning of the twenty-first century.

The anti-Soviet guerrilla campaign began in the Kunar Valley close to Jalalabad, an area adjacent to the border with Muslim Pakistan. At the same time, in neighbouring Persia (Iran) the Shah had just been deposed by the Muslim followers of Ayatollah Khomeini. There, the former stable but authoritarian and unpopular pro-West regime was speedily replaced by an Islamic republic, whose policies and actions were directed by a strict interpretation of the words of the Koran and by the universal and often extreme application of the principles of Islamic fundamentalism. Therefore, while Iran began a repressive and dark period in its own history, Afghanistan had potentially supportive Islamic states on two of its three international borders.

By April 1979, the *jihad* or holy war against the communists and their Soviet backers spread throughout the country and affected all but three of Afghanistan's twenty-eight provinces. Only the major towns remained under government control, and insurgency and protest were rigorously suppressed wherever they appeared. At Herat, on 21 March, 5,000 rebels died in a single battle and more than 17,000 people were executed in the Pul-e-Charki prison in Kabul during the year. But instead of deterring dissent such incidents fuelled the insurgency, whilst Soviet military aid to prop up the Kabul regime and the Democratic Republic of Afghanistan (DRA) army increased dramatically. In a move reminiscent of the more extreme communist actions in South-east Asia, the Taraki government ordered the elimination of the nation's non-communist professional classes and opinion-formers by a systematic campaign of imprisonment and murder. A major influence in this repressive campaign was the hard-line Prime Minister Hafizullah Amin, who had been appointed in March.

By the middle of 1979 the DRA forces, their morale already seriously affected by mujahedin successes, were being closely supervised by a large number of Soviet advisers. Indeed, ever since July that year Moscow had probably anticipated a direct Soviet intervention, following a visit of the Soviet Deputy Minister of Defence, General A. A. Yepishev, to Kabul just as the DRA army suffered a series of crushing defeats in open battle at the hands of the guerrillas.

Meanwhile, true to Soviet doctrine, the DRA was routinely employing chemical offensive weapons[153] against the insurgents, together with a formidable range of Soviet-supplied armour and artillery. Most significantly, the powerful Soviet Mi-24 Hind-D attack helicopter, introduced in the European theatre only as recently as 1973,[154] made its appearance in Afghanistan. This marked its first extensive use in combat and Western military intelligence analysts awaited reports of its operational performance with considerable interest.

Throughout 1979 the level of violence escalated rapidly. As the security situation deteriorated daily, the Kremlin perceived that a communist government inextricably linked to the Soviet Union was in peril of

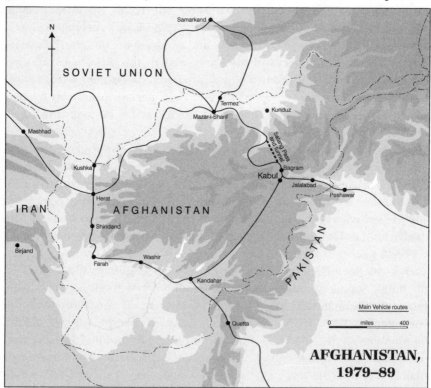

AFGHANISTAN,
1979–89

succumbing to Islamic insurgency. Events in nearby Iran demonstrated very clearly the implications for Afghanistan of an Islamic fundamentalist regime taking power in that country; but for Moscow, with its huge Muslim population in Soviet Central Asia, the implications of such an occurrence were potentially devastating. Just as the United States had expounded the 'domino theory' of communist expansion in South-east Asia, so the Soviet Union now faced its own 'domino effect' as the religious fervour that had consumed Iran threatened to overwhelm Afghanistan, and then flow onward into the Soviet Union itself. There were also important strategic considerations involved, as Afghanistan was an important military base and transit route for future Soviet operations against Pakistan or into the Persian Gulf region.

The political crisis deepened when Taraki was fatally wounded on 14 September, during a coup staged by Prime Minister Amin; he died three days later. The new head of state was an extremist who objected to the somewhat more moderate line that Taraki had by then been forced to adopt by Moscow; but he had in any case deduced that he risked dismissal and so decided to act first. It was immediately clear to President Leonid Brezhnev and his advisers that the new regime would not follow the line they were promoting, and therefore nothing short of direct military intervention could restore the situation. Accordingly, the plans initiated in mid-1979 were finalised. The advisability of this action was confirmed by Lieutenant General Viktov Paputin, who had arrived in Kabul on 2 December ostensibly to serve as Amin's 'military adviser'. Paputin attempted to persuade Amin both to give way to the more moderate Babrak Kamal and to invite Soviet military intervention in Afghanistan to restore the security situation – a measure already provided for in the 1978 Soviet-Afghan Treaty. Amin, however, rejected these proposals and so the die was cast.

In mid-December a full-scale call-up of the Soviet reserves began. Up to 100,000 men were returned to military service. Most of these personnel were Muslims from the Soviet Central Asian and Turkestan Military Districts – a rather perverse decision by the Soviet high command given that their forces would be opposed by Afghan Muslims. At that stage, however, the Kremlin doubtless believed that a benevolent form of invasion was still possible, in which case the use of Muslim soldiers might well have proved beneficial. In the event, with no prospect of a policy change by Amin, the stage was now set for a war that would eventually shake to its very core the confidence and morale of one of the greatest military machines that the world had ever seen.

The invasion was launched on 27 December 1979 and was similar in concept to the operations in Hungary and Czechoslovakia in 1956 and 1968 respectively. Although the Termez-based headquarters of the Soviet 40th Army, commanded by General V. Mikhailov, was nominally in command of the operation, Moscow maintained a direct satellite communications link that enabled the Kremlin to control the Soviet forces on a day-to-day basis. Initially, *spetsnaz* units seized key points and communications facilities, as well as the strategically vital tunnel at the Salang Pass, while the two leading motor rifle divisions of the ground invasion force crossed the Soviet-Afghan border in the north and west of the country. As the 105th Guards Airborne Division – 5,000 men strong – moved out from Bagram airport and secured Kabul, including the Duramalan Palace, Soviet advisers had already neutralised most of the DRA tank units. The Afghans had been informed that their armoured vehicles were about to be removed to the Soviet Union, prior to their replacement with new equipment; so they had already taken most of these vehicles out of service and had stripped out much of the communications, add-on weaponry, fire control and instrumentation.

The long convoys of T-54/55 and T-62 tanks, BMP armoured personnel carriers, trucks, missile launchers, and towed and self-propelled artillery motored south from Kushka to Herat and Shindand, and from Termez towards Kabul and eventually to Kandahar. Overhead, flights of MiG-21 and MiG-23 fighter bombers screamed by, ready to deal with any Afghan force that threatened to impede their progress.

Meanwhile, at the presidential palace two battalions of paratroopers supported by BMDs and ASU-85 airborne self-propelled artillery met brief resistance from a DRA tank regiment. In the course of this clash, Soviet Lieutenant General Paputin was apparently shot by one of Amin's personal guards; possibly while attempting to persuade Amin to relinquish the presidency. Shortly afterwards Amin was himself shot by the Soviet paratroopers.[155] Despite the earlier attempts to present the Soviets as allies assisting the friendly government of a beleaguered neighbouring state, these events finally dispelled any pretence that their intention was other than to subdue and control Afghanistan on their own terms. The immediate Western responses to the invasion were predictable, although their subsequent extent and repercussions had probably been underestimated by the Kremlin when planning the invasion.

Alongside universal international condemnation of the Soviet action, in Washington President Jimmy Carter moved swiftly to implement trade sanctions – specifically restrictions on grain sales – and the transfer of technology to the Soviet Union. The US Congress was also persuaded to postpone ratification of the SALT 2 treaty that had already been negotiated with Moscow. Another target of Western displeasure was the 1980 Moscow Olympic Games, which were boycotted by the United States and others. Later in 1980 the Soviets were also censured by the Non-Aligned Movement, the UN General Assembly and the Organisation of Islamic Nations.

Meanwhile, the United States – with a view to neutralising any threat to the oil-rich Persian Gulf region – indicated an intention to bolster its military presence in that area, in order to deter any Soviet expansion beyond Afghanistan. Washington also took a fateful decision to provide military aid to the mujahedin resistance fighters, and thereby committed America to assist these Muslim 'fighters for the faith' in the conduct of their *jihad* against the communists. By so doing, the United States indirectly enabled the coming to power of the Taliban regime that later supported, sheltered and sustained Osama Bin Laden's Al-Qaeda – the Islamic extremist organisation identified as responsible for the terrorist atrocity in New York on 11 September 2001.

Not surprisingly, Pakistan and certain other Muslim states also supported and provided weapons to the mujahedin. Following the US lead, Britain likewise provided weapons to the mujahedin later in the war – a double irony in light of the British defeats at the hands of earlier generations of Afghan tribesmen during the previous century, and Britain's and the West's present-day problems with Muslim extremism. Pakistan's role was a decisive factor, and the early internationalisation of the conflict by the Afghan resistance was crucial to its ultimate success. The CIA, MI6 and Saudi Arabia worked closely together to support the insurgency and generally agreed that while 'the Pakistanis would run the war, the Western-Arab anti-Communist coalition would foot the bill'.[156] (Incidentally, Afghanistan was to be one of the few sites of Cold War conflicts where Western forces – such as members of the British SAS Regiment – may have been directly engaged in combat against Soviet troops while serving as advisers to the mujahedin.) Western funding notwithstanding, there was also a significant influx of funds from Muslim states and individuals across the world. Much of this activity was co-ordinated by the Muslim Brotherhood, a politically conservative Islamic organisation which had originated in Egypt during the first half of the twentieth century, and now channelled the considerable sums it raised to the mujahedin via Pakistan.

Despite the pre-emptive action of the Soviet advisers, some DRA units did resist the invaders, and more than 2,000 Afghan soldiers died during the first two days of the Soviet invasion. However, the bulk of the 80,000-strong DRA was disarmed by the Soviets without any resistance. More than half of these men deserted early, and a number of them subsequently joined the mujahedin in the mountains. The Soviet intention had always been for the DRA to conduct most of the eventual ground war against the mujahedin forces in the countryside and mountains, while the Soviet forces would provide air power and fire support, and secure the capital, the provincial towns, strategic installations and the main road links. By and large this concept was followed, and the DRA bore the brunt of the fighting, especially during the first four or five years of the conflict. The arrangement was also intended to minimise Soviet casualties, whilst reducing the ability of DRA units to oppose the Soviets in the future. But a series of military defeats at the hands of the guerrillas and the consequent decline of the self-confidence, military capability and morale of the DRA – which also stemmed from its pre-emptive treatment by the Soviets during the first few days of the invasion – meant that Moscow had no choice but to involve Soviet ground forces more and more against the mujahedin in the hinterland.

The initial phases of the invasion were completed with an efficiency culti-vated over three decades of preparing and (in East Germany, Hungary and Czechoslovakia) carrying out such operations to maintain Soviet control of the communist bloc countries. Once the main roads and the capital were secured, headquarters 40th Army relocated to Kabul, although the high command in Moscow still maintained direct control of the operation, as indeed it did throughout the war. Babrak Karmal was installed as prime minister. He had previously been living in East Germany and was therefore a known quantity, having cultivated some support within the Soviet military, and considered to be both politically reliable and controllable. Despite this, it soon became clear to Moscow that Karmal was incapable of leading the Kabul regime in the coming guerrilla war, and the Soviets subsequently contrived the appointment of Dr Muhammad Najibullah as Afghan presi-dent. Najibullah was a former head of the Afghan secret police, the KHAD, and so was well qualified to oversee the counter-insurgency campaign.

Within a month two more Soviet motor-rifle divisions – the 16th and the 54th – reinforced the original four motor-rifle divisions and one airborne division that had carried out the initial invasion. This raised the in-country Soviet force level to about 80,000, with a further 30,000 men readily available from the Soviet Union. Later in 1980 many of the reservists who took part in the original invasion were rotated out of Afghanistan and replaced by regular conscripts. In January and February of 1980, as the severe winter weather constrained operations by both sides (other than in the urban areas), the Soviet forces settled into their newly-acquired territory and prepared for the renewed guerrilla campaign that would begin in the spring. In the moun-tains the mujahedin also readied themselves for the next part of the conflict.

Veterans of the Vietnam War might well have recognised several of the operational techniques and tactics of the Soviet and DRA counter-insur-gency campaign. However, the base-line rationale for the Afghanistan conflict was fundamentally different. Whereas the Americans and their South Vietnamese allies had been defending a beleaguered South Vietnam against the formidable military threat from North Vietnam, the Soviets and their Afghan allies were conducting a campaign against the people of a country that they had invaded and now sought to subdue. Necessarily, therefore, the Soviet campaign was in many respects punitive, divisive and suppressive, and as such it could never have gained popular support in the country.

The course of the conflict was familiar. At first, there were many popular demonstrations against the Soviets and the Karmal administration. However, these were vigorously suppressed wherever they occurred. Typically, a demonstration in Kabul on 22 February 1980 was dealt with by DRA and Soviet troops and resulted in some 300 civilians lying dead on the streets. Strikes were robustly broken by the authorities and student demonstrations were speedily crushed, so that by mid-1980 the main focus of resistance was the mujahedin.

During 1980 Moscow had maintained its original strategy. While the DRA operated on the plains and in the hills and mountains, the Soviets secured the lines of communication, population centres and military bases, and provided airmobility and fire support to the DRA units. Soviet military advisers (about 2,000 in total) also accompanied the DRA units and formations at virtually every level of command. Early in the war, there were also more than one hundred Cuban military and civilian advisers in Afghanistan, while East Germans, Bulgarians and others were also variously involved as consultants to the Kabul regime.

Central to the DRA campaign were extensive clearance operations which often encountered severe resistance, resulting in high casualties. This led to a greater use of Soviet troops from 1981, and to smaller, more focused actions. However, by the end of the year they too had suffered a succession of defeats by the mujahedin. Moscow increased its force levels, but despite the extensive use of air power and helicopter airmobility, further defeats followed in 1982 when the Soviets resumed their large-scale search-and-destroy operations. These costly actions acknowledged the elusive nature of the mujahedin, and were intended to deny the insurgents whole areas of territory that were within striking distance of urban areas and key military targets. Nevertheless, the tempo of guerrilla ambushes, attacks and sabotage – including within Kabul – remained generally unchanged, and although there was no countrywide coalition of the mujahedin forces, the guerrillas still managed frequently to defeat Soviet and DRA units in open battle.

From 1983 the Soviets used bombers to destroy isolated villages and extended the ground denial programme by rendering whole areas uninhabitable. This increased rural hatred for the occupying forces and further fuelled a process begun in 1979, when the Soviets had deliberately set out to destroy Afghanistan's already rudimentary agricultural economy. Clearly, such policies were hardly designed to generate popular backing for the invaders in a land where the threat of starvation was ever-present. The Soviet and DRA forces did, nevertheless, at last achieve a number of battle-field successes in 1984, although the low-level guerrilla attacks continued largely unchecked.

By 1985 armed clashes were taking place at division-level, with both sides suffering heavy casualties, although the mujahedin managed not only to avoid any major defeats but also to overcome entire Soviet and DRA units. The war became increasingly bitter with each passing month, even though it was largely conducted unseen and unreported, as relatively few photo-journalists gained direct or uncensored access. The Afghan tribesmen lived fully up to their savage reputation, and any Soviet soldier unfortunate enough to fall into their hands alive usually suffered a horrific fate. The Soviets repaid the many mujahedin atrocities in kind and – with the full range of modern weapons such as tanks, bombs, napalm and chemical agents available to them – on an even larger scale. War correspondent Doris Lessing filed a first-hand report of insurgent fighters 'tied back to back by Soviet troops, drenched in gasoline, and left ablaze'.[157] The annihilation of whole villages in reprisal or pre-emptive operations by air strikes or ground actions occurred on a number of occasions. The correspondent Eric Margolis, one of the very few journalists who reported the war from the mujahedin side at first-hand, recorded:

As Afghan resistance spread, the Soviets and their Afghan allies, unseen by the outside world, embarked on a ferocious scorched-earth campaign that combined the merciless destructiveness of Genghis Khan's Mongols with the calculated terrorism of Stalin. Villages that had sheltered mujahedin were razed. Crops were burned; farm animals machine-gunned. Tiny butterfly mines, no bigger than a tea saucer, but capable of blowing off a man's foot, were strewn by the millions. Booby-trapped toys were dropped from the air; Afghan children picked them up and had their hands blown off. Irrigation systems that had provided water for eight hundred years were destroyed; wells were poisoned. The dreaded Afghan KHAD secret police, trained and led by the KGB, imprisoned, tortured, and executed tens of thousands of Afghans ... Gravediggers could not keep up with their workload, and complained bitterly to the authorities that their quotas were impossible to meet.[158]

Among the massacres of insurgents and civilians by the Soviet forces those at Kerala in 1979, Rauza in 1983 and Baraki Barak in 1984 are well documented.

However, in Afghanistan relatively few Western journalists made the perilous journey into the country to report on the war. Margolis spent three years reporting the conflict and noted:

> Afghanistan was a most inconvenient, difficult war for journalists. Places like South Africa or the Mideast (sic) had decent accommodation and good telecommunications. You could cover a battle, or the latest bloody outrage, and be back in your Intercontinental Hotel in time for a hot bath and dinner. Getting into Afghanistan usually meant trekking in from Pakistan through the mountains, an arduous and dangerous trip that could take weeks, during which hepatitis and food poisoning were as much a danger as Soviet bullets, rockets, or mines. And every step deeper into Afghanistan meant a longer, more perilous return voyage to the safety of Pakistan. Equally discouraging, TV teams were far too expensive to send on lengthy, dangerous missions into a remote war in the mountains of the Hindu Kush ... Afghanistan was a media-unfriendly war. The few Western news teams that ventured into Afghanistan usually penetrated no more than a few miles, had themselves filmed in Afghan garb beside a knocked-out Soviet tank, and then returned before dark to Pakistan. One American TV newscaster, decked out in Afghan garb, even had a small fake battle staged for his benefit.[159]

Margolis also highlighted the difficulties that he and others experienced trying to have their hard-won stories published in North America, due to 'Afghanistan's remoteness and the West's desire to avoid disturbing the supposed détente with the USSR for the sake of what one newspaper "described as a few Afghan bandits" [which] made people deaf and blind to the industrial-scale butchery in Afghanistan.'

Although the mujahedin were content to combat the DRA forces in the field, they were also prepared to negotiate local ceasefires and other arrangements with them. This revealed the true nature of a war that was still tribal and traditionally Afghan in nature; where the common enemy was the non-Muslim Soviet invader. Consequently, despite the very marked differences between the several mujahedin groups involved in the war, virtually all of Moscow's attempts to capitalise upon these divisions failed.

As the war drew on, the Soviets again increased their force level. By mid-1985 there were three motor-rifle divisions (5th, 108th, 201st), one airborne division (103rd) and twelve independent brigades, regiments and specialist combat and KGB border security units in Afghanistan. There were also two additional motor-rifle divisions (357th, 360th) just over the border in the Soviet Union, which conducted operations into northern Afghanistan from bases at Kushka and Termez. In 1985 the Soviet strength in Afghanistan was about 115,000 combat and combat support troops, plus 40,000 more in the USSR. They were reinforced by about 10,000 air force personnel, with 50,000 support personnel in the USSR. But the overall total was actually somewhat higher, due to the deployment of at least 5,000 KGB border troops and MVD interior ministry troops to Afghanistan. By the mid-1980s the total strength of the guerrillas probably well exceeded 700,000, although the disparate nature of the mujahedin makes any direct comparison of force levels difficult.

The guerrilla casualties were significantly higher than those of the Soviet and DRA forces, and mujahedin losses probably numbered several hundred thousand dead by the mid-1980s, while those of the Afghan civilian population overall (including the guerrilla casualties) may have been as many as a million. Meanwhile, by the end of 1986 the Soviets had lost up to 15,000 killed in action, with about 45,000 wounded. The DRA had lost more than 18,000 killed in action, plus significantly more personnel wounded, missing in action or deserted. Disease also claimed many lives. As the war proceeded, so the casualty toll rose inexorably, and – just as it had in America during that country's war in Vietnam – public opinion in the Soviet Union turned increasingly hostile. Another aspect of the war that mirrored the US experience in Vietnam was the escalating incidence of drug abuse – mainly heroin – by the young Soviet soldiers who were operating in a region that was the world's greatest cultivator of the opium poppy, from which heroin was produced.

The war continued. In Moscow, President Brezhnev died, to be succeeded by Yuri Andropov, and then, following the latter's early death, by Konstantin Chernenko. Against the political changes and trends emerging elsewhere in the world during the 1980s, all of these traditionalist leaders persisted with the Brezhnev doctrine for the security and perpetuation of the Soviet Union and communist bloc. And so, as growing dissent and disquiet led to waning confidence and morale within the Red Army in Afghanistan, the way was finally opened after 1985 for Mikhail Gorbachev to pursue a dramatically different policy, while simultaneously offering the West a pathway to the end of the Cold War.

Meanwhile, in Afghanistan the United States had significantly enhanced the military capability of the mujahedin by the provision of air defence weapons, including hand-held SAM systems.[160] This enabled the guerrillas to combat the helicopters and other low-flying aircraft that were so essential to all Soviet operations. The journalist Eric Margolis witnessed an early use of the American Stinger SAM by the mujahedin:

Fadil pointed. 'There, there, at about two o'clock.' Squinting against the sun, I could just make out dark shapes approaching us from the north, moving fast in the cobalt-blue sky. There was no cover anywhere. The dark shapes drew closer. Fadil watched them calmly through his field glasses. 'Sukhoi-25s. Three!' these were Soviet-built, heavily armoured attack aircraft, probably flying out of the huge Bagram airbase near Kabul. The 25s were configured for ground attack, carrying cannon, rockets, and anti-personnel bombs. The Sukhois were coming because another group of mujahedin had just shelled and were assaulting an isolated Soviet outpost a mile to the west of us. Fadil and his team were in an overwatch position, providing air defence cover for the attack. Intent on the besieged outpost, the Soviet pilots failed to see our group. They deployed their dive brakes, slowed down, and prepared for a strafing run on the mujahedin attacking the outpost's heavily wired perimeter. Fadil directed two of his men who held Stingers on their shoulders. He carefully adjusted their aim points: 'five degrees left, Selim … Lead more, more … wait, wait, wait … Fire,' Fadil said, his voice flat and emotionless. The two Stingers launched with an intense backblast. They flew toward the three Sukhois, corkscrewing slowly …
We heard an explosion in the distance, then saw a puff of black smoke where the Sukhois had been. The first Stinger had found its mark. The other one continued its flight, disappearing from our sight. Moments later, we saw a wing tear off one of the Sukhois. The plane nosed up, then began to cartwheel down, until it smashed into the earth. The two other Soviet aircraft immediately went to full military power, pulled maximum-G turns, and fled the scene at speed … 'Allah Akbar! Allah Akbar!' Fadil and his men cried out, shaking their fists at the fleeing Soviet warplanes.[161]

The provision of American Stinger SAM systems to the mujahedin quickly forced major changes upon Soviet air operations.

Large amounts of financial assistance continued to flow in from Western and Muslim sources, and by 1988 more than 600 million US dollars was reaching Pakistan annually, for use in supporting the mujahedin campaign. The Americans had expanded the USAF presence in Pakistan and had established a worldwide Rapid Deployment Force (RDF). Both measures reflected Washington's continued concerns over the long-term security of the Gulf oilfields and any future Soviet intention to gain control of them. At the time of the invasion in January 1980 the Persian Gulf supplied thirty-two per cent of America's oil needs, seventy per cent of Europe's and seventy-seven per cent of Japan's.[162]

In fact, Washington need not have worried about Soviet intentions, and by supporting the mujahedin whilst limiting Soviet ambitions in the region it actually ensured the stranglehold of the Arab and other Muslim states over the world's principal sources of high-quality crude oil. Indeed, US support for the mujahedin eventually created an even more complex situation in the region, together with a potentially much greater threat to world stability than that posed by the Soviet Union at that stage of the Cold War.

In Pakistan, the government headed by General Zia al-Haq had assessed that the invasion was but the first part of a wider Soviet military campaign designed to overwhelm Pakistan and end at the coast of the Arabian Sea. Accordingly, in early 1980, he had directed General Akhtar Abdul Rahman Khan, the Director General of Pakistan's Inter-Service Intelligence (ISI), to take all necessary action to organise, arm and supply the Afghan resistance fighters. This policy created a safe haven and base for the mujahedin in the south-east of the country and ensured that the insurgency could be prosecuted indefinitely. It also laid a firm foundation of support which the Islamic extremist Taliban movement later exploited with alacrity, to the considerable future discomfort of the Pakistan government.[163]

By the late 1980s the war was threatening the process of East–West détente. It was also prejudicing the rapidly improving bilateral US-Soviet and Anglo-Soviet relations that characterised the years during which President Reagan was in the White House, Prime Minister Margaret Thatcher was in Number 10 Downing Street, and Mikhail Gorbachev – a man with whom both these Western leaders and Chancellor Helmut Kohl in Bonn at last believed they 'could do business' – was in the Kremlin. Militarily, the war was virtually stalemated, although the enormous financial and human costs to the Soviet Union – where the economy was failing and public awareness of the conflict in Afghanistan was widespread – were still escalating.

Consequently, by late 1987 a Soviet withdrawal had become all but inevitable, and following a wide-ranging and pragmatic review of the situation a withdrawal was finally ordered by Gorbachev. This began in May 1988 and was generally completed in February 1989, with the last Soviet elements departing Afghanistan by April that year. Elsewhere, less than a year later the Berlin Wall was little more than a tourist site, the Warsaw Pact was in a state of collapse and would shortly be consigned to oblivion, Russia was on the verge of emerging from the political debris of the former Soviet Union as a sovereign state once more, the Confederation of Independent States (CIS) was in embryo, and the Cold War was to all intents and purposes at an end.

The Soviet military involvement in Afghanistan had ended, but the Najibullah regime, using the vast quantities of matériel inherited from the departing Soviet forces, continued the counter-insurgency campaign. Then, in late 1991 the mujahedin launched a major offensive, several units of the DRA army mutinied, and in May the following year Kabul fell. Najibullah was replaced as head of state by Mojadidi, who was in turn replaced shortly afterwards by Burhanuddin Rabbani. In the inter-factional fighting that persisted throughout 1993 some 10,000 Afghans died, and by the end of 1994 much of Kabul lay in ruins while the country as a whole was in varying states of chaos. From this situation, with the connivance and active support of Pakistan and (to a lesser extent) Iran, there emerged in southern Afghanistan a new Islamic fundamentalist force called the Taliban.

This little-known extreme religious group was headed by Mullah Mohammad Omar Akhund and it speedily transformed itself into a guerrilla army. After a two-year campaign against the Kabul government troops, most of the country was under Taliban domination, and Mullah Omar's forces finally took control of Kabul on 27 September 1996. The strict imposition of Islamic *sharia* law was accompanied by an orgy of killings, reprisals and repression, in which the inhabitants of Afghanistan in general and of Kabul in particular exchanged an authoritarian communist dictatorship for a new and less predictable tyranny: one driven by exclusivity, intolerance, and religious fanaticism. The turbulence continued with a series of campaigns against the Uzbeks and other tribes and factions. By mid-1998, however, it was generally correct to describe the Taliban as the governing power. Thereafter, it mirrored the sort of support it had enjoyed from its Pakistani sponsors by providing a safe haven and active support for organisations such as the Al-Qaeda terrorist movement.

Thus the Soviet invasion in 1979 and its failed military campaign in Afghanistan produced one of the most significant long-term consequences of the Cold War. For from the conflict in Afghanistan there emerged a new threat to world peace and security, the nature and scale of which may yet eclipse the fears, excesses and horrors that characterised the very worst days of Stalin's communist empire. Indeed, although the Taliban regime was finally removed by the US-led military campaign in Afghanistan in 2002, the volatile nature of Afghanistan and its disparate peoples are such that true peace and democracy will probably continue to elude the country. Afghanistan's longer-term future remains almost as uncertain today as it has been during the last two or three centuries.

THE OIL WEAPON AND THE FIRST GULF WAR, 1980–8

Although the United States – followed quickly by Great Britain, the Soviet Union, France, communist China and others – continued to amass arsenals of nuclear weapons throughout the Cold War, there was another much more potent weapon that had existed since the dawn of time, slowly forming upon – or more accurately, beneath – the surface of the world for countless millennia. Whereas nuclear weapons might influence the manner in which a war would be fought, albeit at previously unthinkable levels of destruction, they were never indispensable. But the new weapon that finally emerged as such during the twentieth century was absolutely essential to modern military forces, while it also exhibited wider powers and characteristics that extended far beyond a simple ability to destroy. It was simultaneously an economic weapon and an industrial weapon. It gradually assumed such importance that no modern industrialised nation could exist without it; for it provided warmth, light and – above all else – facilitated mobility and the means of production. At the same time, it was required by every army, navy and air force of the modern world; for without it the matériel, weapons and munitions of war could not be manufactured or employed, warships could not sail, armoured vehicles and military trucks could not move, and aircraft could not fly. Its significance was such that foreign policy was driven by it, wars were fought for it, and campaigns were modified by it. This ultimate weapon – lifeblood of modern warfare and catalyst of conflict – was of course oil.

Throughout that most recent of twentieth-century conflicts – the Cold War – the insatiable needs of the two superpowers and their NATO and Warsaw Pact allies for an uninterrupted and suitably priced supply of oil shaped many of their policies and decisions. Nowhere was this more so than in the Middle East and Asia. There, the vast stocks of oil lying under the otherwise barren hills and deserts assumed increasing prominence for the Americans and Russians (and later the Soviet Union), as their daily requirement for fuel routinely exceeded their own substantial national oil supplies. Thus the existence of Middle East oil shaped the future of that region to a greater extent than history, religion or any other factor, and created a maelstrom of conflict and superpower involvement in a part of the world that might otherwise have been of little or no relevance or significance to the prosecution of the Cold War.

Very large deposits of oil were first discovered in Persia (or Iran) in 1908, then in Iraq in 1927 and subsequently in both Kuwait and Saudi Arabia in

1938; but it was from the 1970s that the oil of the Middle East and southern Asia assumed an unprecedented international importance. During the two world wars the strategic significance of this commodity had been considerable, and then in 1956 the need to safeguard access to Western oil supplies was an important rationale for the abortive Anglo-French operation at Suez. But the enormous potential of oil as a weapon and instrument of foreign policy was only fully appreciated by the West in the aftermath of the Arab attack against Israel during the Yom Kippur War in October 1973, when the one Iranian and five Arab delegates of the Organisation of Oil Producing and Exporting Countries (OPEC) decided at a meeting in Kuwait City to raise the posted price of oil by seventy per cent. By that single historic action oil was transformed from a strategic commodity into a strategic weapon, and at a stroke the Gulf States realised their new-found ability to coerce, influence and shape international policy in much the same way as the superpowers had done for the previous thirty years by using their military and financial muscle.

Début of the Oil Weapon

On 16 October – ten days after the Egyptian attack against Israel – Sheik Yamani of Saudi Arabia told one of the other OPEC delegates: 'This is a moment for which I have been waiting a long time. The moment has come. We are masters of our own commodity.' The very next day, at a meeting with his national security advisers in the White House, President Richard Nixon stated: 'No one is more keenly aware of the stakes: oil and our strategic position.' Meanwhile, on the same day in Kuwait City, at a meeting of the Arab delegates to OPEC called to discuss the use of oil as an instrument or weapon of strategic policy, the Kuwaiti oil minister declared: 'Now the atmosphere is more propitious than [was the case with the Israeli–Arab Six-Day War] in 1967'.[164]

In fact, concepts for the use of oil as a weapon to coerce the West in general and the United States in particular had been raised by Egyptian President Sadat in early 1973. Following this, Arab and Egyptian experts began to plan this in detail, while taking full account of the worsening US energy crisis. In hindsight, all this should have been anticipated by Washington, especially in light of the US commitment to support the post-1967 state of Israel. Now Israel was again at war, and on 17 October the IDF and IAF set about the destruction of the Egyptian and Syrian forces in the wake of their Yom Kippur offensive. Meanwhile, America's own position had already been much weakened by its profligate use of energy. This had led since the 1960s to the extensive use of its own surplus oil reserves, which had virtually eliminated an energy buffer that had safeguarded the West and underwritten its policies and military operations through the Second World War, and then during every subsequent international conflict and crisis up to and including the Six-Day War.

Clearly the Kuwait City meeting that October was a defining moment in world history, with its exposure of the full potential of the oil weapon. The Arab delegates went on to consider a full-scale economic war against the United States – a course proposed and supported most strongly by Iraq. However, Saudi Arabia resisted such an extreme measure, and instead a resolution was adopted for an oil embargo against the United States and any other countries that supported Israel. The delegates agreed to cut oil production by five per cent immediately, and then by a further five per cent each month thereafter until their political objectives were achieved. States friendly to the Arabs and their cause against Israel would continue to receive their full quota of oil supplies. The nine oil ministers present also adopted a secret resolution recommending that 'the United States be subjected to the most severe cuts' with the aim that 'this progressive reduction lead to a total halt of oil supplies to the United States from every individual party to the resolution'. Several countries initiated a ten per cent cut immediately.

Despite the OPEC decision, just one day later Nixon was forced to announce a much extended programme of military aid to resupply the IDF, in order to counter a massive military support programme that the Soviets had implemented for Egypt and Syria. Then, on 19 October he announced a further 2.2 billion US dollar aid package for Israel. The president was already preoccupied with the resumption of North Vietnam's hostilities against South Vietnam and his inability to fulfil his obligations to support Saigon, due in large measure to the rapidly unfolding Watergate scandal. Arab reaction to the massive US aid package for Israel was swift. Led by Saudi Arabia, the plan for progressive reductions was abandoned, and a total oil embargo of the United States was declared and implemented immediately.

The shock effect of the embargo was dramatic, and added considerable impetus to negotiations then being conducted between the United States and the Soviet Union to end the Middle East conflict. Meanwhile, on the battlefield the IDF was in the process of encircling the Egyptian 3rd Army, and President Leonid Brezhnev made it very clear that the Soviets could and would not permit its capture or annihilation. Soviet airborne troops were placed on alert, together with warships in the Mediterranean, and if the United States would not co-operate to halt the war Brezhnev made it clear that the Soviets would intervene unilaterally. The crisis deepened, and at a late-night meeting of Secretary of State Alexander Haig with America's principal military and security advisers on 24 October, the United States prepared to go to war with the Soviet Union. On Haig's advice, the Watergate-weakened and 'too distraught' President Nixon was not awakened for this vital meeting – a telling indication of the parlous state of American leadership at that crucial time. The following morning, the US armed forces worldwide adopted alert state Defence Condition 3 (DEFCON 3), with some units moving to even higher states of readiness. Such measures had not been invoked since the 1962 Cuban missile crisis and now for the second time the Soviet Union and the United States moved to the brink of a war that would almost certainly have involved the use of nuclear weapons.

Fortuitously, however, on 26 October the Israelis halted their forces, the beleaguered Egyptian 3rd Army was resupplied, and the Yom Kippur War ended. Soon thereafter a direct Egyptian–Israeli dialogue began, plus talks between the United States and Cairo. But although the Yom Kippur crisis was ended, the Arabs had in the meantime discovered that they possessed a great new power and almost unlimited source of wealth, so the OPEC oil embargo remained in place. This had momentous consequences for the United States and its Western allies, and threatened to destabilise, divide and diminish the power of the Western Alliance. Daniel Yergin recorded the atmosphere of the times:

> Fear and uncertainty were pervasive and had a self-fulfilling effect: both oil companies and consumers frantically sought additional supplies not only for current use but also for storage against future shortages and the unknown. Panic buying meant extra demand in the market. Indeed, buyers were scrambling desperately to get any oil they could find. 'We weren't bidding just for oil,' said one independent refiner who did not have a secure source of supply. 'We were bidding for our life.' The bidding propelled prices even further upward ... The embargo and its consequences sent shock radiating through the social fabric of the industrial nations ... The age of shortage was at hand. The prospect, at best, was gloomy: lost economic growth, recession, and inflation. The international monetary system could be subject to extreme dislocation ... Moreover, the United States, the world's foremost superpower and the underwriter of the international order had now been thrown on the defensive, humiliated, by a handful of small nations.[165]

In Washington, London, Paris, Bonn, and Tokyo the embargo hit hard those countries not on the Arab list of 'friendly' states. In the United States, a society which had come to believe that unlimited energy and cheap fuel were its birthright was traumatised by soaring petrol prices, queues at the pumps and widespread shortages, rationing and non-availability. The

Arabs continued to exert pressure on the European nations, suggesting that they should disassociate themselves from the United States and its policy of backing Israel. Interestingly, both France and (initially) Great Britain showed a ready willingness to distance themselves from the United States. No doubt Paris recalled the lack of US support for the beleaguered garrison of Dien Bien Phu in 1954, while both France and Britain had suffered from Washington's intervention in the 1956 Suez operation. Also (unlike the United States), France and the other continental European countries were entirely reliant upon access to Middle East oil. In Britain, the situation was further exacerbated by a government in crisis due to rampant industrial action, a national coal-miners' strike, an economy paralysed by power shortages and an enforced three-day working week. With the Western Alliance in danger of fragmenting, the United States convened the Washington Energy Conference in February 1974, with a view to resolving the deepening crisis.

At the Washington conference the Americans widened the discussions and linked the achievement of consensus over the oil crisis to issues such as the role and presence of US forces in Europe. From this conference a general agreement on harmonising Western energy policies emerged. The International Energy Agency (IEA) was established to co-ordinate this, while in the Middle East the Arab leaders saw that the impact of the embargo, although still severe, was now diminishing. Consequently, the Saudi Arabians indicated to Washington that the embargo might be lifted if progress was made with a Syrian–Israeli disengagement on the Golan Heights, and so a US dialogue with Syria was initiated under Saudi auspices. Washington made clear, however, that a peace initiative had to be preceded by the lifting of the embargo (which could anyway easily be reimposed if the United States failed to deliver that which was required of it). After much deliberation by the Arabs, a general agreement to lift it was secured on 18 March 1974, although Libya and Syria both dissented.

This opened the way for a Syrian–Israeli disengagement in May and for a visit by Nixon to Egypt, Syria, Saudi Arabia and Israel in June. Although Watergate and ill-health had by then made him a lame-duck president from the American perspective, this Middle East visit was sufficiently successful to roll back the overall level of tension and – most significantly for the Cold War protagonists – to reduce the threat of global instability and division that had been posed by the Arabs' action. However, just as the discovery of nuclear fission had changed the world forever, so the new comprehension of the potential of oil as a strategic weapon rather than merely a key commodity had changed the fate and fortunes of the industrialised world yet again. As Daniel Yergin observed:

After two decades of talk and several failed attempts, the oil weapon had finally been used, with an impact not merely convincing, but overwhelming, and far greater than even its proponents might have dared to expect. It had recast the alignments and geopolitics of both the Middle East and the entire world. It had transformed world oil and the relations between producers and consumers, and it had remade the international economy. Now [in March 1974] it could be re-sheathed. But the threat would remain.[166]

The Iran–Iraq Conflict, 1980–8

Hardly had the world oil situation regained an acceptable state of equilibrium, when war broke out between Iraq and Iran in 1980. This bitter eight-year conflict followed the Islamic revolution and overthrow of the Shah during the previous year. Both countries had huge oil production facilities, and both had long-standing involvement with the main Cold War protagonists.

On the face of it, the Iran–Iraq War (also known as the First Gulf War) was exclusively an affair between an essentially secular Arab nationalist regime headed by Saddam Hussein in Iraq and the newly established Islamic fundamentalist regime of Ayatollah Khomeini in Iran. The rivalries and disputes between modern Iraq and Iran spanned almost five hundred years of history, and were rooted in the continuing struggle for power and territory between the Ottoman and Persian empires that dated back to the sixteenth century. But the region suddenly assumed a new importance in 1908 when a British oil exploration team discovered oil in commercial quantities near Masjid-i-Suleiman in the Arabistan-Khuzistan region of Persia. Then, almost twenty years later, in 1927 another British team discovered further large oil deposits in northern Iraq. Although Persia and Iraq had long been of importance to imperial Russia and Britain in their struggle for control of the routes to India and to the Arabian Sea, the strategic profile of both countries was raised considerably by these discoveries and their subsequent commercial exploitation.

In the 1940s the region's oil had been vital to the British and Allied war effort, and in the post-1945 world Western influences continued to predominate therein until 1959. However, in July 1958 a nationalist coup overthrew the Iraqi monarchy and in March the following year the Iraqi government withdrew from the Baghdad Pact. This treaty organisation had been set up in 1955, with Great Britain, Iran, Iraq, Turkey and Pakistan as founder members, and was intended to guarantee the security and stability of the whole Gulf and southern Asian region. When Iraq left the Baghdad Pact, it soon forged new diplomatic and military assistance links with the Soviet

Union and the East European bloc. The Shah, who had always been closely involved with Britain and the West, observed this with some concern and from March 1959 sought to strengthen his defence links with the United States. In the intervening years there were numerous armed clashes between Iraq and Iran. These usually involved their rival claims to control the Shatt al Arab waterway, which formed their joint border and also provided access to the Persian Gulf. During the 1973 Yom Kippur War, Western aid was relayed to Israel via Iran, while Iraq sent its troops to Syria to fight against the Israelis.

In March 1974 the Baghdad regime, in furtherance of its ongoing campaign against the Iraqi Kurds, redelineated the boundaries of the Kurdish territory so that all the oil installations fell outside them. The Kurdish guerrilla army was already 45,000 men strong, and had long enjoyed Iranian support, but now the Shah dispatched two regiments of regular troops to fight alongside the guerrillas. The Shia population of Iraq (which had originated in Iran, where Shias were overwhelmingly in the majority) was also suffering growing repression. Full-scale war seemed imminent, but the Shah was reluctant to risk a Kurdish victory in Iraq that might prompt the large number of Iranian Kurds to seek to profit similarly from an uprising against the Tehran government. Also, both nations understood the devastating effect that a war would have upon their oil industries. In any case, Iraq was becoming increasingly isolated internationally due to its repressive internal policies. In due course the signing of the Algiers Accord on 6 March 1975 (in the margins of an OPEC meeting) settled the Shatt al Arab issue and other disputed matters more or less in Iran's favour.

Yet whereas the Shah was well pleased with the Algiers Accord, it actually provided the excuse that Saddam Hussein needed to set Iraq on course for a final military showdown with Iran. Although relatively isolated in 1975, Saddam was not overly concerned about funding such an enterprise, as (following the oil price increases that had been implemented since 1973, linked to the Yom Kippur conflict) he had seen the revenue from his country's oil industry increase from just 75 million US dollars in 1972 to 8,000 million US dollars in 1975; and the value of Iraq's oil income was expected to rise even further by 1980, to about 30,000 million US dollars.[167] Politically, by 1978 Saddam Hussein's Baath Party enjoyed overall control in Iraq, while Saddam himself had achieved total power, and maintained it by favouring the Iraqi military and security services financially and by the bestowal of privileges. Indeed, by 1978 one-fifth of all state employees worked for the security services, and the 'top to bottom' system of internal observing, reporting and informing throughout Iraq was reminiscent of that found in many Eastern bloc countries and other police states. Finally, in a concession made by Iran in the Algiers Accord, the Shah had undertaken to end his support for the Kurds. The Kurdish insurgency promptly collapsed, which removed a long-term commitment for Iraq's armed forces as well as a significant drain on its exchequer. But however ready for war Iraq might be – and its military forces were well equipped with modern Soviet and Eastern bloc tanks, other armoured vehicles and weaponry – the West-equipped forces of Iran were still a formidable enemy. Just then, though, events in Iran took an unexpected turn that changed the whole international and regional situation and ultimately involved various other states in what might otherwise have been an exclusively bilateral clash of arms.

The cleric Ruhollah Musavi Khomeini, or Ayatollah Khomeini as he became known to the world, was an Iranian Shia Muslim who had long believed that his mission in life was to rectify the 'oppressed' position of the Muslims of the Gulf region. He was convinced that the sources of this oppression were the corrupt, flawed and actively non-Muslim leadership of several of the states in and about the Gulf. His views were clearly at odds with those of the increasingly Westernised government of his homeland and he was forced to leave Iran. He then lived in exile in Iraq, but after fourteen years of virtual house arrest in the Shia holy shrine town of Najaf, his continued opposition to Iraq's secular regime and its suppression of the Shias forced him to move again. This time he went to France, where he was able to plan his campaign against the Shah of Iran more or less undisturbed.

Within Iran, despite the country's prosperity and overt stability, there was growing opposition to the Shah's secular, modernising regime and its close-ness to the United States. This was fuelled by the excessive severity of the Iranian secret police and security forces in suppressing any opposition. Despite this, many of the usual prerequisites for a revolution were not in evidence, although the government was undoubtedly complacent about the threat posed by Khomeini and his followers, for:

> Khomeini was a pious, principled man of strong convictions, extremely patient and shrewd, fearless and uncompromising. He led a Spartan life and was incorruptible. All these qualities gave him a charisma which no other Iranian leader, religious or secular, had so far enjoyed. He was rooted completely in Islam; and this enabled him to appeal directly and effectively to the religious masses in Iran, 90 per cent of whom were Shia and another 8 per cent Sunni.[168]

As such, his personal qualities contrasted markedly with those of Shah Reza Pahlavi, and this undoubtedly appealed to many ordinary Iranians, as well as to a number of intellectuals, military officers and decision-makers.

So it was in 1978 that discontent and opposition changed into unrest and revolution. Most of the armed forces declared against the Shah, who was deposed and exiled in January 1979.

On 11 February 1979 Ayatollah Khomeini spoke at a conference on the day the new revolutionary government came to power. He made a policy statement that indicated his further ambitions very clearly.[169] He declared:

> 'We will export our revolution to the four corners of the world because our revolution is Islamic; and the struggle will continue until the cry of "There's no god but Allah, and Muhammad is the messenger of Allah" prevails throughout the world.'[170]

This pronouncement had immediate significance for Iraq and for the monarchies of the Gulf States, as well as wider implications.

A detailed account of the lengthy war between Iraq and Iran is outside the scope of this text; features of the conflict, however, impinged upon or influenced aspects of the Cold War where oil and the oil weapon were once again major factors. Indeed, in 1978 Iran produced eight per cent of the world's oil and twenty-five per cent of that from the Middle East area, while the equivalent statistics for Iraqi oil were four and twelve per cent respectively (Saudi Arabian oil production was the greatest of any state in the region, being about double that of Iran).

Apart from the friction that had long existed between Iraq and Iran, the causes of the war that began in September 1980 were straightforward. Iraq perceived the revolutionary regime in Tehran to be weak and unstable (a view reinforced by the biased assessments of many former highly placed supporters of the Shah who had sought refuge in Iraq). Therefore, Saddam judged that the time was right for a militarily strong Iraq to reverse the 1975 Algiers Accord border agreement and regain control of the Shatt al Arab waterway. In fact, the Iraqi invasion that resulted was repelled by the Iranian forces, albeit at considerable cost, and this strengthened the revolutionary government and increased Khomeini's standing. But then the Tehran leadership allowed religious dogma and ideological aspirations to outweigh pragmatism and common-sense, when Iran launched simultaneous bids to export the Islamic revolution and to overthrow Saddam's secular regime, by invading Iraq in mid-1982. Thus Iran committed both countries to a war of attrition that lasted for a further six years.

During the war the Iranian forces made a number of territorial gains, but at the same time suffered the destruction of many of their towns and cities at the hands of the vastly superior Iraqi air force. And although Iran was already internationally isolated, Khomeini's determination to overthrow what he termed the corrupt and hereditary monarchies of the region meant that an alarmed Saudi Arabia and Kuwait provided aid to Iraq from the outset, and probably even viewed favourably Saddam's aspiration for Iraq to replace Egypt as the leading power in the Arab world.

Once again, this war produced a direct confrontation between the modern Soviet equipment of Iraq and the Western (predominantly US and British) equipment of Iran – although Tehran had experienced serious maintenance and replacement problems once the West's military support for the former Shah ended in 1979. Saddam's 2,500 T-72, T-54/55 and T-62 tanks were opposed by Khomeini's almost 2,000 Chieftain, M-60 and M-48 tanks, while above the battlefields flew Iraq's MiG-21 and MiG-23 aircraft and Iran's F-4, F-5 and F-14 fighters. Both sides also possessed modern Soviet or US transport and attack helicopters.

At the outset, the Iraqi army, 200,000 strong and with half a million reserves and paramilitary forces, contested the ground war with Iran's 150,000 soldiers and 400,000 reserves. By the end of the war in August 1988 Iraq had more than one and a half million soldiers under arms (including 650,000 reserves and paramilitaries), while Iran had by then mustered a huge total of almost four and a half million men, although about three million of these troops were mainly paramilitaries and their reserves.

What then was the Iran–Iraq War's impact upon the superpowers and the Cold War? Despite Iraq's close ties with the Soviet Union, the West was most alarmed by the fall of the Shah and by Iran falling under the control of an extreme regime generally regarded as unstable, repressive and anti-West. It was also a regime with large quantities of Western military hardware, much of which was second in quality and technology only to that then in service with the US and British armed forces. Finally, the concerns of the US administration headed by President Jimmy Carter were confirmed on 4 November 1979 when at 03.00 hours Washington time it was reported that the US embassy in Tehran had been overrun, with the entire staff of sixty-three held hostage. The rationale for this action was the admission of the former Shah into America and to a New York hospital for the treatment of his terminal cancer. However, this was portrayed in Tehran as a conspiracy between the Shah and the US government to restore the Pahlavis to power.

The Iranian hostage affair, the abortive negotiations for their release, and the failed rescue attempt carried out by the US counter-terrorist Delta Force in April the following year, virtually crippled the administration in Washington at a time when the West needed strong, decisive leadership. The Soviets had just invaded Afghanistan, and the industrialised world was still reeling from the effects of the 1973 oil price increases and the embargo on certain states that had persisted until 1975. International terrorism was increasing, and parts of the Middle East region – notably the Lebanon – were fast descending into chaos. Even the kingdom of Saudi Arabia was suffering at the hands of Islamic fundamentalists in Mecca and from Shia Muslims at al-Hasa in the oil-producing region to the east. Amid the international turbulence President Carter's response was limited to banning the import of Iranian oil to America and freezing all Iranian assets – actions that further disrupted an already volatile oil market as OPEC's prices rose again. By mid-1980, however, the situation began to stabilise as demand gradually fell, consumers adopted alternative energy sources, and the Gulf oil ministers understood that they had virtually priced their oil out of the market.

But by that stage the abortive American rescue attempt had taken place and the hostages in Iran had been dispersed in order to foil any further rescue attempts. The hostage affair was a key factor in Carter's defeat in the November 1980 election. He was succeeded by Ronald Reagan, during whose presidency the Cold War was finally won. On the day that Carter relinquished the presidency his humiliation was complete as Tehran released the last of the embassy hostages. Carter, although an idealist and man of principle, was not a strong president, and if the hostage crisis had not happened, and if Reagan had not won in 1980, the outcome of the Cold War might possibly have been somewhat different and certainly much longer in coming.

Meanwhile, the Soviet Union armed, advised and generally supported the Iraqi forces (a process that also involved France – its aid paid for with Iraqi oil and Saudi Arabian and Kuwaiti funding). Moscow also watched carefully for any attempt by Tehran to export its revolution to Afghanistan, and Iran's preoccupation with Iraq from 1980 to 1988 was a useful diversion while the Soviet forces were attempting to subdue the Afghan mujahedin forces.

The West was also unable to remain uninvolved, whether overtly or covertly. In 1983 Washington assessed that an Iraqi defeat would be against US national interests and could well bring about the overthrow of the pro-West regimes in the Gulf States that together contained more than half of the world's oil reserves. The consequences of such an occurrence would be severe, and in November 1983 the US government prepared a secret contingency plan to engage directly any Iranian forces that mounted a major incursion into Iraq. Washington also removed Iraq from its list of nations which supported international terrorism and in January 1984 added Iran to that list. This followed a series of terrorist attacks against US interests and forces in the region, which were attributed directly or indirectly to Iran. Remarkably, until that time the US and many European countries had been supplying arms, spare parts and other matériel to either or both sides in the war.

From the spring of 1984 Iraq attempted to internationalise the war and – still aware of Iran's relative isolation – to involve the superpowers in forcing an advantageous conclusion to it. To that end, Saddam's air force targeted tankers in the Gulf carrying Iranian oil, which in turn compelled Iran to attack those tankers carrying Kuwaiti and Saudi Arabian oil. A number of ships were sunk, and Kuwait requested both superpowers to escort its oil tankers in the region; this led to the deployment of additional US warships to the Gulf (an increase of from six to thirty-two by 1987). But Saddam's wider aims were not realised, due to the surplus of tankers then available. This meant that the owners actually gained more from their insurance claims than they would have done simply by scrapping a vessel. In fact, while oil prices remained generally stable, only the cost of tanker insurance went up. Nevertheless, there were various UN attempts to resolve the war, and it was under that organisation's auspices that a ceasefire was finally agreed in August 1988.

Every US administration seems destined to suffer at least one major scandal. For the Reagan presidency this was the so-called 'Irangate' affair when, during January 1986, in a most bizarre change of policy towards the terrorist-supporting state, the president authorised the CIA to purchase 4,000 TOW missiles from the US Defense Department and sell them on to Iran via Israel. This was but one of several such covert deliveries that even included Hawk air defence missiles, and the arrangements were negotiated directly during secret US–Iran meetings. These arms deals were eventually exposed by the Beirut-based *Al Shiraa* magazine on 3 November 1986, and the repercussions were significant. In reality, the justification for these arms deals was to gain Iranian support for the release of a growing number of American hostages that had been taken and held by Islamic extremist groups in the Lebanon during the previous two and a half years. But despite this, and although Reagan was a very different leader from his predecessor, the Iranian hostage crisis of 1979 and 1980 still haunted the corridors of power in Washington.

On 13 November, in an attempt to explain his actions to his West European NATO allies and to the Arab leaders of the Gulf States, Reagan addressed the strategic perspectives of the affair, that of oil in particular. In a broadcast to the American people, he said: 'Iran encompasses some of the most critical geography in the world. Iran's geography gives it a critical position from which adversaries could interfere with oil flows from the Arab states that border the Persian Gulf. Apart from geography, Iran's oil deposits are important to the long term health of the world economy.' Turning to the political aspect, he said, 'Iranian revolution is a fact of history; [and] between American and Iranian basic national interests there need be no permanent conflict.'[171] Remarkably, Reagan had in effect recognised and legitimised the Tehran regime while it was still categorised by the United States as a supporter of international terrorism. But Irangate could not be disposed of by a single broadcast. In the Middle East, the Gulf States viewed with incredulity what they now interpreted as a US belief that Iran would win the current conflict and consequently they reviewed their own position as supporters of Iraq. They, together with an increasingly vulnerable Iraq, had also noted with concern the US–Israel–Iran links revealed by the affair. This was despite the well-publicised US action in April 1985 to frustrate an Israeli arms deal brokered with Iran to ensure that there would be no Iraqi victory, which involved the provision to Tehran of large quantities of fighter and transport aircraft, tanks, bombs missiles and other matériel. Irangate also had a wider significance. It provided an opportunity for the Soviet Union to capitalise upon US discomfort, reduce Washington's influence in the region, and at the same time increase its own. Moscow quickly supplied Tehran with a large shipment of advanced defensive weaponry, and thereby reinforced the already improving Soviet–Iranian relations.

In September 1986 Moscow indicated that it would not remain passive in the event that the US took military action in the Gulf region and thereafter both superpowers fostered their links with either side in the war, while exerting increasing pressure upon Saddam Hussein to drop his precondition for direct talks with Iran and to accept UN Resolution 598, which called for a ceasefire. And so, with international influences now shaping its progress directly, the Gulf War gradually moved to a conclusion. Both sides had in any case already suffered extensively during the conflict; since September 1980 Iran had lost 262,000 dead and Iraq 105,000. A further 700,000 had been injured on both sides, plus largely unrecorded numbers of civilian casualties.

In Tehran, a more pragmatic view than that of 1982 now prevailed. It was clear by 1988 that the population was war-weary and the mullahs wished neither to impair the Islamic revolution nor the capability to expand it beyond Iran in the future. Indeed, whatever the outcome on the battlefield, Khomeini had always believed that the war would have a consolidating and unifying effect on the Islamic revolution within Iran, and when it looked as if that process had run its course he was prepared to entertain the idea of a ceasefire.

In Baghdad, Saddam Hussein claimed victory in the war, although neither he nor Iran had much to show for the eight-year struggle. Indeed, unlike Khomeini, he had always intended the war to be brief, and following the failure of the 1980 Iraqi invasion he spent much of the final six years of the conflict trying to involve the international community in forcing a ceasefire (on Iraqi terms) upon both sides. Whereas Iran had remained relatively isolated throughout the conflict, Iraq had increasingly depended upon other Gulf States, the two superpowers and various international institutions for support. Finally, Saddam had retained a battle-hardened army of one million men to resume his campaign against the Kurds.

In Cold War terms the first Gulf War had twofold significance. First, there was its impact upon the policies and actions of the superpowers in the 1980s; second, there was the effect of the oil weapon – whether used or merely threatened. At a time when rapprochement, glasnost and perestroika were increasingly influencing day-to-day relations between the United States and the Soviet Union and between East and West, the Iran–Iraq conflict provided an insight into the priorities of both superpowers. Central to this was the impact of the oil factor, while the various US hostage crises also offered a further unwelcome distraction that impacted upon the American national psyche and revived difficult memories of the Vietnam prisoner of war and missing in action (MIA) issues. Certainly, the international status of the United States was diminished as a result of its involvement in the Iran–Iraq War; just as that of the Soviet Union was eroded significantly by its campaign in neighbouring Afghanistan.

Although the United States originally attempted to maintain a neutral position during the Iran–Iraq conflict it was increasingly involved in support of Iraq. There were several reasons for this, and in addition to oil and the hostage issue (which was closely linked to the upcoming 1980 US presidential election) other considerations made this virtually inevitable. These included US identification of an opportunity to decouple Iraq from the Soviet Union and a desire to take positive action against the Islamic revolutionary regime in Tehran, as well as the need to assuage Saudi Arabian fears about the future intentions of that new regime. All this led to the United States supporting Iraq when it invaded Iran, and during the years of war that followed. Moreover, in 1980, Washington had access to similar human intelligence sources as the Saudis and Iraqis, and had therefore probably anticipated an early Iraqi victory. Indeed, in 1983 and 1986 US financial aid to Iraq was critical to Baghdad's ability to continue the war.

But there was another reason that the United States was drawn into the political turmoil of the Middle East, and this went to the very heart of America and its perception by much of the Muslim world as a very alien culture – the 'Great Satan', as the United States was often termed. Although communist criticism of Western capitalism and the sometimes insensitive actions of the United States in the Third World over the previous thirty or so years had been largely dismissed as rhetoric and propaganda, designed principally for communist bloc consumption, the invective that emanated from Tehran after 1979 was of a very different order. The words of the mullahs resonated throughout the world – the Muslim world especially – and provided the first indications of a new ideological confrontation that would soon supplant communism as the principal threat to Western democracy and the peace of the civilised world, including relations with all non-Muslim and non-fundamentalist Muslim states. Dilip Hiro encapsulated the view of the United States from Tehran in the early 1980s:

> Puritanical Iranian revolutionaries regarded America as the prime source of moral corruption on earth, as indicated by the high incidence there of sexual promiscuity and venereal diseases, divorce, broken families, drug abuse and serious crime. They portrayed the United States as the largest devourer of the resources of the Third World, including Muslim states: a superpower which exercised overwhelming political, economic and cultural power over many Muslim countries and their ruling elites.[172]

Whilst there was little doubt that this view was widely held and energetically promoted, there was a broader policy reason for this: Khomeini well understood that his revolutionary republic could only achieve a dominant influence throughout the Gulf region by removing or neutralising the well-entrenched US presence and then imposing the Iranian model of Islam upon the whole region.

Ironically, the Soviet Union was in a similar position to the United States. As a communist atheist state it was also a target of the mullahs' ranting in Tehran. Indeed, with some forty million Muslims populating the southern republics of the Soviet Union and a Muslim mujahedin enemy to fight in Afghanistan, Moscow arguably was much more immediately threatened by the spread of Muslim fundamentalism than the United States. Consequently, although the Soviets might derive some benefit from the Islamic diatribe against the United States, America's enemy had in 1980 become their enemy as well. In practice, Moscow walked a pragmatic and generally successful tightrope between fulfilling its existing treaty commitments to Baghdad while simultaneously improving its relations with Tehran. Therefore, Moscow's policies in the region were in fact conducted more successfully than Washington's; but perhaps the setbacks and humiliations that the United States had endured in the Middle East militated against Washington ever regaining its former stature in the area. Meanwhile, the Kremlin – with large numbers of Soviet troops in neighbouring Afghanistan – never sought to pose a threat to Iran's eastern border, although simply by deploying a large number of units to that area it could greatly have assisted Baghdad by forcing Tehran to move troops away from the Iraqi front. Conversely, Moscow would no doubt have responded speedily to any signs that Iran was about to win an outright victory, as the Iranian forces released would almost certainly have been deployed to support the mujahedin in Afghanistan.

As for Iran and Iraq, the Tehran regime timed its acceptance of UN Resolution 598 astutely: each battlefield success had further diminished its international support, its self-generated level of funding had been reduced considerably following a dramatic drop in oil prices in the mid-1980s, and with a decisive victory over Iraq no longer possible its citizens had become war-weary. But although Iran had lost the war, Ayatollah Khomeini had nonetheless achieved most of his domestic aims. His Islamic revolution was secure, even though he had been unable to expedite his declared intention of exporting it throughout the Gulf region. The Islamic Republic of Iran was an independent and united nation, one that had successfully humiliated and exploited the United States and at the same time achieved a satisfactory accommodation with its Soviet neighbour. In any case, the success of the mujahedin in Afghanistan, plus the rumbles of discontent in Chechnya and other parts of the southern Soviet Union, all indicated to Khomeini that Moscow's defeat at Muslim hands was only a matter of time.

Meanwhile, Saddam Hussein and the all-powerful Baath Party celebrated their victory, and set about planning their next use of the huge Iraqi army. They chose to deploy it both against the Iraqi Kurds and beyond Iraq's borders, and within two years this brought Iraq into direct conflict with the United States, Saudi Arabia and Kuwait, all of whom had supported Baghdad throughout the war against Iran.

But at the beginning and at the end it was really all about oil. Irrespective of the ideological and other issues involved, the Iran–Iraq War and superpower involvement were driven by the possession and control of Middle East oil. In 1978 the region's oil production was 1,059 million tonnes, which was thirty-four per cent of the total world production. The Western industrialised world and Japan depended upon the regular flow of this commodity, at a sustainable price, for their very survival. Had the Islamic Republic of Iran achieved its strategic aim to dominate the whole Gulf region – and therefore to control almost half of the world's oil production – Iran's power and international position would have been virtually unassailable.

The global significance of the oil weapon thus remained paramount throughout the Iran–Iraq conflict, and only by ensuring that Iran was not victorious were the United States and others able to maintain a controlling influence in the region. But for the West this situation can probably last only as long as Saudi Arabia remains an ally of the United States and friend of the West, and the other pro-West Gulf State monarchs continue to rule in the region; and as events in the Middle East since 1945 have already demonstrated time and again the extreme fragility and volatility of the region, the existence of either of these prerequisites cannot be assumed indefinitely.

If ever evidence were needed of the interaction of Middle East politics and the foreign policies of the superpowers – with all of their machinations, complexities, compromises and ambiguities – US policy in the region from 1945 to 1991 had exemplified this. After the Second World War, Washington had supported the pre-1959 Iraqi monarchy. Next, it backed the Shah of Persia (Iran) to counterbalance the new Iraqi regime's links with Moscow. Then, when the Shah was overthrown by the anti-Western Islamic revolution of Ayatollah Khomeini, the United States reverted to supporting Iraq – a country that had been armed and subsidised by the Soviet Union for the previous ten years! Finally, probably against its better judgement and certainly against the American public's perception of the true nature of the Khomeini regime, the US government provided covert assistance to Iran. This policy change was in response to domestic political pressure to secure the release of American hostages held in the region.

It was only when the United States and the Soviet Union, together with the UN, harmonised certain of their policies and actions – and when President Reagan ordered a significant increase in US maritime activity in the Gulf – that their joint approach ended the war. Yet only two years later, early in 1991, in a further bizarre turn of events, the forces of an American-led coalition deployed to the region prior to mounting a major attack upon Iraq from the territory of its former ally Saudi Arabia – a situation that had been precipitated by Iraq's 1990 invasion of Kuwait – Saddam Hussein's erstwhile ally throughout the war with Iran! However, one constant persisted throughout this often unedifying miasma of foreign policy intrigue and incessant change, and that ever-present factor was oil.

The Catalyst of Conflict
Nevertheless, had the needs and policies of the superpowers not created the imperatives that guaranteed their continued involvement in the region during and after the Cold War, the consequences for the developed world might have been disastrous. By manipulating the oil weapon, its production and its price on the world market, Iran, or any other state at the head of a new regional grouping of Islamic republics, could coerce much of the non-Muslim world to satisfy its political, military and ideological agenda, driving the United States and European democracies towards recession and stagnation. The entire focus of industrial development, technology and wealth would eventually shift from America, Japan and Europe to the Gulf.

Yet as Islamic fundamentalism and extremism increasingly impinges upon everyday life in the Middle East, and the Palestine–Israel issue remains unresolved, it is by no means certain that the United States will be able indefinitely to underwrite the security of the region. Indeed, while oil continues to be so vital to the West, any military intervention in the region by the United States or others – no matter how carefully justified for a variety of reasons – will always raise the question as to whether such intervention is in truth motivated by a desire for direct control of the Middle East oil supplies, thereby reducing or removing Western dependence upon the continued goodwill of the Saudis and other Arab states.

The last full-scale Arab–Israeli war was fought almost thirty-years ago, the Iranian Revolution occurred six years later, the Iran–Iraq War ended in 1988, and the Second Gulf War was launched in the immediate aftermath of the Cold War in 1991. Subsequent events showed that the global impact of each of these events was momentous, and highlighted the key role of oil as the catalyst of conflict. Although the world has moved on, with Cold War policies and priorities consigned to history, the global reliance on uninter-rupted supplies of affordable Middle East oil has increased dramatically. Consequently, it is long past time for the developed and industrialised world, with its insatiable and growing appetite for energy, to reduce and eventually eliminate its dependence upon a finite commodity that by and large it does not own, and which it may very well suddenly find that it no longer controls.

THE TRIUMPH OF CAPITALISM

From the account thus far it might be inferred that the West's victory in the Cold War was simply the cumulative result of a myriad of disparate armed clashes at all levels of conflict, each conducted, supported or influenced by the ideological and foreign policies of the United States and its Western allies or by those of the Soviet Union and the communist bloc. But the Cold War was a complex affair, and all kinds of other pressures and non-military factors similarly affected its development and conclusion. Oil was one such weapon, finance was another. Arguably, however, the most crucial aspect of the entire conflict was the economic campaign between the capitalist and communist systems, and the manner in which these two concepts confronted each other in their purest forms.

Of course there was nothing new in the outcome of a war being decided by the ability of one side to resource and sustain its forces beyond its opponent's capability to do so. Since the Second World War, US industrial and economic power had proved decisive, and Washington continued to apply a proven formula of military action underwritten by massive economic power into the Cold War era through the Marshall Aid programme. This was set against a backdrop of military power projection and the constant development of weapons systems by America's huge military-industrial organisation. In 1968, at the midpoint of the Cold War, the declared defence expenditure of the Soviet Union was the equivalent of 39,780 million US dollars, whereas that of the United States was already double that amount at 79,576 million US dollars. The defence expenditure of Great Britain for 1968 equated to a mere 5,450 million US dollars, although this was the largest of any European country except France (at 6,104 million US dollars).[173]

As early as 1968, therefore, the imbalance in East–West defence expenditure was very evident. But perhaps Moscow honestly believed that the capitalist West would succumb to a revolution from within, or that a Third World War would resolve the East–West conflict before the inability of the communist system to sustain itself economically was exposed? Perhaps the Soviet leadership had even begun to believe its own propaganda that expounded the superiority of communism and inevitability of its final victory over capitalism?

The economic equation involved many factors: natural resources, population size, industrial capacity, international trade, gross domestic product (GDP), sustainable economic growth, a stable currency and so on. But ultimately the economic success or failure of a state depended quite simply on its ability to meet its financial obligations. Consequently, by the late 1980s the new Soviet leader Mikhail Gorbachev was finally compelled to acknowledge that – with a failing economy, food shortages, an increasing level of crime, an interminable war in Afghanistan, and growing indications of nationalist unrest in the Soviet republics – his country had lost the economic war. The impact of this was enormous, because it also implied that the great communist experiment, begun in 1917, had finally failed, and that the previous four decades of East–West conflict had been for naught. Yet despite the potential risks, major economic change was unavoidable.

One of the great ironies of the economic reforms subsequently carried out in the Soviet Union was that they were in many cases implemented by those who had been staunch communists for decades, but who now appreciated that it would be very much to their personal financial benefit to introduce a market economy and private enterprise system into the Soviet Union (or Russia, as it was about to become). The alacrity with which these leaders quickly abrogated the ideology that had ensured their power for many years was an eloquent comment upon the deep-seated flaws of the communist system and the integrity of those who had led it for more than seventy years. It also showed their considerable naïveté (mirrored by that of some overoptimistic Western political leaders) in believing that the transformation of Russia into a capitalist economy and its political-military rehabilitation could be accomplished at a similar pace.

A comprehensive analysis of the economic Cold War – a subject in its own right – would require several volumes of text. However, the East–West arms race provided a suitable example with which to illustrate the nature of this contest. Although but one aspect of the equation, the implications for East and West of maintaining up-to-date – both qualitatively and quantitatively – the increasingly expensive forces necessary to carry on the Cold War posed a steadily growing problem for the Soviet Union in the post-Stalin era, as its vast inventory of Second World War military equipment became obsolete. The problem was compounded by the need for large quantities of manpower, equipment and reserve stocks always to be immediately available. This reflected an anticipated lack of warning of war, together with its probable short duration and intense operational tempo.

The ability of East and West to balance (or be perceived to balance) or counter each other's capability at every level from strategic nuclear to tactical conventional was fundamental to the philosophy of deterrence. The emergence of an unbridgeable capability gap would eventually have produced one of three results. The first and most obvious was the dominant side going to war, confident of its final victory. Another possibility was the progressive subjugation of the less capable side by the mere existence of the military threat posed by the other: a permanent state of strategic coercion.

A third alternative was the acquiescence of the less capable side, and its achievement of a mutually acceptable strategic and diplomatic accommodation with the other. This solution obviated the risk of war and (theoretically) removed or reduced the need for either side to perpetuate the cripplingly expensive Cold War levels of defence expenditure. Pragmatically, Gorbachev chose the last of these options, although the manner of its implementation, the break-up of the Soviet Union, the devaluation and removal of the CPSU, and his own dismissal from power were surely not part of his calculations in the late 1980s.

In practice, however, it was the recent development of the Soviet Union that finally frustrated Gorbachev's plans, for by then the Soviet Union had become more urbanised, with a population better informed and better educated than ever before. Most significantly, the peoples of the communist bloc had become aware of the true nature of life and prosperity in the West, as more and more Western media information reached the East. This was especially so in the Warsaw Pact countries that bordered West Germany in Central Europe. Also, by the 1980s the Soviet Union was already dependent upon Western aid and trade, which inevitably reinforced domestic perceptions of the Soviet Union's economic inferiority. For Moscow to meet the growing material aspirations of the Soviet people – and so reduce domestic dissatisfaction and dissent – government expenditure would have to be enormous; and an obvious area in which to make compensating savings was defence. Meanwhile, with its increasing openness and international visibility, the age-old Soviet remedy of suppressing internal dissent by a combination of propaganda and force was much less practicable.

A direct comparison of superpower defence expenditure is virtually impossible, as the United States maintained a veil of secrecy over certain projects and as a matter of principle the Soviet Union treated all defence matters as secret. However, the significant disparity between their declared defence expenditures in the late 1960s provided a general indication of their relative positions and of the sheer scale of funding involved. By the mid-1980s it was abundantly clear that the Soviet Union could compete no longer. A final decisive blow was the need to counter the US Strategic Defence Initiative (SDI) for an anti-ICBM system in space. Irrespective of the technological viability of SDI, the development of measures to overcome it would have imposed an unsustainable financial burden upon the Soviet Union.

At the other end of the war-fighting scale, measures such as Britain's commitment to increase its defence expenditure by three per cent in real terms, plus an upgrading of NATO's combat readiness capability in Central Europe by pre-positioning additional matériel and vehicles in the forward area, all increased the pressure upon the Soviet defence budget just when the Kremlin's main defence focus was necessarily on Afghanistan. The eventual outcome of all this could be foreseen, and by the end of the decade the Soviet leadership knew that they could no longer afford to match the West's military capability. The Soviet war machine had literally been priced out of the market and this simple truth – or perception – meant that Moscow's traditional Cold War policies were no longer sustainable.

Yet although the Soviets were the ultimate losers in this contest, the West was by no means infallible, and it had expended vast sums on several Cold War projects that finally proved non-viable. Examples of such ill-advised and wasted expenditure included Great Britain's Blue Streak IRBM in 1960, the TSR-2 strike aircraft in 1965, and the Nimrod AEW aircraft in the 1980s. In the United States, a new tactical air defence system (Sergeant York) and the MBT-70 tank projects both failed after lengthy and very expensive procurement and development processes. Smaller NATO countries that tried to promote their own major defence projects – such as Canada, which in the 1950s attempted first to develop its own fighter aircraft, then in the 1980s sought to acquire a twelve-boat nuclear submarine fleet – found that they simply could not afford to do so in the post-1945 world. Indeed, the enormous armaments industries of both superpowers ensured that they could always provide the necessary equipment to their allies, but without the latter incurring the huge research and development costs involved. This also provided the superpowers with ready markets, which enabled them to recoup some of their own costs. The prime provider principle attracted inter-operability advantages as well, although there was considerably more equipment diversity within NATO. This meant that, despite the significant operational penalties and financial waste involved, a range of superior weapons, such as the German Leopard and British Centurion tanks and the French Mirage aircraft, emerged from the European defence industry for NATO service.

Finally, however, the critical cost was that of funding readiness – the price of maintaining the necessary capability to go to war. Every technological advance needed to be countered by another as quickly as practicable. Even though the USAF B-1, B-1A and B2 stealth bombers were never required to carry out their Cold War missions, the quantum leap in technology that they utilised meant that the Soviets had to fund a similar quantum leap to develop appropriate counter-measures. The development of Chobham laminated armour by Britain precipitated a complete rethink and redesign of anti-armour weapons; and so it went on throughout the Cold War, as each technological advance demanded a suitable advance to counter it. Routinely, huge amounts of equipment had to be maintained, produced and then replaced virtually unused. The quantities entailed were huge. In 1975 the Soviet Union had about 42,000 tanks, 41,000 armoured personnel carriers,

27,000 artillery pieces and 2,300 helicopters in service. The United States had 9,000 tanks, 23,000 armoured personnel carriers, 9,000 artillery pieces and 9,000 helicopters. In all categories of aircraft, the Soviets outnumbered the United States by several thousand.[174]

The numerical disparity between the superpowers was a major part of Moscow's problem, for its strategic doctrine was firmly founded upon the offensive, and (despite communist propaganda to the contrary) few if any NATO servicemen truly envisaged a situation in which NATO would instigate an invasion of Warsaw Pact territory. Although political reality demanded an active ground defence of NATO territory as far to the east as practicable, NATO's main defensive battles would certainly not have been fought beyond the IGB (apart from a non-NATO tripartite US, British, French defence of West Berlin). But to be successful the Warsaw Pact ground offensive against NATO needed an overall numerical superiority of at least three to one in combat personnel and equipment. Therefore, in order for the Soviet attack plans to match their offensive doctrine and remain credible, Moscow was committed to maintaining and updating these vast forces on a day-to-day basis; and this open-ended expenditure burden finally proved intolerable.

In addition to the expenditure on replacing and modernising equipment, there were also huge personnel costs. Through the 1970s the Soviet Union maintained some 4.8 million men under arms, plus reserves amounting to 7.2 million. The United States had about 2.1 million personnel on active duty, and 1.9 million more in the reserves. Although the Soviet Union and its Warsaw Pact allies made extensive use of conscripts to fill its ranks, its daily manpower bill was substantial. And this recurring expenditure was imposed upon a failing economy and a population that was becoming increasingly disenchanted with communism, and ever more sceptical of the propaganda that a NATO attack on the Soviet Union was imminent.

Meanwhile, although the West suffered its own economic crises – such as the Arab oil embargo of the mid-1970s – its economic structure was fundamentally sound. That of the United States was particularly strong. It had been largely untouched at home by the effects of the Second World War and its defence industry had benefited enormously from that conflict and from the several post-1945 wars. Indeed, in stark contrast to devastated Europe, in America the people had enjoyed a rising standard of living throughout the Second World War, where 'the race tracks were booming, the night clubs were making their greatest profits in history, Miami Beach was so crowded you couldn't get a room anywhere ... this was a boom, this was prosperity'.[175] Little wonder then that America was the rock upon which the economic campaign of the Cold War was originally set, and then fought and won from 1945 to 1990.

LEGACY OF CONFLICT

A Brave New World?

Although it would be nice to relate that the end of the Cold War marked the start of a new golden age of global peace and harmony, for the West the honeymoon period lasted for just ten years and ended in the autumn of 2001. In some other parts of the world – such as the Balkans, Chechnya and the Middle East – it never really began. And sadly each day's news indicates that such an age, whilst a worthy aspiration, is in reality no more than a naïve dream, unachievable in practice. Therefore, instead of the conclusion of the forty-five-year East–West conflict producing a modern utopia, it has in fact ushered in a new level of international tension and uncertainty that in many respects transcends that of the Cold War period. So why was this?

Despite the potentially awesome threat posed by nuclear weapons, as the Cold War developed, rules and procedures were formulated for its management. Many of these were unwritten, but both sides well understood that they were rules nonetheless. Occasionally these were flouted, as with the Soviet deployment of missiles to Cuba in 1962. Sometimes they were bent, as with the construction of the Berlin Wall in 1961. From time to time they were broken, as with the Berlin Blockade of 1948. But notwithstanding such isolated exceptions, the rules of the Cold War were generally understood; and the needs of the world as a whole usually took precedence over the achievement of lesser (albeit sometimes morally higher) goals. For example, direct military intervention by NATO in response to the Soviet operation in Hungary in 1956 would almost certainly have precipitated a full-scale war in Europe, and would probably have led to the use of nuclear weapons. A similar situation obtained when the Warsaw Pact suppressed the 'Prague Spring' in 1968, although by then the first cracks were beginning to appear within units that had been deployed to deal with an illegal uprising but which in reality found themselves suppressing a popular, democratic revolution. Of course the West registered its concern over such activities, but Moscow, Washington and London all knew that direct NATO military intervention within what was acknowledged to be the Soviet sphere of influence was never a serious option. Comparable considerations applied in Afghanistan in 1979, although the matériel and financial support provided surreptitiously to the mujahedin by the United States, Britain, Pakistan and others was significant, and contributed to the guerrillas' eventual victory over the Soviet invaders. Ironically, however, had the Soviets not suffered that defeat and enforced withdrawal, the horrific events of 11 September 2001 might not have been possible.

That devastating terrorist attack by Muslim extremists perhaps typified the new world order – or 'disorder' – that is today the most menacing legacy of the Cold War, and which will prove infinitely more difficult to manage than were the relative certainties of 1945 to 1990. The consequent responsibilities and challenges for today's international leaders are daunting. This is particularly so given the lacklustre leadership and military naïveté of many post-Cold War politicians and governments – a situation compounded in the West by the very nature of modern Western society. There, the removal of the over-arching military threat posed by the Soviet Union during the Cold War, together with the mental and physical softening of Western society through its preoccupation with materialism, consumerism, liberalism and the good life, has created a dangerous lack of awareness of the new threats that have emerged since 1991.

The Nuclear Perspective

History has provided ample evidence that no two major wars are the same. This must be so, as the evolution of mankind, with its technological advances, means that the start point for any future conflict will always differ from that of its predecessors. Accordingly, the Cold War – the longest single period of conflict of the twentieth century – was very different from the preceding Second World War, notwithstanding that much military action in the early years bore a marked similarity to the war-fighting practices of 1939–45. However, the single element above all others that separated the Cold War from the Second World War was the nuclear perspective.

Indeed (Hiroshima and Nagasaki apart), the Cold War constituted the first nuclear conflict, even though no nuclear exchange took place. But the fact that no such weapons were actually used is not the issue; rather it is that from 1949 the potential existed for both sides to do so. The nuclear option had to be taken into account at every point of the Cold War, and the very existence of such an option was the principal reason that the conflict never degenerated into a thermonuclear war. In other words, nuclear deterrence worked; and even the various branches of the anti-nuclear movement – such as the Committee for Nuclear Disarmament and the Greenham Common protest against the deployment of cruise missiles in the United Kingdom – and other pressure groups actually contributed to the concept of nuclear deterrence. By publicly expressing their concerns over these nuclear weapons they reinforced the perception that NATO was ready and willing to use them if necessary. This message emanating from Western sources that were patently not friends of NATO would have been duly noted in Moscow, where any perception of a lack of NATO resolve, capability or readiness to use nuclear weapons would have strengthened the case for a Soviet first strike.

Hiroshima and Nagasaki changed the world and the future nature of warfare forever. Clearly the atomic weapon could not be uninvented after it had fulfilled its immediate purpose, and so the post-1945 generation had to learn to live with the bomb, to come to terms with its existence, and to manage its potentially apocalyptic power. To the credit of the Cold War statesmen of both sides they achieved all this (despite some close calls) with a remarkable degree of success. Eventually, the enforced co-operation made essential by both sides' possession of nuclear weapons contributed to détente, and finally to the end of the East–West confrontation.

The Social Dimension
The Cold War represented a global threat to peace that was much greater than the parochial concerns of any individual state. Consequently, for very many people in East and West the Cold War provided a higher cause and unifying influence – albeit in adversity – that put lesser personal considerations and priorities firmly into perspective. The 1990s would usher in a new world order dominated by market forces, the compensation culture, self-interest and materialism – an age in which much of the population of the developed world knows the cost of everything, but the true value of nothing. One legacy of the Cold War has therefore been a social peace dividend of dubious value, one that has fragmented society and undermined many of the qualities of personal responsibility, self-discipline and respect for authority, patriotism and selflessness that are often found in nations lying under the threat of armed conflict. In the former Warsaw Pact states these trends have been accompanied by widespread lawlessness and corruption on a grand scale.

And in the West, if the positive aspects of the end of the Cold War are not to be squandered or thrown away, the excessively high profile accorded to human rights and civil liberties issues must be rationalised and modified, so that they are at the very least balanced by common-sense and lawfulness to reflect the needs of the majority rather than pandering to the vociferous lobbying of minorities and extremist individuals, groups and organisations. For in the final analysis, surely that should be what the West's Cold War victory and the triumph of democracy over communism in 1989 was really all about.

Border Controls and Illegal Immigration
The abandonment of border controls in Europe after the Cold War satisfied an idealistic and questionable political agenda. History has shown, however,

that sovereign states must have the means to control the inflow and outflow of people, goods and resources, as this bears directly upon the stability and safety of the state and its population. Of course states must communicate with one another and trade as widely as possible: from the former comes understanding and from the latter a sharing and distribution of the limited wealth and resources that the world has to offer. But the idea that the cultures, politics, ethnicity, education, technologies, societies, economies and ideologies of humankind are so similar that the creation of some sort of world nation is imminent, desirable or even practicable is fatally flawed. Nations and peoples have drawn ever closer over the centuries, but very many years will pass before the single world nation might become a realistic goal. The aspiration is thoroughly worthy, but world history, pragmatism and a fair degree of common-sense all indicate that the creation of such an ideal world is several centuries away. The growing problem of illegal immigration is but one indication that the oneness of the 'global village' concept is in most respects little more than a political fantasy. In practice, 'nationalism' is still a much more potent rallying cry than 'globalisation' or 'union of nations', while the most powerful force of all is that which stems from a blend of nationalism and religion.

The end of the Cold War was cited as a justification for the end of border controls in the European Union (EU). This precipitate action resulted in virtually uncontrolled illegal immigration and economic migration, and has proved to be a significant destabilising influence in Europe and Asia. It also provided criminal gangs of 'people smugglers' with a lucrative new source of revenue whilst trading on the human misery of their 'clients' – the illegal immigrants who are now generally, if often somewhat prematurely, categorised as 'asylum seekers' and refugees. Indeed, another result of the end of the Cold War was the rapid change of governmental mindset in many countries on both sides of the former Iron Curtain, but primarily those in the West, which displaced a not unreasonable assumption that anyone entering another country illegally, or who remained in it beyond the validity of their visa, might well have done so with the intention of carrying out some illicit action. During the Cold War this might have included espionage, sabotage or subversion; but since 1990 terrorism must now be added to this list of activities, and probably placed at its head. Whereas the secure detention of illegal immigrants immediately on their discovery or apprehension, pending their deportation or formal acceptance into a country after processing, remains a sensitive political issue and is perceived to be an unpopular measure by some, it is one that should be firmly grasped by any government that truly has the safety, security and interests of the indigenous people and the nation it governs at heart.[176] The failure adequately to security screen and control this highly mobile population was graphically demonstrated by the revelations of the post-11 September 2001 investigation in the United States; and much more recently by the arrests in London, Manchester and elsewhere, in January 2003, of a number of North Africans – including two young men already formally registered in the United Kingdom as 'asylum seekers' – who were apparently in the process of preparing a quantity of the highly toxic poison ricin for a terrorist attack or other illegal use. During what then developed into an ongoing counter-terrorist operation, an unarmed British policeman was murdered by one of these people during a later police arrest operation.

Linked inextricably to illegal immigration has been the growth of Islamic extremism. One of the great tragedies and historic failures of the final decades of the Cold War era has been the misinterpretation and distortion of many of the age-old principles and teaching of Islam in certain countries. The consequence is that one of the world's great religions has gradually become ever more closely identified with Arab nationalism and anti-Semitism, and with extreme anti-Western and anti-American movements. Finally, during the decade or so that has followed the end of the Cold War, Islam is widely perceived (whether or not this perception is justified in fact) to have become inextricably bound up with major acts of terrorism carried out on a global scale.

The rise of Islamic extremism has been evident both in the traditional Islamic countries and in the West, where (until 1990) attention was focused almost exclusively on what was perceived to be the much greater threat posed by world communism. Yet events in the Middle East and Asia since the early 1970s, and more specifically those of 11 September 2001, tend to indicate that this prioritisation of an unequivocal Cold War threat was both naïve and seriously flawed.

In addition to the unlawful practice of 'people smuggling', the trade in illegal drugs has burgeoned within a Europe unfettered by border controls. This has undermined social values, fed domestic crime and destroyed the physical health, self-esteem and lives of ever increasing numbers of young people. The treatment of those using illegal drugs has also imposed an intolerable and avoidable financial burden upon health services that could doubtless better direct their scarce resources elsewhere if the drug problem was eliminated, or at least significantly reduced.

Furthermore, the disbandment of border security and customs units has inevitably resulted in inadequate checks on food imports, and the failure to enforce the regulations for these have placed at considerable risk both the population of Europe and its farming industry. Notwithstanding the substantial natural maritime border that surrounds the British Isles, the disastrous foot-and-mouth epidemic in the United Kingdom and its crippling effect upon the British rural economy in 2001 was but one example of the consequences of the excessively liberal application of this policy. The burgeoning incidence of human diseases such as HIV, AIDS and tuberculosis among the large numbers of illegal immigrants arriving in Western Europe from Third World countries is also a cause for increasing concern. Here, the consequences of an original failure to prevent these people gaining access to the United Kingdom have been significantly compounded by a lack of political will to impose a suitably comprehensive health-screening regime upon them immediately on arrival. Yet while an over-generous social security system has considerably exacerbated the United Kingdom's growing crisis over illegal immigration since the late 1990s, its situation is by no means unique within Western Europe. In large part, this problem stems from the day that the Berlin Wall was finally and irrevocably breached in 1989, together with the subsequent collapse of the former communist states – notably Yugoslavia, Romania and Albania – and the break-up of the Soviet Union, with the consequent implications for Afghanistan, Chechnya and the former Soviet Asian republics.

Indeed, the EU political concept of the unrestricted 'free movement' of people, labour, goods and services was a direct consequence of the Cold War, and it was much lauded by the European politicians of the time. Just over a decade on, however, its blanket application has proved time and again to be an idealist luxury that Europe could not and should not have afforded – one that has contributed both directly and indirectly to many of the social, law enforcement,[177] public health and international security difficulties that exist today. And it is one that will assuredly be further exacerbated in the coming years, as an apparently unstoppable political process of 'enlargement' pushes the borders of the EU even further eastward. The implementation of this policy implies an inevitable increase in east to west migration, with a further dilution of the EU security forces' ability to safeguard the territory and citizens that it is their duty to protect.

The Middle East Powder Keg

The demise of Yugoslavia and the emergence of an independent Bosnian Muslim state was but one such politically contrived legacy of the Cold War. A similar case followed closely the end of the Second World War, with the establishment of the state of Israel at the expense of the Palestinians. This solution, albeit well-intentioned and made by an international community still reeling from the revelation of the concentration camps and genocide carried out by the Nazis, has posed an increasing threat to world peace since 1947. This was especially so after the 1967 Six-Day War, with Israel's

occupation of the West Bank and Gaza Strip and the subsequent establishment of numerous Israeli settlements in these territories. Ultimately, an
Israeli withdrawal from the West Bank – in order to re-create an independent Palestinian state on that land – is probably unavoidable, while the internationalisation of Jerusalem as the focus of three of the world's greatest religions would be both logical and highly desirable. Quite apart, however, from
strategic considerations that have generally not changed since 1967, the
voluntary surrender by Israel of the West Bank and abandonment of its
Jewish settlements, together with any diminution of Israeli control of
Jerusalem, would be political, religious and historical anathema to any
Israeli government and to the Jewish people, and so it is hard to visualise
any form of peaceful settlement that could bring about such a momentous
change. Consequently, the Arab–Israeli dispute, together with the Middle
East oil issue, will almost certainly provide the spark that ignites the Middle
East powder keg yet again in the future. Even more significantly, Israel's
inextricable involvement with the United States, Islamic extremism and
terrorism, Middle East oil and the regional nuclear dimension may eventually make this dispute the catalyst that provokes Armageddon. In the post-
Cold War world there are probably no more important or pressing issues
than resolution of the Arab–Israel–Palestine conflict and the need for the
West to reduce or remove its reliance upon Middle East oil. The first issue
continually threatens international security, and the second prevents any
objective resolution of the first.

It follows that urgent research needs to be pursued to lessen the developed world's dependence upon oil and oil products, so that the strategic and
economic importance of the Middle East and the oil-producing states may be
substantially reduced in the future. Indeed, the West's long-term strategic
goal should be to achieve a level of energy self-sufficiency and capability that
would allow it in extremis to isolate itself from the Middle East and Asia
without serious detriment to its industrial base, economy or way of life. The
financial and economic implications of this are enormous, as neither the
multinational oil companies nor the oil-rich Arab states would welcome a
significant reduction of their oil revenues and their national prosperity, or
the personal prosperity of their rulers. But if this action – necessarily a matter
of decades rather than years – is the price of averting a nuclear Armageddon,
the whole world should judge it a price well worth paying.

The War on Terrorism

Every war lays the foundations of future conflict, and the Cold War was no
exception. The current focus of conflict is the so-called global war on
terrorism. However, this has been an enduring campaign ever since the

1940s with only its tempo, visibility, and the source and nature of the threat changing from time to time. Its high profile in 2002 resulted from the 11 September 2001 attack by the Al-Qaeda terrorists in New York, which dramatically demonstrated to Americans a problem with which much of the world had already lived for many years. A similar wake-up call came for Australia and the Pacific region on 11 October 2002 when a terrorist bomb claimed almost 200 lives – most of whom were young Australians – in the holiday resort of Bali in the predominantly Muslim state of Indonesia. Links between this atrocity and Al-Qaeda and Indonesian extreme Islamic elements were subsequently established, and further such attacks against what might prior to September 2001 have been assessed improbable targets are likely.

The truly global nature of the threat currently posed by Muslim extremists was again demonstrated just two weeks later – this time at the heart of the Russian capital – when more than forty armed Chechens seized a Moscow theatre and took hostage almost 800 people. Although these terrorists were ostensibly seeking a Russian withdrawal from Chechnya, their campaign was underscored by their extreme Islamic faith and the concept of *jihad*; while their readiness to commit suicide in pursuit of their political goals mirrored the method of attack used regularly by Palestinian suicide bombers against Israel. Among the terrorists were a number of girls masked and black-robed in traditional Muslim dress, with explosives strapped about their waists and the means to detonate them at very short notice. Although the form of Islam practised in Chechnya had in past years been less extreme and more tolerant than that typefied in many parts of the Middle East, the attack in Moscow exhibited the extent to which those disputing Russia's authority in Chechnya had by then adopted techniques more usually associated with Arab terrorist groups. Although very effective in ending the crisis, the Russian security forces' response to this act of terrorism with the use of a debilitating gas and *Spetsnaz* troops – the former of which resulted in more than a hundred deaths of hostages and terrorists alike – attracted an immediate surge of media criticism. However, the Kremlin leadership had been left with little option other than to adopt such means, given the unprecedented scale of the terrorist operation and the uncompromising stance adopted by the Chechens involved. Notwithstanding that the terrorists' demand for an immediate Russian withdrawal from Chechnya was unrealistic in any case, the decisive outcome of the incident indicated very clearly the way in which any future acts of terrorism – irrespective of the extremist group involved – would be dealt with by Moscow. Meanwhile, the attack in Moscow on 25 October 2002 has in practice probably set back significantly any eventual achievement of the Chechens' political objectives, although the incident did propel the long-running but otherwise virtually unreported conflict in Chechnya on to the front pages of the international press for a few days.

And this worldwide campaign of terror has continued. Just a month later on 28 November 2002 a hotel in Mombasa, Kenya that was used extensively by Israeli tourists was the subject of a suicide car bomber, while a simultaneous SAM-7 missile attack was carried out against an Israeli civil airliner on take-off from Kenya for Tel Aviv. Whilst the missile failed to hit the aircraft, a dozen people died in the hotel bombing – mostly Kenyans rather than Israelis. Although the dispute with the Palestinians has long made Israel a prime target for international terrorism, this attack in East Africa provided further evidence of the rapidly escalating threat posed to the civilised world by terrorist movements founded upon the teachings of Islamic extremists. While Al-Qaeda was undoubtedly involved directly or indirectly in this attack, its real significance was the fact that it was carried out in Africa: a continent already destabilised by the political machinations of the Cold War years, but which has ever since 1990 been further ravaged by tribal wars, genocide, poverty, famine and disease on an unprecedented scale. Such an environment has proved a fertile recruiting ground for those who expound Islamic fundamentalist principles and its more extreme laws.

Thus the principal terrorist enemy today is the extremist who has in effect declared war upon the West and all that it stands for, while seeking to expunge the West's physical presence and influence from the Muslim world. Increasingly, this threat is interlinked with the nationalist movements in what are now, or aspire to become, predominantly or exclusively Muslim states; and where this situation applies, the threat afflicts East and West, North and South, the Third World and the developed and industrialised worlds alike. The great irony here is the fact that many of today's terrorists originally drew their strength and support from the West, which during the Cold War armed and equipped them to fight against the Soviet Union. The historical parallels with the Western Allies arming communist partisans to fight the Nazis during the Second World War – which was then followed by the need for the United States, France, Nationalist China and Britain to engage these same organisations in combat during the Cold War post-1945 – are striking.

But the use of terror to further political or ideological aims is timeless, and once the current threats have been neutralised, other groups with other agendas will assuredly emerge to inflict their own brand of terror on the world. Peace will, therefore, remain illusory while such groups exist; and the overriding priority of the intelligence, law enforcement and military communities of the whole civilised world must be to forestall the ability of any terrorist group to use nuclear, chemical or biological weapons. Indeed, these agencies and the governments that control them should also be aware that airliners and many other everyday facilities found routinely in the modern industrialised world must now also be categorised for planning purposes as potential weapons of mass destruction. Notwithstanding this, some sections of the media are certainly guilty of providing – through their sensational reporting – the oxygen of publicity upon which the terrorist relies, as well as creating and inflaming the atmosphere of discord, fear and hatred that perpetuates extremist causes and terrorist campaigns. Closely linked to this, it is also all too easy for terrorism and the business of countering it to be exploited for short-term political advantage, while the unequivocal responsibility of the civilised world to deal with terrorism should transcend such parochial considerations.

Whereas the Japanese kamikaze suicide attacks against US naval targets during the Second World War undoubtedly contradicted American norms for war-fighting, their operational value was very clearly understood. However, the advent of the terrorist suicide bomber in recent years has produced a profound feeling of frustration in the West and elsewhere in the civilised world, where the terrorist's total disregard for human life is just as incomprehensible to the Western mind as is the lack of an obvious or viable objective for such wholesale destruction – other than to demonstrate a level of corporate hatred that is itself incomprehensible to modern civilised society. The frustration stems also from the considerable difficulty of pre-empting or countering this particular form of terrorist attack.

As always, however, the keys to successful counter-terrorist operations entail integrated planning by strategic, political and security forces, a credible and carefully managed government information campaign, and sound intelligence which will usually need to emanate directly or indirectly from within the terrorist organisation. Since the several outrages of 2001 and 2002, the world's counter-terrorist forces have moved with unprecedented speed to co-ordinate their national operations and, most importantly, to exchange their locally held intelligence on extremist groups. More evidence of this is emerging all the time – a fact exemplified by the pro-active police operation against Muslim extremists in the United Kingdom and elsewhere in Western Europe from mid-January 2003, based firmly upon a reinvigorated and close working relationship between the French, British, Spanish and Italian security forces (and no doubt with those of several other countries as well). Fundamental to the continued success of these advances will be the use of precisely targeted, high-technology law enforcement and Special Forces operations. In addition there must be a routine public expectation and acceptance of the use of deadly force to eliminate terrorist organisations wherever they are identified. Political leaders and the media alike will need to understand that such operations cannot always be concluded without the collateral loss of innocent lives; but wherever this applies, it should never be forgotten that the instigator of such international terrorism is the terrorist, not the government or its security forces.

Future Security Needs: Armed Forces and Military Service

Since the end of the Cold War, the declining profile of all but the US armed forces, and the abandonment of compulsory military service by most Western nations, has removed an important aspect of national character-building. Quite apart from its function as a source of reserves in time of national crisis, conscription engendered an understanding and acceptance of personal and collective risk as a part of normal life, as well as involving young citizens in matters of international security, and demanding of them the qualities of mental and physical robustness, and of personal responsibility and duty, that are essential to the continuance of free and democratic nation states.[178]

By default, most of today's armed forces – with the notable but very significant exception of those of the United States – are concerned primarily with peacekeeping in its many forms, with the provision of humanitarian aid, and with civil affairs operations. The military balance has swung decisively from destruction to construction and, whilst laudable, this is by definition not the principal purpose of armed forces. Such a change of emphasis owes much to today's obsession with political correctness and to the barely concealed political and legalistic agendas and social experiments that have imposed an ever more debilitating and negative influence upon military capability in the West since the mid-1990s.

Other than in the United States, ever since the successful campaign to liberate Kuwait in 1991, the war-fighting capability of the West, the former Soviet Union and other first world nations has declined significantly. The absence of an obvious threat finds considerable favour with many democratic governments seeking to reduce the size of their defence budgets. In the United Kingdom this precipitate process of restructuring and downsizing was entitled 'Options for Change'; and most West European nations quickly followed suit with similar cost-cutting exercises. Indeed, in the case of the United Kingdom, only the residual existence in Germany in 1990 of the personnel and equipment of a once formidable 1st British Corps enabled a single British armoured division to be formed for the Kuwait operation by the stripping-out of virtually all the corps assets; and if the Gulf War had taken place a couple of years later it is doubtful if the British contribution could have exceeded an armoured brigade group in strength. The irony of

British NATO forces equipped and trained to confront the Soviets on the North German Plain finally fighting a war for which they had prepared for almost fifty years against a Third World army in the Middle East desert was not lost upon many of those then serving. It was also an object lesson in the unpredictability of war and the uncertain nature of the profession of arms.

Nevertheless, despite sweeping reductions in defence capability, armed forces in the post-Cold War era since 1991 have carried out successful operations that involved the threat or actuality of combat; Bosnia, Kosovo, Sierra Leone and (in 2002) Afghanistan are cases in point. For the ground forces involved, however, these limited conflicts were primarily internal security, peace enforcement or policing in nature, and since 1991 such missions have been performed against a background of continuing defence reductions and restructuring.

The Superpower Monopoly

At the end of the Second World War and until 1949 the United States could in theory have carried out an atomic first-strike against the Soviet Union, the PRC or any other state with policies contrary to those of Washington; for until the Soviets acquired the atom bomb the United States enjoyed a situation of global military pre-eminence unique in the history of modern warfare. Not surprisingly, Washington chose not to use this temporary strategic advantage, and the rest became the history of the Cold War. Since the end of the Cold War, however, a comparable situation has occurred. The demise of the Soviet Union and the slow progress of the PRC towards great power status have left the United States as the only superpower, and thus it once again occupies a position of military pre-eminence.

Today, the United States is an exception to the general trend of reducing defence capability – although the thousands of casualties sustained in the 11 September 2001 terrorist attacks was a high price to pay for the wake-up call that alerted Washington to the need to reverse that policy. The United States has already demonstrated in Afghanistan that – while allies and coalitions are a welcome bonus – it is today more than ever before in its history prepared to act alone to resolve issues affecting its national sovereignty and security. The assumption, moreover, that the West can rely upon the American security umbrella indefinitely and free of charge would be extremely naïve. However, a monopoly superpower is subject to enormous temptations, and the risk of Washington inadvertently abusing the power that it now wields is very real. Washington will need to beware of embarking impulsively upon military adventures that cannot be concluded satisfactorily. Since 1990 examples of such 'unfinished business' have included the 1991 Iraq War, the Balkans intervention and the Afghanistan campaign. In the years ahead, US leaders will need to take full account of the two truisms that 'power corrupts and absolute power corrupts absolutely' and 'with great power comes great responsibility'. With no Soviet superpower to check and balance US policies and actions, the burden of responsibility borne by today's White House administrations is probably greater than at any time since 1949.

Indeed, it was unfortunate that Gorbachev so soon lost control of the process of change that he had unleashed and was deposed by Boris Yeltsin in 1991. Certainly the pace of the collapse of communism and the Soviet empire contributed directly to the chaos in the GDR and Romania, and to the Balkan horrors endured by the people of the constituent parts of the former Yugoslavia. Indeed, it would have been much better for the wider world if Gorbachev had remained in power for at least a decade beyond 1990, in order to manage the momentous changes then taking place in the Soviet Union and Eastern Europe at a considered and controlled pace that could have enjoyed the positive influences and involvement of East and West alike.

Consequently, the power now in Washington's hands is formidable, and with no balancing superpower to influence its actions the temptations it faces and the risks it runs are enormous. In foreign and defence policy matters it has the potential to ignore allies, coalitions and the UN alike. It now needs none of these diplomatic appendages in order to wage war and it has the capability to overcome any nation on earth by the use of nuclear weapons, and the majority of them by the use of conventional forces alone. In a vast country that has always, by default, been geographically and cultur-ally isolated from the rest of the world there are potentially huge dangers in this concentration of military power, because American political and military leaders alike know that they can respond to their perception of any threat with relative impunity; the short campaign against the Taliban in Afghanistan in 2002 illustrated this. Therefore, to the more obvious sites and causes of future conflicts must be added the reality of the US superpower monopoly that is yet another legacy of the Cold War. Sadly, Americans will need to understand that the price of their military and economic superiority will be that their country and its forces will be the focus of political and economic envy and extremism so long as the United States occupies this privileged posi-tion; for with great privilege comes great responsibility, and there is always a price to pay. For a very generous if politically naïve nation, whose people crave to be liked and cannot comprehend why anyone should not do so, it will be hard indeed to understand and come to terms with the inevitability of increasing if undeserved unpopularity in many parts of the world.

The Al-Qaeda terrorist atrocity of 11 September 2001 exemplified this in the most horrifyingly dramatic terms, but ordinary Americans need to recognise the implications consequent upon the West's Cold War victory in 1989, and the international loneliness for their country implicit in its super-power monopoly status. The main risk involved in this is of national isola-tionism, paranoia and a feeling of victimisation by the rest of the world – which could lead Washington to over-simplify its foreign policy responses by premature resort to military options, merely because it has the capability to do so. The temptation of such a response to resolve issues is particularly high where the target is a third-rate or third-world nation, organisation or terrorist group, for the suppression of such opponents can so quickly become a matter of national pride rather than considered policy if there is a perception that they have dared to confront the greatest military power on earth. The danger of the United States provoking or involving itself precipi-tately in an armed conflict is probably greater today than it ever was during the Cold War from 1945 to 1990, and the concept of 'regime change' proposed by President George W. Bush in 2002 is but one indicator of this. In several respects the post-Cold War United States seems to be assuming a mantle similar to that which Great Britain enjoyed in the days of its former empire. While this may well be to the long-term betterment of the post-Cold War world, Washington should have no illusions concerning the potential price and the enormous responsibilities that this will involve for the United States, its citizens and its armed forces.

Although the 'special relationship' between the United Kingdom and the United States has ebbed and flowed over the years since 1945, Washington and London have nevertheless maintained a unique association for half a century, and probably the greatest international service that the United Kingdom can perform in the years ahead will be to act as the trusted ally that it is, and counsel and advise on these matters whenever necessary. At the same time London will have to tread carefully, for there is a danger that if it becomes too closely identified with Washington its advice will lack value, and the United Kingdom will by default isolate itself from its neighbours in Western Europe. The post-Cold War dilemma for the United Kingdom has in fact existed ever since the early 1940s, for whenever London's links with Washington grow stronger there is a danger of distancing the United Kingdom further from the aspirations and policies of mainland Europe – particularly from those expressed in Brussels, Paris and Berlin.

A Fragile Future

Geographically, the prime candidates for future conflicts – acts of terrorism apart – continue to be Asia and the Middle East. In the still-volatile Korean peninsula any miscalculation could result in another war, and North Korea's decision in mid-December 2002 to resurrect its dormant nuclear industry, followed by its stated intention on 10 January 2003 to withdraw from the international nuclear non-proliferation treaty, has increased regional tensions and raised considerably the potential for just such a miscalculation. However, although China's reaction and responses cannot be certain, any such incident could probably be contained, given Beijing's increasing readiness to involve China as a full member of the international community. Similarly, with the combined diplomatic and military influence of the United States, Japan, Russia, South Korea and probably China ranged against it, plus that of the rest of the United Nations, even an ill-judged attack by North Korea on the South could probably be controlled and reversed, irrespective of the level of conflict involved, even though this might in the short term be at South Korea's expense. China's acquiescence or non-involvement in the resolution of a new Korean conflict might well involve a Sino-American accommodation over Taiwan; yet at the same time the long-running Taiwan issue could of itself still precipitate an armed conflict between China and the United States in the Asia–Pacific region.

But in two other areas of the world the risk of a nuclear conflict is particularly high. The long-standing territorial and religious differences between India and Pakistan – both nuclear powers – provide cause for considerable concern. Hopefully, the lessons of negotiation and diplomacy learned by the United States and the Soviet Union during the Cold War will not have been lost on the leaders of India and Pakistan, and will allow dialogue to replace rhetoric at those times when the two countries seem to be on a collision course. In a worst case scenario, however, a nuclear exchange on the Indian subcontinent could probably be contained, although the relatively unsophisticated nature of the weapons used might pose collateral hazards beyond those countries.

The second candidate region is, as ever, the Middle East. This must in practice include a wider area embracing much of Arab North Africa, Egypt, Lebanon, Jordan, Syria, Saudi Arabia, the Gulf States, Iraq and Iran – with Israel and its Palestinian community placed at the heart of the area. Indeed, there are two clear strands to the problem of the Middle East and the wider region: the Israel–Palestinian conflict and oil. The problem is exacerbated by an assumption that Israel (and possibly certain of its Arab neighbours) possesses a viable nuclear capability. The implications of this are compounded by the dependence of the civilised world upon the oil produced by the region, and by the immutable military-economic-political links between the United States and Israel.

It is a simple fact that without its unfailing US support the state of Israel would probably not exist today. Even an Israeli capability to strike targets in the region with nuclear weapons might not have deterred Israel's Arab neighbours from attempting to eliminate the Jewish state by military means. But so long as American support for Israel remains firm, the state of Israel is secure. However, the tempo of Palestinian terror attacks has increased in recent years, with the routine use of suicide bombers since 2001. Israel has continued to mount retaliatory and intelligence-led pre-emptive operations against the sources of these terror attacks with each new terrorist atrocity; but with each new incident the need for the creation of a viable Palestinian state becomes ever more immediate, while every new atrocity makes it less likely. But even with the removal of all Jewish settlements from the occupied territories, it is doubtful that a contrived two-part state of Palestine formed from the Gaza Strip and the West Bank would provide a long-term workable solution. At the same time, the extent of Palestinian and Arab hostility to Israel is such that any solution which involves a Palestinian state sharing a border with Israel may not be viable. Indeed, as recently as October 2002 the extreme option of assisting or forcing the removal to other Arab states of all Palestinians from the West Bank was being aired in Israel.

In any event, the intransigence of both sides means that a solution may eventually need to be imposed and overseen by a significant neutral military presence. This should be the task of the UN, although currently the United States and Russia acting in concert are probably the only countries that are realistically capable of doing this. One thing, however, is certain: the achievement of a permanent peace in the Middle East will necessitate very considerable concessions being made by all sides involved in this protracted conflict.

The Cold War victory achieved at no little cost by the West and NATO in 1989 – much assisted by an enlightened regime in Moscow at that time – was momentous, and provided an unrivalled opportunity to advance the welfare of mankind. However, its global potential to build a better world has so far fallen well short of that which might have been, as parochial foreign-policy objectives on both sides of the former Iron Curtain have created a world that is in very many ways less predictable and less secure than that which existed in the late 1970s and 1980s.

The so-called post-1990 'peace dividend' has also bred moral weakness, inappropriate domestic policies and misguided perceptions in many Western states, which are progressively diminishing their real stability and security, as well as providing a fertile recruiting environment for political movements of the extreme right. Thus there is now a very real danger that the benefits attracted by the end of the Cold War will be squandered, and that a great opportunity will be thrown away. In part, this is due to the debilitating effect upon the West caused by the obsession of some governments with political correctness, together with an increasingly unrealistic and

unbalanced approach to the relevance, obligations and practical implementation of the existing human rights conventions and legislation of an earlier
age – generally to the detriment of the wider responsibilities that should
invariably attend such altruistic ideals. The policies concerning these issues
are already urgently in need of pragmatic and non-politicised review in
several EU countries and elsewhere. Once that has been done, they should
then be modified in order to reflect the real needs of these nations and the
majority of their citizens, rather than pandering to the disproportionate
political influence exerted on governments by certain minorities, pressure
groups and organisations. It is irrefutable that democracy and freedom
were the over-arching ideals for which the Cold War was fought and won,
and the misrepresentation, diminution and eventual negation of these great
ideals by such influences and pressures would render the West's success at
the conclusion of forty-five years of conflict a hollow victory indeed.

'SHOCK AND AWE' IN IRAQ

Wars of the Cold War was completed some weeks before the US-led coalition invasion of Iraq in March 2003. However, although this most recent conflict occurred more than a decade after the end of the Cold War, its significance and its indirect linkage to the fallout from that earlier conflict certainly merit a word of comment, in order that this work's consideration of the legacy of the Cold War may be as comprehensive and current as possible. Indeed, it is suggested that much of that which was foretold in the previous chapter has been borne out by what has happened – and continues to happen – in Iraq since March 2003. Furthermore, with the pivotal importance of the United States during the Cold War very much in mind, two or three clearly identifiable aspects of the US involvement in the 2003 Iraq war have already proved instructive in the context of the part played by America in the story of that long-running former conflict, and now in view of its likely role in military operations across the globe in the future.

On 20 March 2003, American and British armoured divisions stormed across the Kuwait border into Iraq. The US force was spearheaded by units of the US Marine Corps and headed for Baghdad, while the British Royal Marines and the 1st UK Armoured Division advanced towards Basra. By 14 April the invading forces had seized their principal objectives, Saddam Hussein and most of his key Baath Party supporters had fled from Baghdad, and the Iraqi army – including the greatly over-rated Republican Guard – had all but melted away. On 1 May, President George Bush declared that the war had been won. However, this declaration proved somewhat premature, and far from being at an end the predominantly US ground forces found that the conventional war they had concluded in relatively short order had turned into a low intensity guerrilla conflict: one that Washington had apparently neither anticipated nor planned for.

The US troops found (after a brief 'honeymoon period') that rather than being perceived as liberators, much of the population of Baghdad, central and northern Iraq viewed them as little more than invaders and occupiers; and as such their physical presence in the country was a welcome propaganda gift to anti-US extremists throughout the region. Ever since the supposed end of the war, the US forces have thus far sustained casualties – including fatalities – at Iraqi or possibly other Islamic extremist hands on an almost daily basis. Although the British forces in Basra and the south of Iraq have by and large fared much better, there is a real danger that over time they also will become synonymous with the US presence, and so attract a similar escalating level of hostility and attacks. Meanwhile, what was billed as a short-term military involvement of the United States and the United Kingdom in Iraq shows every sign of becoming an open-ended commitment – in much the same way that post-Cold War involvements in the Balkans and Afghanistan have run on far beyond the timeframes originally anticipated. Meanwhile, the devastating suicide bombing of the UN headquarters in Baghdad on 19 August, followed soon thereafter by the massive car bomb detonated against Muslim Shia worshippers at Najaf on 29 August, have exacerbated and added important new dimensions to what is currently a deteriorating security situation in Iraq and the wider Gulf region. Indeed, since 1990, only in the case of the Gulf War of 1991 were the coalition ground forces involved able to extricate themselves from that conflict relatively soon after they had achieved their strategic mission of liberating Kuwait (but even then an extensive air campaign continued on a daily basis, in order to enforce the post-war air exclusion zones).

But the 1991 Gulf War was in many respects an aberration, a 'one-off', and as such it was fundamentally different from its 2003 successor. In 1991 the strategic mission was limited and absolutely clear and, although many believed then and since that it should have been expanded to include the destruction of Saddam Hussein and his regime, the mission to liberate Kuwait following the Iraqi invasion of 1990 was patently correct in legal, moral and military terms, and it enjoyed wide support within the UN.

However, by 2003 the world had moved on, and the strategic rationale advanced for the new invasion of Iraq as an extension of the so-called war on terrorism was certainly tenuous and possibly fatally flawed. In the United Kingdom in particular it centred on Iraq's alleged capability to use weapons of mass destruction, but thus far any substantive or definitive evidence of that capability remains elusive. In the United States, the war was justified variously by the weapons of mass destruction argument, its linkage to the war against terrorism and a perceived need to effect regime change in Iraq. At one stage it was also postulated that Iraq had been directly involved in the Al-Qaeda attack of 11 September 2001 – a line actively promoted to motivate US personnel deployed to the conflict, although no substantive evidence for this emotive suggestion was disclosed. In any event, in September 2003 this proposition was laid to rest, when in response to a mounting level of questioning on this issue President George W. Bush finally admitted that no direct link existed between Iraq and the Al-Qaeda attack.

In Washington, President Bush soon became personally identified with the pro-war movement, while in London Prime Minister Tony Blair rapidly assumed the role of Bush's loyal ally and partner on the road to war; albeit that his unwavering adherence to this policy was in direct contravention of the views and wishes of many members of parliament and of much of the United Kingdom population as a whole. Time may eventually show either or both these leaders to have gambled their political futures unsuccessfully on their decision to confront Iraq militarily. Whilst Bush may just survive re-election for a second term – due principally to the 'nine-eleven factor' – the escalating scandal surrounding the questionable legitimacy of Blair's case made to parliament and the nation for involving British forces alongside those of the United States may well presage the end of his time as prime minister. Even worse, it might precipitate a 'lame duck' government in the UK, in the mould of those over which US Presidents Nixon and Carter presided during the final part of their respective Cold War-era administrations. Given all this, the political fallout from the war has so far been fairly inauspicious but, setting that to one side, what are the major military insights and correlations with the Cold War era that might now be discerned in what has become a conflict with no clear end in sight? Here also may be found matters of particular note for the United States – now the sole surviving superpower, still the principal champion of Western democracy, and by default the lead nation in the global fight against terrorism.

First and foremost, the 2003 Iraq War (as with its 1991 predecessor) could not have taken place if the Cold War had still been ongoing. The risk of provoking a wider superpower conflict with the former Soviet Union would assuredly have meant that the United States could not seriously have entertained the idea of launching a full-scale attack against Iraq. Admittedly, in 2003 Russia did oppose the Anglo-US invasion at the diplomatic level, but it was by then no more than a dysfunctional shadow of the mighty Soviet Union that had preceded it and so it was powerless to prevent Washington implementing whatever policy the US leadership chose to adopt. But if Moscow's power had diminished since the Cold War, the very absence of a Soviet threat meant that the Franco-German dependence upon US defence support in former times was now an irrelevance. France and Germany now felt sufficiently confident of their own positions in the new century to oppose the US policy and both countries declared themselves against the impending invasion of Iraq; together with many other European nations and UN member states. Even more significantly perhaps, the emerging superpower China also declared its opposition to the Anglo-US action. Interestingly, Beijing apparently viewed the precedent that it set as a dangerous signal to the Chinese Nationalists in Taiwan – rather than as a possible justification for a future Chinese communist invasion of that island nation. Thus, in very many ways, the 2003 Gulf conflict has demonstrated quite graphically the much changed nature of the post-Cold War world, and the security alignments and new priorities of the states within it.

The argument that the removal of Saddam Hussein's dictatorship was a good thing for certain groups in Iraq (such as the Kurds, non-Sunni Muslim religious sects and various anti-Baath Party movements and individuals) is largely self-evident; but why the Iraqi regime specifically should have attracted this decisive international action remains unclear. Certainly the significance of Iraq's enormous oil deposits must bear upon this issue: not least at a time when the United States is seeking to reduce its presence in Saudi Arabia, with an implied reduction of its influence over Saudi oil assets. In the future, Iraqi oil might provide a suitable substitute source of the mineral – the catalyst of conflict – on which America has become so dependent. Undoubtedly, these matters will attract further debate and controversy in the months and years ahead. This is all the more so where the overthrow of an Arab Muslim state (notwithstanding that Saddam Hussein presided over a primarily secular form of government) by predominantly Western forces – US forces in particular – was bound to attract a storm of political and religious hostility throughout the area; further de-stabilising an already volatile region while fuelling the cause of Muslim extremist groups and reinforcing their real or imagined grievances against the United States. Therefore, however unpleasant Saddam's regime might have been, the legal and moral right of the United States and the United Kingdom to overturn it by launching a high intensity armed conflict against Iraq remains highly questionable, as does the defence and security rationale for this action. This view has tended to be reinforced by numbers of Iraqis who, against all US and British expectations and conflict projections, are at present (some four months after the official end of the war) showing their continued hostility to what they perceive to be forces of occupation. Unfortunately, the US 'iron fist' concept of operations and the consequent actions of some of their troops tend day-by-day to confirm rather than to refute this perception. And it is here that the military legacy of the Cold War experience may be seen truly to have impacted upon this latter-day conflict.

Increasingly, as the nature of the conflict has changed, more and more pundits, defence analysts and commentators have drawn comparisons between the relative success enjoyed by the British forces in Basra and the major security problems that the US forces in Baghdad and towards the north of the country are still experiencing; although such comparisons need to be balanced by an awareness of the traditionally much greater support for Saddam and the Baath Party in what are today the US-controlled areas. Understandably, serving British personnel have been reluctant to criticise their US allies, but certain basic military truths are self-evident and these need to be exposed and acted upon if the US armed forces of the future are to be able to support effectively a superpower in the post-Cold War world.

This goal may well demand a 'root and branch' review of the US way in war and of a core military culture that has changed little since the 1970s.

Between 1945 and 1990 the United States learnt well the Cold War lessons of high-intensity war-fighting on a global scale; it remains pre-eminent in the use of overwhelming firepower, state of the art technology and superlative mobility to defeat any opponent in such a war. The US armed forces first built successfully upon their experience of the campaign in North-West Europe in 1944-45; they were then well prepared to counter thereafter a Cold War threat in post-war Europe that had developed from the Soviet experience of the Great Patriotic War 1941-45. Consequently, the US military today is equipped, organised, trained and motivated to conduct devastatingly effective combined, joint and all-arms combat at a level of violence that its own high command has characterised as delivering 'shock and awe' against its enemy. This capability is not in doubt. However, once the scale and tempo of the conflict reduce, the vast majority of US servicemen and women are ill-prepared to conduct lesser, but often more complex, low-intensity operations. Despite the burgeoning number of Special Forces, Civil Affairs, Psychological Operations and other specialist units, the problem has thus far not been noticeably redressed. There are several reasons for this.

The men and women of the all-regular US armed forces currently operating in Iraq are very different from those that fought in Vietnam in the 1960s and 1970s; just as those forces – the conscripted personnel especially – bore little resemblance to the men and women who had fought in Korea. And none of those armed forces bore more than a passing resemblance to the mighty war machine that had been developed to fight the war in North-West Europe from mid-1944. Yet all of these conflicts have together contributed to shaping the US forces that are today attempting with varying degrees of success to control and impose the rule of law and order in the Balkans, Afghanistan, Iraq and elsewhere. Many of the problems these forces now face are a direct consequence of the US experience of the Cold War; being both politically-inspired and a product of the military culture that has developed in the United States.

Ever since US forces became engaged in the Balkans in late-1995 the negative legacy of the Vietnam War and the 'body bag factor' has become ever more apparent in the policy of 'force protection' applied at all levels throughout any US forces involved in operations. In simple terms this policy reflects the politically immutable unacceptability of incurring US casualties, and consequently the over-riding responsibility of US commanders to avoid these at all costs. The unbending implementation of this policy stifles tactical options and actually reduces the real capability of US ground forces. It also tends to breed an ethos of self-protection, uncertainty and fear of being in harm's way that can all too easily result in the premature or excessive use of deadly force. This in turn can both threaten the mission and also produce an operating environment for US forces precisely the opposite of that which the Pentagon seeks to achieve.

At the individual level, soldiers are required as a matter of standard operating procedure to wear helmets and body armour – with the usual addition of ballistic-grade sun glasses or eye protectors – they are equipped with automatic weapons and routinely operate from armoured vehicles rather than on foot. Nuclear, biological and chemical warfare protection suits (whether worn or carried) often complete the US soldier's ensemble and appearance. These measures result in a larger than life physical image of the 'modern US warrior' that is actively cultivated and promoted by many soldiers and their commanders at all levels. However, whilst these measures are entirely prudent for high intensity combat, when there is a real need to interact directly with a civilian population in order to pacify, stabilise and re-build a nation they create an almost tangible barrier which prejudices the success of the mission before it has even begun.

As an aside, where perception management and the impact of the visual image have become key considerations in the conduct of modern war and its reporting by the media, the adoption by the US forces of the so-called 'Fritz' helmet in the 1990s was perhaps somewhat unfortunate, given that its shape – however suitable in terms of the protection it offered – was very similar to that of the German steel helmet of the First and Second World Wars.

The Pentagon should certainly remove the millstone of its current force protection policy from about the necks of its commanders and forces in the field. Not only will they be better able to achieve their missions, but they will also probably find in practice that they actually sustain fewer casualties once they are able to connect and interact more directly with civilian populations. The best forms of force protection are not physical, but comprise a thorough knowledge of the threat together with an informed understanding of the operational environment and the people that populate it. In this environment military professionalism is blended with interpersonal skills – including a measure of compassion and a ready sense of humour – to achieve operational success. The British army's experience of conflict during the last three or four decades has provided irrefutable evidence of the validity of this way of doing business.

The contrast of the US troops' approach with that of the British ground forces, who habitually move into 'soft' head-dress rather than helmets and reduce their overall offensive posture as soon as possible when conducting operations short of war-fighting, could not be more marked; and the merits of this application of perception management are usually reflected in the responses and reactions of the civilian population to the ordinary British soldier – which in turn bring operational and intelligence benefits. In low-intensity operations it was ever thus.

Over time, the US doctrine and concept of military service have developed and today stress what within the military is widely termed the 'warrior culture'. Taken a stage further, this begets the 'iron fist' concept and the impersonal or professionally detached nature of the American fighting man's approach to the business of war. Firepower, technology and the application of overwhelming force are pre-eminent; and (by inference) displaying, compassion, individualism or a human face all risk being judged weak by an enemy. In the same way, with a huge variety of white, black, Hispanic, and other ethnic groups from every band of the American socio-economic and cultural spectrum represented in its armed forces there is evidence in the training regime of a positive policy of reducing all new members – whether enlisted personnel or officers – to a common denominator and then re-shaping them into the Pentagon-required mould of a US serviceman or servicewoman.

Given the polyglot nature of US society and sheer size of the US armed forces, this approach may well be the only way to achieve the aim, but at the same time it risks de-humanising these personnel and dividing them too far from the civilian personnel of the democracy that they exist to serve and protect. It also tends to diminish and denigrate the national characteristics of a nation against or within which US forces are engaged and thus isolate the latter to the detriment of their mission. The US military culture also contrasts markedly with the military training approach of most Western European nations – notably that of the United Kingdom – which aims to capitalise and build upon an individual's existing attributes, rather than risking stifling his or her individuality in order to create some sort of 'standard' soldier. If Washington intends to embark upon other such operations short of all-out war, the Pentagon might benefit from the British experience and approach to the profession of arms.

Interestingly, a mood of change may already be emerging from within the US forces in Iraq. In early August, Lieutenant General Ricardo Sanchez, overall commander of the US-led coalition forces in Iraq, announced that the US forces would henceforth modify their 'iron fist' tactics in dealing with the civilian population, against the background of a worsening security situation. However, it may prove difficult to change in short order – other than superficially – what has thus far been accepted military doctrine.

Irrespective of the eventual verdict of history on the invasion of Iraq, there will assuredly be some pragmatic benefits that the US and British forces engaged can derive from it. Every war – win or lose – is a learning experience for the forces and political leadership involved, and just as the British forces will have been able to hone and maintain their capability to conduct high tempo war-fighting, Iraq may well be the catalyst that forces a sea change in US military thinking: in order much better to prepare the American armed forces for operations of the sort in which they have now become involved in the war against terrorism. At the same time the political fallout and lessons of Iraq are already assuming significant proportions, and may well indicate for the United States and other Western nations in the future a preferred policy of military containment rather than direct inter-vention such as that in Iraq and Afghanistan.

In the new terminology of conflict, the war against terrorism is 'asym-metric'; it is certainly atypical. But if it is largely unprecedented, so also is the nature of the post-Cold War world and international scene in which it is being conducted. Not since the heyday of the Roman Empire has a single power – the United States – enjoyed such a position of strategic dominance. But, ironically, the same advances in technology that – more than anything else – have allowed America to achieve this are now liable positively to threaten its security.

Technology has always been the key to US military success, whilst less affluent nations have of necessity relied more on the quality of their indi-vidual servicemen and servicewomen than upon the quantity and scale of resources they can afford to give them. But now the new technology of the twenty-first century has empowered the individual – including the terrorist – and so has provided him with destructive capabilities which, until 1990, were almost exclusively the preserve of large, well-funded military forces. Although US military technology will undoubtedly continue to increase apace, that of the terrorist, guerrilla or small armed force will probably increase disproportionately in terms of scale and speed. It follows that the traditional and well-tried US reliance on overwhelming qualitative strength, firepower and technology to resolve armed conflicts will become ever less relevant in the years ahead. The Iraq conflict has already provided some early indications of this, and it has also demonstrated that the US approach to war-fighting of 1941 to 1990 has run its course. Indeed, much of the remarkable military capability that finally defeated the Soviet Union and Warsaw Pact at the close of the 1980s may prove largely irrelevant in the new century.

Arguably, the Cold War to 1990 was a 'Third World War' in all but name: certainly its scale was global and its many thousand casualties were all too real. And if this was truly so, the verdict of history may well be that the Al-Qaeda terrorist attack using that organisation's own 'weapons of mass destruction' – four hijacked civilian airliners piloted by suicide bombers – was in fact the opening action of what is already a 'Fourth World War': one in which two responsive campaigns against terrorism have been initiated thus far: in Afghanistan and Iraq – but with counter-strokes by a terrorist enemy having been launched already in places as far apart as Indonesia, Kenya, Casablanca, Moscow, and (as ever) the Middle East. Undoubtedly further such terrorist attacks are planned. But whereas the main protagonists in 1914-18, 1939-45 and 1945-90 were nations broadly similar in military and philosophical terms, this new conflict pits the unconventional against the conventional, the lawless against the lawful and the militarily very small against the very big; and since time immemorial smaller military forces and organisations have usually proved much better able to adapt and react than their larger opponents – despite the more obvious advantages that the latter might superficially appear to enjoy. Thus the immediate and future challenge for the United States and others is to adapt their military capability effectively and sufficiently fast so that they stay ahead of the terrorist organisationally and conceptually, while still maintaining their existing and inherent technological and resource advantages.

The US experience of the war in Iraq in 2003 has already indicated that this will be an enormous challenge, but it is one that America, its allies and the other free, civilised and democratic nations of the world must confront and overcome. Ultimately, this 'Fourth World War' in embryo may well evolve into a struggle for the very survival of a way of life and the maintenance of personal and corporate freedoms and security that are today the product of more than two thousand years of world history.

NOTES

1 Miller is particularly comprehensive on NATO and the Warsaw Pact.

2 John Newhouse, *The Nuclear Age: From Hiroshima to Star Wars* and Lawrence Freedman *The Evolution of Nuclear Strategy* both provide a comprehensive view of the nuclear hardware, policies and strategies.

3 See David Stone, *Cold War Warriors – The Story of the Duke of Edinburgh's Royal Regiment (Berkshire and Wiltshire), 1959–1994*.

4 Charles Whiting, *'45: The Final Drive from the Rhine to the Baltic*.

5 Charles Whiting, *The Last Battle – Montgomery's Campaign April–May 1945*, pp. 238–9. Whiting noted that the Russians had earlier been drinking 'a potent mixture of vodka and V-1 [rocket] fuel!'

6 Apart from incidental contacts between Soviet troops and members of the US or British Special Forces who were advising the mujahedin guerrillas in Afghanistan during the 1980s.

7 Karl von Clausewitz, *On War*.

8 During the nineteenth and early twentieth centuries the long-running contest between Russia and Britain for control of Afghanistan, Persia and the North-West Frontier region, which provided ready access into British India, was termed 'the Great Game'. See Jennifer Siegel, *Endgame: Britain, Russia and the Final Struggle for Central Asia*.

9 The sum borrowed was equivalent to £70 billion at 2002 values, and a final payment of 346 million US dollars is currently due to be made by 31 December 2006. The loan followed US withdrawal of wartime lend-lease arrangements and ensured in practice that Britain would never be able to resume its pre-war primacy or challenge the United States for leadership of the West. See also the report by David Smith and Christopher Morgan in *The Sunday Times*, 2 June 2002 (p. 4 of the News Review).

10 William J. Koenig, *Americans at War*, p. 212.

11 Apart from the wars against Britain in 1812 and Mexico in 1836.

12 France – which had also suffered extensively at German hands in two world wars (as well as in 1870–1) – originally opposed Dulles's promotion of German rearmament. However, Paris subsequently bowed to American pressure and supported the political and military rehabilitation of West Germany in the 1950s.

13 Following their first successful atomic detonation on 23 September 1949, the Soviets' subsequent nuclear milestones during the 1950s included the M-4 Bison strategic bomber becoming operational in 1956, the hydrogen bomb taken into service in about 1956, and the SS-6 ICBM becoming operational in 1959.

14 For a full account of the abortive Iran hostage rescue attempt see Colonel Charlie A. Beckwith and Donald Knox, *Delta Force*, pp. 186–300.

15 Although the Provisional IRA also favoured the use of the Colt AR-15 assault rifle and the M-60 machine-gun, both of which weapons were of American origin.

16 Nuclear weapons development and deployment was also at varying stages in Great Britain, France, China, and elsewhere in the world during the 1950s and 1960s, albeit nowhere on a scale approaching that of the two superpowers.

17 Peter Hennessy, *The Secret State*, p. 39.

18 Robert A. Divine (Ed.), *The Cuban Missile Crisis*, p. 36; quoted by Fred Inglis, *The Cruel Peace*, p.159.

19 Hennessy, p. 40.

20 Hennessy, pp. 42–3.

21 See the account by Mark Franchetti at p. 29 of *The Sunday Times*, 20 October 2002.

22 Interview BBC Radio 4 (*Today*), 16 October 2002.

23 *Military Balance 1969–1970*, p. 55.

24 The ABM Treaty expired on 13 June 2002, following President George W. Bush's decision not to renew it.

25 1980 nuclear weapons statistics extracted

from Eric Morris, *Nuclear Confrontation (War in Peace)*, p. 267.

26 The characteristics, capabilities and application of the ER weapon are dealt with in considerable detail by David Miller in *The Cold War – A Military History*. At p. 386 he quotes from a letter by President Jimmy Carter, in which (while not dismissing the possible use of ER weapons) his reservations about them are clear. He wrote: 'The decision to use nuclear weapons of any kind, including enhanced radiation weapons, would remain in my hands, not in the hands of local theatre commanders. A decision to cross the nuclear threshold would be the most agonizing decision to be made by any President ... [the existence of] enhanced radiation weapons, would not make that decision any easier.' (Extract from President Carter's letter to Senator John C. Stennis dated 11 July 1977, quoted in van Cleave and Cohen, *Tactical Nuclear Weapons*, p. 8.)

27 France subsequently withdrew from the NATO integrated command structure in 1966, and required all NATO forces and installations to be removed from France at that time. This reflected de Gaulle's desire for the country to be free of foreign influences, especially Washington's. However, France continued to participate in NATO activities where they accorded with French national interests. Indeed, although clearly a national asset, the French nuclear forces and 1st French Army would undoubtedly have been involved alongside or in support of NATO forces in any war. Accordingly, the French armed forces were taken fully into account in NATO planning after 1966, and French military liaison staffs and observers proliferated throughout much of the post-1966 NATO structure.

28 The Republic of Ireland was also considered for NATO membership in 1948, but this possibility was dropped when Dublin indicated that its membership would be dependent upon Britain transferring to the Republic the six counties that comprised Northern Ireland.

29 For a comprehensive account of the creation and development of NATO see Miller, pp. 16–53.

30 The US, British and French forces in Berlin were not under NATO command.

31 *NATO Military Guide 1987, Volume I (NATO Unclassified)*, pp. 24 and 25.

32 David Pryce-Jones, *The War That Never Was*, pp. 123–4 (including the quoted first-hand observations of Charles Powell, who was Private Secretary to Mrs Thatcher from 1984 to 1991).

33 In practice, Albania had been a non-participant in the Warsaw Pact since 1 February 1962, and on 13 September 1968 it formally withdrew from the pact in protest over the Soviet military intervention in Czechoslovakia.

34 Uniquely among the member states, the national armed forces of the GDR (probably the most effective non-Soviet troops in the Warsaw Pact) were also under the command of the Combined Supreme Command in peacetime – a reflection of the Soviet Union's continuing fear of a resurgence of German militarism.

35 The number of divisions in the Soviet groups of forces stationed in the Warsaw Pact countries fluctuated over the life of the pact. The figures indicated were extracted originally from Friedrich Wiener, *The Armies of the Warsaw Pact Nations*, pp. 19–33. Throughout the Cold War the national intelligence communities of the United States and of some other NATO nations produced varying totals for the Soviet and Warsaw Pact forces, although a NATO-agreed version of the Soviet and Warsaw Pact order of battle was normally used for NATO exercise scenarios.

36 However, the sheer scale of manpower, resources and funding provided to NATO by the United States meant that de facto it led the Alliance and (where necessary) exerted a decisive influence on key policy issues. Nationally, the United States adhered absolutely to a principle that stemmed from its experience during the final year of the Second World War: that its armed forces would only serve under American command. This meant that a number of senior US commanders in NATO appointments (such as SACEUR, who commanded ACE from his headquarters at SHAPE in Belgium) also had US national command responsibilities, and were thus in the unenviable position of

reporting and responding to two separate chains of command, one of which led ultimately to the Secretary General of NATO in Brussels, the other to the US President in Washington.

37   Sir Robert Thompson, *When Greek Meets Greek*, p. 17.

38   Thompson, p. 20.

39   In later years a discrete planning headquarters ('Live Oak') at SHAPE (with a naval planning facility at SACLANT in Norfolk, Virginia) continued to develop a range of contingency plans for use in the event of another Soviet blockade of Berlin. These plans were far-reaching and included maritime, air and ground options. As Berlin was not a NATO responsibility, these plans were developed on a tripartite basis and Live Oak was manned exclusively by US, British and French personnel. Live Oak was commanded by a British major-general in peacetime, and by a senior US officer who reported direct to SACEUR in wartime. See also Miller, pp. 334–8.

40   Tony Le Tissier, *Berlin Then and Now*, p. 357.

41   Statistics from Le Tissier, p. 358.

42   Troop strengths and casualty figures from Miller, pp. 58–9.

43   Hennessy, pp. 36–7.

44   'Checkpoint Alpha' was at the West German end of the autobahn to West Berlin, and 'Checkpoint Bravo' was at the West Berlin end. Logically, therefore, 'Checkpoint Charlie' was the next checkpoint to the east.

45   The issue centred upon Western Allied personnel seeking to cross into East Berlin while wearing civilian clothes, as the East Germans clearly could not readily identify them as such. Shortly after 22 October the British agreed that their military personnel would only enter the East in uniform. However, as was their right, the Americans insisted on free and unhindered access whether in uniform or not.

46   Interview recorded in Rainer Hildebrandt, *Vom '13 August' zur 'Modernen Grenze'*.

47   Statistics collated from Miller, Le Tissier and Hildebrandt.

48   Despite the gravity and sincerity of the occasion, Kennedy's intended statement ('I am a Berliner') gave rise to some amusement, as the literal translation of this phrase is 'I am a doughnut' (a 'Berliner' is a type of cake): he should have omitted 'ein' and simply said 'Ich bin Berliner'. The error was no doubt much appreciated by the people of a city renowned for their love of political satire!

49   Colonel A. D. Meek, *Operation Centre*.

50   Although Romania had been directly involved in the imprisonment and subsequent elimination of the Hungarian leaders following the 1956 uprising, in the case of Czechoslovakia in 1968 the Romanian government declared its support for the Czech reforms and made it clear to Moscow that it would not participate in any action against Czechoslovakia. It was the only Warsaw Pact country to support Dubcek's reforms.

51   Stalin's ready agreement with Germany to partition Poland in 1939 and the massacre of about 15,000 Polish officers, officials and political leaders by the Soviets in the Katyn Forest in 1940 were but two reasons for Poland's uneasy relationship with its Soviet neighbour.

52   In accordance with a 1948 secret agreement between the US and the UK, North Korea fell into that area of the world in which the US was responsible for gathering signals intelligence (SIGINT), or technical eavesdropping. This intelligence could have reduced or negated the surprise achieved by the DPRK. However, due to serious failings in this branch of the US intelligence community between 1948 and 1952 and 'largely as a result of the lack of co-ordination, North Korea did not become a priority SIGINT target until after it had attacked the South'. (Hennessy, p. 26).

53   Korea became a Japanese colony in 1910, and since 1942 it had been treated as an integral part of Japan.

54   Max Hastings, *The Korean War*, pp. 45–7.

55   Despite this, MacArthur ordered the USAF to bomb targets north of the 38th parallel. This was a correct military decision, but it foreshadowed the difficulties that later arose between Truman and MacArthur.

56   Fred Inglis, *The Cruel Peace*, p. 112.

57   The 24th US Infantry Division was the same formation that had been based at

Schofield Barracks, Hawaii at the time of the Japanese attack on Pearl Harbor in December 1941. Its readiness on that occasion had also attracted criticism.

58 Extract from an article by Jerry Shane in the journal of the American Society of Military Insignia Collectors (ASMIC), March 2002. General Dean was the most senior US officer captured during the Korean War. Despite the performance of his division and his personal ability as a senior commander (see comments by Colonel John Michaelis in Max Hastings, *The Korean War*, pp. 85 and 111), Dean's personal courage was not in doubt. He spent three years in solitary confinement in a prison near Pyongyang, throughout which he was constantly subjected to Marxist-Leninist indoctrination, which prompted him to remark on his release: 'I'm an authority now on the history of the Communist party and much of its doctrine.' General Dean was awarded the Congressional Medal of Honor – the highest US military award – after the war. Interestingly, Lieutenant Colonel James Carne, who commanded the 1st Battalion, the Gloucestershire Regiment at the battle of the Imjin in April 1951, was eventually captured after the conclusion of that battle, and subsequently also received his own country's highest award for valour, the Victoria Cross.

59 Hastings, p. 44.

60 Hastings, pp. 150–4 and 162–3.

61 Lieutenant Colin Mitchell again achieved fame in 1967, when commanding the 1st Battalion, Argyll & Sutherland Highlanders. Then, his battalion's uncompromising but effective operations in the town of Crater during the final days of the Aden Protectorate, earned him the nickname 'Mad Mitch', together with the largely undeserved criticism of several British politicians and senior officers of the time.

62 Hastings, p. 164.

63 Hastings, p. 168.

64 Hastings, p. 194.

65 By then, a second British brigade, the 29th Infantry Brigade, had arrived in Korea and was deployed on the line of the Han River, a little to the south of Seoul.

66 Both men displayed very different quali-ties and personalities. Almond was an energetic and dedicated officer and a capable corps commander; but was excessively self-confident and possibly over-concerned with achieving personal glory. Conversely, Smith was slow, cautious and methodical; but he was a caring and consummately professional leader at the operational level of command – all very appropriate skills during the division's fighting withdrawal from Chosin to the port of Hamhung (where it finally embarked in good order for Pusan). Inevitably, both men had their critics and their champions.

67 'A shortage of transportation and escort personnel makes it impossible to accomplish the mission of supplying the troops. As a result our soldiers frequently starved … They ate cold food, and some had only a few potatoes in two days. They were unable to maintain their physical strength for combat; the wounded could not be evacuated … The firepower of our entire army was basically inadequate. When we used our guns, there were often no shells, or the shells were duds.' Extract from a PLA 26th Army document dated November 1950 (Hastings, p. 204).

68 See the objective but highly critical secret report written for the British Chiefs of Staff by General Sir Robert Mansergh, Commander-in-Chief of the British Forces in Hong Kong, summarised at Hastings, pp. 207–9.

69 The manner of Walker's death was uncannily similar to that of his great mentor General Patton in Germany five years earlier. General Walker's fitness for high command had already attracted concern in Washington, Tokyo and within his own command, and his performance as commander of the 8th US Army in Korea tended to bear this out. He was undoubtedly a courageous and committed soldier, but simply lacked the intellect necessary for high command in the post-1945 era. MacArthur's lack of confidence in him was evident when he consistently denied him overall command of the ground forces in Korea, whilst at the same time declining to replace him with a more suitable army commander.

70 In fact, US nuclear contingency planning

for Korea was still proceeding apace, although this was not disclosed to the British at that meeting. Given the extent of support in Washington for the use of atom bombs against communist China, it was probably only the PLA's failure to demonstrate a clear capability to defeat the UN in the winter of 1950–1 that prevented China from becoming the first state to suffer atomic attack since 1945.

71 Edited extract from HQ 8th US Army, APO 301, message dated 21 January 1951, on the subject 'Why We Are Here'. The message was signed 'Matthew B. Ridgway, Lieutenant General, United States Army, Commanding'. It was issued down to unit level throughout 8th US Army.

72 Hastings, p. 235.

73 Although General Ridgway remained loyal to his erstwhile commander, he later commented that MacArthur's wish to extend the war into China risked 'igniting World War III and [the] consequent over-running of Western Europe, with the loss of our oldest and staunchest allies sure to follow'. Ridgway's awareness of the wider global issues involved in the Cold War era contrasted with MacArthur's views, which reflected his very different experience of high command during and immediately after the Second World War (see Hastings, p. 244).

74 The 27th Commonwealth Brigade comprised 1st Battalion the Middlesex Regiment, Princess Patricia's Canadian Light Infantry (PPCLI), and 3rd Battalion the Royal Australian Regiment (3 RAR).

75 Despite this observation, the Centurion medium tank – which had been developed at the close of the Second World War, but entered service in 1945 just too late to see action – was one of the best post-war NATO tanks. It remained in service with the British Army into the early 1970s, and much longer with some other armies.

76 Hastings (p. 268) attributed the idea for this morale-boosting initiative to Captain Farrar-Hockley, and 'The moment when Buss stood at attention on the position, playing in succession "Reveille", "Cook-house", "Defaulters" and "Officers Dress for Dinner" passed into the legend of the Imjin battle.'

77 Colonel D. E. Whatmore, *1 Glosters at Imjin – April 1951*, an article published in 'The Sphinx and Dragon' (The Regimental Journal of the Royal Gloucestershire, Berkshire and Wiltshire Regiment), Volume 3, No. 2 (2000).

78 Lieutenant Colonel Carne, together with WO1 (RSM) Hobbs and some others, evaded capture for twenty-four hours before they too joined the soldiers of A, B and C Companies already in captivity. Some thirty Glosters who had survived the battle subsequently died while prisoners of the Chinese and North Koreans.

79 The other units that received this US honour following the battle on the Imjin in April 1951were the PPCLI, 3 RAR, and C Troop 170 Independent Mortar Battery RA.

80 See also S. L. A. Marshall, *Pork Chop Hill*.

81 Bruce Jacobs, *Korea's Heroes*, pp. 151–2.

82 William J. Koenig, *Americans at War*, p. 293.

83 During the Korean War, the United States made 131 awards of the Congressional Medal of Honor – the nation's highest award for valour – to its servicemen (US Army 78, USMC 42, USN 7, USAF 4). The last of these was for an action less than twenty-four hours before the armistice was signed, and six days after the terms of the armistice had been agreed in practice. The award was made posthumously to USMC Staff Sergeant Ambrosio Guillen of El Paso, Texas, who died of wounds sustained while leading his platoon in the successful defence of an isolated outpost against a massive Chinese attack. He did not survive long enough to witness the end of the fighting on 27 July.

84 Koenig notes at p. 262 that although MacArthur 'was ostensibly acting as a United Nations Commander of United Nations troops ...' he 'took his orders from the American Joint Chiefs of Staff and was never in direct contact with the UN at any time during the Korean conflict'.

85 Hastings, p. 413.

86 Koenig, p. 275.

87 See also Hastings, p. 89 et seq.

88 See the detailed explanation and analysis at John J. McCuen, *The Art of Counter-Revolutionary War* (Chapter 3).

89 David Stone, *Out of the Shadows...The Re-emergence of the British Army's Psycho-*

logical Operations Capability pp. 3–4.

90 Tony Geraghty, *Who Dares Wins – The Story of the SAS 1950–1980*, p. 36.

91 Subsequently these Malayan aborigines, the Senoi Pra'ak, were formed into ad hoc units on the government side. Armed only with their traditional weapon – the blowpipe – during the final two years of the Emergency these units killed more guerrillas than did all the rest of the security forces during the period.

92 Geraghty, p. 38.

93 Templer was later promoted to field marshal. He was replaced in Malaya by his former deputy, Sir Donald MacGillivray, who oversaw the continuance of Templer's policies and achievements after 1954, including the crucial elections in 1955.

94 Tony Geraghty, *March or Die*, p. 227.

95 Geraghty, p. 227.

96 One such was Ho Chi Minh's agreement to the stationing of 25,000 French and French-officered Vietnamese troops in the major urban areas (to be followed by a French withdrawal in five annual stages, with completion in 1952), in return for French recognition of the Democratic Republic of Vietnam as a free state within both an Indochinese Federation and the French Union.

97 Geraghty, p. 239.

98 Eight years later, as a lieutenant colonel, Jeanpierre commanded 1 REP (1er Régiment Étranger de Parachutistes) in Algeria, where he was killed in action while leading his legionnaires against ALN guerrillas on 29 May 1958. See Lieutenant Colonel D. J. A. Stone, *The Supreme Adventure: The Life and Death of Lieutenant Colonel Pierre Jeanpierre of the French Foreign Legion*.

99 The base at Na San was subsequently evacuated without any loss of French lives during a rationalisation and reduction of the number of French outstations in August 1953.

100 The name 'Dien Bien Phu' translated literally as the 'administrative centre of the border region'. However, while Dien Bien Phu was a name infrequently used by the local T'ai villagers and Viet Minh forces of the time, it was by this name that the valley – and specifically the site of the sizeable village of Muong Thanh at its centre – was known to the French Union forces of the mid-1950s.

101 By February 1954, the Viet Minh 308th and 312th Divisions had been joined by the 304th, 316th Divisions and the 351st Heavy Division. The last was a combat support division, which comprised two artillery regiments (with field and anti-aircraft artillery) and an engineer regiment.

102 The details of these MRLs varies considerably between separate accounts of Dien Bien Phu, but they were most probably the Soviet BM-13 MRL, with its sixteen 132mm barrels, which had been used extensively by the Red Army during the Second World War. The BM-13 was also in service with the Chinese PLA in 1954. At least twelve MRLs were used by the Viet Minh at Dien Bien Phu.

103 Four of the six parachute battalions that had originally jumped into Dien Bien Phu for Operation Castor had subsequently been replaced by non-parachute units, which had been airlifted into the base.

104 John Pimlott, *Operation Castor: The Seizure of Dien Bien Phu*, p. 75.

105 The circumstances of de Castries's promotion and of his beleaguered command echoed those of Hitler's promotion of General Paulus to field marshal shortly before the collapse and surrender of the German 6th Army at Stalingrad in February 1943.

106 See also Geraghty, pp. 247–9. US Secretary of State John Foster Dulles was apparently in favour of Operation Vulture – an interesting fact, given his lack of support for the strategically much more worthy Anglo-French Suez operation in 1956. However, from the American perspective, Indochina was all about combating communism, whereas Suez was viewed by many in Washington as an Anglo-French attempt to perpetuate the pre-war European empires – which was anathema to post-1945 US administrations.

107 Geraghty, p. 242.

108 Bernard Fall, *Street Without Joy*, p. 31.

109 See Fall, p. 319. Viet Minh *strengths* were assessed to within 10 per cent accuracy. However, their *capabilities* were not, and the relative capabilities of the French forces were consistently overestimated.

110 On 7 March 1954 Giap also inflicted an important blow against the air support upon which the garrison of Dien Bien Phu depended, when a force of Viet Minh regular troops from People's Army Battalion No. 204, led by its deputy commander, Captain Minh Khanh, infiltrated Cot-Bi military airfield close to Haiphong and destroyed four B-26 bombers and six reconnaissance aircraft on the ground. This Viet Minh operation into the very heart of French-controlled territory shortly preceded the start of the main communist offensive at Dien Bien Phu. Other accounts of Viet Minh commando attacks and sabotage operations against Cot-Bi and Gia-Lam airfields in March 1954 state in one case that some thirty-eight transport aircraft were destroyed in a single raid, while another account quotes a (probably more accurate) figure of eighteen supply aircraft destroyed during what was presumably the same attack. Despite the variations in these accounts, airpower was critical to the French at Dien Bien Phu and the loss of any number of aircraft from the small force available to them was very significant. Although they commandeered every available civilian aircraft in an effort to make good those lost at Cot-Bi and elsewhere, the French were subsequently unable to sustain and support Dien Bien Phu at the levels required.

111 MAAG-V had been established in 1953, under the command of General J. W. O'Daniel. Lieutenant General Williams replaced O'Daniel in 1955.

112 The attacks on the USS *Maddox* and USS *C. Turner Joy* on 4 August were confirmed by both destroyer captains, who reported that two North Vietnamese boats were sunk and two damaged by naval gunfire and air support. However, this incident subsequently attracted much controversy when some US intelligence personnel asserted that the 'hostile patrol craft' were in fact radar blips that had been misread by an inexperienced radar operator on the *Maddox* – an assertion strongly disputed by the USN commanders involved.

113 Dr William Michael Hammond, *The Vietnam War*, p. 76.

114 Although the Commander MACV was the in-theatre commander-in-chief and was therefore responsible for every aspect of America's war within South Vietnam, MACV was organisationally subordinate to the US regional commander – the Commander-in-Chief Pacific (CINCPAC).

115 The battle at Ia Drang was featured in the film 'We Were Soldiers Once ...', based upon the book *We Were Soldiers Once, and Young*, by Lieutenant General Harold G. Moore and Joseph L. Galloway.

116 The historical lineage of the 1st US Cavalry Division ('The First Team') can be traced back to its activation at Fort Bliss, Texas in 1921. It assumed the infantry role in 1943 and then served in the Pacific theatre, subsequently joining the US Army of Occupation in Japan. In 1950 it was one of the ill-fated units rushed to Korea to counter the North Korean invasion. In June 1965, at Fort Benning, Georgia, the 11th Air Assault Division (Test) provided the nucleus of the reformed 1st Cavalry Division (Airmobile) immediately prior to its deployment to South Vietnam; the first complete US division to be deployed there.

117 Shelby L. Stanton, *Anatomy of a Division: The 1st Cav in Vietnam*, p. 41.

118 Lieutenant Colonel D. J. A. Stone, *Airmobility and Air Assault: The American Experience 1945–75*.

119 Australian units operating in Phuoc Tuy Province assessed that the evacuation time from a casualty occurring until he was on the hospital operating table would usually be no more than forty minutes. The US target evacuation time from battlefield to hospital was a maximum thirty minutes.

120 Lieutenant Colonel D. J. A. Stone, *Airmobility and Air Assault: The American Experience 1945–75*.

121 The M-16 (the US military version of the AR-15 Armalite) was issued to the division not long before its deployment to Vietnam; replacing the well-tried but heavier 7.62mm M-14 rifle.

122 See also Stanton, *Anatomy of a Division: The 1st Cav in Vietnam* for a detailed account of the development and application of the US air cavalry organisations and operational concepts.

123 Shelby L. Stanton, *Vietnam Order of Battle*, p. 347.

124 Statistics from Stanton, pp. 333 and 349.

125 Rick Atkinson, *The Long Gray Line*, p. 266.

126 Charles B. MacDonald, *Communist Thrust – The Tet Offensive of 1968 (The Vietnam War)*, p. 150.

127 Koenig, p. 329.

128 MacDonald, pp. 152 and 153.

129 MacDonald, p. 153.

130 Statistics from Sir Robert Thompson, *Vietnam*, p. 219.

131 Potentially lethal attacks by their subordinates upon those officers and non-commissioned officers whom they perceived to be over-zealous or otherwise unpopular. 'Fragging' was so-called due to the oft-used technique of rolling a fragmentation grenade into the subject's bunk or office.

132 Atkinson, pp. 300–1.

133 Koenig, p. 334.

134 The Pentagon Papers ran in the *New York Times* from 13 June 1971. The leaked documents upon which the newspaper reports were based comprised a detailed analysis, commissioned by McNamara on 17 June 1967, of US policy in South-east Asia from 1945 to 1968. This covered the governments of Truman, Eisenhower, Kennedy and Johnson. The study revealed major underestimates of the communist capabilities and intentions, the failure of US political leaders to understand the realities of the war, the misrepresentation of the US commitment and responsibility to South Vietnam, and finally the failure to explain and brief openly and honestly the progress of the war to the American people.

135 The former US headquarters of MACV in Saigon moved to Nakhon Phanom in Thailand, where it was redesignated HQ US Support Activities Group. In Saigon, a predominantly civilian presence was established to safeguard residual US interests, administer the ongoing provision of aid to South Vietnam and provide technical advice and assistance as required.

136 David Butler, *The Fall of Saigon*, p. 493.

137 However, the US Special Forces Joint Casualty Resolution Centre (JCRC), originally established following the signing of Article 8 (prisoner accountability) of the Paris Peace Agreement, was based in Saigon to assist in the recovery or resolution of status of unaccounted for US personnel. Following the final US evacuation in 1975 the JCRC relocated its main South-east Asia office to Bangkok in Thailand. In 1990, the JCRC was permitted to maintain a liaison team in Hanoi for the purpose of locating and recovering the remains of US servicemen.

138 Butler, pp. 502–4. The two flag bearers were Pham Duy Do and Pham Huy Nghe, a two-man sapper team. Shortly after fixing one of their flags to the palace flagpole, while searching the building, they found General Duong Van Minh and the members of the South Vietnam government in a room at the palace. Nghe guarded them until Do brought four political officers to the room, one of whom accepted Minh's unconditional surrender of the armed forces of South Vietnam.

139 Statistics from Stanton, p. 346.

140 Koenig, p. 340.

141 The importance of the Jewish vote in the United States is often overstated. There are today about six million American Jews within a population of 280 million. Of these, about two million live in New York. In an analysis by Alistair Cooke – an authoritative commentator on all aspects of American life and politics – of the political significance of the Jewish vote, broadcast by Radio 4 on 13 April 2002, Cooke observed that 'even if [the American Jews] all voted the same ticket, it would not be a decisive factor'.

142 In June 1967, Egypt fielded 240,000 men, 1,200 tanks and 450 aircraft; Jordan 50,000 men, 200 tanks and 40 aircraft; Syria 50,000 men, 400 tanks and 120 aircraft; and in fact a total of 250,000 men, 2,000 tanks and 939 aircraft actually opposed the IDF during the Six-Day War. However, the higher total figures included the potential involvement of Kuwait, Algeria, Saudi Arabia and Iraq, and it is these worst case figures that the Israeli cabinet must have considered on 3 June 1967.

143 Christopher Angeloglou and Brian Haynes (Ed.), *The Holy War June 1967*, p. 34. Text © Times Newspapers Limited, London, 1967 and Murray Sayle.

144 Angeloglou and Haynes (Ed.), p. 64. Original text by Donald McCullin.

145 H. P. Wilmott (*The Yom Kippur War*) states

at p. 236 that SA-9 (Gaskin) SAM systems were also used. However, David C. Isby (*Weapons and Tactics of the Soviet Army*) indicates quite clearly at p. 266 that (as at March 1981) 'The SA-9 has never seen action ...' and at p. 264 that it was not introduced into service until 1974.

146 See Robert Fisk (*Pity the Nation: Lebanon at War*), pp. 201, 255 and p. 359 et seq.

147 The Israeli Likud government's policy in the Lebanon in 1982 – with its support for the Lebanese Christian militias – echoed many aspects of David Ben Gurion's much earlier plans for the Lebanon in 1948. These had included the division of the Lebanon, with the creation of a new Lebanese Christian state north of the Litani River (which would provide a defensive bulwark for Israel). Ben Gurion's other policies of 1948 included preventing the creation of a Palestinian state and the systematic expulsion of the indigenous Arab population from Israeli territory.

148 Statistics from H. P. Wilmott, *Kenya in Revolt*, p. 113.

149 See Tony Geraghty, *March or Die*, p. 305.

150 John Pimlott, *The Algerian Revolution*, p. 132.

151 PAIGC: Partido Africano da Independência da Guiné e Cabo Verde; FRELIMO: Frente de Libertação de Moçambique; FNLA: Frente Nacional de Libertação de Angola; UNITA: União Nacional Para a Indepéndencia Total de Angola; MPLA: Movimento Popular de Libertação de Angola.

152 The BMD (*Bronevaya Maschina Desantnaya*) was the airborne forces' air-droppable version of the BMP armoured personnel carrier. It mounted a 73mm turret gun and a Sagger ATGM launcher rail above the gun barrel.

153 The DRA use of riot control and incapacitating agents like CS and CN was supplemented by older lethal agents such as phosgene, and possibly by the various nerve agents that had long been in the Soviet chemical weapons inventory, notably sarin, soman, mustard gas and VR-55 thickened nerve gas. The use of chemical offensive weapons was a standard tactical option for the Soviet armed forces, and once engaged in Afghanistan the then current range of mycotoxin

nerve agents (lethal and incapacitating) also became available to them. Afghanistan was undoubtedly a useful proving ground for these weapons.

154 The Hind-A was designed in the late 1960s, and took full account of US helicopter gunship operations in Vietnam. The Hind first flew in 1969, with the Hind-A reaching GSFG in the GDR in 1973. Hind-D came into service from 1975 and was not exported beyond the Warsaw Pact until the late 1970s. The Hind could be armed with alternative or mixed weapons fits of missiles, machine-guns, rockets, bombs and cannon. Although primarily an attack helicopter, it had a limited troop-carrying capability, albeit at the expense of other equipment.

155 Michael Orr, *Invasion of Afghanistan*, p. 289. Orr and Laffin (*The World in Conflict*, p. 16) both state that 'Amin was killed in the fighting', while Isby (*Russia's War in Afghanistan*, p. 6) states that 'Amin was executed by his erstwhile allies'. However, if the Soviets had definitely intended to murder Amin from the outset, there would probably have been much greater *Spetsnaz* involvement in the palace seizure. Therefore, even as late as 27 December, the Soviets may still have hoped to present themselves as allies rather than invaders.

156 Eric S. Margolis, *War at the Top of the World*, p. 21.

157 Fred Inglis, *The Cruel Peace*, p. 266 (quoting from Doris Lessing, *The Wind Blows Away Our Words*, p. 162).

158 Margolis, p. 18.

159 Margolis, pp. 17–18.

160 The mujahedin used the US Stinger SAM system against fighters, transport aircraft and helicopters. Prior to the arrival of the Stingers, the mujahedin were provided with the British Blowpipe SAM and Chinese-manufactured copies of the Soviet SAM-7, but both these shoulder-launched systems proved generally unsuitable and 'worthless in combat' (see Margolis, p. 34).

161 Margolis, pp. 35–6.

162 Prudently, from 1980 the United States progressively reduced its dependence on Middle Eastern oil supplies, so that by 2001 only four per cent of its needs came from the Gulf.

163 Pakistan's leader, General Zia, and the Director General of the ISI, General Akhdar, may have paid the ultimate price for Pakistan's support of the mujahedin. In June 1988 the Soviet representative in Kabul, Yuri Vorontsov, indicated that Zia would 'pay personally' for his part in the Soviet defeat in Afghanistan. Subsequently, on 17 August 1988, a C-130 military transport carrying both men, plus US Ambassador Arnold Raphael and thirty senior Pakistani officers, took off from Bahawalpur. It crashed minutes later, killing all on board. The initial crash investigation indicated sabotage, but the Pakistan government (by then headed by Benazir Bhutto) and the FBI blocked further investigation. Following his own investigation of the incident, Eric Margolis came to the conclusion that the crash resulted from a US–Soviet agreement made in spring 1988 to replace the pro-Islamic Zia with the anti-Islamic Bhutto, while at the same time ending the war without embarrassing Gorbachev. Thus, this event may well have been engineered by the CIA and KGB, with assistance from Bhutto's supporters in Pakistan. See Margolis, pp. 45–8.

164 For a full account of the OPEC decisions and actions on 16 and 17 October 1973 see Daniel Yergin and Joseph Stanislaw, *The Prize – The Epic Quest for Oil, Money and Power*, pp. 606–12.

165 Yergin and Stanislaw, pp. 615–16.

166 Yergin and Stanislaw, p. 632.

167 Dilip Hiro, *The Longest War*, pp. 21 and 38.

168 Hiro, p. 34.

169 Although President Abolhassan Bani-Sadr was the nominal head of state, the real power in Iran from 1979 was always that exerted by Ayatollah Khomeini.

170 Hiro, p. 32.

171 Hiro, p. 219 (extract from the *International Herald Tribune* 14 November 1986).

172 Hiro, p. 262.

173 *The Military Balance 1969–70*, p. 57. However, during the late 1960s the United States was also extensively engaged in Vietnam.

174 Statistics from Ray Bonds (Ed.), *The Soviet War Machine*, p. 235.

175 Stephen Ambrose, *Band of Brothers*, p. 232. Extract from observations recorded by David Kenyon Webster in February 1945.

176 Interestingly, of the non-communist or 'Westernised' states, only Australia – originally a country of immigrants with the notable exception of the aboriginal native Australians – has implemented a firm but effective policy of border controls, with the detention of illegal immigrants while their applications to remain in Australia are processed: a pragmatic but (in some quarters) unpopular policy that has attracted a predictable level of criticism from human rights' activists both within Australia and from elsewhere.

177 The escalating influx of large numbers of immigrants from conflict areas in Asia and Eastern Europe since the end of the Cold War has in recent years paralleled a dramatic increase in gun-related crime and the gang ethos within these communities in the United Kingdom. The long-term impact of this imported and accelerating culture of violence has already changed – possibly for ever – the core nature of several of Britain's inner cities, and unless checked it also threatens eventually to overwhelm the country's wider law enforcement and justice systems.

178 See Michael Yardley and Dennis Sewell, *A New Model Army*, pp. 101–26.

BIBLIOGRAPHY AND SOURCES

Ambrose, Stephen E. *Band of Brothers.* Simon & Schuster UK, London, 2001

Angeloglou, Christopher and Haynes, Brian (Ed.). *The Holy War June 1967.* Clive Irving & Cornmarket Press Ltd., Manchester, 1967. Extracts reproduced by permission of *The Sunday Times*, London

Atkinson, Rick. *The Long Gray Line.* Collins, London, 1990. Extracts reproduced by permission of the author

Austin, Greg and Muraviev, Alexey D. *The Armed Forces of Russia in Asia.* I. B. Tauris & Co., London, 2000

Beckwith, Col US Army (Retd) Charlie A. and Knox, Donald. *Delta Force.* Arms & Armour Press, London, 1984

Bergot, Erwan. *1954: 'Eliane' – La Bataille des Paras.* Histoire et Collections, Paris, 1987

Bonds, Ray (Ed.). *The Soviet War Machine.* Hamlyn Publishing Group, London, 1977

Butler, David. *The Fall of Saigon.* Sphere Books, London, 1986

Carver, F. M. Lord. *Britain's Army in the 20th Century.* Pan Books, London, 1999

Clausewitz, Karl von. *On War.* Germany, 1832

Clay, Lucius D. *Decision in Germany.* William Heinemann, Netherlands, 1950

Divine, Robert A. (Ed.), *The Cuban Missile Crisis.* Markus Wiener, New York, 1988

Fall, Bernard. *Street Without Joy.* Pall Mall Press, London, 1963

Fisk, Robert. *Pity the Nation: Lebanon at War.* André Deutsch, London, 1990

Forty, George. *At War in Korea.* Arms & Armour Press, London, 1997

Freedman, Lawrence. *The Cold War.* Cassell, London, 2001

— *The Evolution of Nuclear Strategy.* Macmillan, London, 1981

Geraghty, Tony. *BRIXMIS.* HarperCollins, London, 1996

— *March or Die.* Grafton Books, London, 1986

— *Who Dares Wins: The Story of the SAS 1950–1980.* Arms & Armour Press, London, 1981

Godfrey, F. A. *War in Peace: Crisis in Korea.* Orbis Publishing, London, 1981

Halliday, Jon and Cummings, Bruce. *Korea, The Unknown War.* Viking, London, 1998

Hammond, Dr William Michael, (Ed. Ray Bonds). *The Vietnam War.* Salamander Books, London, 1979

Hastings, Max. *The Korean War*. Pan Books, London, 2000. Extracts reproduced by permission of Macmillan Publishers Ltd

Hennessy, Peter. *The Secret State: Whitehall and the Cold War*. Allen Lane, London, 2002. Extracts reproduced by permission of Peter Hennessy and Allen Lane, The Penguin Press

Hiro, Dilip. *The Longest War: The Iran–Iraq Military Conflict*. Paladin and Grafton Books, London, 1989

Horne, Alistair. *A Savage War of Peace: Algeria 1954–1962*. Macmillan, London, 1977

Inglis, Fred. *The Cruel Peace: Living Through the Cold War*. Aurum Press, London, 1992

Isaacs, Jeremy and Downey, Taylor. *Cold War*. Bantam Press, London, 1998

Isby, David. *Russia's War in Afghanistan*. Osprey, London, 1987

— *Weapons and Tactics of the Soviet Army*. Jane's Publishing Co., London, 1981

Jacobs, Bruce. *Korea's Heroes*. Berkley Publishing, New York, 1961

Koenig, William J. *Americans at War*. Bison Books. London, 1980

Laffin, John. *The World in Conflict*. Brassey's, London and Washington 1997

Lassus, Dennis. *6 Mois de Combat à Dien Bien Phu*. Histoire et Collections, Paris, 1989

Lessing, Doris. *The Wind Blows Away Our Words*. Vintage Books, New York, 1987

Le Tissier, Tony. *Berlin Then and Now*. After the Battle, Battle of Britain Prints, Plaistow Press, London, 1992

Macdonald, Charles B. *The Vietnam War: Communist Thrust, The Tet Offensive of 1968*. Salamander Books, London, 1979. Extracts reproduced by permission of Chrysalis Books PLC

Margolis, Eric S. *War at the Top of the World*. Routledge, New York, 2001. All extracts © 2001, reproduced by permission of Routledge, Inc., part of The Taylor & Francis Group

Marshall, S. L. A. *Pork Chop Hill*. Panther Books, London, 1956

McCuen, John J. *The Art of Counter-Revolutionary War*. Faber and Faber, London, 1966

Meek, Col A. D. *Operation Centre*. British Army Review No. 104, 1994

Mercer, Charles. *The Foreign Legion*. Four Square Books, London, 1964

Military Balance 1969–1970. The Institute for Strategic Studies, London, 1969

Miller, David. *The Cold War: A Military History*. Pimlico (Random House), London, 2001. Extracts and information reproduced by permission of John Murray (Publishers) Ltd

Moore, Lt Gen Harold G. and Galloway, Joseph L. *We Were Soldiers Once, and Young*. Random House Inc., New York, 1992

Morris, Eric. *War in Peace: Nuclear Confrontation*. Orbis Publishing, London, 1981

NATO Military Guide: Volume I (unclassified). Published by the NATO School (SHAPE), D-8103 Oberammergau, Federal Republic of Germany 1987

Newhouse, John. *The Nuclear Age: From Hiroshima to Star Wars*. Michael Joseph, London, 1989

Newman, Bernard. *Background to Viet-Nam*. Robert Hale, London, 1965

Orr, Michael, *War in Peace: Invasion of Afghanistan*. Orbis Publishing, London, 1981

Palit, Maj Gen D. K. *The Lightning Campaign – The Indo-Pakistan War 1971*. Compton Press, Salisbury, 1972

Perrett, Brian. *The Taste of Battle*. Cassell, London, 2000

Pimlott, John. *War in Peace: The Algerian Revolution*. Orbis Publishing, London, 1981

— *War in Peace: Ho Chi Minh's Triumph*. Orbis Publishing, London, 1981

Ponton, Geoffrey. *The Soviet Era: Soviet Politics from Lenin to Yeltsin*. Blackwell Publishers, Oxford 1994

Pryce-Jones, David. *The War That Never Was: The Fall of the Soviet Empire 1985–1991*. Orion (Weidenfeld & Nicolson), London, 1995. Extracts reproduced by permission of The Orion Publishing Group Ltd

Shane, Jerry. '24th Infantry Division in the Korean War': article in *The Trading Post*, journal of the American Society of Military Insignia Collectors (ASMIC), January–March 2002, USA. Extract reproduced by permission of ASMIC

Sheehan, Neil. *A Bright Shining Lie*. Jonathan Cape, London, 1989

Siegel, Jennifer. *Endgame: Britain, Russia and the Final Struggle for Central Asia*. I. B. Tauris & Co., London and New York, 2002

Sphinx and Dragon: The Regimental Journal of the Royal Gloucestershire, Berkshire and Wiltshire Regiment Volume 3, Number 2. Forces & Corporate Publishing, Rushden, Northamptonshire 2000. Extracts reproduced by permission of the Royal Gloucestershire, Berkshire & Wiltshire Regiment

Stanton, Shelby L. *Vietnam Order of Battle*. Galahad Books, New York, 1987

— *Anatomy of a Division: The 1st Cav in Vietnam*. Presidio Press, Novato, USA, 1987

Stone, Lt Col David J. A. *'SHAPE Within NATO: The First Forty Years'*. Unpublished text of an unclassified presentation provided to SACEUR and the SHAPE staff at Mons, Belgium 4 April 1989

— *Cold War Warriors: The Story of the Duke of Edinburgh's Royal Regiment (Berkshire and Wiltshire) 1959–1994.* Leo Cooper/Pen & Sword Books, Barnsley 1998

— 'Out of the Shadows … The Re-emergence of the British Army's Psychological Operations Capability'. *British Army Review* No. 114, December 1996

— 'The Supreme Adventure: The Life and Death of Lieutenant Colonel Pierre Jeanpierre of the French Foreign Legion'. *British Army Review* No. 98, August 1991

— 'Airmobility and Air Assault: The American Experience 1945–75'. *British Army Review* No. 94, April 1990

Thompson, Sir Robert. *War in Peace: Vietnam.* Orbis Publishing, London, 1981

Watson, Dr George M. and O'Neill, Richard. *The Vietnam War: The End of French Rule in Indochina.* Salamander Books, London, 1979

Whiting, Charles. *'45: The Final Drive from the Rhine to the Baltic.* Century, London, 1985

— *The Last Battle: Montgomery's Campaign April–May 1945.* Crowood Press, Marlborough, Wiltshire, 1989

Wiener, Friedrich. *The Armies of the Warsaw Pact Nations.* Carl Ueber-reuter, Vienna 1978

Wilmott, H. P. *War in Peace: The Yom Kippur War.* Orbis Publishing, London, 1981

— *War in Peace: Kenya in Revolt.* Orbis Publishing, London, 1981

Wintle, Justin. *The Vietnam Wars.* Weidenfeld and Nicolson Ltd, London, 1991

Yardley, Michael and Sewell, Dennis. *A New Model Army.* W. H. Allen, London, 1989

Yergin, Daniel and Stanislav, Joseph. *The Prize: The Epic Quest for Oil, Money and Power.* Simon & Schuster, London, 1993. All extracts © Daniel Yergin, 1991

Young, Marilyn B. *The Vietnam Wars 1945–1990.* HarperCollins/Harper Perennial, New York, 1991

INDEX

329